Analytical Marketing

THE HARBRACE SERIES IN BUSINESS AND ECONOMICS

Analytical Marketing

LEONARD S. SIMON
The University of Rochester

MARSHALL FREIMER
The University of Rochester

HARCOURT, BRACE & WORLD, INC.
New York Chicago San Francisco Atlanta

ISBN: 0-15-502645-3

Library of Congress Catalog Card Number: 78-105697

Printed in the United States of America

Foreword

Management science is rapidly taking its place as an important underlying discipline of marketing. Mathematical models are being used more and more as aids in problem solving, and the advice of model builders is being sought in an ever wider range of situations. The growing importance of this field is confirmed by the number of "quantitative marketing" books and articles now being published.

The turning point in the application of quantitative methods to marketing came when management scientists were able to demonstrate practical uses for formal models and their machinery, such as probability theory, statistical inference, and mathematical programming. Conceptual models and general theories are useful, especially in an elementary exposition of the subject, but they do not nearly exhaust the power of formal methods. The hallmark of the successful book on applied management science is the degree to which it deals with models that are directly relevant to decision making. Thus, a book on quantitative marketing must stress models and model building.

This approach depends as much on the marketing insights of the authors as on their mathematical abilities. Taken together, the authors of *Analytical Marketing* represent a rare combination of training and experience in marketing management and quantitative skills. They have developed sophisticated models and applied powerful techniques, while keeping marketing relevance paramount.

Analytical Marketing is not intended to be merely a survey of management science applications in marketing, although, in fact, a great many applications are covered. Rather, it is designed for the student who wishes to investigate the structure of representative marketing models, to determine the critical factors in their design and application, and to assess their adequacy. In other words, this book is for the serious student of marketing models—the person who may one day participate in their creation. It is a book on harmony and composition, rather than on music appreciation.

The authors have expended considerable effort to provide a broad coverage of the basics of marketing management as well as the applications of models. This is important because management concepts and modeling considerations are closely intertwined in practice. Students who have already studied marketing management will have a context in which to test the applicability of the models. Students of quantitative methods will be able to learn about marketing management as they go along. Thus, *Analytical Marketing* should be relevant to both the marketing student with a quantitative interest and the student of management science who wishes to apply his skills in this exciting and rapidly growing field.

William F. Massy

Preface

This book stems from a latent need we perceived in our joint research work. During our construction of analytical models for various decision problems in marketing, the question arose as to whether the type of output we were producing would be taught to students specializing in marketing. A search of available materials revealed that there was no marketing text of a level adequate to enable students to evaluate and criticize quantitative research work in marketing. We were not under the illusion that many students would want to develop sufficient skills to be researchers. Rather, it was our belief that the coming generation of marketing managers would wish to have a sufficiently good command of analytical models and their uses that they could provide appropriate and comprehensible guidance to those persons immediately responsible for conducting marketing research efforts. At the same time, the reasonably well trained manager could maintain a critical faculty for evaluating the output of these researchers. Thus, we found the necessary stimulation to write this book from the joining of our belief about the future character of marketing management with the existing lack of appropriate text materials.

Analytical Marketing can be used in any of several ways. Probably, it is most generally suitable for an advanced marketing management course in which the instructor wishes to emphasize the analytical tools available for attacking decision problems in the principal policy areas in marketing. However, it could also be used in conjunction with a more traditional, descriptive, and less quantitative text in an introductory marketing management course or, possibly, with several other texts, each representing a principal policy area such as advertising or sales force management.

The student must bring to this text more than a cursory knowledge of mathematics if the proper benefit is to be derived from the analytical materials. Both elementary probability theory (as contained, say, in a first course in statistics emphasizing theoretical underpinnings) and mathematics covering the basic concepts of the calculus and linear algebra are requisites for the materials discussed. On the other hand, we have attempted to provide each model described with the following framework: (1) a delineation of the assumptions on which the model rests; (2) suggestions as to how else the problem might have been attacked; and (3) discussion of the applicability of the results, particularly emphasizing whether the models are primarily useful for the insights they yield or because they produce valid solutions to real world problems. We may have not succeeded in accomplishing all of this in every case, but at least it should be clear to the student that we are not merely running through a series of mathematical exercises.

Chapters 2, 3, and 4 review some of the mathematical training we feel is desirable and also introduce certain other material generally applicable to managerial decision making in marketing. These introductory chapters are also referenced at many points in succeeding chapters when it might be advisable for the student to refresh himself regarding the mathematics in a particular analysis. Chapters 5 through 9 discuss each of the basic policy areas in marketing. Chapter 10 focuses on mathematical approaches to the analysis of consumer behavior, which—although not a policy area—is of pivotal importance to decisions in the policy areas and frequently the vehicle by means of which the effects of such decisions are assessed. Chapter 11 is a brief introduction to the concept of management information systems applied to marketing. This area, an entirely separate subject in itself, is introduced here primarily to alert the student to the magnitude of the problem of structuring an adequate data base in order to utilize the models discussed in earlier chapters.

The book concludes with a series of five case studies, each derived from a real situation. These cases are of a sufficiently broad nature that materials from many different sections of the text may be applied in developing solutions. However, it is our hope that students will not confine themselves solely to the application of models from the text but will employ the more basic methodologies or tools to structure new, possibly unique, approaches to the managerial problems presented. The cases are offered primarily for their illustrative value and are not intended to represent either good or bad managerial practices.

Any book is the product of the ideas of many people. We are particularly indebted to the vast number of researchers whose earlier work produced the models and analytical techniques discussed here. Numerous colleagues have offered criticism and advice that have strengthened the book; in particular we would like to thank Marcus Alexis, William Gavett, George Haines, and P. S. R. S. Rao. Lawrence Bumpus, Douglas Dobson, Walter

Foertsch, Robert Gagan, and Linda Reinschmidt are a few of our students who deserve special note for their help in the preparation of the cases. We also owe a major debt to the many executives who gave so freely of their time in helping us develop the case materials. William Massy contributed far more than could reasonably have been expected of an advisory editor. For the necessary financial support, we are indebted to the Ford Foundation, Community Savings Bank, and Dean William Meckling of the College of Business Administration of The University of Rochester. Finally, a special note of thanks is due to Elizabeth Eggleton, Janet Evangelista, Rochelle Plascoe, and Martha Riley, who struggled through typing, editing, and proofing the numerous versions of this manuscript. We confess complete responsibility for the final product, although the temptation is great to make all jointly liable.

Leonard S. Simon
Marshall Freimer

Contents

CASES

Analytical Marketing

MODELS AND DECISION MAKING IN MARKETING

CHAPTER ONE

Our purpose in this chapter is to provide some of the history and rationale for mathematical analysis of marketing problems. In addition, we suggest how such work may be applied in the construction of a total marketing strategy for the firm, and we end by reviewing the factors that will most strongly influence future developments.

Mathematical models in marketing

The use of mathematical techniques in marketing is by no means new. Even the early marketing researchers performed fundamental, classical statistical analyses on the information they had collected. But the mathematical techniques employed and the attitudes of the people developing and utilizing them have become more sophisticated. Where the marketing researcher may once have been satisfied with a nose count and a few logical inferences from the data, he now concerns himself with building models of real-world processes from which he can draw inferences regarding the marketing environment. Similarly, where an executive may once have been satisfied merely to accept results and interpretations from researchers, he may now demand an explanation of the underlying structure of their work and evaluate for himself the credibility of their assumptions. This change in philosophy and operations has made it necessary for marketing managers to be conversant with mathematics as it may be applied to marketing decision making. One objective of this book is to encourage the development and use of the necessary skills. A second objective is to provide those who prefer the analytical work of constructing models and analyzing data with a taste of the probable future character of analytical marketing. If we do our job well, we should help managers and staff analysts to improve their communication with each other and to become more cognizant of the particular contributions each can make in building models of marketing processes.

Since the early 1950s, the scope of the mathematical techniques employed in marketing has expanded so far beyond the classical statistics that there probably no longer exists any class of marketing problems that has not been attacked with a mathematical model. The principal reason for this change is the development of operations research techniques, beginning with their application to military problems in World War II and followed by their rapid absorption into industrial environments after the war. Marketing has probably been the slowest of the functional areas in industry to adopt the tools of operations research. This is not because the problems are not amenable to such tools, but rather because it is so much more difficult to identify cause and effect in marketing than in, say, production or finance. For instance, the production planner knows that if a certain process is carried out, the product is altered in a particular way. Unfortunately, the interrelationships are not that clear-cut in marketing; for example, no one has yet been able to describe precisely how advertising affects sales volume. The problem is additionally complicated by the fact that it is not always clear what variables are relevant to a particular marketing problem. To illustrate, if we were exploring the question of the rate at which a new product would be adopted by the consuming public, could we unequivocally identify the total set of appropriate variables on which to take measurements?

The second enormous difficulty in marketing involves the question of measurement. What is an appropriate measurement of a specific consumer attitude that affects the decision to purchase a product? If we could decide what to measure, how would we scale it? Moreover, the definition, measurement, and scaling problems in marketing are particularly complicated by the question of allocation. In a production process, we may clearly demonstrate that a given machine has been responsible for producing certain defects. But in marketing, if we examine a given sales territory, we cannot necessarily attribute all the sales in that territory to the salesman's effort; advertising and technical service, for example, may have played a major role in helping that salesman achieve a particular level of success, but their contribution is not readily determinable.

Our principal concern in this book, however, is not with the philosophy of measurement. Our goal is to give the reader a feeling for the principal decision areas in marketing and how their problems can be attacked with mathematical techniques. We do not wish to embroil ourselves with the questions of scaling, measurement, accuracy and validity of data, and so on, in each model we present. On occasion, we have made comments on such questions, but appropriate treatment of them in every case would be impractical. Rather, we hope that, once he has been seduced into modeling marketing processes, the reader will take it upon himself to explore the problems involved in the definition and measurement of variables.[1]

Managerial decision areas in marketing

There are several ways in which the study of marketing can be approached. One is via an analysis of the types of institutions, such as agent wholesalers, brokers, and retailers, which make up a marketing system. Another is by examination of the particular functions, such as credit and collections, warehousing, and order processing, that are included in marketing. A third is what is sometimes referred to as the *descriptive approach*, in which the emphasis is on describing the character of the marketplace and its components; an example would be material dealing with information on where consumers are located, their income distributions, and other demographic and socioeconomic data. Still a fourth approach is the *commodity approach*, in which a thorough description is provided of how a particular good is marketed and the student is exposed to many of these descriptions to give him an overall impression of the character of marketing. Obviously, these categories are by no means mutually exclusive and depend on each other to some extent. In this book we take a fifth approach, which focuses on the examination of the key decision areas which confront the marketing manager. We shall be concerned with decisions having to do with product development and mix, pricing, physical distribution systems and channel management, sales force, advertising, and consumer behavior. The reader will find chapters devoted to the principal approaches to constructing analytical models for each of these areas. Some elaboration upon these will indicate what each area embodies.

In the *product decision* area the concern is with the nurturing and development of new product ideas into full-fledged, marketable products, the interaction of the products in a firm's product line with each other, and so on. *Pricing* is involved primarily with establishing the number of dollars at which the firm would be willing to offer its goods or services in the marketplace and with consideration of various trade-offs, such as maintenance service, that have value as against selecting a particular higher or lower price. *Physical distribution* concerns the inventorying and transportation of goods from the time they are produced until they are placed in the hands of the ultimate consumer, whereas *channel management* focuses on the relationships between the originator, or manufacturer of goods and services,

---

[1] To this end, the following references may be helpful: C. West Churchman, *Prediction and Optimal Decision*, Prentice-Hall, Englewood Cliffs, N.J., 1961; C. West Churchman and P. Ratoosh, *Measurement: Definition and Theories*, Wiley, New York, 1959; Peter Langhoff, Ed., *Models, Measurements and Marketing*, Prentice-Hall, Englewood Cliffs, N.J., 1965; and Warren S. Torgenson, *Theory and Methods of Scaling*, Wiley, New York, 1958.

and the independent firms that handle the goods en route from the producer to the consumer. The scope of the next two managerial areas, *sales force* and *advertising*, is self-evident. The principal distinction between the two is based on the extent of personal effort involved—advertising centers on mass communication, whereas sales force efforts are highly personalized. The last decision area, *consumer behavior*, is important because it provides the framework upon which decisions in all the preceding areas are based. In other words, it is ultimately through analysis of consumer behavior that management estimates the effects of its strategies with respect to pricing, sales force, channels, and so on. Just as important, it is also through an analysis of consumer characteristics and behavior that the particular market target group for which we are going to design a given product or service is established.

Strategy formulation

A marketing strategy has two principal components: (1) selection of the market target group toward whom the effort of the firm will be devoted and (2) development of a marketing mix. The latter is essentially the set of policies in each of the decision areas outlined above by which the firm hopes to convince the potential customers in the market target group to buy its product. The first component is quite stable over time and cannot be changed rapidly. If a commitment is made to a market comprising farm families, it would be extremely difficult for an organization to take a product that has unique value for these families and sell the same product to suburbanites without substantially altering its character. Further, as the firm develops special skills in serving a particular market target group, it is only reasonable that it will attempt to build on these skills and thus develop more and more products for that group. Consequently, the firm is usually committed to its market target groups for a fairly substantial time.

On the other hand, the marketing mix is a highly dynamic set of factors. If, for example, it is discovered that the wrong strategy is being used with respect to media allocation to reach the families in the market target group, the delay in changing this strategy need be, at most, no more than the few months required to give appropriate notice to the various media of the desire to withdraw or introduce material. The main problem in the marketing mix concept is not that of commitment but rather that the interactions of the various strategies are not well defined, so that it is difficult to define or determine an *optimal* marketing mix.

The purpose of the models developed in this book is to provide the decision maker with information that will be useful to him in selecting particular strategies. It can easily be seen that the person with the responsibility for establishing price would like to know with the best possible precision what the effects of different price levels might be. Similarly, if the concern happens to be physical distribution, it would be important to know the effects of locating a warehouse in a particular area upon the level of customer service. The ensuing models are meant to produce such aids to strategy formulation. They do not give definitive answers that say that *this* is the only reasonable course to follow. One reason is that there are frequently nonquantifiable elements in the environment which the strategist himself has to examine and estimate the effect of upon the quantitative conclusions reached. Another reason is that these models are frequently solved under a specific set of assumptions. If this set of assumptions were to change, a different solution might be obtained. Again, it is the strategist, in concert with the analyst, who determines the reasonableness of the assumptions employed in a given model. Our view, then, is that the models are nothing more than aids to managerial decision making and are not themselves determiners of policy or strategy.

Future development of mathematical models in marketing

Given the substantial expansion that has occurred in the use of mathematical techniques in marketing, the reader may well ask whether this trend is likely to continue or if, perhaps, it is more like the fads that strike professional groups every now and then, such as the motivation research fuss[2] in marketing in the 1950s. Although we cannot be sure of the answer to this question, we shall discuss several factors that will influence future developments. (Since we have written this book, our own opinions are obvious.)

The first, and probably the most important, factor will be the proven ability of the models developed to date. It is reasonable to examine the historical record with respect to how useful and comprehensive the existing models have been before deciding whether to invest more heavily in this type of work in the future. When evaluating models, emphasis should be on the long-run record. It would also be appropriate to focus on identifiable changes in a manager's behavior and in the quality of his decisions after he has begun utilizing mathematical models in his work. There should also be periodic reviews of the accomplishments resulting from application of management science techniques to marketing decisions. Unfortunately, this review process has not been routinized as it has in other areas, and frequently no one assesses the impact of particular models as they are applied to given decisions. We offer no general assessment of the value of mathematical models, because much of the evaluation has to be company specific.

One hindrance to the evaluation of past success is that a manager often

---

[2] This was "exposed" by Vance Packard in *The Hidden Persuaders* (McKay, New York, 1957).

does not have very good information about the success other firms are having with mathematical modeling. Efficient exchange of information about developments in the use of mathematical techniques in marketing is important to further model development. Professional societies can play a valuable role here, but it is also the manager's responsibility to assure himself of adequate information flow regarding other companies' developments.

Another factor affecting future development of mathematical decision models is whether there is top management support in the form of money for research purposes and a corresponding removal of human organizational barriers. Clearly, developmental work is expensive. Conducting a field experiment involving several sales zones and, say, manipulation of price incurs costs for the firm well beyond those of the experiment itself. For example, the firm must bear opportunity costs in those cases where business is lost because the research design calls for a high price, and, similarly, it must bear some losses in cases where the item is sold for a price less than might otherwise be obtained. When one considers that field experiments may be carried on for many months, it can be seen that the cost to the firm could be very large. A related problem is that there will always be members of the organization who are fearful of innovation and who oppose new approaches because of the potential impact on their own specialties. Management must be prepared to make it clear that those conducting the research in the area of analytical marketing models are to be given the necessary cooperation, and to deal with balkiness and even minor sabotage of the project on the part of its opponents.

The computational capability of electronic data processing systems will also affect modeling applications. The importance of this factor may be illustrated through some examination of what has happened in the past. Not long ago, it took many days to perform a complete multiple regression analysis; a computer may now do the same job in a few minutes. The ability to undertake certain kinds of analysis and extract implications is highly dependent upon the data processing capabilities of the computer. As the scope of what computers can do becomes even broader, we may expect more complex marketing models to be structured.

Finally, both the availability and the pertinence of data influence the types of models that can be built and the cost of structuring them. Lack of data, however, is not likely to be much of a problem in the future because of the present trends toward data collection and dissemination: (1) The number of surveyors and others concerned with collection of market data is increasing profusely; (2) business firms themselves are exhibiting a growing tendency to spend substantial funds on data collection; and (3) information management is becoming a specialized area within the firm. On the other hand, the pertinence of the data obtained must be evaluated in terms of the questions raised earlier in this chapter regarding measurement, and thus this is a problem likely to remain for a long time to come.

INTRODUCTION TO MATHEMATICAL PROGRAMMING

CHAPTER TWO

We would like to assume that our readers are already familiar with mathematical programming. However, we are aware that this will not always be the case, so we have included this chapter in order to acquaint the uninitiated reader with a few topics in this field that he will find particularly valuable. For those who have already been introduced to mathematical programming, this chapter may provide a useful review.

The first three sections are devoted to linear programming,[1] which is the optimization of linear functions subject to linear inequality constraints. Included under this heading is the important *transportation problem.* In order to make this material immediately accessible to the reader, we present it on an elementary mathematical level.

The final section is concerned with the optimization of nonlinear functions subject to linear or nonlinear equality constraints, with particular emphasis on the use of Lagrange multipliers. This section is on a more advanced mathematical level and assumes that the reader is familiar with differential calculus.

Linear programming—the simplex method

The mathematical argument that follows may be aided substantially if the reader has in mind a marketing example to which this technique can be applied. Assume that we are in the business of selling products through

[1] Although there are several excellent books on linear programming, the one most commonly cited is G. Hadley, *Linear Programming*, Addison-Wesley, Reading, Mass., 1962.

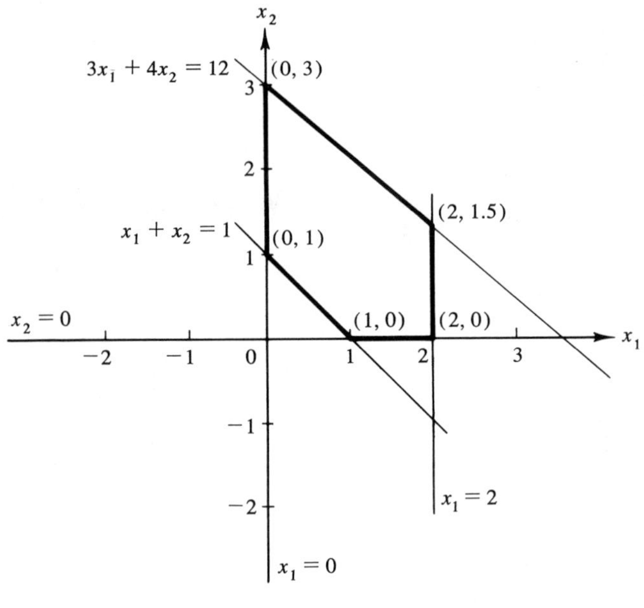

FIGURE 2-1

the use of literature sent through the mails. Assume further that a client has come to us with an item particularly suited for sale to professional persons, such as physicians and attorneys; in other words, let us say it is something that improves record keeping of services rendered. Before embarking on a large-scale mailing, we wish to test the salability of the product via a mailing to just two groups, physicians and attorneys, who were picked because they tend to be representative of the professions as a whole. We have a given number of dollars to spend on this test, \$1200.00, and the question confronting us is how many pieces to mail to physicians and how many to attorneys. Additional information we have available to aid in making this decision is: (1) Each mailing to an attorney costs \$.30, whereas each mailing to a physician costs \$.40 because of the greater difficulty of securing lists of physicians' names (these figures include the cost of preparation of the literature, as well as handling and postage); and (2) it is the management's judgment that a physician is about twice as likely to purchase the product because it was originally designed for use in a physician's office and then restructured for general applicability to all the professions. We also want to assure the following: that some mailings get to each group, that the total number of mailings is at least 1000 pieces, and that attorneys receive no more than 2000 pieces.

This problem can be formulated mathematically as follows. Let

x_1 = number of test mailings to attorneys

x_2 = number of test mailings to physicians

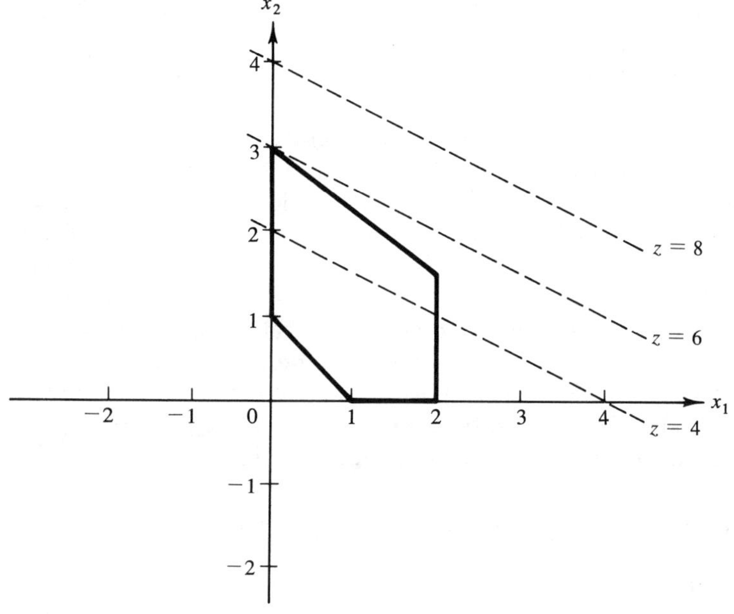

FIGURE 2-2

The following conditions are imposed on these variables:

$$
\begin{aligned}
.30x_1 + .40x_2 &\leq 1200 \qquad &\text{cost constraint} \\
x_1 \qquad\quad &\leq 2000 \qquad &\text{attorney constraint} \\
x_1 + \quad x_2 &\geq 1000 \qquad &\text{minimum mailing constraint}
\end{aligned}
$$

If we measure the number of mailings in thousands rather than individual units, then we have the following problem.

Suppose that we are required to

maximize
$$z = x_1 + 2x_2 \tag{2-1}$$

subject to
$$
\begin{aligned}
3x_1 + 4x_2 &\leq 12 \\
x_1 \qquad &\leq 2 \\
x_1 + x_2 &\geq 1
\end{aligned}
\tag{2-2}
$$

$$x_1 \geq 0, \quad x_2 \geq 0 \tag{2-3}$$

The points whose coordinates satisfy the system of inequalities (2-2), (2-3) lie on and within the pentagon outlined in Figure 2-1. The vertices and the equations of the boundaries of the pentagon are also shown in Figure 2-1. In Figure 2-2 the pentagon is repeated, together with the lines $z=4$, $z=6$, and $z=8$. We see that the lines of constant z are parallel to one another, with larger values being farther from the origin. We further see that the largest value of z that can be reached is $z = 6$, and that this is achieved at the vertex (0, 3) of the pentagon.[2]

Returning to our marketing example, we interpret this result as stating that the most effective test mailing is 3000 pieces to physicians and none to attorneys. But this violates the requirement that some mailings be made to each group. In fact, this requirement was not included in our mathematical formulation (2-1), (2-2), (2-3). If we did include some minimum number to be reached in each group, say 100 individuals, then it is clear from Figures 2-1 and 2-2 that this minimum number of pieces is all that would be mailed to attorneys.

At this point we might also comment that the use of relative expected sales as a measure of effectiveness may not be appropriate when we are gathering information. Instead, we might use the expected value of sample information,[3] which would be a nonlinear objective function.

Generalizing the preceding problem, we might be required to

maximize
$$z = c_1x_1 + c_2x_2 + \cdots + c_nx_n \tag{2-4}$$

subject to[4]
$$\begin{array}{ccccccccc} a_{11}x_1 & + & a_{12}x_2 & + & \cdots & + & a_{1n}x_n & \leq & b_1 \\ a_{21}x_1 & + & a_{22}x_2 & + & \cdots & + & a_{2n}x_n & \leq & b_2 \\ \cdot & & \cdot & & \cdot & & \cdot & & \cdot \\ \cdot & & \cdot & & \cdot & & \cdot & & \cdot \\ \cdot & & \cdot & & \cdot & & \cdot & & \cdot \\ a_{m1}x_1 & + & a_{m2}x_2 & + & \cdots & + & a_{mn}x_n & \leq & b_m \end{array} \tag{2-5}$$

$$x_1 \geq 0, \quad x_2 \geq 0, \quad \ldots, \quad x_n \geq 0 \tag{2-6}$$

In generalizing the original result, we would expect the maximum to occur at a vertex of the n-dimensional hyperpolygon defined by inequalities (2-5) and (2-6). The difficulty is that in the absence of an n-dimensional diagram comparable to Figure 2-2, it is impossible by this method to tell at which vertex the maximum occurs.

What we need is a more usable algebraic representation of the system of inequalities (2-5), (2-6), in particular one that emphasizes the vertices of the hyperpolygon. In order to introduce this new representation, we will return to the two-dimensional system of inequalities (2-2), (2-3). We define *slack variables*:

---

[2] We might as well note that if we were trying to minimize z, the smallest value would be $z = 1$, and that this too would be achieved at a vertex, here (1, 0).

[3] See Chapter 4.

[4] It is simpler to write all our inequalities in the less-than or equal-to format. Thus, the inequality $x_1 + x_2 \geq 1$ would be written as $-x_1 - x_2 \leq -1$. In effect, this is already accomplished when we write the equation $-x_1 - x_2 + x_5 = -1$ in (2-9).

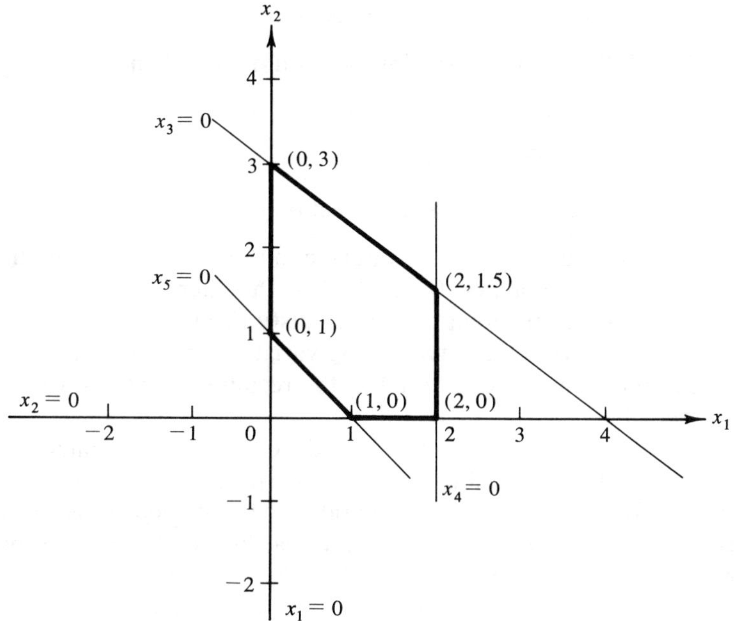

FIGURE **2-3**

$$
\begin{aligned}
x_3 &= 12 - 3x_1 - 4x_2 \\
x_4 &= \ \ 2 - \ \ x_1 \\
x_5 &= -1 + \ \ x_1 + \ \ x_2
\end{aligned}
\tag{2-7}
$$

In terms of these new variables, inequalities (2-2) and (2-3) can be written as

$$x_1 \geq 0, \quad x_2 \geq 0, \quad x_3 \geq 0, \quad x_4 \geq 0, \quad x_5 \geq 0 \tag{2-8}$$

The five variables x_i are related by the system of three equations (obtained from (2-7)):

$$
\begin{aligned}
3x_1 + 4x_2 + x_3 \qquad\qquad &= 12 \\
x_1 \qquad\qquad + x_4 \qquad &= \ \ 2 \\
-x_1 - \ \ x_2 \qquad\qquad + x_5 &= -1
\end{aligned}
\tag{2-9}
$$

As we have already seen, the vertices of the pentagon in Figure 2-1 are of particular interest to us. Each of these can be represented as the intersection of two of the boundary lines of the pentagon. In our five-variable notation, these lines have the equations $x_i = 0$, $i = 1, 2, \ldots, 5$ (see Figure 2-3). Each vertex[5] is the intersection of two such boundaries:

[5] The values of x_3, x_4, and x_5 are obtained from equations (2-7).

$(0, 3, 0, 2, 2)$ is the intersection of $x_1 = 0$ and $x_3 = 0$

$(2, 1.5, 0, 0, 2.5)$ is the intersection of $x_3 = 0$ and $x_4 = 0$

$(2, 0, 6, 0, 1)$ is the intersection of $x_2 = 0$ and $x_4 = 0$

$(1, 0, 9, 1, 0)$ is the intersection of $x_2 = 0$ and $x_5 = 0$

$(0, 1, 8, 2, 0)$ is the intersection of $x_1 = 0$ and $x_5 = 0$

There are, of course, points of intersection of two boundaries that are not vertices. For example, $(4, 0, 0, -2, 3)$ is the intersection of $x_2 = 0$ and $x_3 = 0$. Since $x_4 < 0$, this point does not satisfy (2-8). Thus, we see that although we can always set any two of the variables equal to zero and solve (2-9) for the remaining three variables, the resulting point is a vertex only if (2-8) is satisfied.

At this point it is convenient to introduce some new terminology. We shall call a set of five variables $(x_1, x_2, x_3, x_4, x_5)$ that satisfies the three equations (2-9) a *solution*. If, in addition, the five inequalities (2-8) are satisfied, we have a *feasible solution*; the feasible solutions correspond to the points on and within the pentagon. Finally, if two of the x's are equal to zero, rather than merely non-negative, then we have a *basic feasible solution*; as we have already seen, this corresponds to a vertex of the pentagon. In a basic feasible solution, the two x's that equal zero are said to be *nonbasic*, whereas the remaining three positive x's are *basic*.

The system (2-9) of three equations in five variables is written in a format that can be described as being solved for the variables x_3, x_4, and x_5, in the sense that we can immediately read off the values of these variables in terms of the two remaining variables x_1 and x_2. If, in an attempt to find a basic feasible solution, the latter two variables were set equal to zero,[6] we would obtain $x_3 = 12$, $x_4 = 2$, $x_5 = -1$, which is not feasible, because $x_5 < 0$. A feasible solution[7] is obtained if x_2 and x_5 are set equal to zero, in which case $x_1 = 1$, $x_3 = 9$, and $x_4 = 1$. We must rewrite equations (2-9) as solved for the basic variables in this solution, x_1, x_3, and x_4. This is accomplished by dividing the third equation by the coefficient of x_1, -1, and eliminating x_1 from the other two equations:

$$\begin{aligned} x_2 + x_3 \qquad + 3x_5 &= 9 \\ -x_2 \qquad + x_4 + x_5 &= 1 \\ x_1 + x_2 \qquad\qquad - x_5 &= 1 \end{aligned} \tag{2-10}$$

[6] This point corresponds to the origin in Figure 2-3, which, although it is the intersection of two boundary lines, is not a vertex.

[7] Finding a basic feasible solution is not quite as trivial as it might appear to be. In this example, we can read one off from Figure 2-3, but the whole point of the algebraic technique is to make do without a diagram. In some business applications, current practice will furnish a basic feasible solution. For a general method of finding a basic feasible solution, see G. Hadley, *op. cit.*, p. 116.

The function we are trying to maximize is $z = x_1 + 2x_2$. Substituting the value $x_1 = 1 - x_2 + x_5$ obtained from the final equation in (2-10), we have

$$z = 1 + x_2 + x_5 \tag{2-11}$$

This is an *identity* in that the value of z for any *solution* can be obtained from this formula. In particular, if $x_2 = 0$ and $x_5 = 0$, then $z = 1$. This is the value of z at one basic feasible solution, but we would like to find another basic feasible solution with a larger value of z. From equation (2-11) we see that if either of the currently nonbasic variables x_2 and x_5 is made positive, z will increase. Supposing, then, that we decide to make x_2 positive; how large can it get? Rewriting equations (2-10) with x_5 held equal to zero we obtain

$$\begin{aligned} x_3 &= 9 - x_2 \\ x_4 &= 1 + x_2 \\ x_1 &= 1 - x_2 \end{aligned} \tag{2-12}$$

We see that x_1 and x_3 decrease and x_4 increases as x_2 increases. Since feasibility must be maintained, x_2 can only be increased until x_1 or x_3 reaches zero. This occurs when $x_2 = 1$, at which point $x_3 = 8$ and $x_4 = 2$ but $x_1 = 0$. With $x_1 = 0$ and $x_5 = 0$, the basic variables are now x_2, x_3, and x_4, and equations (2-10) must be rewritten as solved for these variables.

$$\begin{aligned} -x_1 \qquad + x_3 \qquad + 4x_5 &= 8 \\ x_1 \qquad\qquad + x_4 \qquad &= 2 \\ x_1 + x_2 \qquad\qquad - \; x_5 &= 1 \end{aligned} \tag{2-13}$$

Once again $z = x_1 + 2x_2$ can be expressed in terms of the nonbasic variables, this time by substituting $x_2 = 1 - x_1 + x_5$ into (2-11):

$$z = 2 - x_1 + 2x_5 \tag{2-14}$$

It is now apparent that x_5 must be increased, leaving $x_1 = 0$, if we are to increase z. This can only be done as far as $x_5 = 2$, because at that value $x_3 = 0$ (see equations (2-13)). The basic variables are now x_2, x_4, and x_5, and the equations are

$$\begin{aligned} -.25x_1 \qquad + .25x_3 \qquad + x_5 &= 2 \\ x_1 \qquad\qquad + x_4 \qquad &= 2 \\ .75x_1 + x_2 + .25x_3 \qquad\qquad &= 3 \end{aligned} \tag{2-15}$$

$$z = 6 - .5x_1 - .5x_3 \tag{2-16}$$

Remember that equation (2-16) is an identity holding for all solutions. Thus, any feasible change in x_1 and x_3 can only decrease z, and we have finally arrived at the maximum.

This is, of course, the same maximum at $x_1 = 0$, $x_2 = 3$ that was found earlier by graphical methods. Again we stress that the reason for using the algebraic method just presented is to solve multidimensional problems for which the graphical method is unavailable.

Returning now to inequalities (2-5) and (2-6), we see that if we introduce the m slack variables

$$x_{n+i} = b_i - a_{i1}x_1 - a_{i2}x_2 - \cdots - a_{in}x_n \qquad i = 1, 2, \ldots, m \tag{2-17}$$

then we require $n + m$ inequalities

$$x_j \geq 0 \qquad j = 1, 2, \ldots, n + m \tag{2-18}$$

where the $n + m$ x's are related by the m equations

$$\begin{aligned}
a_{11}x_1 + a_{12}x_2 + \cdots + a_{1n}x_n + x_{n+1} \qquad\qquad &= b_1 \\
a_{21}x + a_{22}x_2 + \cdots + a_{2n}x_n \qquad + x_{n+2} \qquad &= b_2 \\
\vdots \qquad\qquad\qquad\qquad & \quad \vdots \\
a_{m1}x_1 + a_{m2}x_2 + \cdots + a_{mn}x_n \qquad\qquad + x_{n+m} &= b_m
\end{aligned} \tag{2-19}$$

A *solution* is now defined as any set of x's satisfying (2-19). It is *feasible* if all the x's are non-negative (2-18), and it is *basic* if n of the x's are equal to zero. Since the maximum value of z will occur at a basic feasible solution, with n x's set equal to zero, only m x's, including slack variables, will be positive, where m is the number of constraints (2-5). The algebraic method of solution[8] is conceptually no harder to carry out with m equations and $n + m$ variables than it was with three equations and five variables, but the arithmetic may turn out to be so extensive as to make desirable the use of a computer.

Duality

If we rewrite the maximization problem (2-4), (2-5), and (2-6) using summation symbols, we obtain

$$\text{maximize} \qquad z = \sum_{j=1}^{n} c_j x_j \tag{2-20}$$

$$\text{subject to} \qquad \sum_{j=1}^{m} a_{ij}x_j \leq b_i \qquad i = 1, 2, \ldots, m \tag{2-21}$$

$$x_j \geq 0 \qquad j = 1, 2, \ldots, n \tag{2-22}$$

Closely related to this is the so-called dual problem:

---

[8] The maximization problem, (2-4), (2-5), and (2-6), is known as *linear programming*; the algebraic method of solution is the *simplex method*.

minimize
$$w = \sum_{i=1}^{m} b_i y_{n+i} \tag{2-23}$$

subject to
$$\sum_{i=1}^{m} a_{ij} y_{n+i} \geq c_j \qquad j = 1, 2, \ldots, n \tag{2-24}$$

$$y_{n+i} \geq 0 \qquad i = 1, 2, \ldots, m \tag{2-25}$$

The relationship is best viewed by associating the dual variable y_{n+i} with the ith inequality (2-21) in the original problem,[9] and the original variable x_j with the jth inequality (2-24) in the dual problem. The coefficient b_i of y_{n+i} in the minimization function w is also the constraining value in the ith original inequality, whereas the coefficient c_j of x_j in the maximization function z is also the constraining value in the jth dual inequality. Furthermore, a_{ij} is both the coefficient of x_j in the ith original inequality and the coefficient in the jth dual inequality of y_{n+i}.

In further discussion of duality, we shall resort to our example. The dual of the maximization problem (2-1), (2-2), and (2-3) is[10]

minimize
$$w = 12y_3 + 2y_4 - y_5 \tag{2-26}$$

subject to
$$\begin{aligned} 3y_3 + y_4 - y_5 &\geq 1 \\ 4y_3 \qquad - y_5 &\geq 2 \end{aligned} \tag{2-27}$$

$$y_3 \geq 0, \quad y_4 \geq 0, \quad y_5 \geq 0 \tag{2-28}$$

When we introduce slack variables y_1 and y_2, we obtain

$$y_1 \geq 0, \quad y_2 \geq 0, \quad y_3 \geq 0, \quad y_4 \geq 0, \quad y_5 \geq 0 \tag{2-29}$$

$$\begin{aligned} -y_1 \qquad + 3y_3 + y_4 - y_5 &= 1 \\ -y_2 + 4y_3 \qquad - y_5 &= 2 \end{aligned} \tag{2-30}$$

Consider expression (2-11) for z, which corresponded to the basic variables x_1, x_3, and x_4 in the original problem. We shall rewrite this expression as

$$-z + 1 = 0x_1 - 1x_2 + 0x_3 + 0x_4 - 1x_5 \tag{2-31}$$

If we set y_j equal to the coefficient of x_j, we obtain

$$y_1 = 0, \quad y_2 = -1, \quad y_3 = 0, \quad y_4 = 0, \quad y_5 = -1 \tag{2-32}$$

These values of y_j satisfy equations (2-30); they constitute a solution. Furthermore, three of them equal zero, and since three is the number of variables in the system (2-27), the y_j are a basic solution. However, they do not satisfy the feasibility conditions (2-29), so what we have is a basic infeasible solution.

---

[9] In this context, this will also be called the *primal* problem.

[10] Recall that the inequality $x_1 + x_2 \geq 1$ has been rewritten as $-x_1 - x_2 \leq -1$.

If we similarly rewrite the expression (2-14) for z that corresponded to the basic variables x_2, x_3, and x_4 in the original problem as

$$-z + 2 = 1x_1 + 0x_2 + 0x_3 + 0x_4 - 2x_5 \tag{2-33}$$

we again obtain from the coefficients a basic infeasible solution to the dual problem. If, however, we rewrite the expression (2-16) for z that corresponded to the basic variables x_2, x_4, and x_5 as

$$-z + 6 = .5x_1 + 0x_2 + .5x_3 + 0x_4 + 0x_5 \tag{2-34}$$

we obtain a basic feasible solution.

This example illustrates the general principle that the coefficients of the maximization function of the original problem written in the "$-z$" format form a basic solution to the dual problem that is feasible if, and only if, the corresponding solution to the original is optimal.

Another basic relation between the primal and dual problems can be derived as follows. Suppose that x_1, x_2 satisfy (2-2), (2-3) and that y_3, y_4, y_5 satisfy (2-27), (2-28). Then the fact that multiplying both sides of an inequality by a non-negative number preserves the inequality enables us to make the chain of substitutions

$$z = 1x_1 + 2x_2 \tag{2-35}$$

$$\begin{aligned} &\leq (3y_3 + y_4 - y_5)x_1 + (4y_3 - y_5)x_2 \\ &= (3x_1 + 4x_2)y_3 + (x_1)y_4 + (-x_1 - x_2)y_5 \end{aligned} \tag{2-36}$$

$$\leq 12y_3 + 2y_4 - 1y_5 = w \tag{2-37}$$

Thus, the value of the objective function corresponding to any feasible solution of the primal problem is always less than or equal to the value of the objective function corresponding to any feasible solution of the dual problem.

If we now consider the maximizing feasible solution to the primal problem $x_1 = 0$, $x_2 = 3$, we obtain $z = 6$. If we also consider the corresponding feasible solution to the dual problem (see equation (2-34)) $y_3 = .5$, $y_4 = 0$, $y_5 = 0$, we obtain $w = 6$. Thus, there is at least one pair of feasible solutions to the primal and dual problems at which the objective functions are equal. In view of the above inequality, this common value of the objective functions must provide simultaneously the maximum for the primal problem and the minimum for the dual problem.

The transportation problem

Let us now consider a new problem. Assume that we operate a steel products distributorship over a rather large geographic region.[11] The re-

[11] Another illustration of the transportation problem can be found in Chapter 7, "Distribution Systems."

gion may be divided roughly into n marketing areas $M_1, M_2, \ldots, M_n$; it also contains m warehouses. It is physically possible to serve any of the market areas from any of the warehouses, but the costs of doing so differ. The management's concern is to identify which markets should be served from which warehouses in order to minimize the costs of transporting the goods. The demand for each market is translated into tons of product demanded daily, and we also know the capabilities of the warehouses in terms of tons of merchandise that can be shipped each day. Finally, our cost accounting group has supplied us with the cost of moving a ton from any warehouse to any market.

We may suppose that we are required[12] to

minimize
$$z = \sum_{i=1}^{m} \sum_{j=1}^{n} c_{ij}x_{ij} \qquad (2\text{-}38)$$

subject to
$$\sum_{j=1}^{n} x_{ij} = a_i \qquad i = 1, 2, \ldots, m \qquad (2\text{-}39)$$

$$\sum_{i=1}^{m} x_{ij} = b_j \qquad j = 1, 2, \ldots, n \qquad (2\text{-}40)$$

$$\text{all } x_{ij} \geq 0 \qquad (2\text{-}41)$$

This problem is one of minimizing the *transportation cost* z if we have quantities a_i available at *sources* (warehouses), $i = 1, 2, \ldots, m$, that must be shipped to *destinations* (marketing areas), at which quantities b_j are required, $j = 1, 2, \ldots, n$, with unit costs of shipment c_{ij}.

Aside from the facts that we are required to minimize rather than maximize and that some of the constraints start off as equations rather than inequalities, this is clearly a linear programming problem. We shall solve it by a variant of the simplex method that makes use of the convenient tabular format:

$$\begin{array}{cccc|c}
x_{11} & x_{12} & \cdots & x_{1n} & a_1 \\
x_{21} & x_{22} & \cdots & x_{2n} & a_2 \\
\cdot & \cdot & & \cdot & \cdot \\
\cdot & \cdot & & \cdot & \cdot \\
\cdot & \cdot & & \cdot & \cdot \\
x_{m1} & x_{m2} & \cdots & x_{mn} & a_m \\
\hline
b_1 & b_2 & \cdots & b_m &
\end{array} \qquad (2\text{-}42)$$

[12] In order to be able to require both (2-39) and (2-40), we must have

$$\sum_{i=1}^{m} a_i = \sum_{j=1}^{n} b_j$$

In this case, one of the $n + m$ equations will be redundant, so basic solutions will contain $n + m - 1$ basic variables.

According to requirements (2-39), the rows in (2-42) must add up to the marginal value; according to (2-40), the columns must also. We shall refer to (2-42) as the *requirements table.*

Suppose, for example, that we have three warehouses with availabilities $a_1 = 50$, $a_2 = 75$, $a_3 = 50$ and four marketing regions with requirements $b_1 = 30$, $b_2 = 40$, $b_3 = 20$, $b_4 = 45$. Since the sum of the requirements, 135, is less than the sum of the availabilities, 175, we introduce a fictional fifth marketing area with $b_5 = 175 - 135 = 40$ and zero associated costs; this corresponds to adding slack variables in the general linear programming problem. These requirements are shown in (2-43).

In using the simplex method, we need an initial basic feasible solution. In a transportation problem, this is readily obtained by the *northwest corner* method, which is illustrated in the example in table (2-43).

30	20				50
	20	20	35		75
			10	40	50
30	40	20	45	40	

(2-43)

Starting with $x_{11} = 30$, we have worked our way from upper left to lower right, successively exhausting row or column totals before moving on to the next position. We have written in only the seven[13] basic variables, leaving blank spaces in the positions corresponding to the nonbasic variables.

The format in table (2-43) is not quite equivalent to that in equations (2-10), (2-13), or (2-15) in that we do not have an explicit representation of the basic variables in terms of the nonbasic variables. The explicit representation was used for two purposes: to determine the effect on z of making a nonbasic variable positive, and to determine which basic variable decreases to zero and so is nonbasic in the next solution. We will now see how both of these purposes can be accomplished using table (2-43).

Suppose that some nonbasic variable is made positive, say $x_{31} = +\theta$. In order to maintain the row and column balances, various adjustments in the basic variables must be made; these are shown in table (2-44).

$30 - \theta$	$20 + \theta$				50
	$20 - \theta$	20	$35 + \theta$		75
$+\theta$			$10 - \theta$	40	50
30	40	20	45	40	

(2-44)

If we now introduce the matrix (c_{ij}) of costs,[14]

[13] $n + m - 1 = 5 + 3 - 1 = 7$; see footnote 12.

[14] In this example, the last column of the cost matrix is zero, which corresponds to the last column in the requirements table (2-42) consisting of slack variables.

$$\begin{bmatrix} 2 & 1 & 7 & 4 & 0 \\ 3 & 5 & 2 & 8 & 0 \\ 4 & 6 & 3 & 1 & 0 \end{bmatrix} \tag{2-45}$$

we can see, by referring to equations (2-38) and (2-44), that for each unit x_{31} is increased, z is changed by

$$\begin{aligned} \delta_{31} &= c_{31} - c_{11} + c_{12} - c_{22} + c_{24} - c_{34} \\ &= 4 - 2 + 1 - 5 + 8 - 1 = 5 \end{aligned} \tag{2-46}$$

Since we are trying to minimize z, we will not increase x_{31}. On the other hand, we see from (2-47) and (2-48) that increasing x_{25} decreases z.

(2-47)

30	20				50
	20	20	$35-\theta$	$+\theta$	75
			$10+\theta$	$40-\theta$	50
30	40	20	45	40	

$$\begin{aligned} \delta_{25} &= c_{25} - c_{35} + c_{34} - c_{24} \\ &= 0 - 0 + 1 - 8 = -7 \end{aligned} \tag{2-48}$$

If we do decide to increase x_{25}, table (2-47) tells us that x_{24} decreases to zero and becomes nonbasic for the next solution when $\theta = 35$. All we need do to obtain this new solution is to set θ equal to 35 and omit the new nonbasic variable:

(2-49)

30	20				50
	20	20		35	75
			45	5	50
30	40	20	45	40	

Although table (2-49) represents a solution for which z is $7 \times 35 = 245$ lower than initially, it is not the desired minimum. It is still necessary to investigate the further use of nonbasic variables. Without any of the details of this investigation, we present the final solution:

(2-50)

10	40				50
20		20		35	75
			45	5	50
30	40	20	45	40	

The method we have just presented for solving the transportation problem is, in fact, just the simplex method with most of the calculations omitted. A further improvement can be made in the method of calculating the quantities δ_{ij} that determine the change in z per unit increase in the nonbasic variables x_{ij}. If we define quantities u_i and v_j such that[15]

$$u_i + v_j = c_{ij} \quad \text{if } x_{ij} \text{ is basic} \tag{2-51}$$

then we find that

$$\delta_{ij} = c_{ij} - (u_i + v_j) \quad \text{if } x_{ij} \text{ is nonbasic} \tag{2-52}$$

Equation (2-52) follows the observation that in the previous method of computing δ_{ij} all c's but the first satisfy equation (2-51), and when these substitutions are made, consecutive u's and v's will cancel in pairs. For example, from equation (2-46) we have

$$\begin{aligned}\delta_{31} &= c_{31} - (u_1 + v_1) + (u_1 + v_2) - (u_2 + v_2) + (u_2 + v_4) - (u_3 + v_4) \\ &= c_{31} - (u_3 + v_1)\end{aligned} \tag{2-53}$$

Equation (2-51) is most readily visualized in a tabular format:

	v_1	v_2	v_3	v_4	v_5
u_1	2	1			
u_2		5	2	8	
u_3				1	0

(2-54)

The entries in the body of table (2-54) are the c_{ij} corresponding to the basic x_{ij} in table (2-43); the interpretation is that $u_i + v_j$ must equal these c_{ij}. There are seven equations in eight variables, which allows us to set one of the variables arbitrarily; it is customary to set u_1 equal to 0. Once we have done this, we can see that $v_1 = 2$ and $v_2 = 1$. From this latter we find that $u_2 = 4$, which in turn leads to $v_3 = -2$ and $v_4 = 4$. The complete solution is shown in table (2-55).

	2	1	−2	4	3
0	2	1			
4		5	2	8	
−3				1	0

(2-55)

We readily verify that equation (2-53) agrees with equation (2-46):

[15] The astute reader will find equations (2-51) and (2-52) to be related to the dual of the transportation problem given by equations (2-38), (2-39), (2-40), and (2-41).

$$\begin{aligned}\delta_{31} &= c_{31} - (u_3 + v_1) \\ &= 4 - (-3 + 2) = 5\end{aligned} \tag{2-56}$$

Lagrange multipliers

In this section we shall consider optimization of nonlinear functions. Because we wish to consider only elementary examples here, we shall not attempt to provide a marketing context as we did for the linear programming and transportation models. For a somewhat more advanced example, we refer the reader to the first model in Chapter 8, "Sales Force Management." Suppose that we are required to

maximize $$z = x_1 x_2 \tag{2-57}$$

subject to $$3x_1 + 4x_2 = 12 \tag{2-58}$$

We can solve equation (2-58) for x_2 and substitute into equation (2-57), obtaining

$$z = x_1 \frac{12 - 3x_1}{4} = 3x_1 - \tfrac{3}{4}x_1^2 \tag{2-59}$$

The maximum of this quadratic function of one variable is readily obtained (by setting the derivative equal to zero):

$$z_{\max} = 3 \text{ occurs at } x_1 = 2$$

In Figure 2-4 we plot both the curve $z = 3$ and the constraining line $3x_1 + 4x_2 = 12$. We see that they are *tangent* at the point (2, 1.5). Analytically, for their curves to be tangent, it is required that the two functions have

FIGURE 2-4

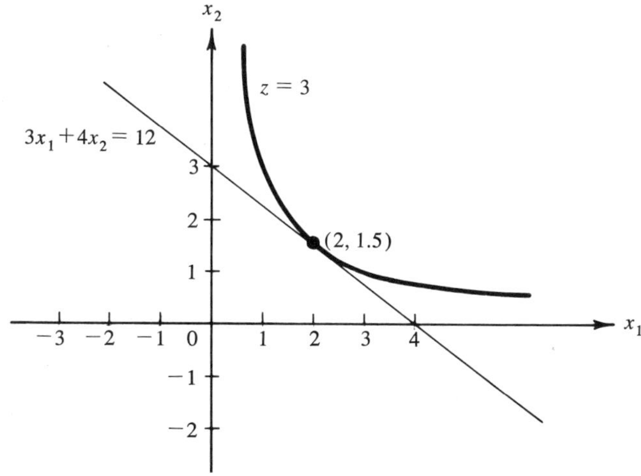

proportional partial derivatives at the point of tangency. An easy mnemonic device for imposing this requirement[16] is the introduction of a *Lagrange multiplier* λ. We first form the *Lagrangian* expression

$$z_\lambda = x_1x_2 - \lambda(3x_1 + 4x_2 - 12) \tag{2-60}$$

the first term of which is the function to be maximized, whereas the second is the constraint multiplied by $-\lambda$. At this stage of the analysis, λ is some as yet undetermined constant. We then set the partial derivatives of the Lagrangian equal to zero.

$$\begin{aligned} 0 &= \frac{\partial z_\lambda}{\partial x_1} = x_2 - 3\lambda \\ 0 &= \frac{\partial z_\lambda}{\partial x_2} = x_1 - 4\lambda \end{aligned} \tag{2-61}$$

Eliminating λ from these two equations, we obtain $x_2 = \frac{3}{4}x_1$; combined with the constraint (2-58), this yields the point (2, 1.5). We can also obtain $\lambda = .5$.

In general, if we are required to

$$\text{maximize} \qquad z = f(x_1, x_2, \ldots, x_n) \tag{2-62}$$

$$\text{subject to} \qquad g(x_1, x_2, \ldots, x_n) = 0 \tag{2-63}$$

we will form the Lagrangian

$$z_\lambda = f(x_1, x_2, \ldots, x_n) - \lambda g(x_1, x_2, \ldots, x_n) \tag{2-64}$$

and set its partial derivatives equal to zero:

$$0 = \frac{\partial z_\lambda}{\partial x_j} = \frac{\partial f}{\partial x_j} - \lambda\frac{\partial g}{\partial x_j} \qquad j = 1, 2, \ldots, n \tag{2-65}$$

These equations state that the partial derivatives of $f(x_1, x_2, \ldots, x_n)$ and $g(x_1, x_2, \ldots, x_n)$ are proportional, with λ the constant of proportionality. Taken together with the constraining equation (2-63), they form a system of $n + 1$ equations in the $n + 1$ variables $x_1, x_2, \ldots, x_n, \lambda$. In the example above, these equations were linear and readily solved; in general, of course, they can be well nigh impossible.

In order to illustrate the use of equation (2-65), consider the following three-variable problem:

$$\text{maximize} \qquad z = x_1x_2x_3 \tag{2-66}$$

$$\text{subject to} \qquad x_1^2 + 2x_2^2 + 3x_3^2 - 36 = 0 \tag{2-67}$$

Equation (2-65) then provides three equations

[16] That this device does in fact impose this requirement will be seen in the discussion of equations (2-65).

$$
\begin{aligned}
0 &= x_2x_3 - \lambda(2x_1) \\
0 &= x_1x_3 - \lambda(4x_2) \\
0 &= x_1x_2 - \lambda(6x_3)
\end{aligned}
\tag{2-68}
$$

Eliminating λ from equations (2-68) yields

$$\frac{x_2x_3}{2x_1} = \frac{x_1x_3}{4x_2} = \frac{x_1x_2}{6x_3} \tag{2-69}$$

which can be seen to be equivalent to

$$x_1^2 = 2x_2^2 = 3x_3^2 \tag{2-70}$$

Combining equations (2-67) and (2-70), we find that

$$x_1 = \pm\sqrt{12}, \quad x_2 = \pm\sqrt{6}, \quad x_3 = \pm 2 \tag{2-71}$$

The maximum value of z is $(\sqrt{12})(\sqrt{6})(2) = 12\sqrt{2}$, which is achieved at four different points since, in addition to all the x's being positive, we could have any two of them negative.

We may as well note that (2-71) also yields four different points at which the minimum value, $z = -12\sqrt{2}$, is achieved. One of the difficulties with the Lagrange multiplier method is that it does not offer a simple test to distinguish maximum from minimum, and care must be exercised with regard to this point.

More generally, we can consider the problem with several constraining equations:

maximize $$z = f(x_1, x_2, \ldots, x_n) \tag{2-72}$$

subject to $$g_i(x_1, x_2, \ldots, x_n) = 0 \qquad i = 1, 2, \ldots, m \tag{2-73}$$

We now form the Lagrangian with m multipliers λ_i:

$$z_\lambda = f(x_1, x_2, \ldots, x_n) - \sum_{i=1}^{m} \lambda_i g_i(x_1, x_2, \ldots, x_n) \tag{2-74}$$

and set its n partial derivatives equal to zero:

$$0 = \frac{\partial z_\lambda}{\partial x_j} = \frac{\partial f}{\partial x_j} - \sum_{i=1}^{m} \lambda_i \frac{\partial g_i}{\partial x_j} \qquad j = 1, 2, \ldots, n \tag{2-75}$$

Taken together with the constraints (2-73), these now give us a system of $n + m$ equations in as many variables.

For example, consider the three-variable, two-constraint problem:

maximize $$z = x_1x_2x_3 \tag{2-76}$$

subject to
$$
\begin{aligned}
x_1 + 2x_2 + 3x_3 - 18 &= 0 \\
2x_1 - x_2 + x_3 - 11 &= 0
\end{aligned}
\tag{2-77}
$$

In this example, two multipliers, λ_1 and λ_2, are required, and (2-75) represents the three equations

$$\begin{aligned} 0 &= x_2x_3 - \lambda_1(1) - \lambda_2(2) \\ 0 &= x_1x_3 - \lambda_1(2) - \lambda_2(-1) \\ 0 &= x_1x_2 - \lambda_1(3) - \lambda_2(1) \end{aligned} \tag{2-78}$$

There are two solutions to the system of five equations, (2-77) and (2-78):

$$x_1 = 6,\ x_2 = 3,\ x_3 = 2,\ \lambda_1 = 6,\ \lambda_2 = 0 \quad \text{for which } z = 36 \tag{2-79}$$

and

$$x_1 = \tfrac{4}{3},\ x_2 = -\tfrac{5}{3},\ x_3 = \tfrac{20}{3},\ \lambda_1 = \tfrac{4}{3},\ \lambda_2 = -\tfrac{56}{9} \quad \text{for which } z = -\tfrac{400}{27} \tag{2-80}$$

It would appear that, as in the immediately preceding example, we have found both the maximum and minimum values of z. In fact, as we shall now see, we have found neither. If we solve equations (2-77) for x_1 and x_2, we obtain

$$\begin{aligned} x_1 &= 8 - x_3 \\ x_2 &= 5 - x_3 \end{aligned} \tag{2-81}$$

Substituting into formula (2-76) for z, we find that

$$z = x_3^3 - 13x_3^2 + 40x_3 \tag{2-82}$$

This is graphed in Figure 2-5. We see that solution (2-79) corresponds to the *relative maximum* at $x_3 = 2$, while solution (2-80) corresponds to the *relative minimum* at $x_3 = \frac{20}{3}$, but that z has neither an *absolute maximum*

FIGURE 2-5

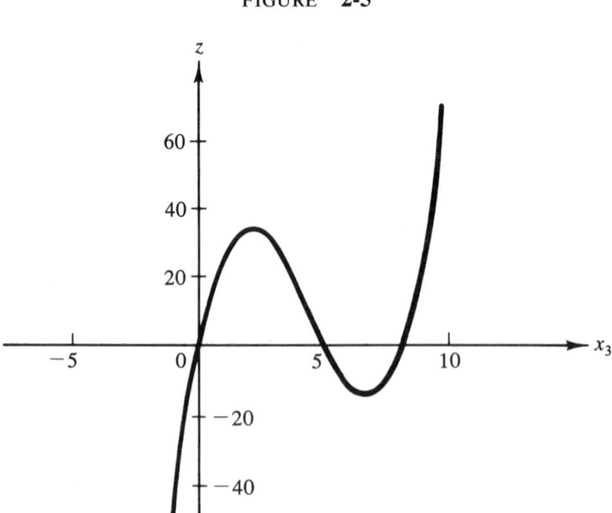

nor an *absolute minimum.* This problem is not, of course, peculiar to the Lagrange multiplier technique but pervades the use of differential calculus in optimization problems.

We close with one final note. As the astute reader has undoubtedly already noticed, in this section we have not considered optimization of nonlinear functions subject to inequality constraints. Although this is an important and useful topic, it is too advanced mathematically to be presented in this book.

PROBLEM 1

A manufacturer has been able to identify the amount of contribution margin he receives on each of the four products, x_1, x_2, x_3, x_4, in his product line. Since he operates in highly competitive markets, the prices at which the products are sold do not vary according to customers. However, sales are limited by the total amount of time the salesmen can put in per week, the total amount of money available for promotion, and the firm's capability for doing installation and repair work. The manufacturer is thus able to express his problem in terms of a series of equations, one that expresses the rate at which each product contributes to the total contribution margin and three others that specify the rate at which each of the four products consumes scarce resources. The problem is thus:

$$\begin{aligned} &\text{maximize} && 3x_1 + 4x_2 + x_3 + 7x_4 \\ &\text{subject to} && 8x_1 + 3x_2 + 4x_3 + x_4 \leq 7 \\ &&& 2x_1 + 6x_2 + x_3 + 5x_4 \leq 3 \\ &&& x_1 + 4x_2 + 5x_3 + 2x_4 \leq 8 \\ &&& \text{all } x_i \geq 0 \end{aligned}$$

How many of each product should the firm set as its sales goal?

PROBLEM 2

An oil company has three refineries, any one of which can deliver gasoline to any of five major East Coast marketing areas. The capacities of the refineries are $S_1 = 10$, $S_2 = 11$, and $S_3 = 15$. The demands at each of the marketplaces are $D_1 = 4$, $D_2 = 5$, $D_3 = 7$, $D_4 = 9$, $D_5 = 9$. The various costs for each refinery to deliver to each market are as follows:

$$
\begin{array}{lll}
C_{11} = 4 & C_{21} = 6 & C_{31} = 5 \\
C_{12} = 1 & C_{22} = 4 & C_{32} = 2 \\
C_{13} = 2 & C_{23} = 3 & C_{33} = 6 \\
C_{14} = 6 & C_{24} = 5 & C_{34} = 4 \\
C_{15} = 9 & C_{25} = 7 & C_{35} = 8
\end{array}
$$

How much gasoline should each refinery deliver to each market?

PROBLEM 3

Show that the maximum of the product

$$z = x_1 x_2 \cdots x_n$$

subject to

$$a_1 x_1 + a_2 x_2 + \cdots + a_n x_n = b \qquad b \text{ and all } a_i \text{ positive}$$

and

$$x_1 \geq 0, \quad \ldots, \quad x_n \geq 0$$

occurs when

$$a_1 x_1 = a_2 x_2 = \cdots = a_n x_n = b/n$$

PROBLEM 4

Find the minimum of

$$z = (x_1 - 2)^2 + (x_2 - 3)^2 + (x_3 - 4)^2$$

subject to

$$
\begin{aligned}
x_1 + x_2 + x_3 &\leq 4 \\
x_1 + x_2 \qquad &\leq 3 \\
x_1 \geq 0, \quad x_2 \geq 0, &\quad x_3 \geq 0
\end{aligned}
$$

A REVIEW OF RANDOM VARIABLES

CHAPTER THREE

In this chapter, we assume that our readers have already had an introduction to probability and statistics and therefore shall not discuss the basic laws of probability that constitute its definition. This chapter[1] is meant to review and extend the reader's knowledge of probability, especially as it concerns random variables.

Because this material is mostly review, it is presented formally with only limited explanation and no numerical examples. The one exception to this procedure is the discussion of discrete Markov chains, which we expect to be totally new to many of our audience.

We start the chapter with the definition, properties, and some examples of discrete random variables. The main difficulty we anticipate for the reader here is the concept of the probability generating function.

The second section is devoted to discrete Markov chains, with examples as previously mentioned.[2] The next two sections present the definitions and some examples of continuous and compound random variables. There is nothing particularly new or difficult here, but the latter material does involve some rather complicated algebraic manipulation.

The final section is concerned with sums of independent random variables.

---

[1] The best overall reference for this material is W. Feller, *An Introduction to Probability Theory and Its Applications*, Vol. 1, 3rd ed., Wiley, New York, 1968.

[2] A useful reference on this subject is R. Howard, *Dynamic Programming and Markov Processes*, M.I.T. Press, Cambridge, Mass., 1960.

Discrete random variables

If X is a variable that takes on only non-negative integral values, with

$$p_r = \text{prob } (X = r) \geq 0 \qquad r = 0, 1, 2, \ldots \tag{3-1}$$

$$\sum_{r=0}^{\infty} p_r = 1 \tag{3-2}$$

then we shall refer to X as a *discrete random variable*.[3]

The *expected value* of any function $f(x)$, defined for all non-negative integers x, is specified by the formula

$$Ef(X) = \sum_{r=0}^{\infty} f(r) p_r \tag{3-3}$$

Using this concept, we can define the *mean* and the *variance* of X as

$$\mu = EX = \sum_{r=0}^{\infty} r p_r \tag{3-4}$$

and

$$\sigma^2 = E(X - \mu)^2 = \sum_{r=0}^{\infty} (r - \mu)^2 p_r \tag{3-5}$$

respectively.

We also define the *probability generating function*[4] of X:

$$P_X(z) = Ez^X = \sum_{r=0}^{\infty} z^r p_r \tag{3-6}$$

The probability generating function is a function of one real (or complex) variable z that incorporates all the information contained in the individual probabilities p_r. For example, we have

$$p_r = \frac{1}{r!} \frac{d^r}{dz^r} P_X(z) \Big|_{z=0} \qquad r = 0, 1, 2, \ldots \tag{3-7}$$

$$\mu = \frac{d}{dz} P_X(z) \Big|_{z=1} \tag{3-8}$$

$$\sigma^2 = \frac{d^2}{dz^2} P_X(z) \Big|_{z=1} + \mu - \mu^2 \tag{3-9}$$

Whether we use the individual probabilities, the probability generating func-

---

[3] Although this is not the most general form a discrete random variable may take, it will suffice for our purposes.

[4] This is closely related, but not identical, to the *moment generating function*.

tion, or both in a particular application will depend on which is most convenient for our purposes.

EXAMPLE 1: If

$$p_r = p_P(r|m) = \frac{e^{-m}m^r}{r!} \quad \text{for all } r \tag{3-10}$$

then X has a *Poisson* distribution. We find that

$$\mu = m \tag{3-11}$$

$$\sigma^2 = m \tag{3-12}$$

$$P_X(z) = e^{-m(1-z)} \tag{3-13}$$

EXAMPLE 2: If[5]

$$p_r = p_b(r|n, p) = \begin{cases} \binom{n}{r} p^r (1-p)^{n-r} & \text{for } r \leq n \\ 0 & \text{for } r > n \end{cases} \tag{3-14}$$

then X has a *binomial* distribution. We find that

$$\mu = np \tag{3-15}$$

$$\sigma^2 = np(1-p) \tag{3-16}$$

$$P_X(z) = (1 - p + pz)^n \tag{3-17}$$

The special case $n = 1$ is also known as a *Bernoulli* distribution.

EXAMPLE 3: If

$$p_r = p_{nb}(r|k, p) = \binom{k-1+r}{r}(1-p)^k p^r \quad \text{for all } r \tag{3-18}$$

then X has a *negative binomial* distribution. We find that

$$\mu = k\frac{p}{1-p} \tag{3-19}$$

$$\sigma^2 = k\frac{p}{(1-p)^2} \tag{3-20}$$

$$P_X = \left(\frac{1-p}{1-pz}\right)^k \tag{3-21}$$

The special case $k = 1$ is also known as a *geometric* distribution.

---

[5] The binomial coefficient

$$\binom{n}{r} = \frac{n!}{r!(n-r)!}$$

is the number of combinations of n objects taken r at a time. It is therefore sometimes symbolized by ${}_nC_r$.

Discrete Markov chains

A sequence of random variables $X_1, X_2, X_3, \ldots$ for which[6]

$$\text{prob } (X_{n+1} = r_{n+1} | X_1 = r_1, \ldots, X_n = r_n) = \text{prob } (X_{n+1} = r_{n+1}) \quad \text{for all } n \text{ and all } r_1, \ldots, r_{n+1} \tag{3-22}$$

is said to be a *sequence of independent random variables*. Although such sequences are important, they can be studied by examining the individual X's separately, so there is no need for us to say anything further about them here.

A sequence of random variables $X_1, X_2, X_3, \ldots$ for which

$$\text{prob } (X_{n+1} = r_{n+1} | X_1 = r_1, \ldots, X_n = r_n) = \text{prob } (X_{n+1} = r_{n+1} | X_n = r_n) \quad \text{for all } n \text{ and all } r_1, \ldots, r_{n+1} \tag{3-23}$$

is said to be a *discrete first-order Markov chain*. In contrast to sequences of independent random variables, there is much that needs to be said about Markov chains.

To begin with, the customary interpretation is that the different X's represent the *state* of the same *system* at different times n. For example, the system might be a customer's purchases and the state a quantitative measure thereof. With n measured in weeks, we might have

$$X_n = r \quad \text{if a specific customer purchases } r \text{ units in the } n\text{th week}$$

If we were not interested in the quantity purchased, we might formulate this alternatively as

$$X_n = \begin{cases} 0 & \text{if the customer made no purchase in the } n\text{th week} \\ 1 & \text{if the customer made a purchase in the } n\text{th week} \end{cases}$$

in which case values of $r > 1$ would not be possible.[7]

We can now interpret equation (3-23) as stating that, given the history of the system up to time n, only the current state is needed in predicting the forthcoming state. It is natural in this context to call

$$\text{prob } (X_{n+1} = s | X_n = r) = p_{rs}(n) \tag{3-24}$$

the *state transition probability* from state r at time n to state s at time $n + 1$.

---

[6] We recall that for any two events A and B we define the *conditional probability* of B given A as

$$\text{prob } (B|A) = \frac{\text{prob } (A, B)}{\text{prob } (A)}$$

[7] Compare equation (3-14) for the binomial distribution in which values of $r > n$ were not possible.

If these state transition probabilities do not depend on the time of transition, that is, if

$$\text{prob }(X_{n+1} = s | X_n = r) = p_{rs} \quad \text{all } n \text{ and all } r, s \tag{3-25}$$

we have a *stationary* Markov chain. Because it is very difficult to obtain sufficient data to estimate time-dependent state transition probabilities (3-24), we will assume stationarity whenever we can plausibly do so. For the remainder of this section we will consider only stationary Markov chains.

Using some elementary laws of probability, we calculate

$$\begin{aligned} \text{prob }(X_{n+1} = s) &= \sum_{r=0}^{\infty} \text{prob }(X_n = r, X_{n+1} = s) \\ &= \sum_{r=0}^{\infty} \text{prob }(X_n = r) \text{ prob }(X_{n+1} = s | X_n = r) \end{aligned} \tag{3-26}$$

If we now introduce the notation

$$p_r(n) = \text{prob }(X_n = r) \tag{3-27}$$

then from equations (3-25) and (3-26) we obtain

$$p_s(n+1) = \sum_{r=0}^{\infty} p_r(n) p_{rs} \tag{3-28}$$

If we define the matrix of state transition probabilities[8]

$$P = ((p_{rs})) \tag{3-29}$$

and if we write the state probabilities at time n as a row vector

$$p(n) = (p_1(n) p_2(n) \ldots) \tag{3-30}$$

then equation (3-28) can be written in vector-matrix form[9] as

$$p(n+1) = p(n)P \qquad n = 1, 2, \ldots \tag{3-31}$$

Equation (3-31) can be iterated to yield

$$\begin{aligned} p(2) &= p(1)P \\ p(3) &= p(2)P = p(1)P^2 \\ p(n+1) &= p(n)P = p(1)P^n \end{aligned} \tag{3-32}$$

---

[8] Because the conditional probabilities (3-25), like any other complete set (3-2), must add up to 1, each of the rows of the matrix P adds up to 1. Such a matrix is called *stochastic*.

[9] Although we have left open the possibility of infinite-dimensional vectors and matrices, in practice these are rarely used. All the examples in this book will be finite-dimensional.

If

$$P^{\infty} = \lim_{n\to\infty} P^n \tag{3-33}$$

exists, as it usually will, then

$$p(\infty) = \lim_{n\to\infty} p(n) \tag{3-34}$$

also exists and, from (3-32),

$$p(\infty) = p(1)P^{\infty} \tag{3-35}$$

Also, from (3-31), we obtain the *steady-state* condition

$$p(\infty) = p(\infty)P \tag{3-36}$$

The vector $p(\infty)$ of limiting state probabilities is found more readily from equation (3-36) than from equation (3-35).

EXAMPLE 1[10]

$$P = \begin{pmatrix} \frac{1}{2} & \frac{1}{2} & 0 \\ \frac{2}{5} & \frac{3}{5} & 0 \\ \frac{1}{3} & 0 & \frac{2}{3} \end{pmatrix}$$

It can be shown that[11]

$$P^n = \begin{pmatrix} \frac{4}{9} & \frac{5}{9} & 0 \\ \frac{4}{9} & \frac{5}{9} & 0 \\ \frac{4}{9} & \frac{5}{9} & 0 \end{pmatrix} + (\tfrac{1}{10})^n \begin{pmatrix} \frac{5}{9} & -\frac{5}{9} & 0 \\ -\frac{4}{9} & \frac{4}{9} & 0 \\ -\frac{50}{153} & \frac{50}{153} & 0 \end{pmatrix} + (\tfrac{2}{3})^n \begin{pmatrix} 0 & 0 & 0 \\ 0 & 0 & 0 \\ -\frac{2}{17} & -\frac{15}{17} & 1 \end{pmatrix}$$

Thus,

$$P^{\infty} = \begin{pmatrix} \frac{4}{9} & \frac{5}{9} & 0 \\ \frac{4}{9} & \frac{5}{9} & 0 \\ \frac{4}{9} & \frac{5}{9} & 0 \end{pmatrix}$$

and, by (3-35),

$$p(\infty) = p(1) \begin{pmatrix} \frac{4}{9} & \frac{5}{9} & 0 \\ \frac{4}{9} & \frac{5}{9} & 0 \\ \frac{4}{9} & \frac{5}{9} & 0 \end{pmatrix} = (\tfrac{4}{9} \quad \tfrac{5}{9} \quad 0)$$

---

[10] In these examples, only states 0, 1, and 2 can occur. We therefore omit the values of p_{rs} whenever r or s exceeds 2, enabling us to write P as a 3×3 matrix. See the preceding footnote.

[11] See R. Howard, *op. cit.*, pp. 9–11, for a simple explanation of the method.

no matter what $p(1)$ may be. We could also have obtained this result from (3-36) by verifying that the equation

$$(p_0(\infty)p_1(\infty)p_2(\infty)) = (p_0(\infty)p_1(\infty)p_2(\infty))\begin{pmatrix} \frac{1}{2} & \frac{1}{2} & 0 \\ \frac{2}{5} & \frac{3}{5} & 0 \\ \frac{1}{3} & 0 & \frac{2}{3} \end{pmatrix}$$

holds for $(\frac{4}{9} \quad \frac{5}{9} \quad 0)$ and for no other state probability vector.

EXAMPLE 2

$$P = \begin{pmatrix} 1 & 0 & 0 \\ 0 & 1 & 0 \\ \frac{1}{3} & \frac{1}{3} & \frac{1}{3} \end{pmatrix}$$

It can be shown that

$$P^n = \begin{pmatrix} 1 & 0 & 0 \\ 0 & 1 & 0 \\ \frac{1}{2} & \frac{1}{2} & 0 \end{pmatrix} + (\tfrac{1}{3})^n \begin{pmatrix} 0 & 0 & 0 \\ 0 & 0 & 0 \\ -\frac{1}{2} & -\frac{1}{2} & 1 \end{pmatrix}$$

so that

$$P^\infty = \begin{pmatrix} 1 & 0 & 0 \\ 0 & 1 & 0 \\ \frac{1}{2} & \frac{1}{2} & 0 \end{pmatrix}$$

and, by (3-35),

$$p(\infty) = p(1)\begin{pmatrix} 1 & 0 & 0 \\ 0 & 1 & 0 \\ \frac{1}{2} & \frac{1}{2} & 0 \end{pmatrix} = \left(p_0(1) + \frac{p_2(1)}{2} \qquad p_1(1) + \frac{p_2(1)}{2} \qquad 0\right)$$

In this example, the steady-state probabilities depend on $p(1)$.

In both examples there were states for which

$$p_r(\infty) = \lim_{n\to\infty} p_r(n) = 0 \tag{3-37}$$

(state 2 in each case). Any state r for which equation (3-37) holds is *transient*; with probability 1 we will sooner or later leave such a state, never to return.

In both examples there were also states for which

$$p_r(\infty) = \lim_{n\to\infty} p_r(n) > 0 \tag{3-38}$$

(states 0 and 1 in each case). Any state r for which (3-38) holds is *recurrent*. As Example 2 shows, it is *not* true that we will sooner or later return to each recurrent state; even though both states 0 and 1 are recurrent, once the system is in either of these states it becomes trapped there, never to return to the other.

Continuous random variables

If X is a variable and f a function for which

$$f(x) \geq 0 \qquad \text{all } x \tag{3-39}$$

$$\text{prob } (a \leq X \leq b) = \int_a^b f(x)\, dx \qquad \text{all } a, b \tag{3-40}$$

$$\int_{-\infty}^{\infty} f(x)\, dx = 1 \tag{3-41}$$

then we shall refer to X as a *continuous random variable* and to f as the *probability density function* of X. We will also be interested in the *cumulative distribution function* of X:

$$F(x) = \text{prob } (X \leq x) = \int_{-\infty}^{x} f(t)\, dt \tag{3-42}$$

The *expected value* of any function $g(x)$ defined for all real numbers x, is specified by the formula

$$Eg(X) = \int_{-\infty}^{\infty} g(x)f(x)\, dx \tag{3-43}$$

Using this concept, we can define the *mean* and the *variance* of X as

$$\mu = EX = \int_{-\infty}^{\infty} xf(x)\, dx \tag{3-44}$$

and

$$\sigma^2 = E(X - \mu)^2 = \int_{-\infty}^{\infty} (x - \mu)^2 f(x)\, dx \tag{3-45}$$

respectively.

EXAMPLE 1: If

$$f(x) = f_n(x|\mu, \sigma) = \frac{1}{\sqrt{2\pi}\,\sigma} \quad \exp \left[\frac{-(x - \mu)^2}{2\sigma^2}\right] \tag{3-46}$$

then X has a *normal (Gaussian)* distribution with mean μ and variance σ^2.

EXAMPLE 2: If

$$f(x) = f_\gamma(x|b, a) = \begin{cases} \dfrac{a^b x^{b-1} e^{-ax}}{(b-1)!} & x \geq 0 \\ 0 & x < 0 \end{cases} \tag{3-47}$$

then X has a *gamma* distribution. We find that

$$\mu = \frac{b}{a} \tag{3-48}$$

$$\sigma^2 = \frac{b}{a^2} \tag{3-49}$$

The special case $b = 1$ is also known as an *exponential* distribution.

EXAMPLE 3: If

$$f(x) = f_\beta(x|a, b) = \begin{cases} \dfrac{x^{a-1}(1-x)^{b-1}}{B(a, b)} & 0 \leq x \leq 1 \\ 0 & \text{otherwise} \end{cases} \tag{3-50}$$

where the *beta function* is defined by

$$B(a, b) = \int_0^1 x^{a-1}(1-x)^{b-1}\, dx = \frac{(a-1)!(b-1)!}{(a+b-1)!} \tag{3-51}$$

then X has a beta distribution. We find that

$$\mu = \frac{a}{a+b} \tag{3-52}$$

$$\sigma^2 = \frac{ab}{(a+b)^2(a+b+1)} \tag{3-53}$$

Compound random variables

For each of the examples we have given of both discrete and continuous random variables, the probabilities of X depended on one or more parameters. If these parameters are themselves random variables, jointly distributed with X, then we shall be interested, among other things, in the marginal distribution of X.

EXAMPLE 1: If X is Poisson (formula (3-10)) and its parameter m has a gamma distribution, then the marginal distribution of X is

$$\text{prob } (X=r) = \int_0^\infty \frac{e^{-m}m^r}{r!} \frac{a^b m^{b-1} e^{-am}}{(b-1)!}\, dm$$

$$= \frac{a^b}{r!(b-1)!} \int_0^\infty m^{r+b-1} e^{-(1+a)m}\, dm \tag{3-54}$$

$$= \binom{b-1+r}{r} \left(\frac{a}{1+a}\right)^b \left(\frac{1}{1+a}\right)^r$$

If we compare this with formula (3-18), we see that marginally X has a negative binomial distribution with

$$\mu = \frac{b}{a} \tag{3-55}$$

$$\sigma^2 = b\frac{1+a}{a^2} \tag{3-56}$$

EXAMPLE 2: If X is binomial (formula (3-14)) and its parameter p has a beta distribution, then the marginal distribution of X is

$$\text{prob } (X=r) = \int_0^\infty \binom{n}{r} p^r (1-p)^{n-r} \frac{p^{a-1}(1-p)^{b-1}}{B(a,b)}\, dp$$

$$= \binom{n}{r} \frac{1}{B(a,b)} \int_0^\infty p^{r+a-1}(1-p)^{n-r+b-1}\, dp \tag{3-57}$$

$$= \binom{n}{r} \frac{B(r+a,\, n-r+b)}{B(a,b)}$$

with probability zero for all values of $r > n$. This distribution is not one that we have previously studied, but it is useful in statistical decision theory.[12] It can be shown that its mean and variance are

$$\mu = \frac{na}{a+b} \tag{3-58}$$

$$\sigma^2 = \frac{nab(n+a+b)}{(a+b)^2(a+b+1)} \tag{3-59}$$

EXAMPLE 3: If X is normal with parameters μ and σ and its parameter μ is in turn normal with parameters μ_0 and σ_0, then the marginal distribution of X is obtained as

[12] This distribution has been named the *beta-binomial*; see H. Raiffa and R. Schlaifer, *Applied Statistical Decision Theory*, Harvard Business School, Cambridge, Mass., 1961, p. 237. It is closely related to the hypergeometric distribution.

$$f(x) = \int_{-\infty}^{\infty} \left(\frac{1}{\sqrt{2\pi}\,\sigma} \exp\left[-\frac{(x-\mu)^2}{2\sigma^2}\right]\right)\left(\frac{1}{\sqrt{2\pi}\,\sigma_0} \exp\left[-\frac{(\mu-\mu_0)^2}{2\sigma_0^2}\right]\right) d\mu$$

$$= \frac{1}{\sqrt{2\pi}\,\sqrt{\sigma^2+\sigma_0^2}} \exp\left[-\frac{(x-\mu_0)^2}{2(\sigma^2+\sigma_0^2)}\right] \tag{3-60}$$

which is still the probability density function of a normal distribution. We shall also require the conditional distribution of μ given x; the density function of this distribution, obtained from equation (3-60) by dividing the integrand by the final expression for $f(x)$,

$$f(\mu|x) = \frac{\sqrt{\sigma^2+\sigma_0^2}}{\sqrt{2\pi}\,\sigma\sigma_0} \exp\left\{-\frac{[\mu - (\sigma_0^2 x + \sigma^2\mu_0)/(\sigma^2+\sigma_0^2)]^2}{2\sigma^2\sigma_0^2/(\sigma^2+\sigma_0^2)}\right\} \tag{3-61}$$

is once again normal. In particular, the mean of this distribution is

$$E(\mu|x) = \frac{\sigma_0^2 x + \sigma^2\mu_0}{\sigma^2+\sigma_0^2} \tag{3-62}$$

Sums of independent random variables

If X and Y are discrete random variables such that the joint probability equals the product of the marginal probabilities

$$\text{prob}\ (X=r\quad Y=s) = \text{prob}\ (X=r)\cdot\text{prob}\ (Y=s) \qquad \text{all } r, s \tag{3-63}$$

then X and Y are *independent*. If we define a new random variable, Z, to be the sum of X and Y,

$$Z = X + Y \tag{3-64}$$

then we can readily calculate, using (3-63), that

$$\text{prob}\ (Z=t) = \sum_{r=0}^{t} \text{prob}\ (X=r,\ Y=t-r)$$

$$= \sum_{r=0}^{t} \text{prob}\ (X=r)\cdot\text{prob}\ (Y=t-r) \tag{3-65}$$

The final summation in equation (3-65) is called a *convolution*. If t is large, a fair amount of arithmetic is involved in calculating a convolution sum. On the other hand, it is easy enough to derive the following product rule for the probability generating functions of the random variables X, Y, and Z from the convolution relationship:

$$P_Z(z) = P_X(z)\cdot P_Y(z) \tag{3-66}$$

The obvious generalization to sums of more than two random variables is correct.

From equation (3-66) we can obtain all sorts of useful results. To give just one example: If X has a Poisson distribution with parameter m_X and Y a Poisson distribution with parameter m_Y, then, using equation (3-13) for the probability generating function of a Poisson distribution, Z also has a Poisson distribution, with parameter $m_X + m_Y$.

If X and Y are continuous random variables such that the joint probability density function equals the product of the marginal density functions

$$f_{X,Y}(x, y) = f_X(x) f_Y(y) \qquad \text{all } x, y \tag{3-67}$$

then X and Y are independent. If we once more define the sum

$$Z = X + Y \tag{3-68}$$

then we can calculate that

$$f_Z(t) = \int_{-\infty}^{\infty} f_X(x) f_Y(t - x)\, dx \tag{3-69}$$

This formula is known as a *convolution integral.*

If X and Y are independent, normally distributed random variables with means and standard deviations μ_x, σ_x and μ_y, σ_y, respectively, then from (3-46) and (3-69) we can obtain

$$f_Z(t) = \frac{1}{\sqrt{2\pi}\,\sigma_Z} \exp\left[-\frac{(t - \mu_Z)^2}{2\sigma_Z^2}\right] \tag{3-70}$$

where

$$\begin{aligned} \mu_Z &= \mu_x + \mu_y \\ \sigma_Z^2 &= \sigma_x^2 + \sigma_y^2 \end{aligned} \tag{3-71}$$

Thus, the sum of two independent normal random variables is again normal, with mean and variance equal to the respective sums.

PROBLEM 1

(a) If $p_0 = 1 - p$

$p_1 = p$

$p_r = 0 \qquad r \geq 2$

calculate the probability generating function.

(b) Calculate the probability generating function for a sum of n independent random variables, each of which has the above distribution. Use this to identify the distribution of the sum.

PROBLEM 2

Suppose that we focus our interest on whether or not a given customer purchases a product in a given week. Evidence indicates that the sequence of purchases forms a stationary first-order Markov chain with transition probabilities

This week	Next week: purchase	Next week: no purchase
purchase	.3	.7
no purchase	.2	.8

If the customer makes a purchase this week, what is the probability of his purchasing

(a) two weeks from now?
(b) five weeks from now?
(c) infinitely many weeks from now?

PROBLEM 3

The probability density function of a normal random variable X having mean $\mu = 0$ and with variance replaced by *precision* $h = 1/\sigma^2$ is (from (3-46))

$$f(x) = \sqrt{\frac{h}{2\pi}} \exp\left\{-\frac{hx^2}{2}\right\}$$

If h is a random variable with a gamma distribution (3-47), show that the marginal distribution of X has probability density function

$$f(x) = \frac{(b + \frac{1}{2} - 1)!(2a)^b}{\sqrt{\pi}(b-1)!(2a + x^2)^{b+1/2}}$$

Note: If $a = b = n/2$, then the marginal distribution of X is Student's t with n degrees of freedom.

INTRODUCTION TO STATISTICAL DECISION THEORY

CHAPTER FOUR

Although it is more than ten years since the publication of Schlaifer's elementary book on statistical decision theory,[1] we find that it is best to proceed on the assumption that our readers have had limited acquaintance with this subject. Most recent introductory statistics texts[2] now contain a section or two, or possibly a short chapter, on this subject, but we fear that most basic statistic courses pay little attention to it.

In the first two sections of this chapter, we introduce statistical decision theory by means of a simple example. Then we present the same material formally. In the final two sections, which are also formal, we develop the special results that hold for linear utility functions.

A simple decision problem

Suppose that in setting out for the day a pushcart operator anticipates the possibility of rain. Three choices are open to him: He may make no special preparation; he may make a modest preparation, such as taking a

---

[1] R. Schlaifer, *Probability and Statistics for Business Decisions,* McGraw-Hill, New York, 1959. See also H. Raiffa and R. Schlaifer, *Applied Statistical Decision Theory*, Graduate School of Business Administration, Harvard University, Boston, Mass., 1961, for a mathematical presentation.

[2] A notable exception is William A. Spurr and Charles P. Bonini, *Statistical Analysis for Business Decisions*, Richard D. Irwin, Homewood, Ill., 1967, which devotes 5 out of 25 chapters to decision theory.

raincoat; or he may make full preparation including raincoat, hat, rubbers, and umbrella for himself and a selection of plastic rainhats for sale. As a first step in deciding what to do, the vendor must make a personal evaluation of the consequences of each combination of weather condition and level of preparation. The results of this evaluation should be set forth in terms of a numerical utility,[3] as in Table 4-1. In this table, states refer to possible weather conditions, acts refer to possible actions that can be taken to counter these conditions, and the utility scale is set up with a maximum of 5 (corresponding to the best combination of state and act) and a minimum of 0 (corresponding to the worst). If the vendor also knows the probability of rain to be equal to .4, according to the weather bureau, for example, then he could calculate the expected utilities:

$$\begin{aligned} u(a_1) &= (.6)(5) + (.4)(0) = 3.0 \\ u(a_2) &= (.6)(4) + (.4)(2) = 3.2 \leftarrow \\ u(a_3) &= (.6)(2) + (.4)(3) = 2.4 \end{aligned} \tag{4-1}$$

Under the circumstances, his best choice is to make a modest preparation for rain.

Now suppose that before making a choice the vendor can consult an oracle, such as his wife. Like all such, she is inclined to hedge her answers, but the pushcart operator can distinguish three possible predictions: fair, doubtful, and foul weather. Furthermore, from previous observations of the oracle's performance, the vendor knows the conditional probabilities of the forecasts given that it is going to rain or not; these probabilities are shown in Table 4-2. Note that this table is set up to give the relative frequencies of the various forecasts conditional on the state of weather; in symbolic terms this is $p(x|\theta)$. In the usual decision theory terminology, these conditional probabilities are *likelihoods*.

TABLE **4-1**

Utilities

	States	
Acts	θ_1 (no rain)	θ_2 (rain)
a_1 (no preparation)	5	0
a_2 (modest preparation)	4	2
a_3 (full preparation)	2	3

[3] For a thorough discussion of the concept of utility, see Chapter 2 of R. Duncan Luce and H. Raiffa, *Games and Decisions*, Wiley, New York, 1957.

If we now multiply the likelihoods of the various forecasts by the probabilities of the conditioning states of weather, we obtain the joint probabilities

$$p(x, \theta) = p(x|\theta) \cdot p(\theta)$$

$$= \text{probability that forecast } x \text{ and weather condition } \theta \text{ will both hold}$$

These joint probabilities are displayed in Table 4-3.

Also given in Table 4-3 are the marginal probabilities. For the states, these are the same as the weather bureau's probabilities since the identity

$$\sum_{\theta} p(x|\theta)p(\theta) = p(\theta)$$

follows from the fact that the sum of the likelihoods in any column in Table 4-2 equals 1. For the forecasts, however, the marginal probabilities give useful new information. For example, the probability of a forecast of fair weather from the oracle is .44.

What happens if the forecast is for fair weather? The conditional probability of rain is, from Table 4-3, equal to $.08/.44 = .182$, so the expected utilities of our choices are

TABLE **4-2**

Likelihoods

	States	
Forecasts	θ_1 (no rain)	θ_2 (rain)
x_1 (fair)	.60	.20
x_2 (doubtful)	.25	.30
x_3 (foul)	.15	.50

TABLE **4-3**

Joint and marginal probabilities

	States		
Forecasts	θ_1	θ_2	
x_1	.36	.08	.44
x_2	.15	.12	.27
x_3	.09	.20	.29
	.60	.40	

$$u(a_1|x_1) = (.818)(5) + (.182)(0) = 4.090 \leftarrow$$
$$u(a_2|x_1) = (.818)(4) + (.182)(2) = 3.636 \qquad (4\text{-}2)$$
$$u(a_3|x_1) = (.818)(2) + (.182)(3) = 2.182$$

Thus, if the forecast is for fair weather, the best choice is to make no special preparation for rain.

Similarly, if the forecast is for doubtful weather, the conditional probability of rain is $.12/.27 = .444$, and the expected utilities are

$$u(a_1|x_2) = (.556)(5) + (.444)(0) = 2.780$$
$$u(a_2|x_2) = (.556)(4) + (.444)(2) = 3.112 \leftarrow \qquad (4\text{-}3)$$
$$u(a_3|x_2) = (.556)(2) + (.444)(3) = 2.444$$

so the best choice is to make a modest preparation for rain.

Finally, if the forecast is for foul weather, the conditional probability of rain is $.20/.29 = .690$, and the expected utilities are

$$u(a_1|x_3) = (.310)(5) + (.690)(0) = 1.550$$
$$u(a_2|x_3) = (.310)(4) + (.690)(2) = 2.620 \qquad (4\text{-}4)$$
$$u(a_3|x_3) = (.310)(2) + (.690)(3) = 2.690 \leftarrow$$

so the best choice is to make full preparation for rain.

With the data of this example, it has turned out that the best choice is always to accept the oracle's prediction.

We would now like to evaluate the overall expected utility when the vendor's choice is based on the oracle's prediction. From the marginal probabilities in Table 4-3, we obtain the probabilities of the various predictions. From equations (4-2), (4-3), and (4-4) we obtain the largest possible utilities conditional on the predictions. The expected utility is then

$$(.44)(4.090) + (.27)(3.112) + (.29)(2.690) = 3.420 \qquad (4\text{-}5)$$

which is $3.420 - 3.2 = .220$ higher than the expected utility if the vendor makes the best choice without a forecast. Thus, it would be worth paying the oracle up to .22 utility units to obtain her prediction.

Analysis using opportunity losses

It will often be desirable to perform analyses like the foregoing using opportunity losses rather than utilities. For any state of nature, the opportunity loss of an act is defined as the difference between its utility and the best obtainable utility for that state. For the above example, we would proceed as follows.

1. From Table 4-1 we find that the best possible utility for state θ_1 is 5, and that for state θ_2 is 3.

2. Subtracting the utility for each act from the best possible utility for each state, we obtain the opportunity losses given in Table 4-4.

If we use opportunity losses rather than utilities, then equations (4-1) through (4-5) are replaced by (4-6) through (4-10).

$$\begin{aligned} l(a_1) &= (.6)(0) + (.4)(3) = 1.2 \\ l(a_2) &= (.6)(1) + (.4)(1) = 1.0 \leftarrow \\ l(a_3) &= (.6)(3) + (.4)(0) = 1.8 \end{aligned} \tag{4-6}$$

The smallest expected opportunity loss based only on the weather bureau's probabilities is 1.0. This is the most that should be paid for a perfect forecast in the face of those probabilities.

$$\begin{aligned} l(a_1|x_1) &= (.818)(0) + (.182)(3) = .546 \leftarrow \\ l(a_2|x_1) &= (.818)(1) + (.182)(1) = 1.000 \\ l(a_3|x_1) &= (.818)(3) + (.182)(0) = 2.454 \end{aligned} \tag{4-7}$$

$$\begin{aligned} l(a_1|x_2) &= (.556)(0) + (.444)(3) = 1.332 \\ l(a_2|x_2) &= (.556)(1) + (.444)(1) = 1.000 \leftarrow \\ l(a_3|x_2) &= (.556)(3) + (.444)(0) = 1.668 \end{aligned} \tag{4-8}$$

$$\begin{aligned} l(a_1|x_3) &= (.310)(0) + (.690)(3) = 2.070 \\ l(a_2|x_3) &= (.310)(1) + (.690)(1) = 1.000 \\ l(a_3|x_3) &= (.310)(3) + (.690)(0) = .930 \leftarrow \end{aligned} \tag{4-9}$$

$$(.44)(.546) + (.27)(1.000) + (.29)(.930) = .780 \tag{4-10}$$

Action based on the oracle's prediction results in an opportunity loss that is $1.000 - .780 = .220$ lower than if the vendor makes his best choice using only the weather bureau's probabilities. This reduction in opportunity loss is exactly equal to the gain in utility calculated in the previous section.

TABLE **4-4**

Opportunity losses

Act	States θ_1	θ_2
a_1	0	3
a_2	1	1
a_3	3	0

Formal presentation

In general, we call the various unknown possibilities that await us *states of nature*, and our choices *acts*. We define

$u(a, \theta)$ = utility of the consequences of act a and state of nature θ
$p(\theta)$ = initial assessment of the probability of state θ, also known as the prior probability of θ
$u(a)$ = expected utility of act a

Equations (4-1) above are calculations based on the general formula

$$u(a) = \sum_{\theta} u(a, \theta)p(\theta) \tag{4-11}$$

Before acting, we may have the opportunity to gather additional data to guide us in our assessments of the states of nature. Such data will typically not be a perfect guide but will consist of random outcomes with probabilities depending on the true (but unknown) state of nature. We define

$p(x|\theta)$ = conditional probability of outcome x given state θ, also known as the *likelihood function*
$p(x, \theta)$ = joint probability of x and θ
$p(x)$ = marginal probability of outcome x
$p(\theta|x)$ = conditional probability of state θ given outcome x, also known as the *posterior probability* of θ

According to the basic laws of probability, these satisfy

$$p(x, \theta) = p(x|\theta)p(\theta) \tag{4-12}$$

$$p(x) = \sum_{\theta} p(x, \theta) \tag{4-13}$$

$$p(\theta|x) = \frac{p(x, \theta)}{p(x)} \tag{4-14}$$

These equations have already been used to calculate Table 4-3.

With respect to the posterior probability distribution of θ, the expected utility of act a is

$$u(a|x) = \sum_{\theta} u(a, \theta)p(\theta|x) = \frac{\sum_{\theta} u(a, \theta)p(x, \theta)}{p(x)} \tag{4-15}$$

Since we are free to observe x before we choose a, we will naturally make that choice $a(x)$ that maximizes the posterior expected utilities (see equations (4-2), (4-3), and (4-4)). Such a choice of the act as a function of the observed outcome is called a *decision rule*. Since the outcomes themselves are random, we calculate the expected utility of the decision rule:

$$E_x u(a(x)) = \sum_x u(a(x)|x)p(x) = \sum_{\theta,x} u(a(x), \theta)p(x, \theta) \tag{4-16}$$

Equation (4-5) was calculated using the first equality in (4-16), but the same result is obtained from the second; recalling that $a(x_i) = a_i$ happens to hold in our weather example, we obtain from Tables 4-1 and 4-3

$$(5)(.36) + 0(.08) + 4(.15) + 2(.12) + 2(.09) + 3(.20) = 3.42 \tag{4-17}$$

If we define

$l(a, \theta) =$ opportunity loss of the consequences of act a and state θ

then we have the relationship

$$l(a, \theta) = [\max_a u(a, \theta)] - u(a, \theta) \tag{4-18}$$

For our weather example, we determined the maxima from Table 4-1, and Table 4-4 calculated the opportunity losses.

Equations (4-11), (4-15), and (4-16) carry over to opportunity losses if u is replaced by l. Naturally, we choose the act that minimizes expected opportunity loss; this always results in the same act as maximizing expected utility. For example, if we calculate expected losses with respect to the prior distribution

$$\begin{aligned} l(a) &= \sum_\theta l(a, \theta)p(\theta) \\ &= \sum_\theta \left\{[\max_a u(a, \theta)] - u(a, \theta)\right\}p(\theta) \\ &= \sum_\theta \max_a u(a, \theta)p(\theta) - \sum_\theta u(a, \theta)p(\theta) \end{aligned} \tag{4-19}$$

the first term does not depend on a, and the second is just $-u(a)$. Of course, the corresponding result will hold for $l(a|x)$.

The minimum expected loss with respect to the prior distribution is called the *expected value of perfect information* (EVPI). Thus, using (4-19),

$$\begin{aligned} \text{EVPI} &= \min \sum_\theta l(a, \theta)p(\theta) \\ &= \sum_\theta \max_a u(a, \theta)p(\theta) - \max_a \sum_\theta u(a, \theta)p(\theta) \end{aligned} \tag{4-20}$$

The expected value of perfect information is the difference between the expected utility we would obtain if we could tailor the act to the state of nature and the expected utility we can achieve not knowing the state of nature. For this reason, it is also known as the *cost of uncertainty*.

In the weather example, the expected value of perfect information, obtained from equations (4-6), was 1.0. The expected loss when the outcome x could be observed before choosing an act was .780, a reduction of .220 from the prior cost of uncertainty. This reduction is known as the *expected value of sample information* (EVSI). If we use equation (4-16) as written for expected losses, and then equation (4-18), we obtain

$$\begin{aligned} E_x l(a(x)) &= \sum_{\theta,x} l(a(x), \theta) p(x, \theta) \\ &= \sum_{\theta,x} \left\{ [\max_a u(a, \theta)] - u(a(x), \theta) \right\} p(x, \theta) \\ &= \sum_{\theta,x} [\max_a u(a, \theta)] p(x, \theta) - \sum_{\theta,x} u(a(x), \theta) p(x, \theta) \\ &= \sum_{\theta} [\max_a u(a, \theta)] p(\theta) - \sum_{\theta,x} u(a(x), \theta) p(x, \theta) \end{aligned} \tag{4-21}$$

Thus, from (4-20) and (4-21),

$$\begin{aligned} \text{EVSI} &= \text{EVPI} - E_x l(a(x)) \\ &= \sum_{\theta,x} u(a(x), \theta) p(x, \theta) - \max_a \sum_{\theta} u(a, \theta) p(\theta) \\ &= E_x u(a(x)) - \max_a \sum_{\theta} u(a, \theta) p(\theta) \end{aligned} \tag{4-22}$$

This shows that the expected value of sample information can also be calculated by subtracting the maximum prior expected utility from the maximum expected utility achievable after x has been observed. This has already been verified for the weather example.

Linear utility functions

Suppose, now, that the states of nature θ are describable by means of real numbers, and that the utility of the consequences of act a and state θ is a linear function of θ:

$$u(a, \theta) = K(a) + k(a)\theta \tag{4-23}$$

Then, from (4-15),

$$\begin{aligned} u(a|x) &= \sum_{\theta} u(a, \theta) p(\theta|x) \\ &= \sum_{\theta} [K(a) + k(a)\theta] p(\theta|x) \\ &= K(a) + k(a)\bar{\theta}_x \\ &= u(a, \bar{\theta}_x) \end{aligned} \tag{4-24}$$

where we have introduced the notation

$$\bar{\theta}_x = \sum_{\theta} \theta p(\theta|x) \tag{4-25}$$

for the *posterior expected value* of θ.

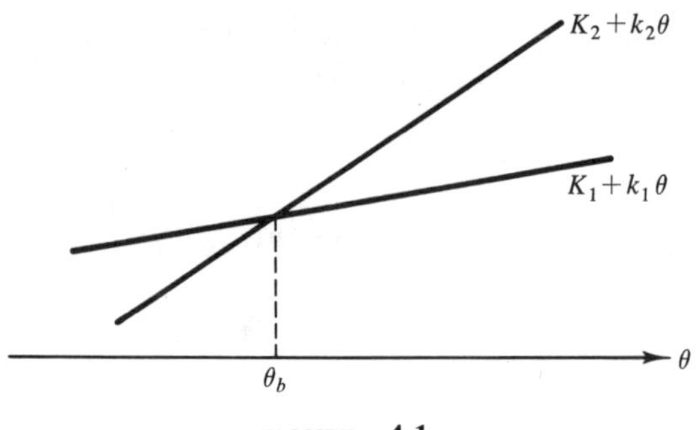

FIGURE **4-1**

Utility functions

Under these circumstances, it is the posterior expected value and not the value of x that is relevant to the choice of the best act. Writing $p(\bar{\theta})$ for the probability of a particular posterior expected value, and $a(\bar{\theta})$ for the best act given that value, we have, from (4-24),

$$u(a(\bar{\theta})|\bar{\theta}) = u(a(\bar{\theta}), \bar{\theta}) = \max_a u(a, \bar{\theta}) \tag{4-26}$$

and, by analogy with (4-16),

$$\begin{aligned} E_{\bar{\theta}}\, u(a(\bar{\theta})) &= \sum_{\bar{\theta}} u(a(\bar{\theta})|\bar{\theta})p(\bar{\theta}) \\ &= \sum_{\bar{\theta}} \max_a u(a, \bar{\theta})p(\bar{\theta}) \end{aligned} \tag{4-27}$$

If we substitute (4-27) into (4-22), we obtain

$$\text{EVSI} = \sum_{\bar{\theta}} \max_a u(a, \bar{\theta})p(\bar{\theta}) - \max_a \sum_{\theta} u(a, \theta)p(\theta) \tag{4-28}$$

which is of the same form as equation (4-20) for EVPI. Thus, if utility is a linear function of the state θ, then the expected value of sample information is the difference between the expected utility we would obtain if we could tailor the act to the posterior expected value of the state of nature and the expected utility we can achieve knowing only the prior distribution.

Linear utilities, two acts, normal probability distributions

Denoting the unknown state of nature by θ, suppose that we must choose between two acts having utility functions

$$u(a_i, \theta) = K_i + k_i\theta \qquad i = 1, 2 \tag{4-29}$$

These utility functions are shown in Figure 4-1. The *break-even value*, θ_b, can be obtained by equating the two functions and solving for θ:

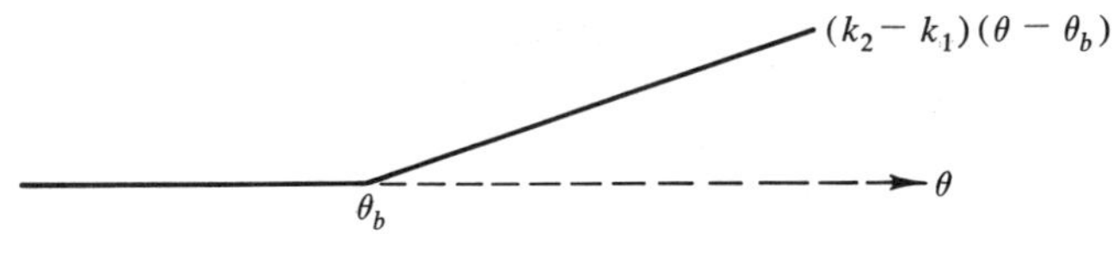

FIGURE 4-2

Loss function for a_1

$$\theta_b = \frac{K_1 - K_2}{k_2 - k_1} \tag{4-30}$$

We see that if we know θ, then a_1 is preferred for any $\theta < \theta_b$. Thus, the opportunity loss function of a_1 is

$$l(a_1, \theta) = \begin{cases} 0 & \theta \leq \theta_b \\ (k_2 - k_1)(\theta - \theta_b) & \theta > \theta_b \end{cases} \tag{4-31}$$

This is shown in Figure 4-2.

Now suppose that θ has a normal distribution with mean θ_0 and variance σ_0^2. Then the expected utilities are

$$u(a_i) = K_i + k_i\theta_0 \qquad i = 1, 2 \tag{4-32}$$

and a_1 is preferred if $\theta_0 < \theta_b$. The expected loss of a_1 is

$$\begin{aligned} l(a_1) &= \int_{\theta_b}^{\infty} (k_2 - k_1)(\theta - \theta_b) \frac{1}{\sqrt{2\pi}\,\sigma_o} \exp\left[-\frac{(\theta - \theta_0)^2}{2\sigma_0^2}\right] d\theta \\ &= (k_2 - k_1)\sigma_0 \int_{t_{b0}}^{\infty} (t - t_{b0}) \frac{1}{\sqrt{2\pi}} \exp\left[-\frac{t^2}{2}\right] dt \end{aligned} \tag{4-33}$$

where

$$t_{b0} = \frac{\theta_b - \theta_0}{\sigma_0} \tag{4-34}$$

The final integral in equation (4-33), known as the *unit normal loss integral*, is a function[4] of just the one quantity t_{b0}.

Similarly, if $\theta_0 > \theta_b$, then a_2 is preferred, and

$$\begin{aligned} l(a_2) &= \int_{-\infty}^{\theta_b} (k_2 - k_1)(\theta_b - \theta) \frac{1}{\sqrt{2\pi}\,\sigma_0} \exp\left[-\frac{(\theta - \theta_0)^2}{2\sigma_0^2}\right] d\theta \\ &= (k_2 - k_1)\sigma_0 \int_{-\infty}^{t_{b0}} (-t + t_{b0}) \frac{1}{\sqrt{2\pi}} \exp\left[-\frac{t^2}{2}\right] dt \\ &= (k_2 - k_1)\sigma_0 \int_{-t_{b0}}^{\infty} (t - (-t_{b0})) \frac{1}{\sqrt{2\pi}} \exp\left[-\frac{t^2}{2}\right] dt \end{aligned} \tag{4-35}$$

[4] See R. Schlaifer, *Probability and Statistics for Business Decisions*, McGraw-Hill, New York, 1959, p. 706, for a table.

Since the EVPI is the expected opportunity loss of the preferred act, and taking into account the fact that when a_1 is preferred t_{b0} is positive, whereas when a_2 is preferred $-t_{b0}$ is positive, we have

$$\text{EVPI} = (k_2 - k_1)\sigma_0 \int_{|t_{b0}|}^{\infty} (t - |t_{b0}|) \frac{1}{\sqrt{2\pi}} \exp\left[-\frac{t^2}{2}\right] dt \tag{4-36}$$

Now suppose that before choosing an act we can observe data x, which is normally distributed with mean θ and *known* variance σ^2. According to equation (3-60), the unconditional distribution of this data is also normal, with mean θ_0 and variance $\sigma^2 + \sigma_0^2$. Furthermore, from equation (3-62) the posterior mean is

$$E(\theta|x) = \frac{\sigma_0^2 x + \sigma^2\theta_0}{\sigma^2 + \sigma_0^2} \tag{4-37}$$

which is then normally distributed with mean θ_0 and variance $\sigma_0^4/(\sigma^2 + \sigma_0^2)$. But from the previous section of this chapter we know that with linear utilities the EVSI is of the same form as the EVPI, but with the distribution of the posterior mean replacing the prior distribution of the state. Thus,

$$\text{EVSI} = (k_2 - k_1) \frac{\sigma_0^2}{\sqrt{\sigma^2 + \sigma_0^2}} \int_{t_{b\bar{\theta}}}^{\infty} (t - |t_{b\bar{\theta}}|) \frac{1}{\sqrt{2\pi}} \exp\left[-\frac{t^2}{2}\right] dt \tag{4-38}$$

where

$$t_{b\bar{\theta}} = \frac{\theta_b - \theta_0}{\sigma_0^2/\sqrt{\sigma^2 + \sigma_0^2}} \tag{4-39}$$

Since the same function is involved, the table previously referred to can be used to evaluate (4-38).

PROBLEM 1

A mail-order company is about to send out a mailing of 100,000 pieces. Using an old mailing list, its fixed costs for this mailing are \$10,000, and it is rather certain that it will get a 2 percent response. Since the gross profit per response is \$7.50, the net profit of the mailing is expected to be $(100{,}000)(.02)(7.5) - 10{,}000 = \$5{,}000$.

Before sending out the mailing, the company decides to consider a new mailing list. The fixed costs remain at \$10,000, but the exact percent response is unknown. However, it is estimated that the percent response will be either 1, 2, or 3, with the following probabilities:

Percent response	Probability
1	.50
2	.25
3	.25

(a) Set up the utility and loss tables for this problem using the two mailing lists as the acts and the three percent responses for the second list as the states. (Does the utility of the old list depend on the percent response to the new list? Does the opportunity loss?)

(b) Which is the preferred act, and what is the expected value of perfect information?

PROBLEM 2

Now suppose that, before deciding between the two lists in Problem 1, the company decides to obtain more information. A random sample of 5 customers from the new list is sent the mailing, and 1 of the 5 responds. From a table of the binomial distribution it is found that the following are the probabilities of the number of responses in a random sample of 5 customers as a function of the overall percent response of the list:

Number of responses	Percent response 1	2	3
0	.951	.904	.858
1	.048	.092	.134
2	.001	.004	.008

(a) Now which is the preferred act, and what is its expected opportunity loss?

(b) Considering also the other outcomes that might have occurred, what is the expected value of sample information of the mailing to 5 customers chosen randomly from the new list?

PROBLEM 3

It may be instructive to redo Problems 1 and 2 using normal approximations to the distributions. For this purpose, it is more convenient to use the fractional, rather than percent, response. The original distribution for the fractional response (Problem 1) had

$$\text{mean} = \theta_0 = .0175$$

$$\text{standard deviation} = \sigma_0 = .0083$$

The average number of responses in a sample of five (Problem 2) has

$$\text{mean} = \theta$$

$$\text{standard deviation}^{5} = \sigma = .0626$$

Calculate the EVPI and EVSI, and compare them with the answers obtained in Problems 1 and 2.

[5] We have substituted $\theta = .02$ in the formula $\sigma^2 = \theta(1-\theta)/5$.

PRODUCT DECISIONS

CHAPTER FIVE

Most managerial product decisions are in some way related to the introduction of new products to the firm's markets. For example, even when a company attempts to reduce the number of items in its product line, the impetus for this move is often the desire to add a product to the existing line. The principal questions on which product operating policies must be evolved are: (1) Should the firm be a multiproduct or a single-product firm? (2) To what extent will the firm seek new products as opposed to variations of existing products? (3) Should the new products or variations of existing products predominate among the items ultimately commercialized? (4) Which products should be brought to the marketplace? (5) What is an appropriate control system for the number of products in the product line? (6) Should the firm be a leader or a follower in product improvement and development? Although the material in this chapter is written from the viewpoint of a manufacturer, the same set of decisions and the same techniques apply to firms offering services and to other members of the channel of distribution.

What is a product?

One of the most difficult managerial problems in the product area is the determination of what constitutes an individual product. The introduction of a new product requires quite a different set of decisions than does the addition of a new feature to an already existing product. The question of identifying separate products can be approached by examining (1) the coincidence of the production and marketing systems for the product of concern with the systems for other products in the firm's line, (2) the set of benefits the consumer may receive, and (3) the nature of directly competitive product offerings. The greater the separation of two products on this three-dimensional scale, the clearer it is that different products are being dealt with. Obviously, we are not restricted to a three-dimensional system if some larger set of factors lends more clarity to the issue; in any case, the useful concept is that of spatial separation. Thinking of the problem in this manner avoids many of the difficulties commonly encountered in considering whether a particular item is a variation of other items or a distinct product. For example, the Chevrolet automobile is much closer dimensionally to the Cadillac than to a General Motors bus because of the similarities in (1) marketing channels and promotional methods; (2) functional and, to some extent, psychological motivations and satisfactions of the consumer; (3) competitors' products (that is, degree of similarity on the preceding points); and so on. Thus, Chevrolet and Cadillac are really varieties in one of General Motors' product lines, automobiles, whereas buses constitute a separate product line. The structure of the firm is not a relevant concern; separate divisions and different product managers may deal with the same product.

An important question arises concerning the meaning of newness to the firm as compared to newness to the industry. The firm must plan principally on the basis of what is new to it, even though other firms may manufacture similar products. One danger here is that if the product is new only to the particular company, the company's planners may be too greatly influenced by what competitors have done. On the other hand, a company may have to imitate a competitor because it has failed to anticipate shifts in consumer preferences, and must then attempt to make its product line the equivalent of the competitor's.

Forces favoring the multiproduct firm

Of the forces influencing the firm to adopt the multiproduct position, none is more powerful than the character of the society itself. A consumption-oriented society in which consumers have vast spending power and are able to indulge their tastes for a tremendous variety of goods leads to relative instability in a product's position in the marketplace. In economies less developed than that of the United States, the firm concerns itself much less with shifts in consumer tastes or industrial technology; further, those shifts that do occur take place over relatively long periods of time, and the economic penalty for not quickly diagnosing these changes and responding appropriately is not so severe.

The trend toward more equal distribution of the wealth of the society is a primary force in moving the firm toward a multiproduct position. Changes in styles of living affect the demand for various products. For example, the incurring of debt as a means of acquiring goods very rarely constrains the consumer in a society that has developed a highly refined credit mechanism for the consumer as well as for the enterprise.[1] A shorter work week means that the consumer is free to pursue a variety of interests beyond those concerned with earning a living and operating the household unit. The bulk of American society is now urban (or suburban) in character, living in megalopolises and subject to a different and more varied set of wants than existed in a predominantly rural nation.

A more detailed illustration may aid in understanding the effect of changes in styles of living as a stimulus to product development. A substantial increase in home ownership in the United States has occurred since World War II. In turn, particularly in suburban areas, sizable plots of lawn have to be tended. Manufacturers first responded by producing power lawn mowers to lighten the chore of the suburbanite. Some time later, manufacturers again improved their offerings by producing power mowers that could be ridden, lightening the chore still further. It is such differences between similar responses to the same set of consumer needs that create some of the instability a manufacturer is confronted with in the marketplace.

Many changes have also occurred in the ways individuals accomplish their routine tasks. These changes, in turn, may stimulate the growth of products. For example, continuing technological changes in communications and transportation clearly affect consumer tastes. Consumers may develop a habit of using television as a principal source of information upon which to base decisions about certain classes of purchases. Purchases of other types may then partially depend upon what the consumer is exposed to via television, bringing about a more generalized shift in his taste toward those kinds of products most amenable to television advertising. In children's toys, for example, television advertising forces emphasis on active toys, such as hula hoops and slot racing cars, at the expense of passive toys, such as dolls and board games. Similarly, changes in transportation, especially the increased use of the automobile by housewives, have given rise to the development of large shopping plazas and have produced changes in consumer shopping patterns, with appropriate responses by manufacturers and resellers.[2]

It is extremely difficult for the manufacturer to forecast shifts in consumer tastes. Therefore, he may try to lead these consumers by means of product innovation. An example may be taken from an industrial manufacturing situation. For a number of years, the Goodyear Rubber Company has

---

[1] James Bayton also points out that the psychological inhibitions regarding the use of credit, and conversely the importance of building savings, have declined. See "Motivation, Cognition, Learning—Basic Factors in Consumer Behavior," *Journal of Marketing*, Vol. 22, January 1958, pp. 282–289.

[2] A list of social and economic trends influencing product development may be found in Martin Zober, *Marketing Management*, Wiley, New York, 1964, p. 63.

produced a latex-based additive for the asphalt used in road paving. In early tests, the additive increased the road life of a surface by a significant factor so that it was frequently many years before any maintenance was required; it made the road more pliable—more responsive to temperature changes, allowing easier expansion and contraction—and generally gave a longer-lasting black appearance that contrasted well with the painted road markings. In spite of the test results, the highway engineers and the public officials responsible for allocating highway funds were reluctant to use this additive because it added from two to twenty cents per square yard to paving costs. However, in recent years, several state highway departments have experimented with the additive on an extensive scale, increasing the demand to the extent that two other rubber companies have entered the field. What has occurred is a shift over time in the institutional consumer's value system. Certainly the economic values were as great ten years ago as they are now, if not greater, in terms of the savings to be incurred. However, it is only recently that the product has been widely accepted. The manufacturer who led the way, Goodyear, of course stands to benefit in that its sales engineers have been pointing out the merits of this product to highway engineers across the country for a number of years, and the company name is probably strongly associated with the generic product.[3]

The preceding discussion has attempted to demonstrate the interrelationship between changes in consumer preferences and product line expansion. There are also several other sets of factors that move the firm toward the multiproduct position. One of these is the nature of the competitive system. A prime motivation for the development of new products, or even variations of existing products, is to beat one's competitors to the marketplace. That is, the firm tries to anticipate consumers' changing wants and respond to them before competitors do. If a manufacturer fails to do this, his incentive for new product development then becomes the need to equalize his offering in the marketplace by imitating his competitor. In either case, there are pressures for product line expansion.

There are also certain industry-wide effects that influence manufacturers. In some industries, such as clothing and appliances, periodic model changes are a trade practice, whereas in others there is a need to convert excess materials, left over after production of the basic products, into marketable products. An unusually strong example of the latter would be the petroleum industry, in which both natural gas and petrochemicals have taken their place with basic petroleum products as a source of profit. In addition, the perseverance of the firm in seeking out new products is strongly related to the rate of technological innovation in the firm's industry as it results in technological obsolescence of existing products. If this rate is high, then the firm must have a regular program devoted to developing new

[3] New York *Times*, November 7, 1965, p. 46.

products; if the rate is low, the firm may periodically introduce new products as a result of windfall discoveries or marketing propositions from other firms.

It is quite clear, then, that the primary influence on product expansion comes from the ultimate consumer market with some secondary considerations from the manufacturer's own competitive situation. As markets become more segmented, in terms of both use opportunities and consumer tastes, the possibilities and hence the competitive need for new products grow rapidly. Given these factors, it is difficult to see how a firm can elect to be a single-product firm. Of course, many firms start out with only one product, but it is evident that all firms will, in the long run, decide in favor of the multiproduct position. Once this decision has been made, the firm is then confronted with the second product decision, which is the extent to which it will emphasize new products as opposed to seeking variations in the existing products.

Factors influencing the search for new products

An important factor in successful introduction of new products is compatibility with the present resource structure of the firm. The process whereby this situation is analyzed is well described in several other publications, and the following is intended only as a summary of some of the considerations.[4]

First, the production and marketing of the proposed new products must be compared to the arrangements in force for existing products. Obviously, a firm would prefer to develop new products that had either the same production requirements or the same marketing requirements as some of their existing products.[5] If neither of these were coincident, the chances are that the firm would either have to defer marketing of such a product until some future time when its capital resources were very large or borrow capital if the expected payoff could be demonstrated to be very high. The second point, then, has to do with the availability of capital and the comparative opportunity costs of the various alternatives. Clearly, there are times of capital shortage in the life of any firm. In addition, it may be that although a new product appears to have excellent chances of success, a similar sum of money invested in more intensive marketing of the existing products will

---

[4] See, for example, Martin Zober, *op. cit.* pp. 41, 42; Fred M. Jones, *Introduction to Marketing Management*, Appleton-Century-Crofts, New York, 1964, pp. 238–239; or Charles H. Kline, "The Strategy of Product Policy," *Harvard Business Review*, Vol. 33, July-August 1955, p. 92.

[5] An excellent discussion of convergence and divergence in production and marketing systems is given in Thomas A. Staudt and Donald A. Taylor, *A Managerial Introduction to Marketing*, Prentice-Hall, Englewood Cliffs, N.J., 1965, ch. 9.

produce greater returns to the firm or returns with less uncertainty. Third, not only must the marketing or distribution system be evaluated in terms of similarity of the marketing mixes required, but also the coincidence, or lack thereof, of market target groups with the present customer groups must be examined. Finally, the extent to which present executive talent can be devoted to marketing this new product is very important, as is the availability of new executive personnel if the present staff is insufficient.

Product variation vs. new product development

There are many difficulties involved in marketing new products that act as hindrances to their addition to the product line and favor the development of variations of existing products. For example, one of the key factors is the uncertainty about demand for the new product, which, in turn, leads to uncertainty on how to price the product, how to advertise it, and so on. It is not nearly so difficult to establish price for a product variation because of the wealth of information that has been collected on similar products. A second hindrance has to do with the transferability of knowledge. A new product may require new technology or, say, new sales techniques that would require extensive training of both the manufacturer's own sales force and middlemen. The same constraint holds for the production facilities or any other part of the enterprise. This point is related to the one in the previous paragraph having to do with the extent of the utilization of the present marketing structure—if the coincidence is high, then the capacity to absorb the new product may not be there; on the other hand, if coincidence is low, then organizational problems may result in terms of structuring the new organization. Still another drawback to the introduction of new products is the generally greater risk involved in marketing them. The marketing of new products is extremely risky; some estimates indicate that approximately 80 percent of the product ideas that are developed and brought to the market fail. Many firms tend to prefer conservative alternatives, even if the expected value of risky ones is high. The safer alternative is usually the addition of varieties. In general, it can be seen that there are rather strong forces favoring expansion in the direction of variations of existing products over the introduction of new ones.

Given the apparently large drawbacks just discussed, it is not unreasonable to ask why many firms continue to expend so much effort in marketing new products. If the frequent changes that occur in consumer tastes are considered, it may be suspected that firms decide in favor of accepting the risks involved in taking new products to the marketplace because of the tremendous cost of failure to keep up with these shifts in consumer preferences. That is, the relative risk involved in not innovating is much greater in terms of its effect upon profits than that involved in having a high product failure rate. In addition, this decision is directly affected by what might be called the "style" of the management. Some managers, either as a reflection of their own personalities or as a result of the philosophy prevailing within their organizations, place a very high premium on "being first" or pioneering within their industries. It is not that the monetary rewards are proved greater for following such a course, but the management believes them to be so. Such a belief is likely to produce a style of leadership and an organizational environment that push for new product development.

Steps in the product development process

There are many schemes for formalization of the process, whereby a product idea is taken from its inception through various evaluative and design stages until it is finally marketed. The steps commonly found can be categorized as follows: (1) a product idea accumulation phase; (2) a screening phase, in which the many ideas uncovered in the first stage are reduced to a few worthy of further exploration; (3) a product structuring phase, in which the physical characteristics of the product that are most amenable to the firm's production and marketing systems,[6] or contemplated systems, are worked out; (4) a market testing phase; and (5) the addition of the product to the firm's regular product line, or commercialization. Figure 5-1 illustrates the system used by the B. F. Goodrich Company for product development.

At one time, the uncovering of new product ideas for the firm was something that was left mostly to chance. However, two structural changes have occurred in the business environment that have made this course of action all but impossible: first, the rapid growth of technological knowledge, and second, the previously mentioned adoption of a strong consumer orientation by a great many enterprises. In industries with an advanced state of product technology, the probability of any other than very crude product ideas originating outside the firm's research and development laboratory is quite low; the principal reason for this situation is the tremendous cost of appropriate laboratory facilities for experimentation. Following the lead of the science-oriented companies, other firms established research and development operations, and these then became the primary basis for new product ideas. There are, however, other sources that, although their contribution may be less than that of the research and development groups, occasionally bring forth new product ideas. Among these are a firm's own employees, suppliers, customers, governmental agencies, and so on. In addition, merger and acquisition, as well as the leasing of patent rights, are means of expanding the product line, and the potential products involved should be subjected to much the same kind of evaluation process as a new product idea. Of the multitude of ideas that a firm considers during this initial discovery period, very few go beyond the next phase, that of screening.

The screening stage may have two steps: first, to take raw ideas and de-

[6] *Marketing system* as it is used here is taken to include consumer preferences.

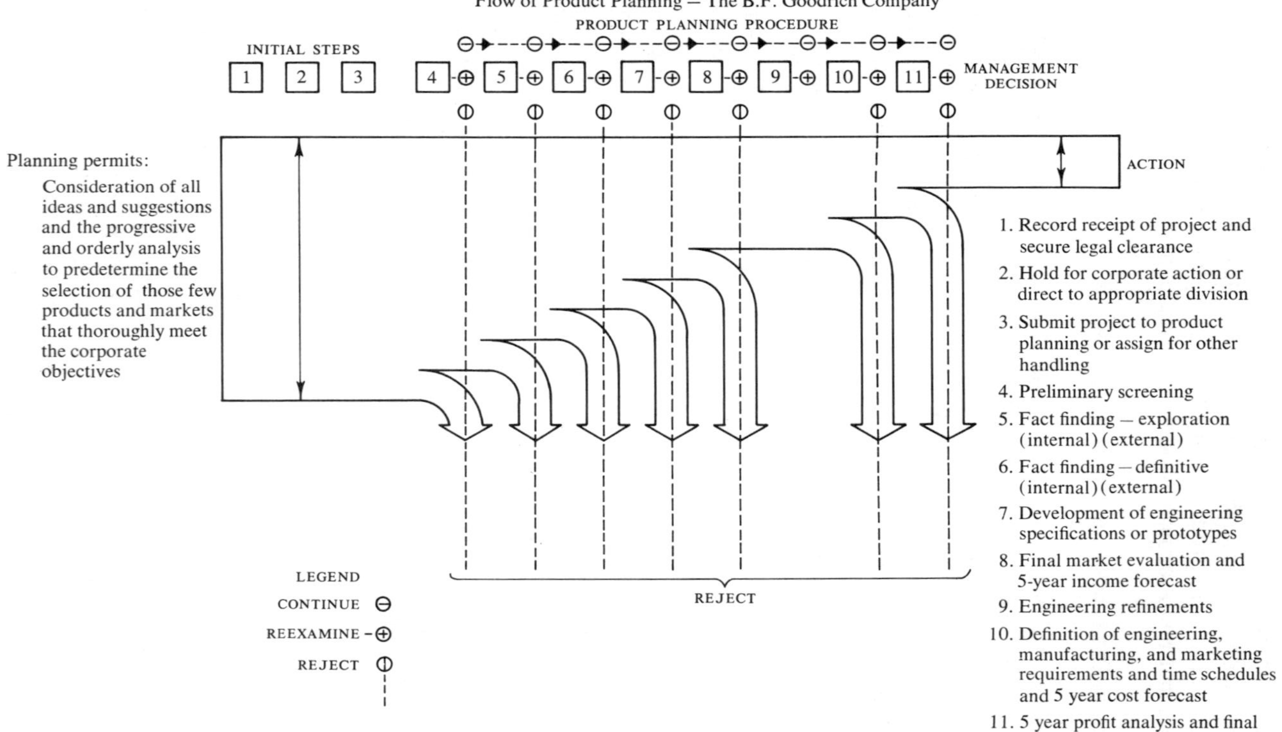

FIGURE **5-1**

Flow of product planning—the B. F. Goodrich Company. SOURCE: *"Appraising the Market for New Industrial Products," National Industrial Conference Board,* Studies in Business Policy *No. 123, New York, 1967, p. 9.*

velop them into potential products, and second, to filter out those potential products that are not consistent with the firm's objectives and resource structure. This type of work is frequently done by a committee because of the necessity of viewing the new idea from a variety of angles. An idea that may seem perfectly capable of achieving market success may have almost insurmountable production, financial, or personnel difficulties; marketing may, of course, also be the problem area with all the others being favorable.

The product structuring phase, which follows next, is the one in which the basic nature of the product is determined; certain features, such as color, can still be revised after the marketing testing stage but not the product's function or the basic means by which it accomplishes this function. Since no product actually yet exists, the information collection process at this point is frequently referred to as *concept testing*. Some of the data sought may concern[7];

1. Applications and situations for which the new product might be used
2. Identification of various types of users for the proposed product, and the specific needs of each
3. Desired product attributes
4. Relative importance of proposed features and intended functions of the product to different classes of users
5. Design parameters for the product
6. Economic utility of the product to potential users and general evidence about pricing possibilities
7. Preliminary indications of potential sales volume
8. How the product could best be marketed, for example, advance clues to suitable channels of distribution, promotional requirements, etc.
9. Estimates of production capabilities and attendant costs

The structuring of the marketing strategy for the new product goes hand in hand with the structuring of the product itself. Information such as that above is essential for developing the marketing mix (that is, the combination of promotion, channel, and price strategies) to be used for the prospective product. For example, low production costs may permit a price for the new product that results in rapid market penetration. Kotler points out that it is extremely important to evaluate simultaneously the profit potentials of the various marketing mixes contemplated at this phase in the product development process.[8] It is in the product structuring phase that investment first becomes substantial, particularly as a result of the development and pro-

---

[7] National Industrial Conference Board, "Appraising the Market for New Industrial Products," *Studies in Business Policy*, No. 123, New York, 1967, p. 33.

[8] Philip Kotler, "Marketing Mix Decisions for New Products," *Journal of Marketing Research*, Vol. 1, No. 1, February 1964, p. 43. All the special problems that arise in the development of the marketing mix for a new product could be discussed here, but it would be redundant since these are principally variants on the subjects taken up in other chapters.

duction of the prototype product. From here on, each phase is likely to be more expensive than the preceding one, so the commitment at the product structuring phase must be particularly carefully evaluated.[9]

The market testing phase may include either or both of the following: (1) laboratory testing for purposes of comparing performance to that of competitive or substitute products, an example of which would be an automobile tire manufacturer's tests for tread wear, puncture resistance, traction, and so on; and (2) actual sales tests in selected cities, possibly with other cities serving as controls if the characteristics of the product and its marketing mix are to be manipulated. In addition, consumer-use tests are frequently undertaken to determine if consumers can and do use the product properly, for example, to ascertain if a product is used according to instructions. One packaged foods manufacturer withdrew from the market a new powder for making hot chocolate after it was learned that housewives were still using two to three teaspoons per cup when directions specified that only one was to be used because of the greater "chocolatiness" of the new product. After these tests, the manufacturer still may delay entry into the market. A frequently overlooked evaluation affecting this decision that should take place at this point is balancing the "engineering" maturity of the product against the market opportunity. If the technical aspects of the product can be further improved prior to full-scale production but if such a delay would reduce its sales potential, the firm may elect to proceed immediately to commercialization. The hope, then, is to make appropriate technical adjustments in the field, as in the case of an industrial product or a consumer durable, or on subsequent production runs.

After completion of the market tests, the probable success of the new product is again evaluated, and this is the last opportunity to do so before the company becomes fully committed. At this point, the manufacturer has close to the maximum amount of information he is likely to get on which to base his forecast of success. He can, of course, elect to wait longer, but then a problem arises concerning the appropriate timing of the product's introduction; this will be discussed subsequently.

The final phase is that of making the product available in the marketplace on the scale intended under the program outlined in the previously developed marketing plan. The goal of this phase is to carry out the marketing plan until the product becomes a regular feature of the firm's product line, at which time the marketing emphasis must shift to other kinds of problems.

A brief comment about the role of marketing personnel in the developmental process may be useful. The marketing people should be involved in every phase of the developmental process, particularly in supplying much of the information on which the decisions must be based. Obtaining their identification with the product early in its developmental process is also

[9] Ralph W. Jones, "Management of New Products," *Journal of Industrial Engineering*, Vol. II, No. 5, September–October 1958, p. 432.

important because it commits them to the product's ultimate success or failure.

Product profile analysis: a method for evaluating potential new product alternatives

In this and the next two sections, we present a means of evaluating the potential of a new product idea through improvements in existing methodology and incorporation of the decision theoretic approach. This model probably has its greatest applicability at the screening stage in the product development process. It can be designed primarily to focus on the marketing aspects—as we do in our discussion of the model—or as a broad instrument to determine the overall compatibility of the product idea with the firm's resource structure.[10] The successful use of the model, in either event, is a function of how well the important factors, or criteria for evaluation, have been identified.

One of the most commonly accepted means for evaluating potential products is the use of some sort of rating scheme.[11] However, directly estimating overall performance ratings on a single scale for each of several product opportunities would be akin to crystal-ball gazing. Consequently, in order to be more meaningful, most rating systems estimate individual scores on a number of important criteria of evaluation. A rating scale ranging from, say, 10 points for "very good" down to 2 points for "very poor" might be used for each criterion. An overall weighted score could then be calculated using weights for the individual criteria based on their relative importance.[12] This single number can then be used to answer such questions as whether a particular product is sufficiently promising to promote, or which of a number of products is most promising. This method, frequently referred to as *product profile analysis*, has widespread acceptability among executives, particularly because (1) it is not highly abstract, permitting a person with limited mathematical skill to comprehend the methodology, and (2) it appears to be a quantification of the reasoning process that an executive might actually follow. Some of the important deficiencies of this method have been pointed out by Alderson and Green,[13] but these need not concern us here.

---

[10] See Table 5-1, which gives an idea of the breadth of the variables that may be included within the framework of the model.

[11] John T. O'Meara, Jr., "Selecting Profitable Products," *Harvard Business Review*, Vol. 39, No. 1, January–February 1961, pp. 83–99; Wroe Alderson and Paul Green, *Planning and Problem Solving in Marketing*, Richard D. Irwin, Homewood, Ill., 1964, pp. 204–207; or Herbert Terry, "Comparative Evaluation of Performance Using Multiple Criteria," *Management Science*, Vol. 39, No. 3, April 1963, pp. 431–442; Edgar A. Pessemier, *New Product Decisions: An Analytical Approach*, McGraw-Hill, New York, 1966.

[12] Later in this section we develop these weights from a different point of view.

[13] Wroe Alderson and Paul Green, *loc. cit.*

Tables 5-1 and 5-2 reproduce two of the tables devised by O'Meara.[14] We shall use them as the basis for illustrating our approach to new product evaluation. On referring to Table 5-1, we see that there are 17 individual subfactors; thus, each potential product gives rise to 17 individual subfactor scores that may be thought of as a 17-dimensional vector. Data on these subfactors would usually be in the form of analyses conducted by the marketing research, economic analysis, and other groups. For example, the purchasing department may assess the availability of raw materials and the quality of the potential suppliers. The results of these analyses, though, do not have to be in as judgmental a form as Table 5-1 but can actually be quantitative estimates; for example, growth potential could be expressed as five different rates at which sales might be expected to grow within a well-defined time period.

On the other hand, in the usual approach to product profile analysis, the weights are most frequently the result of either singular or combined subjective evaluations by managers and staff involved in the problem.[15] We suggest the following alternative method for obtaining the weights. Given the objective of determining whether the product will be successful or not, we can suppose two 17-dimensional probability distributions, one of scores from successful products and one of scores from unsuccessful products.[16] The two likelihoods of the observed vector from these distributions can now be computed. Assuming a multivariate normal distribution, the probability density function of x (the observed value) given Σ (the variance–covariance matrix) and μ (the mean) is[17]

$$\frac{1}{\sqrt{(2\pi)^n|\Sigma|}} \exp\left[-\tfrac{1}{2}(x-\mu)^t\Sigma^{-1}(x-\mu)\right] \tag{5-1}$$

The likelihood ratio, LR, is the ratio of the probability density function of success, subscripted 1, to that of failure, subscripted 2.

$$\mathrm{LR} = \frac{[1/(\sqrt{(2\pi)^n|\Sigma_1|})] \exp\left[-\tfrac{1}{2}(x-\mu_1)^t\Sigma_1^{-1}(x-\mu_1)\right]}{[1/(\sqrt{(2\pi)^n|\Sigma_2|})] \exp\left[-\tfrac{1}{2}(x-\mu_2)^t\Sigma_2^{-1}(x-\mu_2)\right]} \tag{5-2}$$

[14] John T. O'Meara, *loc. cit.*

[15] A procedure for obtaining these judgments is outlined in C. West Churchman, R. S. Ackoff, and E. L. Arnoff, *Introduction to Operations Research*, Wiley, New York, 1952, ch. 6.

[16] At the screening stage, this dichotomy should suffice; at later stages, the range from total success to total failure must be broken down more finely. For the mathematical analysis of this problem, see: T. W. Anderson, *An Introduction to Multivariate Statistical Analysis*, Wiley, New York, 1958, sect. 6.4, "Classification into one of two known multivariate normal populations," pp. 133–137.

[17] In general, $x-\mu$ is an n-dimensional column vector, its transpose $(x-\mu)^t$ is an n-dimensional row vector, and Σ is an $n \times n$ square matrix with determinant $|\Sigma|$. We would, of course, take $n = 17$.

TABLE **5-1**

Factor and Subfactor Ratings for a New Product

	Very Good	Good	Average	Poor	Very Poor
I. MARKETABILITY					
A. *Relation to present distribution channels*	Can reach major markets by distributing through present channels.	Can reach major markets by distributing mostly through present channels, partly through new channels.	Will have to distribute equally between new and present channels, in order to reach major markets.	Will have to distribute mostly through new channels in order to reach major markets.	Will have to distribute entirely through new channels in order to reach major markets.
B. *Relation to present product lines*	Complements a present line which needs more products to fill it.	Complements a present line that does not need, but can handle, another product.	Can be fitted into a present line.	Can be fitted in a present line but does not fit entirely.	Does not fit in with any present product line.
C. *Quality/price relationship*	Priced below all competing products of similar quality.	Priced below most competing products of similar quality.	Approximately the same price as competing products of similar quality.	Priced above many competing products of similar quality.	Priced above all competing products of similar quality.
D. *Number of sizes and grades*	Few staple sizes and grades.	Several sizes and grades, but customers will be satisfied with few staples.	Several sizes and grades, but can satisfy customer wants with small inventory of nonstaples.	Several sizes and grades, each of which will have to be stocked in equal amounts.	Many sizes and grades which will necessitate heavy inventories.
E. *Merchandisability*	Has product characteristics over and above those of competing products that lend themselves to the kind of promotion, advertising, and display that the given company does best.	Has promotable characteristics that will compare favorably with the characteristics of competing products.	Has promotable characteristics that are equal to those of other products.	Has a few characteristics that are promotable, but generally does not measure up to characteristics of competing products.	Has no characteristics at all that are equal to competitors' or that lend themselves to imaginative promotion.
F. *Effects on sales of present products*	Should aid in sales of present products.	May help sales of present products; definitely will not be harmful to present sales.	Should have no effect on present sales.	May hinder present sales some; definitely will not aid present sales.	Will reduce sales of presently profitable products.

(continued)

TABLE **5-1** *(continued)*

Factor and Subfactor Ratings for a New Product

	Very Good	Good	Average	Poor	Very Poor
II. DURABILITY					
A. *Stability*	Basic product which can always expect to have uses.	Product which will have uses long enough to earn back initial investment, plus at least 10 years of additional profits.	Product which will have uses long enough to earn back initial investment, plus several (from 5 to 10) years of additional profits.	Product which will have uses long enough to earn back initial investment, plus 1 to 5 years of additional profits.	Product which will probably be obsolete in near future.
B. *Breadth of market*	A national market, a wide variety of consumers, and a potential foreign market.	A national market and a wide variety of consumers.	Either a national market or a wide variety of consumers.	A regional market and a restricted variety of consumers.	A specialized market in a small marketing area.
C. *Resistance to cyclical fluctuations*	Will sell readily in inflation or depression.	Effects of cyclical changes will be *moderate*, and will be felt *after* changes in economic outlook.	Sales will rise and fall with the economy.	Effects of cyclical changes will be *heavy*, and will be felt *before* changes in economic outlook.	Cyclical changes will cause extreme fluctuations in demand.
D. *Resistance to seasonal fluctuations*	Steady sales throughout the year.	Steady sales—except under unusual circumstances.	Seasonal fluctuations, but inventory and personnel problems can be absorbed.	Heavy seasonal fluctuations that will cause considerable inventory and personnel problems.	Severe seasonal fluctuations that will necessitate layoffs and heavy inventories.
E. *Exclusiveness of design*	Can be protected by a patent with no loopholes.	Can be patented, but the patent might be circumvented.	Cannot be patented, but has certain salient characteristics that cannot be copied very well.	Cannot be patented, and can be copied by larger, more knowledgeable companies.	Cannot be patented, and can be copied by anyone.
III. PRODUCTIVE ABILITY					
A. *Equipment necessary*	Can be produced with equipment that is presently idle.	Can be produced with present equipment, but production will have to be scheduled with other products.	Can be produced largely with present equipment, but the company will have to purchase some additional equipment.	Company will have to buy a good deal of new equipment, but some present equipment can be used.	Company will have to buy all new equipment.

B. *Production knowledge and personnel necessary*	Present knowledge and personnel will be able to produce new product.	With very few minor exceptions, present knowledge and personnel will be able to produce new product.	With some exceptions, present knowledge and personnel will be able to produce new product.	A ratio of approximately 50-50 will prevail between the needs for new knowledge and personnel and for present knowledge and personnel.	Mostly new knowledge and personnel are needed to produce the new product.
C. *Raw materials' availability*	Company can purchase raw materials from its best supplier(s) exclusively.	Company can purchase major portion of raw materials from its best supplier(s), and remainder from any one of a number of companies.	Company can purchase approximately half of raw materials from its best supplier(s), and other half from any one of a number of companies.	Company must purchase most of raw materials from any one of a number of companies other than its best supplier(s).	Company must purchase most or all of raw materials from a certain few companies other than its best supplier(s).
IV. GROWTH POTENTIAL					
A. *Place in market*	New type of product that will fill a need presently not being filled.	Products that will substantially improve on products presently on the market.	Product that will have certain new characteristics that will appeal to a substantial segment of the market.	Product that will have minor improvements over products presently on the market.	Product similar to those presently on the market and which adds nothing new.
B. *Expected competitive situation—value added*	Very high value added so as to substantially restrict number of competitors.	High enough value added so that, unless product is extremely well suited to other firms, they will not want to invest in additional facilities.	High enough value added so that, unless other companies are as strong in market as this firm, it will not be profitable for them to compete.	Lower value added so as to allow large, medium, and some smaller companies to compete.	Very low value added so that all companies can profitably enter market.
C. *Expected availability of end users*	Number of end users will increase substantially.	Number of end users will increase moderately.	Number of end users will increase slightly, if at all.	Number of end users will decrease moderately.	Number of end users will decrease substantially.

SOURCE: John T. O'Meara, Jr., "Selecting Profitable Products," *Harvard Business Review*, Vol. 39, No. 1, January–February 1961, pp. 84–85.

TABLE **5-2**

Example of the Use of an Evaluation Sheet

Proposed product: Product X   Evaluated by: John Smith

Factor: Marketability

1	2	3		4		5		6		7		8	9
Subfactor	Subfactor Weight	Very Good (10)		Good (8)		Average (6)		Poor (4)		Very Poor (2)		Total EV	Subfactor Evaluation (Col. 2 × Col. 8)
		EP	EV	EP	EV	EP	EV	EP	EV	EP	EV		
Relative to present distribution channels	1.0	0.1	1.0	0.2	1.6	0.5	3.0	0.2	0.8	–	–	6.4	6.4
Relative to present product lines	1.0	0.1	1.0	0.2	1.6	0.4	2.4	0.2	0.8	0.1	0.2	6.0	6.0
Quality/price relationship	3.0	0.3	3.0	0.4	3.2	0.2	1.2	0.1	0.4	–	–	7.8	23.4
Number of sizes and grades	1.0	0.1	1.0	0.2	1.6	0.5	3.0	0.2	0.8	–	–	6.4	6.4
Merchandisability	2.0	0.5	5.0	0.4	3.2	0.1	0.6	–	–	–	–	8.8	17.6
Effects on sale of present products	2.0	–	–	0.2	1.6	0.5	3.0	0.3	1.2	–	–	5.8	11.6
	10.0											Total factor value	71.4

SOURCE: John T. O'Meara, Jr., "Selecting Profitable Products," *Harvard Business Review*, Vol. 39, No. 1, January–February 1961, p. 86.

Note: EP = estimated probability as judged by management; EV = expected value computed by multiplying the rating's numerical value by the estimated probability.

If the two distributions are multivariate normal with the same variance–covariance matrix,[18] that is,

$$\Sigma_1 = \Sigma_2 = \Sigma$$

then

$$\mathrm{LR} = \exp\left[-\tfrac{1}{2}(x-\mu_1)^t\Sigma^{-1}(x-\mu_1) + \tfrac{1}{2}(x-\mu_2)^t\Sigma^{-1}(x-\mu_2)\right] \quad (5\text{-}3)$$

$$= \exp\left[x^t\Sigma^{-1}(\mu_1-\mu_2) - \left(\frac{\mu_1+\mu_2}{2}\right)^t\Sigma^{-1}(\mu_1-\mu_2)\right] \quad (5\text{-}4)$$

$$= \exp\left[x^t\Sigma^{-1}\mu - v^t\Sigma^{-1}\mu\right] \quad (5\text{-}5)$$

where $\mu = \mu_1 - \mu_2$ is the difference and $v = (\mu_1 + \mu_2)/2$ is the average of the mean vectors for the two probability distributions.

We have just shown that the likelihood ratio depends on the observed score x through the linear function (weighted sum)

$$z = x^t\Sigma^{-1}\mu \quad (5\text{-}6)$$

Since this likelihood ratio measures the credence placed on each of the two probabilities, the same may be said of the linear function of the scores on which it depends. Thus, large values of the linear function will correspond to high expectation of success, and low values to failure. Let us further investigate this linear function.

If the individual scores had no interactions, then the covariances would all equal zero—a rather dangerous assumption—and we could write the linear function (5-6) as

$$z = \sum_{i=1}^{17} (\mu_i/\sigma_i^2)x_i \quad (5\text{-}7)$$

The coefficient μ_i/σ_i^2 of x_i can be interpreted as the relative importance of the ith subfactor. We want to compare this result with what we obtain when we do not assume zero covariances. Because 17-dimensional vectors and matrices are unwieldy, the six marketing subfactors of Table 5-1 shall be used to illustrate the computation.

Suppose that

$$\Sigma = \begin{pmatrix} 2 & 0 & 0 & 0 & 0 & 0 \\ 0 & 3 & 0 & -1 & 0 & 1 \\ 0 & 0 & 1 & 0 & 0 & 0 \\ 0 & -1 & 0 & 2 & 0 & 0 \\ 0 & 0 & 0 & 0 & 2 & 1 \\ 0 & 1 & 0 & 0 & 1 & 2 \end{pmatrix} \qquad \mu = \begin{pmatrix} 2 \\ 4 \\ 3 \\ 1 \\ 6 \\ 7 \end{pmatrix}$$

[18] The data may be suitably transformed to more nearly fit this assumption.

are the variance–covariance matrix and the difference of the mean vectors for the two probability distributions.[19] Then

$$\Sigma^{-1}\mu = \begin{pmatrix} \frac{1}{2} & 0 & 0 & 0 & 0 & 0 \\ 0 & \frac{6}{11} & 0 & \frac{3}{11} & \frac{2}{11} & -\frac{4}{11} \\ 0 & 0 & 1 & 0 & 0 & 0 \\ 0 & \frac{3}{11} & 0 & \frac{7}{11} & \frac{1}{11} & -\frac{2}{11} \\ 0 & \frac{2}{11} & 0 & \frac{1}{11} & \frac{8}{11} & -\frac{5}{11} \\ 0 & -\frac{4}{11} & 0 & -\frac{2}{11} & -\frac{5}{11} & \frac{10}{11} \end{pmatrix} \begin{pmatrix} 2 \\ 4 \\ 3 \\ 1 \\ 6 \\ 7 \end{pmatrix} = \begin{pmatrix} 1 \\ 1 \\ 3 \\ 1 \\ 2 \\ 2 \end{pmatrix} \tag{5-8}$$

are the respective weights for the six marketing subfactors. (These have been made to coincide with O'Meara's weights in Table 5-2.) Note that even though only three of the fifteen covariances were taken to be different from zero, the optimal weights are quite different from the μ_i/σ_i^2 values that would have held if all covariances had been equal to zero. In that case, we would have had

$$\frac{\mu}{\sigma^2} = \begin{pmatrix} 1 \\ \frac{4}{3} \\ 3 \\ \frac{1}{2} \\ 3 \\ \frac{7}{2} \end{pmatrix}$$

In particular, the sixth weight of O'Meara is much smaller than μ_6/σ_6^2 as seen above, reflecting the fact that the "effect of sales on present products" is already somewhat taken into account when we measure "relation to present product lines," "number of sizes and grades," and "merchandisability."

The cost of uncertainty in the new product decision

The numbers in $\Sigma^{-1}\mu$ are the same as those in column 2 of Table 5-2. If the observed scores are those given in column 8, then the weighted score is 71.4, as shown in column 9 of Table 5-2. The natural question to ask is whether this is a high or a low score. If we refer to equation (5-5), we see that an average weighted score would be $\nu^t\Sigma^{-1}\mu$, where ν is the average of the mean vectors for the two probability distributions. For example, if

[19] These values could be established by the usual combination of historical data from previous projects and expert opinion concerning the present ones.

$$v = \begin{pmatrix} 7 \\ 6 \\ 6.5 \\ 6.5 \\ 6 \\ 6 \end{pmatrix}$$

then $v^t\Sigma^{-1}\mu = 63.0$. Thus, the observed weighted score of 71.4 for the product in question would be 8.4 above the average weighted score. From (5-5), the likelihood ratio is equal to the exponential of the difference of the observed weighted score and the average weighted score, which here is $e^{8.4} = 4447$.

With the preceding likelihood ratio of 4447, almost any prior probabilities of success or failure and costs of misclassification would still result in the superior decision being to classify the product as potentially successful.

For example, if the opportunity loss of not marketing a product that would have been successful is five times the cost of marketing an unsuccessful product, then the opportunity loss table is (in some appropriate units) as shown in Table 5-3. If the prior probability of a successful product is π_0 and the likelihood ratio of successful to unsuccessful outcomes is LR, then the posterior probability of success is

$$\pi_1 = \frac{\pi_0 \text{LR}}{\pi_0 \text{LR} + (1 - \pi_0)} \tag{5-9}$$

If 1 percent of all products that have reached this stage of evaluation are successful, then $\pi_0 = .01$ and

$$\pi_1 = \frac{\text{LR}}{\text{LR} + 99} \tag{5-10}$$

The expected loss of marketing conditional on knowing LR is $1 - \pi_1 = 99/(\text{LR} + 99)$, whereas that of not marketing is $5\pi_1 = 5\text{LR}/(\text{LR} + 99)$. Marketing is the better decision if $99/(\text{LR} + 99) < 5\text{LR}/(\text{LR} + 99)$, that is, if $\text{LR} > 99/5 = 19.8$. Since the natural logarithm of 19.8 is 2.99, the observed weighted score would merely have to exceed $63.0 + 2.99 = 65.99$ in order to justify continuing the project.

TABLE **5-3**

	Act	
Event	Market	Do not market
Successful	0	5
Unsuccessful	1	0

TABLE **5-4**

Calculation of Overall Mean and Standard Deviation for Criteria of Evaluation

	z	$p(z)$	$E(z)$	$E(z^2)$	
Subfactor 1	10	.1	1.0	10.0	
	8	.2	1.6	12.8	
	6	.5	3.0	18.0	
	4	.2	.8	3.2	
	2				
			6.4	44.0	$\sigma^2(z) =$ 3.04
Subfactor 2	10	.1	1.0	10.0	
	8	.2	1.6	12.8	
	6	.4	2.4	14.4	
	4	.2	.8	3.2	
	2	.1	.2	.4	
			6.0	40.8	$\sigma^2(z) =$ 4.80
Subfactor 3	30	.3	9.0	270.0	
	24	.4	9.6	230.4	
	18	.2	3.6	64.8	
	12	.1	1.2	14.4	
	6				
			23.4	579.6	$\sigma^2(z) =$ 32.04
Subfactor 4	10	.1	1.0	10.0	
	8	.2	1.6	12.8	
	6	.5	3.0	18.0	
	4	.2	.8	3.2	
	2				
			6.4	44.0	$\sigma^2(z) =$ 3.04
Subfactor 5	20	.5	10.0	200.0	
	16	.4	6.4	102.4	
	12	.1	1.2	14.4	
	8				
	4				
			17.6	316.8	$\sigma^2(z) =$ 7.04
Subfactor 6	20				
	16	.2	3.2	51.2	
	12	.5	6.0	72.0	
	8	.3	2.4	19.2	
	4				
			11.6	142.4	$\sigma^2(z) =$ 7.84

Overall mean = 71.4
Overall variance = 57.80
Overall standard deviation = 7.60

If there were absolute certainty that the observed weighted score was 71.4, then the project should be continued. But examination of columns 3 through 7 of Table 5-2 shows that there is considerable uncertainty about the individual subfactor scores.[20] These subfactor scores can be treated as random variables. The observed weighted score is then a random variable whose mean is the sum of the subfactor means and whose variance is the sum of the subfactor variances, provided the scores on the separate subfactors are independent. If the subfactor scores are not independent, then we would also include the appropriate covariance terms in calculating the variance of their weighted sum.

In Table 5-4 we calculate that for the data given in Table 5-2 the observed weighted score has mean 71.4 and standard deviation 7.60. Using a normal approximation, there is a

$$P_N\left(\mu < \frac{65.99 - 71.4}{7.60}\right) = .24$$

chance of the score for the product under consideration actually being below the break-even value 65.99. This leads us to consider the cost of uncertainty and the possibility of obtaining additional information before making our decision.

TABLE **5-5**

Calculation of expected loss of marketing
(Relative to perfect information about potential success of product)

Observed weighted score (z)	Conditional loss	$\frac{\text{Observed score} - \text{Mean}}{\text{Standard deviation}^a}$ A	B	Probability	Expected loss
⩾76	.000		.474	.318	.000
74	.002	.342		.099	.000
72	.012	.079		.104	.001
70	.083	−.184		.103	.009
69	.400	−.447		.095	.038
66	.831	−.710		.082	.068
64	.973	−.974		.065	.063
62	.996	−1.237		.049	.049
60	.999	−1.500		.034	.034
⩽58	1.000		−1.632	.051	.051
					.313

[a] Column A is used to obtain the probabilities in the body of the distribution, whereas column B is used for the right and left tails of the distribution and contains a correction for continuity.

[20] Also, there may be uncertainty about our estimates of Σ and μ.

Since z is actually a random variable, so is $\text{LR} = \exp(z - 63.0)$. For any given value z, the losses of marketing and not marketing are, respectively,

$$\text{Loss of marketing conditional on } z = \frac{99}{\exp[z - 63.0] + 99} \qquad (5\text{-}11)$$

$$\text{Loss of not marketing conditional on } z = \frac{5e^{z-63.0}}{\exp[z - 63.0] + 99} \qquad (5\text{-}12)$$

The probability distribution of z, normal with mean 71.4 and standard deviation 7.60, can be used to compute expected, or unconditional, losses. Because of the nature of the nonlinearities in equations (5-11) and (5-12), these calculations require numerical integration. A crude form of numerical integration, sufficient for our purposes, is used in Table 5-5 to show that the expected loss of marketing is .313 (in the same units used in Table 5-4).[21]

Since the conditional loss of not marketing equals 5(1 − conditional loss of marketing), the same relationship holds between the expected losses. Thus, the expected loss of not marketing is 3.435. Marketing is the better decision, and its expected loss, .313, is the cost of uncertainty. Note that this amounts to 31.3% of the loss if the product is not successful. Since this same result would have been obtained if we had first computed the expected posterior probability of failure with respect to the distribution of observed weighted scores, this expected probability must also equal 31.3%. Thus,

---

[21] These calculations make use of the following formula for the probability that a normal random variable with mean μ and variance σ^2 lies between a and b:

$$\int_a^b \frac{1}{\sqrt{2\mu}\,\sigma} \exp\left[-\frac{(x-\mu)^2}{2\sigma^2}\right] dx = \int_{(a-\mu)/\sigma}^{(b-\mu)/\sigma} \frac{1}{\sqrt{2\pi}} \exp\left[-\frac{t^2}{2}\right] dt$$

In a probability in the body of the table, we let

$$a = z - \tfrac{1}{2}\,\Delta z$$
$$b = z + \tfrac{1}{2}\,\Delta z$$

where Δz is the spacing between consecutive z values. The result is

$$\int_{(z-\mu)/\sigma-\Delta z/2\sigma}^{(z-\mu)/\sigma+\Delta z/2\sigma} \frac{1}{\sqrt{2\pi}} \exp\left[-\frac{t^2}{2}\right] dt \doteq \frac{\Delta z}{\sigma} \cdot \frac{1}{\sqrt{2\pi}} \exp\left[-\frac{(z-\mu)^2}{2\sigma^2}\right] = \frac{\Delta z}{\sigma} f\left(\frac{z-\mu}{\sigma}\right)$$

where f is the probability density function of the standardized normal distribution (mean 0 and variance 1).

For the left tail probability, we let

$$a = -\infty$$
$$b = z + \tfrac{1}{2}\,\Delta z$$

obtaining

$$\int_{-\infty}^{[z+(1/2)\Delta z-\mu]/\sigma} \frac{1}{\sqrt{2\pi}} \exp\left[-\frac{t^2}{2}\right] dt = F\left(\frac{z + \frac{1}{2}\,\Delta z - \mu}{\sigma}\right)$$

where F is the cumulative distribution function of the standardized normal distribution. In this latter context, $\frac{1}{2}\,\Delta z$ is known as the "correction for continuity."

The right tail probability is obtained in similar fashion.

there is a good chance that this product will fail. Nevertheless, because of the highly favorable relative losses, the project should be continued.

The value of additional information in the new product decision

If the point at which a final decision must be made concerning our potential product has been reached, then the method just presented would be complete. However, at the rough screening stage described in O'Meara's article, a final decision is probably not yet required, and the project would go ahead, conditionally, subject to later determination. The costs involved in studying this situation further before making a final decision are probably not so much direct costs of experimentation and data gathering as they are opportunity losses caused by getting the product to market later than we might have if we had decided immediately to start production. Although this might affect the losses in Table 5-4 unequally, we shall assume that it does not so that we may avoid the complication of having the cost of experimentation depend on the act finally chosen.

In deciding to postpone a final decision for further study, it must be made clear what additional information can be obtained. Surely, not much can be discovered about the underlying probability distributions of successful and unsuccessful products, because the additional study will focus on the potential product rather than on a new sample of marketed products. This means that Σ, μ, and v as previously calculated will not change, but that knowledge of x may improve. It also means that the cost of uncertainty calculated above, .313, is not the correct measure of ignorance, since even perfect knowledge of x will result in some finite expected loss, however small.

It is simpler again to consider the scalar $z = x^t\Sigma^{-1}\mu$ rather than the vector x. To obtain the expected value of perfect information about z, recall that the expected losses of the two terminal decisions, conditional on knowing z, are

$$\text{Loss of marketing conditional on } z = \frac{99}{\exp[z - 63.0] + 99}$$

$$\text{Loss of not marketing conditional on } z = \frac{5\exp[z - 63.0]}{\exp[z - 63.0] + 99}$$

These curves are drawn in Figure 5-2, which once again shows that the break-even score is $z = 65.99$. The conditional opportunity losses of the two decisions are not the heights of their respective curves but the differences between the lower curve and the curve in question, as shown in Figure 5-3. In Table 5-6 we calculate the expected opportunity loss of .196 for marketing, using the normal prior probability distribution previously obtained for z. Using this result we can calculate the expected opportunity loss of not marketing as follows. If we let M represent the loss of marketing conditional on

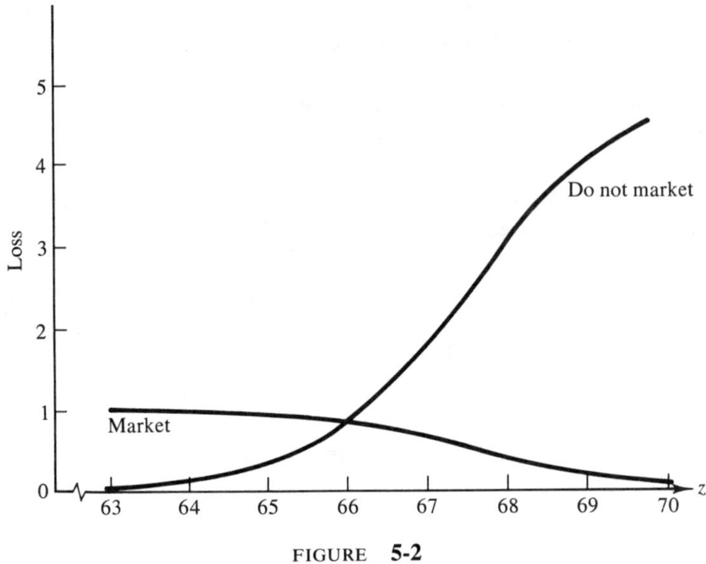

FIGURE 5-2

Expected loss curves

z, what we have calculated in Table 5-6 is $E_0^{66}\{M - 5(1 - M)\} = E_0^{66}\{6M - 5\}$. Then

$$\begin{aligned}\text{Expected loss of not marketing} &= E_{66}^{\infty}\{5(1 - M) - M\} = E_{66}^{\infty}\{5 - 6M\} \\ &= E_0^{\infty}\{5 - 6M\} + E_0^{66}\{6M - 5\} \qquad (5\text{-}13) \\ &= 5 - 6(.313) + .196 = 3.318\end{aligned}$$

TABLE 5-6

Calculation of expected loss of marketing (Relative to perfect information about likelihood ratio)

Observed weighted score (z)	Conditional loss	Probability	Expected loss
≥66	0	.781	.000
65	.583	.037	.022
64	.840	.033	.028
63	.940	.028	.026
62	.978	.024	.023
61	.992	.021	.021
60	.997	.017	.017
59	.999	.014	.014
≤58	1.000	.045	.045
		1.000	.196

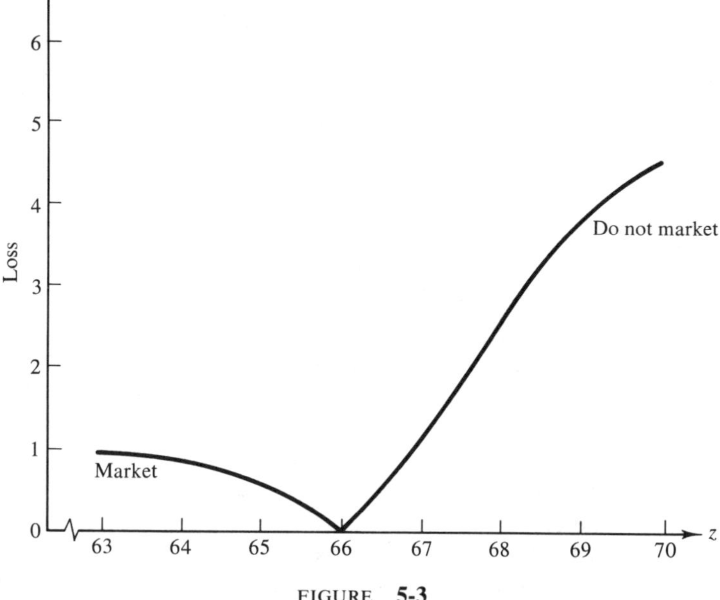

FIGURE 5-3

Conditional loss curves

Thus, .196 is the expected value of perfect information about z and is the most that should be paid for such. For anything less than perfect information about z, we would, accordingly, be willing to pay less. Suppose, for example, that the additional information gained by further study comes to us in the form of a sample of size n from a normal population with mean equal to the true (but unknown) value of z and variance equal to σ^2 (known). Then the sample mean m, say, is sufficient to determine the posterior distribution of z, which is again normal, with[22]

$$\text{Posterior mean} = \frac{(\sigma^2/n)(71.4) + (7.60)^2(m)}{(\sigma^2/n) + (7.60)^2} \tag{5-14}$$

$$\text{Posterior variance} = \frac{(\sigma^2/n)(7.60)^2}{(\sigma^2/n) + (7.60)^2} \tag{5-15}$$

Before we gain the information, m is a random variable. If the loss curves in Figure 5-2 were linear, then the posterior mean would be all that were required to compute expected losses. Since the preposterior (prior distribution of the posterior) mean is also normal, with[23]

---

[22] See equation (3-61).

[23] See R. Schlaifer, *Probability and Statistics for Business Decisions*, McGraw-Hill, New York, 1959, sect. 34.3.

$$\text{Preposterior mean} = \text{prior mean}$$

$$\text{Preposterior variance} = \text{prior variance} - \text{posterior variance}$$

then the expected value of sample information would be calculated as in Table 5-6, using the preposterior distribution in place of the prior distribution.

At this point, however, difficulties set in. The curves in Figure 5-3 are highly nonlinear, so the previous preposterior analysis is inapplicable; although the preposterior mean still has the distribution described above, the posterior mean is no longer sufficient to determine the expected loss. Thus, the expected value of sample information cannot be calculated by using the preposterior distribution in place of the prior distribution in Table 5-6. For example, if $\sigma^2/n = 1$, the preposterior standard deviation is 7.54. This is so close to the prior standard deviation of 7.60 that the calculations in Table 5-6 would remain unchanged, and (to the accuracy of the approximation involved), the expected value of sample information would appear to equal the expected value of perfect information, .196.

The correct calculation is much more laborious. For each value of the sample mean m, the posterior mean must be calculated. Then, using the entire posterior distribution and the loss curves in Figure 5-3, the expected opportunity losses of marketing and not marketing can be calculated. The smaller of these two expected losses is the posterior loss for that value of m. Using the prior (marginal) distribution of the sample mean, which is normal, with[24]

$$\text{Mean of sample mean} = \text{prior mean}$$

$$\text{Variance of sample mean} = \text{prior variance} + \text{sampling variance}$$

we then calculate the preposterior expected loss.

For example, if $\sigma^2/n = 1$, then the posterior mean and standard deviation for any value of m are given by

$$\text{Posterior mean} = \frac{71.4 + (7.60)^2 m}{1 + (7.60)^2} \tag{5-16}$$

$$\text{Posterior variance} = \frac{(7.60)^2}{1 + (7.60)^2} = .983$$

$$\text{Posterior standard deviation} = .99 \tag{5-17}$$

The probability of any value of z can then be found by using the normal tables, and the two expected losses can be calculated. The calculations for $m = 65.7$ are shown in Table 5-7 (the posterior mean is 65.8). Note that even though the posterior mean is below the break-even value, marketing is the

[24] See equation (3-60).

better act. The expected loss of marketing, .271, is entered as the loss conditional on knowing $m = 63.7$ in Table 5-8. The other conditional losses in Table 5-8 are computed similarly. The probabilities in Table 5-8 are obtained from the normal tables using

$$\text{Mean of sample mean} = 71.4$$

$$\text{Variance of sample mean} = (7.60)^2 + 1 = 58.76$$

$$\text{Standard deviation of sample mean} = 7.66$$

As calculated in Table 5-8, the preposterior expected loss is then .017, and the expected value of sample information is .196 − .017 = .179.

TABLE 5-7

Computation of expected opportunity losses conditional on $m = 65.7$

		Loss of marketing		Loss of not marketing	
z^a	Probability	Conditional	Expected	Conditional	Expected
⩾70	.000				
69.5	.000				
69	.001			3.818	.004
68.5	.005			3.272	.016
68	.017			2.599	.044
67.5	.046			1.857	.085
67	.072			1.133	.082
66.75	.063			.803	.051
66.5	.078			.504	.039
66.25	.091			.240	.022
66	.099			.012	.001
65.75	.101	.181	.018		
65.5	.096	.343	.033		
65.25	.086	.475	.041		
65	.073	.583	.042		
64.75	.058	.670	.039		
64.5	.043	.740	.032		
64.25	.030	.796	.024		
64	.029	.840	.024		
63.5	.014	.902	.013		
63	.004	.940	.004		
62.5	.001	.963	.001		
⩽62	.000	.978	.000		
	1.007		.271		.344

[a] Note the variation in the intervals between successive values of z to give finer gradations in more critical regions.

The commercialization decision

The last of the several phases that constitute the process by which a product finally takes its place in the company's product line is that of com-

TABLE **5-8**

Computation of preposterior expected loss

m^a	Probability	Conditional loss	Expected loss
⩾68	.680	.001	.0007
67.5	.023	.018	.0004
67.0	.022	.041	.0009
66.5	.021	.098	.0021
66.0	.014	.194	.0027
65.8	.006	.244	.0015
65.7	.004	.271	.0011
65.6	.004	.297	.0012
65.5	.004	.260	.0010
65.4	.006	.216	.0013
65.2	.008	.157	.0012
65.0	.013	.111	.0014
64.5	.017	.040	.0007
64.0	.016	.012	.0002
⩽63.5	.159	.001	.0002
	.997		.0166

[a] See footnote to Table 5-7.

mercialization. Rarely, however, does the firm enter commercialization full-scale, committing all its resources at once. During the period of the product's initial acceptance and growth, there is still continual evaluation taking place. The firm is interested not only in assessing whether the new product is likely to be a success and the order of magnitude of such success, but also in collecting information that will be useful in developing marketing strategy for the product. We shall now discuss a model that addresses itself to the preceding problem.[25] Although most of the analytical work in this area has focused on packaged goods because of the much greater frequency with which new products are introduced, the theoretical structures that have been laid out appear reasonably adaptable to other product categories.

The DEMON planning system

DEMON is an acronym for DEcision Mapping via Optimum Networks. The model consists of two distinct parts: (1) a procedure for the

[25] Several other analyses useful for this purpose are the following: (a) Louis A. Fourt and Joseph W. Woodlock, "Early Prediction of Market Success for New Grocery Products," *Journal of Marketing*, Vol. 25, April 1960, pp. 31–38; (b) William R. King, "Early Prediction of New Product Success," *Journal of Advertising Research*, Vol. 6, June 1966, pp. 8–13, and "Marketing Expansion—A Statistical Analysis," *Management Science*, Vol. 9, May 1963, pp. 563–573; and (c) Harlan D. Mills, "Dynamics of New Products Campaigns," *Journal of Marketing*, Vol. 28, October 1964, pp. 60–63.

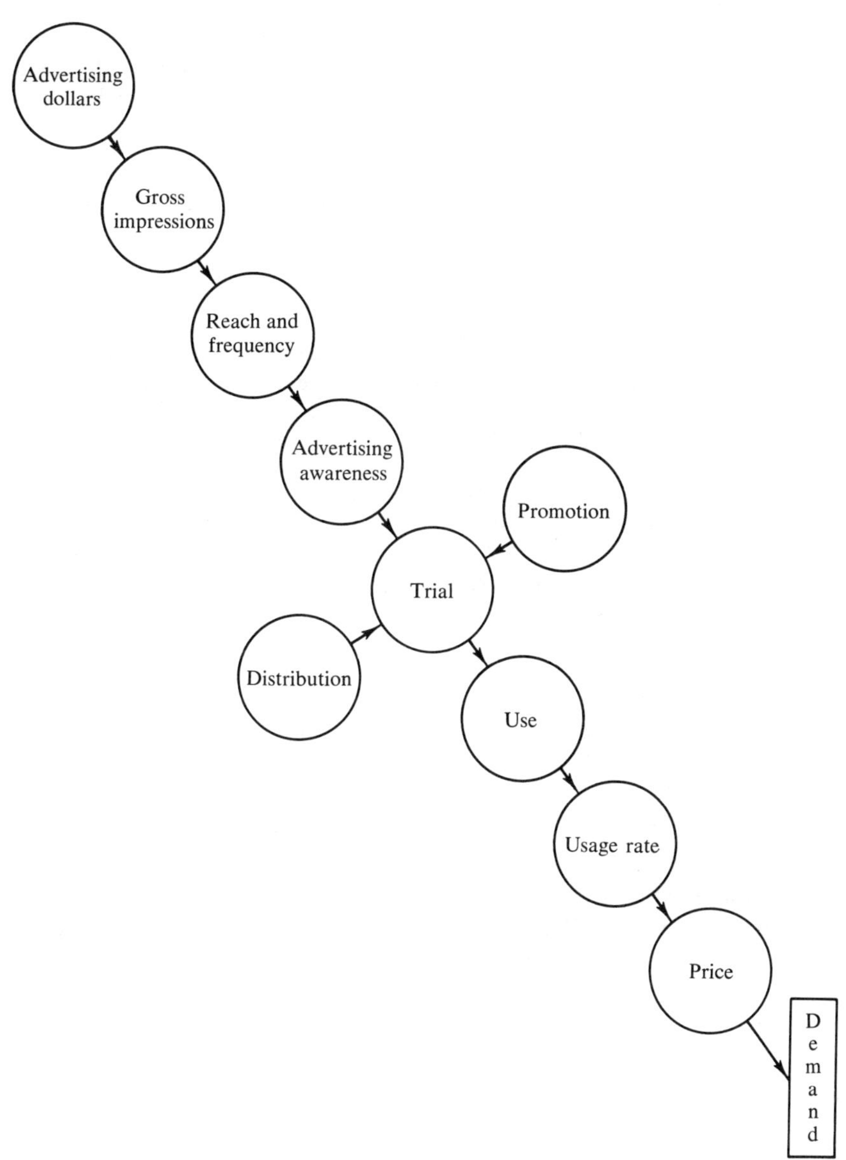

FIGURE 5-4

DEMON planning system

development and analysis of the effect of strategy decisions on estimated demand and profits, and (2) a decision system for deciding whether to continue evaluations of the product, drop the product, or proceed to full-scale commercialization of the product.

The first part, the marketing planning system,[26] is diagrammed in Figure 5-4. A definition of each variable is helpful before proceeding to a discussion of their functional relationships. In the list that follows, asterisks denote decision variables.

*ADVERTISING DOLLARS ($) the amount spent in all media forms.
GROSS IMPRESSIONS (GI)[27] the total number of potential exposures to advertising, or the cumulative total of the audiences of the vehicles used, regardless of media form.
REACH (R)[27] the percentage of the total audience exposed to at least one advertisement.
FREQUENCY (f)[27] the distribution of impressions among those who have been reached, that is, the number of persons exposed once, twice, etc.
AWARENESS (AW) the fraction of the total audience that can recall the brand advertising. Measured by field surveys focusing on recall of thematic content, not brand recall.
TRIAL (T) first full price purchase of the product.
USE (U) second full price purchase.
USAGE RATE (UR) frequency distribution of purchases per user unit for any specified time period, a random variable.
*PRICE (P) full retail price.
DEMAND (d) a random variable that reflects, in part, the effects of different levels of each of the decision variables.
*PROMOTION alternative means of inducing trial based on such techniques as couponing for special price-off opportunities, distribution of samples, etc.[28]
*DISTRIBUTION availability of the product in the outlets where it is sold. This is a function of such factors as the number of salesmen, the number of sales calls, and other sales force performance measures, and the relationship is fairly readily determinable.

The relationships of each pair of successive variables in Figure 5-4 have been studied for over 200 packaged goods products in 16 product categories and the following general results obtained.

$$GI = (b_1\$)^{1+E} \tag{5-18}$$

where E reflects media discounts available. If $E = 0$, the relationship is perfectly linear.

$$R = a_2 + b_2 \ln GI \tag{5-19}$$

[26] See James K. DeVoe, "Plans, Profits, and the Marketing Program," in *New Directions in Marketing, Proceedings*, Frederick E. Webster, Jr., Ed., American Marketing Association, Chicago, Ill., 1965, pp. 473–488.

[27] These concepts are discussed in more detail in Chapter 9, "Mass Communications."

[28] For a comparison of the efficacy of different methods, including use of mass media, see George H. Haines, Jr., "A Study of Why People Purchase New Products," in *Science, Technology, and Marketing, Proceedings*, Raymond M. Haas, Ed., American Marketing Association, Chicago, Ill., 1966, pp. 685–697.

This relationship is concave, as would be expected, since the percentage of the population not reached must get smaller at a diminishing rate as more dollars are expended.

$$AW = b_3 \exp\,[-R^{-a_3}] \tag{5-20}$$

The parameters b_3 and a_3 must be estimated: b_3 is the maximum obtainable level of awareness. This may be determined by field surveys that attempt to measure the maximum awareness obtainable in a product category—a feasible tactic if one believes that very few products are genuinely new. The variable a_3 has not been amenable to operational definition; it does, however, appear to be related to the creative aspects of the advertisements and may be determined via survey measurements. Past studies for the relevant product category should help in establishing bounds for the range in which a_3 lies.

The relationship between awareness and trial was, surprisingly, linear:

$$T = a_4 + b_4AW \tag{5-21}$$

Trial is not solely a function of the level of awareness; it is affected by both promotion and distribution. The relationships between various forms of promotion and specific trial rates are reasonably well known, as is the case for sales force effort and distribution. In the DEMON model, the percentage distribution is simply factored in multiplicatively, resulting in a reduction in the trial rate. This assumption of independence in the achievement of awareness and distribution is not unreasonable, although efforts to achieve both may be concentrated in the same geographic region. For example, Haines and Silk have completed a study in which they show that the obtaining of shelf space in outlets is not related to the extent of the advertising expenditure.[29]

At this point, the management has an allocation problem, that is, how to distribute its expenditures among the advertising, promotion, and distribution factors, and the substrategies within each of these, in order to maximize trials. This is done under the assumption that full price is a constant; obviously, price affects purchase, but the analysis is repeated separately for the array of prices under consideration. Each of these various combinations may be considered the equivalent of a different marketing strategy or plan.

The relationship between trial and usage is also linear:

$$U = a_5 + b_5T \tag{5-22}$$

Given the above estimate of the number of users and information on the distribution of rates at which the product is used per specified time period, an estimate of demand can be obtained for a particular price or prices. This estimate is the principal input into the second part of the DEMON model,

[29] George H. Haines, Jr., and Alvin J. Silk, "Does Consumer Advertising Increase Retail Availability of a New Product?" *Journal of Advertising Research*, Vol. 7, No. 3, September 1967, pp. 9–15.

which deals with whether to go full-scale, drop the product, or explore the opportunity further. Before proceeding to this part of the model, a few additional comments are necessary to help in evaluating the planning system we have just described.

There are several assumptions in the model that appear to be contrary to one's intuition. For example, one would be inclined to believe that the relationship between usage and trial should be affected by other variables whose impact is introduced earlier in the system; for instance, advertising frequency should directly influence conversion from trial to use, the rationale being that many exposures may help to reinforce the consumer in believing that he made the right decision in making the initial trial. The developers of DEMON maintain, however, that this intuitive logic is not verified by the substantial evidence they have compiled. The only factor they have uncovered that seems to affect the conversion rate from trial to usage is the technical character of the product, and this notion would support an equally viable and different intuitive hypothesis: Experience with use of the product is the most potent influence on the consumer's future purchase decisions. This, by the way, would also explain the effectiveness of sampling (giving away the product) in inducing trial.

One possible drawback in the DEMON model that cannot be disputed is that of the diminution of competitive advantage as more time is spent securing information in the marketplace. Each time survey work or testing in the field is undertaken to develop more accurate descriptions of the various relationships and marketing mix alternatives, valuable information is provided to competitors about the firm's intentions. If the product is sufficiently innovative, the firm may have to accept a greater degree of uncertainty to protect its advantage. If, on the other hand, the product is quite similar to existing ones, much of the desired information can be collected by analyzing these near substitutes; the danger here, however, is that there may be some product attributes that produce quite different parameters in the various equations even though the general form remains the same. More generally, the DEMON model in no way directly takes account of competitive actions. This is a conscious decision in that the model was designed to ignore those things that the firm cannot directly control, and, of course, competitive actions are reflected in the uncertainty surrounding the estimate of demand.

The DEMON decision system[30]

We shall now examine the second part of the DEMON model, which begins with the estimate of demand, *d*, already derived.

---

[30] See A. Charnes, W. W. Cooper, J. K. DeVoe, and D. B. Learner, "DEMON Mark II: An Extremal Equation Approach to New Product Marketing," *Management Science*, Vol. 14, May 1968, pp. 513–524.

Consider a situation in which the chief uncertainty in deciding whether to market a new product lies in not knowing the precise demand for the product. In line with our usual practices, we shall treat such uncertainty by means of random variables. Thus, we define the random variable

$$d = \text{demand per unit time}$$

In d is normally distributed[31] with mean μ and variance σ^2.

If π is the profit per unit sold, then the total profit in time T is $\pi T d$. Depending on the profit picture, we may decide to

GO = market the product nationally

KILL = discontinue the product

or

CONTINUE = study the situation further before making a terminal decision

In making our decision, two time periods are of interest to us:

$$T_0 = \text{payback period}$$

$$T_1 = \text{horizon period for market planning}$$

The expected profit over the horizon period is

$$\pi T_1 E(d) = \pi T_1 \exp\,[\mu + \sigma^2/2] \tag{5-23}$$

One requirement for national distribution might be that the expected profit exceed some desired level, P_G. Thus,

$$\pi T_1 \exp\,[\mu + \sigma^2/2] \geq P_G \tag{5-24}$$

or

$$\mu + \sigma^2/2 \geq \ln(P_G/\pi T_1) = P'_G \tag{5-25}$$

---

[31] We choose a lognormal distribution for d because demand is always non-negative and because independent influences on demand are more likely to be multiplicative than additive. The density function of the lognormal distribution is

$$f_L(z|\mu, \sigma) = \frac{1}{\sqrt{2\pi}\,\sigma z} \exp\left[-\frac{1}{2}\frac{(\ln z - \mu)^2}{\sigma^2}\right]$$

We can readily calculate that

$$\text{mean} = \exp\left(\mu + \frac{\sigma^2}{2}\right)$$

$$(\text{coefficient of variation})^2 = \frac{\text{variance}}{(\text{mean})^2} = \exp(\sigma^2) - 1$$

so σ is more directly inferred from the relative than from the absolute spread of the distribution. The theory of the lognormal distribution, analogous to our results in Chapters 3 and 4 for the normal distribution, can be found in Gordon M. Kaufman, *Statistical Decision and Related Techniques in Oil and Gas Exploration*, Prentice-Hall, Englewood Cliffs, N.J., 1963, ch. 7.

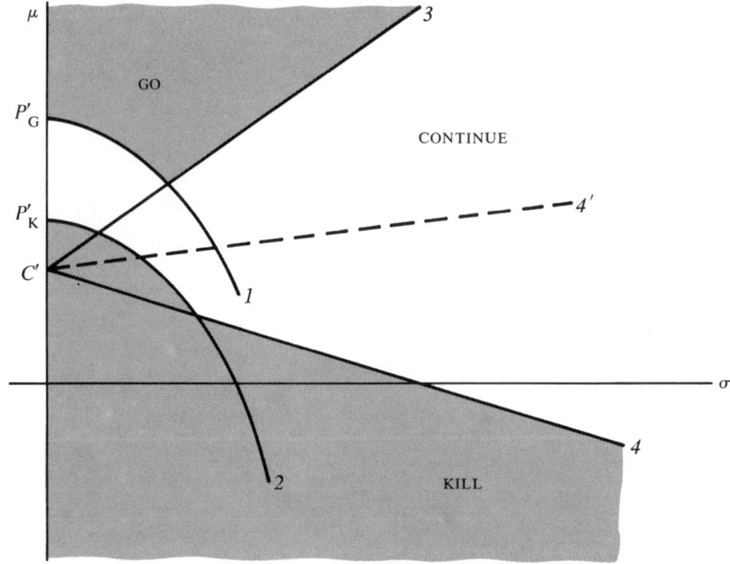

FIGURE **5-5**

Decision regions for DEMON commercialization decision

(*1*) $\mu + \frac{1}{2}\sigma^2 = P'_G$. (*2*) $\mu + \frac{1}{2}\sigma^2 = P'_K$.
(*3*) $\mu + t_{1-\alpha_G}\sigma = C'$. (*4*) $\mu + t_{\alpha_K}\sigma = C'$.

This is illustrated by curve *l* in Figure 5-5; in order to GO we must have (μ, σ) above the curve. Similarly, if the expected profit over the planning period were less than some minimum, P_K, that is,

$$\pi T_1 \exp\,[\mu + \sigma^2/2] \leq P_K \tag{5-26}$$

or

$$\mu + \sigma^2/2 \leq \ln(P_K/\pi T_1) = P'_K \tag{5-27}$$

then we would KILL. Thus, all points (μ, σ) below curve *2* in Figure 5-5 are marked for KILL.

A second consideration might concern the net cash position at the end of the payback period. If fixed costs in the amount C were required by GO, then this would equal $\pi T_0\, d - C$. Before going national we might require that there be a satisfactory high probability of a positive net cash position, say

$$\text{prob}\,\{\pi T_0\, d - C \geq 0\} \geq \alpha_G \tag{5-28}$$

where α_G is close to 1. This is the same as requiring

$$\text{prob}\left\{\frac{\ln d - \mu}{\sigma} \geq \frac{\ln(C/\pi T_0) - \mu}{\sigma}\right\} \geq \alpha_G \tag{5-29}$$

or

$$\text{prob}\left\{\frac{\ln d-\mu}{\sigma}\le\frac{\ln(C/\pi T_0)-\mu}{\sigma}\right\}\le 1-\alpha_G \tag{5-30}$$

Since $(\ln d-\mu)/\sigma$ is $N(0, 1)$, normal with mean 0 and variance 1, this is equivalent to

$$\frac{\ln(C/\pi T_0)-\mu}{\sigma}\le t_{1-\alpha_G} \tag{5-31}$$

or

$$\mu+t_{1-\alpha_G}\sigma\ge\ln\frac{C}{\pi T_0}=C' \tag{5-32}$$

where $t_{1-\alpha_G}$ is the $(1-\alpha_G)$ percentile of $N(0, 1)$. Because α_G is close to 1, $1-\alpha_G$ is close to 0, and $t_{1-\alpha_G}$ is negative. Line *3* in Figure 5-5 then illustrates this requirement. Note that in order to employ GO, a point (μ, σ) must lie above both curve *1* and line *3*; that is, *both* requirements are necessary for GO.

Once again, we can obtain a sufficient condition for KILL from similar considerations. This time we would look for a sufficiently large probability of a negative net cash position at the end of the payback period, say,

$$\text{prob}\ \{\pi T_0 d-C\le 0\}\ge\alpha_K \tag{5-33}$$

Equivalently,

$$\text{prob}\left\{\frac{\ln d-\mu}{\sigma}\le\frac{\ln(C/\pi T_0)-\mu}{\sigma}\right\}\ge\alpha_K \tag{5-34}$$

$$\frac{\ln(C/\pi T_0)-\mu}{\sigma}\ge t_{\alpha_K} \tag{5-35}$$

$$\mu+t_{\alpha_K}\sigma\le\ln(C/\pi T_0)=C' \tag{5-36}$$

If α_K is greater (smaller) than $\frac{1}{2}$, then t_{α_K} is positive (negative). Line *4* (*4'*) in Figure 5-5 then illustrates this condition for KILL. Note that in order to imply KILL, it is sufficient for a point (μ, σ) to lie below either curve *2* or line *4*; that is, *either* condition is sufficient for KILL.

The acceptable constraints in the model are not limited to profit or cash position. Any factor that reflects an area of managerial decision would be appropriate for inclusion. For example, another possibility is a budget limitation on expenditures for study of the relationships among the different variables and examination of different marketing mixes. As above, these constraints can be probabilistic or chance constrained. Essentially, this latter procedure maximizes an objective function of random variables subject to a constraint on these variables that must be maintained at prescribed levels of probability.[32]

---

[32] This approach is developed in A. Charnes and W. W. Cooper, "Chance Constrained Programming," *Management Science*, Vol. 5, October 1959, pp. 73–79.

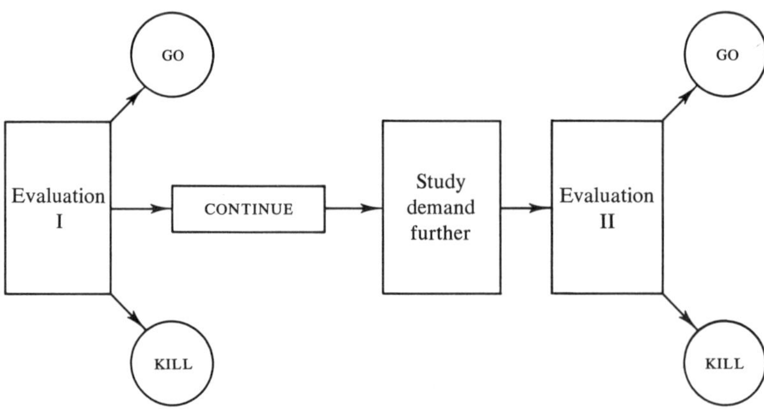

FIGURE **5-6**

DEMON evaluation system

The region in Figure 5-5 that is neither GO nor KILL is CONTINUE. If μ and σ lie in this region, we do not have enough information to make a terminal decision. In the sequence of decisions pictured in Figure 5-6, we would be to the right of the first evaluation stage. As pictured, we make a further study of the demand by reinvestigating the relationships in the planning system (see Figure 5-4), and would then make a terminal decision. In principle, we could extend the sequential process further, postponing a terminal decision as long as further study seemed profitable, but we shall not do this here.

In order to simplify our discussion of the value of further study, let us suppose that we have decided to base our decision on the payoff over the horizon period for market planning. Since we are ignoring the payback period, because we are in the CONTINUE region we must have

$$P_K < \pi T_1 E(d) < P_G \tag{5-37}$$

If instead of the mean, $E(d)$, we used the exact value of demand, d, then presumably we would make a terminal decision on the basis of some required profit P, where $P_K < P < P_G$. Our net (excess) profit is then $\pi T_1 d - P$ if we choose GO, and 0 if we choose KILL. This is a two-action problem with linear losses in which the unknown demand is a lognormally distributed random variable. The basic ideas are the same as when the random variable is normally distributed, but the details are somewhat different.

For prior analysis we would use $E(d) = \exp(\mu + \sigma^2/2)$. We choose GO if $\pi T_1 E(d) - P > 0$ or $E(d) > P/\pi T_1$, which is the incorrect decision if $d < P/\pi T_1$. The expected value of perfect information is then

$$\begin{aligned} \text{EVPI} &= \pi T_1 \int_0^{P/\pi T_1} \left(\frac{P}{\pi T_1} - z\right) f_L(z|\mu, \sigma)\, dz \\ &= P - \pi T_1 E(d) + P L_L^*\left(\frac{\pi T_1 E(d)}{P}, \sigma\right) \end{aligned} \tag{5-38}$$

where

$$L_L^*(R, \sigma) = \int_0^R (R - z) f_L(z| - \sigma^2/2, \sigma)\, dz$$

is a function tabulated by Kaufman,[33] where R is the standardized break-even value. If $\sigma^2 = 0$, then we have $L_L^*(R, 0) = R - 1$, so EVPI = 0. This corresponds to the fact that if $\sigma^2 = 0$ we already know $d = E(d)$ with certainty. Similarly, if $\sigma^2 = \infty$, we have $L_L^*(R, \infty) = R$, so EVPI = P. This corresponds to the fact that we really do not know d very well.

Since

$$\frac{\text{EVPI}}{P} = 1 - \frac{\pi T_1 E(d)}{P} + L_L^*\left(\frac{\pi T_1 E(d)}{P}, \sigma\right)$$

we can readily calculate the EVPI in any situation as a fraction of the required profit, P. Some values of this ratio are given in Table 5-9.

In order to calculate the EVSI, we need the prior distribution of the positive mean, $E(d|x)$. If the information obtained by sampling is in the form of a lognormal random variable x with parameters d, σ_s, then $E(d|x)$ is also a lognormal random variable,[34] with parameters

$$\mu + \frac{\sigma^2\sigma_s^2}{2(\sigma^2 + \sigma_s^2)}, \quad \frac{\sigma^2}{\sqrt{\sigma^2 + \sigma_s^2}}$$

Then

$$\begin{aligned} \text{EVSI} &= \pi T_1 \int_0^{P/\pi T_1} \left(\frac{P}{\pi T_1} - z\right) f_L\left(z|\ \mu + \frac{\sigma^2\sigma_s^2}{2(\sigma^2 + \sigma_s^2)}, \frac{\sigma^2}{\sqrt{\sigma^2 + \sigma_s^2}}\right) dz \\ &= P - \pi T_1 E(d) + P L_L^*\left(\frac{\pi T_1 E(d)}{P}, \frac{\sigma^2}{\sqrt{\sigma^2 + \sigma_s^2}}\right) \end{aligned} \tag{5-39}$$

TABLE **5-9**

Expected value of perfect information[a]

$\frac{\pi T_1 E(d)}{P}$	$\sigma = .25$ (c.v. = .064)	$\sigma = .5$ (c.v. = .284)	$\sigma = .833$ (c.v. = 1.01)	$\sigma = 1.25$ (c.v. = 3.77)
1	.0995	.1974	.3231	.4680
2	.0003	.0261	.1272	.2899
3	.0000	.0042	.0595	.2009
4	.0000	.0008	.0312	.1484
5	.0000	.0002	.0177	.1143

[a] c.v. = coefficient of variation.

[33] Gordon M. Kaufman, private communication, 1964.

[34] See Gordon M. Kaufman, *Statistical Decision and Related Techniques, op. cit.*, p. 166.

Note that all that has happened to the formula is that the prior parameter σ has been replaced by the preposterior parameter

$$\frac{\sigma^2}{\sqrt{\sigma^2 + \sigma_s^2}} = \sigma\sqrt{\frac{\sigma^2}{\sigma^2 + \sigma_s^2}} < \sigma$$

Since L_L^* is an increasing function of its second variable, EVSI is less than EVPI, as was to be expected.

If there is more than one further study that could have been chosen, then the different studies must be characterized not only by their values of σ_s^2 but also by the costs of undertaking the study. By subtracting the cost of a study from its EVSI, we obtain the expected net gain of sampling, which enables us to chose the most profitable study to undertake.

Unfortunately for the simple analysis above, payback constraints cannot always be ignored, there is usually a restriction on the amount of money available for studies, and, in general, all sorts of managerially imposed requirements prevail under the guise of a "marketing plan." DEMON is designed so that for any given set of constraints it searches out the maximum expected profit that can be achieved. If several alternative sets are given, DEMON will study them simultaneously to obtain the best plan.

Simplification of the product line

The forces that typically lead a manufacturer to expand his product line have already been discussed. However, in the limiting case, these forces would result in an almost infinite expansion of the product line until each product was tailor-made for each customer. Obviously, this might result in a very poor profit performance for the firm. Thus, the firm must develop a systematic method for controlling the size of the product line and preventing the proliferation of variations of products; this process is referred to as *simplification*, or *reduction*.

Some of the problems necessitating deletion of an item from the firm's line are that an old product "is likely to generate more than its share of small unprofitable orders, to make necessary short, costly production runs, to demand an exorbitant amount of executive attention, and to tie up capital that could be used profitably in other ventures."[35] In addition, there are certain effects that result just from the size of the line itself. The success of any item in the product line is not independent of the effects of the total line upon that product; that is, interaction occurs in both directions. If the product line is extended too far, the manufacturer's chances for success on the total product line are reduced, and, at the same time, the cost structure of

[35] Ralph S. Alexander, "The Death and Burial of Sick Products," *Journal of Marketing*, Vol. 28, April 1964, p. 1. Alexander also discusses how managerial fondness for old members of the product line hinders their deletion.

the total line is likely to increase, particularly in terms of inventory and handling costs. Similarly, too broad a product line generally affects the sales force effort adversely. The more products a salesman has to sell, the less attention he can devote to each. Some products may thus become unprofitable, not due to inherent weaknesses in their design or lack of demand for them, but rather due to the fact that salesmen's efforts have been misplaced, resulting in low volume. The firm may be reinforced in its opinions in this case by the fact that the product is not selling well and instruct the salesmen to deemphasize further effort on this product. Reduction, or simplification, of the product line may also result from factors concerned with the maintenance of quality, the duplication of organizational structure, the desire to have relatively simple channels of distribution, and the approach to full utilization of facilities.

Another reason for reduction, one which is possibly more important than any of the above, is the opportunity cost of maintaining the product in the line. It is easy enough to argue that a product should surely be dropped when not even the marginal costs of producing and selling it can be recovered, but the decision can be substantially improved by the more appropriate approach of evaluation of opportunity cost. Essentially, the firm should periodically reevaluate the manner in which it has committed its resources among the products in its line. It may well be that profits can be increased by a shift in effort and resources even when an existing product is making a profit. And, of course, this approach is important in evaluating the merit of a new product opportunity *relative* to existing products.

Simplification usually takes the form of reduction of the varieties of a given item in the product line rather than elimination of one of the members of the line. For example, if a manufacturer has many different kinds of hammers, with varying combinations of claws, heads, weights, colors, sizes, and so on, he may elect to reduce the number of these, but he would not be likely to stop producing hammers. A manufacturer will rarely eliminate a *type* of product from his product line. Further, there is a strong reluctance on the part of management to admit that a product is unsuccessful, and a typical way to retain the item in the product line is to try to improve its profitability by reducing the number of varieties.

The product life cycle and timing

The essence of successful new product introduction or of simplification may lie in the appropriate timing of the action. The importance of timing is best understood by studying the characteristics of a generalized product life cycle shown in Figure 5-7.

A few comments about the nature of Figure 5-7 are necessary before proceeding with its analysis. First, the lines graphed are highly generalized and may not be precise representations of the life cycle for any one product;

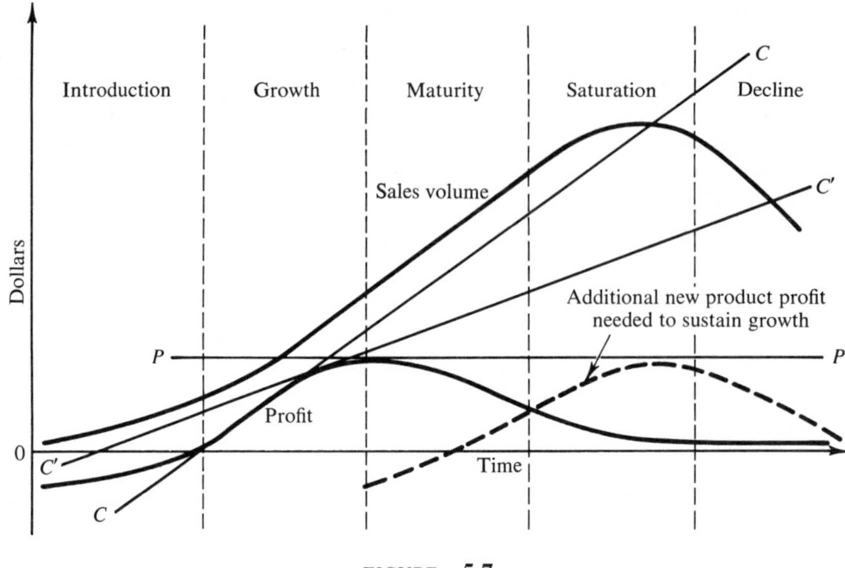

FIGURE 5-7

Generalized product life cycle. SOURCES: *Management Research Department, Booz, Allen, and Hamilton, Inc. (as reported in Thomas L. Berg and Abe Shuchman, Editors,* Product Strategy and Management, *Holt, Rinehart and Winston, New York, 1963, p. 28) and Jay W. Forrester, "Advertising: A Problem in Industrial Dynamics,"* Harvard Business Review, *March–April 1959, p. 108.*

however, this does not preclude its use as a basis for planning. Second, the relationship between sales and profit is not precise, but again this situation will not interfere with the analysis that follows. Third, the decline stage is left incomplete since its duration is indeterminate—as is the total length of the cycle or any of the delineated stages, for that matter. Finally, the rate at which consumers adopt the product will determine the slope of the sales curve during the introductory and growth phases.

The introduction of new products may be used as the takeoff point for consideration of timing. One of the things the firm wishes to do is to phase appropriately the introduction of new products so that, as a minimum effect, the current level of profit is maintained; of course, the firm's objective probably is to increase profit. The key to successful timing is to space the profit peaks of different products over time such that a straight line, such as *PP*, can be drawn across the top of the profit peaks with the sum of the profits from each product amounting to whatever value is represented by *PP*; this behavior pattern would maintain a particular profit level. For increasing profits, the desired rate of growth can be achieved by timing introduction of new products closer together so that profit peaks build on each other with a very slight lag, as in lines *CC* and *C′C′*. This procedure has long-run limitations in that to maintain an established rate of growth in profits the products would have to be introduced closer and closer together; at some point, there either may be no new products available, or the rate of introduction called for may be beyond the company's capabilities. Either objective requires very astute forecasting of life cycles, and most firms are not very successful at this. However, this does not mean that the attempt should not be made. Similarly, a product that is in the declining phase can be eliminated in such a fashion that it does not reach the point at which it no longer contributes to profit. If at the same time as this product is deleted a new one is pressed on the scene, the energies formerly spent attempting to make the first product successful can now be devoted to the new product. Some products are, naturally, kept in the product line even though they make no contribution to profit and possibly none to overhead, in order to present the image in the marketplace of having a complete product line or for public service reasons; an example of the latter is the manufacture of ethical drugs with extremely low demand.

Another possible policy with respect to timing may be to let one product almost complete its life cycle before taking on another. In this way the firm may attempt to gain a larger and larger share of the declining market, increasing short-run profits, but this course does not hold very enticing long-run opportunities. In a sense, the basis for such action is retrenchment. This policy is usually followed by firms that have unexpectedly found themselves with a product that is rapidly becoming obsolete; that is, this kind of behavior is typical of companies that have not been particularly forward-looking in their industries and have failed to respond to the forces that dictate expansion of the product line. An excellent example is that of the steam locomotive manufacturers who refused to recognize that the diesel locomotive was making their product outmoded.

In order for a company to use the concepts just put forth, it is essential to determine position in the life cycle for each of its products. Recall that it was mentioned earlier that Figure 5-7 presents a generalized picture. It is extremely difficult for a company to identify the stage in the life cycle of its own product, which may not be in phase with the industry product category. However, a starting point for the company is the identification of the position of the industry product. This may be accomplished in one of several ways. First, the growth record for a product or a product group within an industry in terms of its sales curves, profit curves, etc., may be compared with the generalized graph given in Figure 5-7. Then, if the factors that influence each phase are considered—for example, the degree of competition, which is certainly most intense in the maturity and saturation phases—the position of the product in its life cycle may be approximated. A second method would be to look at historical trends in the industry. These, of course, would influence the general shape of the curvature for the product, but they are useful in an even more specific fashion. For example, in the chemical industry, it is known that the entire product line except for a very few basics may turn every ten years; similarly, the decline in price as a product moves from specialty to commodity status is a fairly stable phenomenon.

In studying the product life cycle analytically, we can make use of the three-parameter family of functions

$$f(t) = at^b e^{-ct} \tag{5-40}$$

If all three parameters are positive, (5-40) will have the general shape required for the sales curve in Figure 5-7. Since

$$f'(t) = a\left(\frac{b}{t} - c\right)t^b e^{-ct} \tag{5-41}$$

the maximum occurs at $t = b/c$ and is independent of a. Brockhoff[36] has found it useful to write sales at time t as

$$S_t = at^b e^{-ct} + dR_t \tag{5-42}$$

where a, b, c, and d are parameters, and the additional variable R is the sum of sales of related products manufactured by the same company. It is clear from (5-41) that

> Variation in the parameters has the following consequences: (i) as a becomes larger, every point of the function (except 0) grows larger; (ii) as b increases, the upswing tends to be faster and the maximum of sales S is reached later; (iii) as c becomes larger, the decline tends to be faster, and the maximum of S is reached earlier; (iv) if d is positive, sales tend to be greater, if it is negative they are smaller. Measures can easily be imagined that the firms might take to produce such changes in the values of the parameters.[37]

A method for estimating the parameters in (5-42) is developed by Brockhoff.[38] He then applies the estimation method to data supplied by a German automobile manufacturer. Different models of cars were defined largely on the basis of mechanical aspects, such as horsepower and cylinder volume, as opposed to styling elements. Eleven different models of automobiles, most of which had two- to five-year life cycles, were subjected to analysis. The results show quite a close fit between the calculated, or derived, and empirical curves. Two illustrations of this agreement are given in Figure 5-8; because $d \neq 0$, these curves do not have the smooth shape shown in Figure 5-7.

Admittedly, the number of cases upon which Brockhoff has tested his methodology is not large and, further, they are all confined to one industry. On the other hand, it does seem that he has pioneered a useful way of validating the general form of the life cycle.

---

[36] See Klaus Brockoff, "A Test for the Product Life Cycle," *Econometrica*, Vol. 35, July–October 1967, pp. 472–484.

[37] *Ibid*, p. 475.

[38] This material involves a specialized technique beyond the scope of this text.

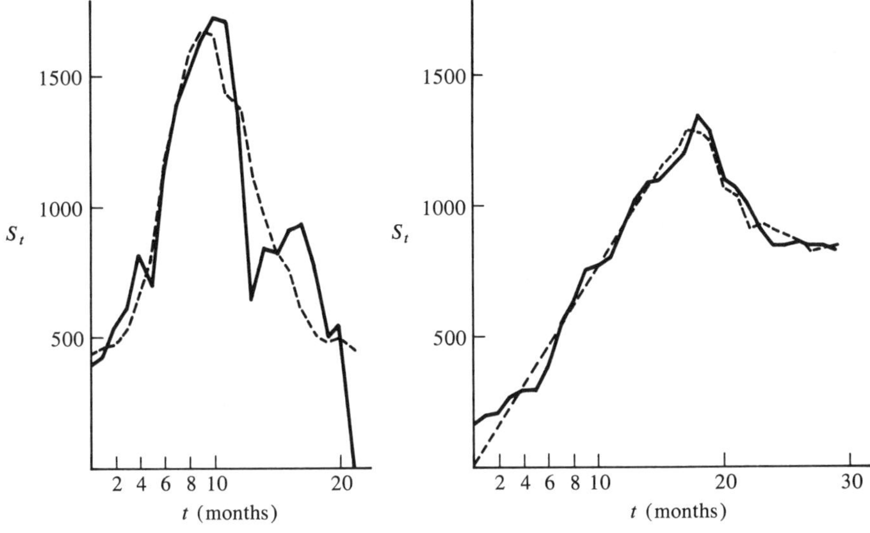

FIGURE **5-8**

Empirical and calculated sales curves for product life cycles

One difficulty with using the life cycle concept is that it requires point estimate accuracy for the timing of introductions or deletions. A product cannot be eliminated "sometime within this period" or introduced "sometime within that period." Ultimately, a decision has to be arrived at identifying which month and day. If it were possible to identify the months on the generalized graph, this would be of great benefit to the company, but unfortunately this is not usually the case.

Another problem involved in use of the product life cycle concept is determination of what market saturation really is. At one time, the objective of automobile manufacturers was to have every family own a car; this was viewed as the relevant definition of market saturation. At that point, the product would have achieved a peak in its sales growth curve—mostly replacements would be produced from then on, with the exception of demand generated by growth in the population—and the product would begin a long, slow decline. With the increased personal wealth in our society, the hypothetical saturation level for Detroit has become a two-car family, and it is not improbable to imagine that someday the saturation level may be the one-person, one-car concept. It can be seen from this illustration that the definition of market saturation very decidedly affects the shape of the product life cycle curve. Thus, if manufacturers are able either to expand the heretofore believed market constraints in terms of the size of the potential market or to evolve new uses for their products, the life cycle may be lengthened considerably. However, it is not clear that the same product is really being dealt with in those instances where a new use has been evolved.

Leader or follower

The final product issue on which the company must decide, which is really a question of philosophy, is whether the company wishes to be a leader or a follower in product development and expansion. The same question does not apply to reduction because of the reduced visibility of the action and the resultant smaller market impact. Reduction decisions usually take place after the demand for a product has substantially diminished so that neither consumers nor competitors will view the act as having particular importance; little market benefit or glory accrues to management for being a leader in reduction, though substantial profits may.

The development of a reputation for innovations in product development by a firm can, on the other hand, frequently yield a loyal group of customers who look to this firm for such innovations, general public respect for the managerial capabilities of the people operating the organization, and the attraction to the firm of creative persons, such as researchers and inventors, interested in developing new ideas. Similarly, there are advantages in the firm's market system; for example, the successfully innovating firm has relatively less trouble in introducing a new product to the members of its channels of distribution or to its sales force. Over the long run, the firm that chooses to be a leader will have both its internal and external systems changed in such a way that it almost totally loses the ability to be a follower; innovation becomes a way of life and the organization's character reflects it. Of course, the follower firm is introducing a product new to itself each time it follows someone else's lead, but the effect of the action upon the firm's production and distribution systems is less permanent; for this reason, it is easier for a follower to attempt to convert to a leader.

The decision to be a leader or a follower rests on the balance between the profits to be gained from innovation and the costs of development of new products. The innovator is likely to reap substantial profits for being the first into the market, particularly if as the market expands the product becomes widely accepted. The follower, on the other hand, avoids all those costs associated with large-scale research and development enterprises, does not take the risk of possible error in marketing a product that will not achieve market acceptance, and generally can benefit from all the mistakes of the innovator. However, at the time the follower arrives in the marketplace, considerable barriers to entry into the industry may already have been built up. For example, a high degree of loyalty may exist for the innovator's product[39]; this is a very definite advantage in maintaining market share. Finally, because only one firm can be the innovator of any given product,

[39] The follower usually enters into the life cycle of the industry product in the growth stage, but possibly late in the introductory stage or early in the maturity stage (see Figure 5-7). The later the follower enters, the greater the disadvantages, so the conscientious follower would usually be entering in the latter part of the introduction period.

the rest have to be followers. Consequently, the firm that elects following as a regular policy will at all times be facing a larger number of competitors and invading established markets, as compared to the firm that elects to be the occasional innovator. In essence, there are only two requisites for leadership: a management that wants leadership and a resource structure that permits leadership. The lack of either of these is not a drawback in the long run, because either can be altered—by the stockholders in the former case and the management in the latter.

Summary

This is the first chapter in which we have dealt with one of the primary decision areas in marketing. In this and each of the succeeding chapters we shall attempt to summarize from three viewpoints the material that has been covered: (1) the principal models presented, (2) the "proven" quality of such models, and (3) the state of the art in quantifying the particular decision area.

This chapter has stressed only models which focus on the development and introduction of new products. However, arguments were initially put forth concerning why it is appropriate to treat almost all product decisions from this viewpoint. The first model is most appropriate for evaluation of product ideas at early stages of development. The format of the model, product profile analysis, is a widely used tool. It is certainly not limited to marketing problems of manufacturers; for example, the format is quite appropriate for a retailer deciding whether to add a particular department or some product lines within the department—only the factors evaluated would change. What we have done in the preceding material is simply to cast product profile analysis into a decision theoretic framework so that the decision maker is better able to estimate the risk under which he is proceeding.[40]

A second model presented herein, DEMON, in contrast to the product profile model, is as yet too new to have received widespread acceptance. Part of the reason is that managers (and researchers) find it hard to believe that the rather simplistic, linear relationships between many pairs of variables in the model actually do hold. DEMON has been applied to one or more new product introductions by seven companies, resulting in a variety of opinions on the part of the different managements.[41] Despite this limited

---

[40] We have demonstrated elsewhere that the high rate of product failures may be due to the fact that the basic product profile analysis format was not designed to evaluate risk explicitly. See Marshall Freimer and Leonard S. Simon, "Screening New Product Ideas," in *Marketing and the New Science of Planning*, Robert L. King, Ed., American Marketing Association, Chicago, 1968, pp. 99–104.

[41] We received this information in a private communication from one of DEMON's developers. As usual, the results are all confidential; about all we can report is that the developers were satisfied with the predictive results of the model.

trial, DEMON is a very valuable theoretical tool. It is one of the few models that integrate the effects of varying strategies in each of the decision areas in the marketing mix. Further, in contrast to some of the other models that purport to accomplish this integration, DEMON uses demonstrated results as opposed to simulated ones; that is, the feasibility of possible strategies is tested first and then integrated into the model as opposed to developing hypotheses about useful strategies via simulation and then subsequently having to determine if the strategies are feasible. In general, DEMON provides a useful way of developing an integrated marketing mix and determining whether or not to commit the full array of the company's resources to marketing the product.

On the whole, quantification in the principal product decision areas is probably less developed than in other decision areas relative to the magnitude and number of problems. But significant progress is being made in converting some of the previously suggested verbal models into quantitative statements—consider, for example, Brockhoff's work. Two areas which should be particularly productive are (1) development of new product ideas through analysis of the n-dimensional state space described by generic product and substitute product characteristics and (2) simplification of the product line.[42]

[42] Since this chapter was written, much has already been accomplished in the first area.

THE PRICING DECISION

CHAPTER SIX

In the writing of any marketing-oriented textbook there is always the question of what material to present on pricing decisions. An extensive literature on price theory exists in economics, but there is not much evidence that the practicing businessman uses this theory as a normative model in developing prices for his output. This discrepancy may be due primarily to either or both of two factors: (1) There is a communications problem in that businessmen do not speak the price theorist's language or, alternatively, are not able to articulate the procedures they actually do follow; and (2) the price theorist's models are poor representations of the marketplace.[1] To effect a reconciliation between theory and practice, we present in this chapter sufficient material to enable the reader to grasp the nature of the firm's important pricing decisions and the factors that influence them, along with some models of how these decisions might be resolved. We shall start by reviewing the limiting cases in economic theory, monopoly and competition, move to the middle ground of oligopoly and monopolistic competition, and then develop various decision rules and models for the establishment of price given particular economic environments.[2]

[1] Oxenfeldt has tried to assess both of these possibilities. See Alfred R. Oxenfeldt, "How Well Existing Market Models Meet the Needs of Businessmen," in *Models of Markets*, Alfred R. Oxenfeldt, Ed., Columbia University Press, New York, 1963, pp. 61–92.

[2] The following are good introductory source material for those who wish to enhance their knowledge of price theory and pricing practices: Robert Dorfman, *The Price System*, Prentice-Hall, Englewood Cliffs, N.J., 1964; Donald V. Harper, *Price Policy and Procedure*, Harcourt, Brace & World, New York, 1966; Alfred R. Oxenfeldt, *Industrial Pricing and Market Practices*, Prentice-Hall, Englewood Cliffs, N.J., 1951; Robert A. Lynn, *Price Policies and Marketing Management*, Richard D. Irwin, Homewood, Ill., 1967; A. D. H. Kaplan, Joel B. Dirlam, and Robert F. Lanzillotti, *Pricing in Big Business*, The Brookings Institution, Washington, D.C., 1958.

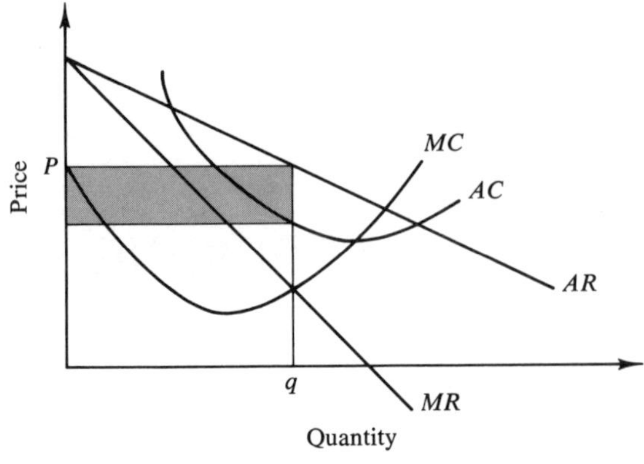

FIGURE 6-1

Monopoly price

Monopoly

There are very few situations in which a firm totally controls the supply of a given product or service and its offering in the marketplace. In those few instances where such a situation does exist, the industry's demand and supply schedules are obviously identical to those of the firm. Because of existing beliefs about the "waste" of resources that may occur in monopoly, most societies or economic systems make an effort to inhibit the development of monopoly. Occasionally, however, monopoly is thought to lead to more efficient distribution, and "regulated" monopolies are permitted to operate; prime examples are the public utilities in the United States.

An understanding of monopoly pricing is important because in competitive situations the firm strives toward the goal of being able to price as the monopolist would, since the monopolist's pricing decisions have the potential for yielding the maximum industry, or company, profit. In Figure 6-1 we show the standard diagram for determination of the short-run monopoly price. Profits are maximized at the point where marginal revenue (MR) equals marginal cost (MC), and the shaded area shows the amount of such profits. Although the firm could produce without loss up to the point at which average revenue (AR), or the demand function, equals average cost (AC), or the supply function, it would be in violation of its own best interests because profits would be reduced. Thus, the monopolist may have substantial incentive to constrain output.

The mathematical structure will make this clearer. Suppose that the equation of the demand curve can be written as

$$p = f_1(q) \tag{6-1}$$

and that the cost (supply) function is

$$c = f_2(q) \tag{6-2}$$

Then total profit is

$$qf_1(q) - qf_2(q) \tag{6-3}$$

which is maximized when

$$\frac{d}{dq} qf_1(q) = \frac{d}{dq} qf_2(q) \tag{6-4}$$

that is, when marginal revenue equals marginal cost. Although profit is positive as long as $f_1(q) > f_2(q)$, it steadily decreases as output is increased, finally falling to zero when $f_1(q) = f_2(q)$.

These theoretical statements are easily made, but the truly difficult problem is the determination of the demand and cost functions. Since the firm rarely gets to offer a product to potential customers in the same marketplace at several different prices, the nature of the demand function must be largely deduced.[3] Demand estimation is a subject extensively covered in the economic literature, and much of it focuses on developing point estimates of the firm's sales volume for different price levels. However, the literature does not limit itself to the relationship between price and sales. Obviously, even in a monopolistic situation, many other factors influence sales volume—advertising and general economic conditions, for example. Thus, demand is more properly described as a multivariate function, with price as one of many variables:

$$q = f(p, x_1, x_2, \ldots, x_n)$$

The other variables may be described as causing shifts in the demand curve when it is described only in terms of the price–quantity relationship. One author's conception of the variables and information flows in demand estimation is given in Figure 6-2. Various approaches may be utilized to estimate the coefficients in the demand function,[4] but a discussion of these is not appropriate here. Two additional problems frequently encountered in demand estimation are (1) the inadequacy of data on factors that have been

[3] Experimental work in estimating individual purchasers' demand functions for products sold on a mass market basis has increased in the past few years; an excellent example is Edgar Pessemier, *Experimental Methods of Analyzing Demand for Branded Consumer Goods with Applications to Problems in Marketing Strategy*, Washington State University Press, Pullman, Wash., 1963.

[4] A basic discussion of single-equation models may be found in Milton H. Spencer and Louis Siegelman, *Managerial Economics*, Richard D. Irwin, Homewood, Ill., 1964, pp. 120–257, and a discussion of multiple-equation models in E. Z. Beach, *Economic Models*, Wiley, New York, 1957, pp. 182–203. Another individual customer-oriented approach may be found in Robert S. Weinberg, "Multiple Factor Break-Even Analysis: The Application of Operations-Research Techniques to A Basic Problem of Management Planning and Control," *Operations Research*, Vol. IV, No. 2, April 1956, pp. 152–186.

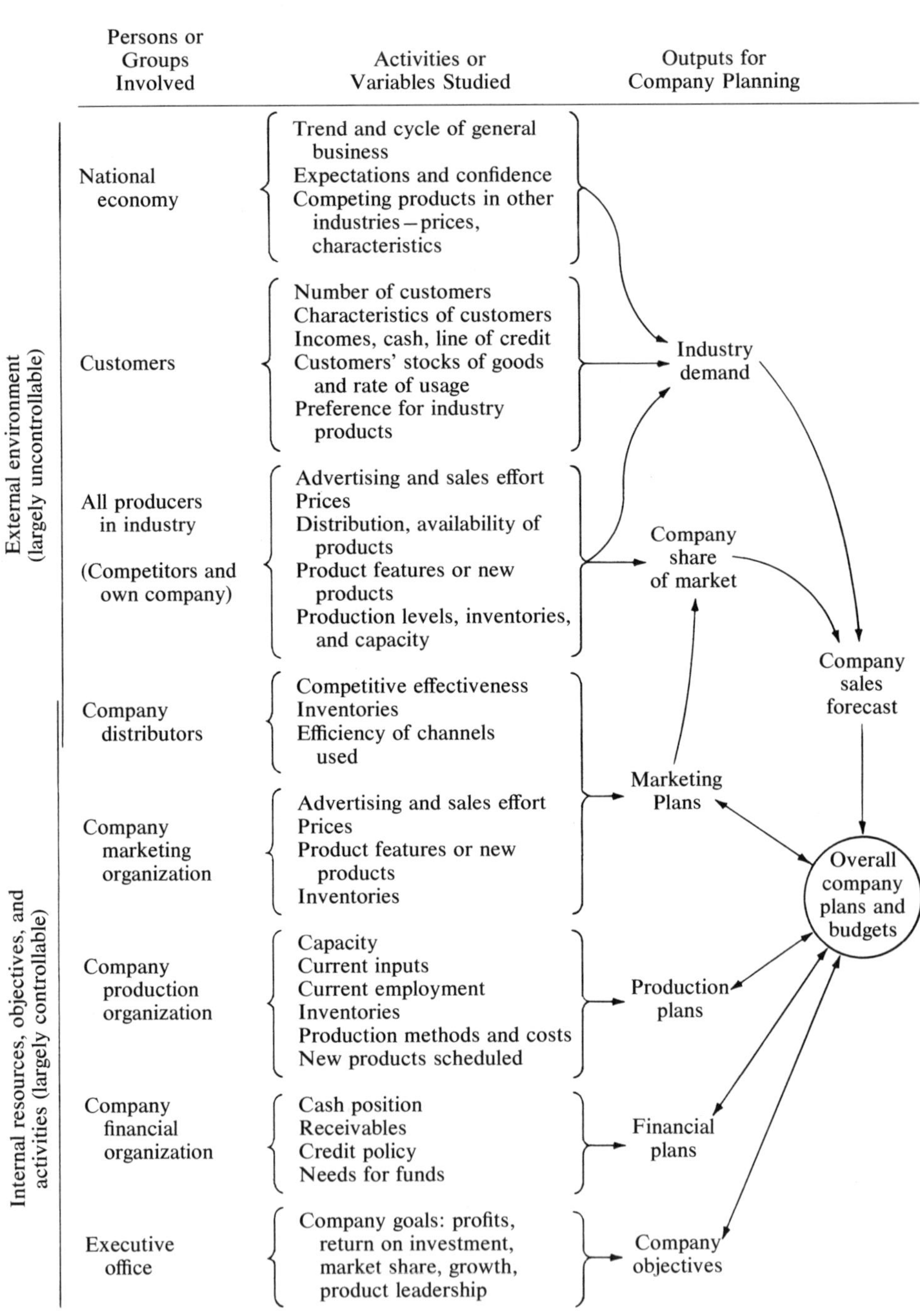

FIGURE **6-2**

Information flows in sales forecasting and business planning. TAKEN FROM *Vernon G. Lippitt, "Modern Sales Forecasting for Effective Management," unpublished manuscript.*

proved to have a substantial influence on demand, and (2) the question of the quality of the data that are available. The latter factor would include the size of the error term in the data concerning the phenomena described and possible biases introduced into the data collection and analysis procedures.

Another concept useful in estimating the effect of price on the quantity demanded is that of *elasticity*. For a specific segment of the demand curve, this is the percentage change in quantity divided by the percentage change in price for the relevant price increase or decrease being evaluated, or

$$\eta = \frac{(q_2 - q_1)/\frac{1}{2}(q_1 + q_2)}{(p_2 - p_1)/\frac{1}{2}(p_2 + p_1)} \quad \text{or} \quad \frac{(q_2 - q_1)(p_2 + p_1)}{(q_1 + q_2)(p_2 - p_1)} \tag{6-5}$$

The average of the prices or quantities is used to counter arguments over which base should be used for establishing the percentage change. If $\eta > 1$, the curve is defined as elastic; if $\eta < 1$, it is inelastic; and if $\eta = 1$, the term used is *unitary elasticity*. Essentially, elasticity measures the relative sensitivity of sales volume to price changes at any given point on the demand curve and thus should be a great aid to the manager in selecting price – given, of course, that the demand curve portrays the situation accurately. Obviously, elasticity is simply the relative rate of proportional change function; that is,

$$\eta = \frac{p\,dq}{q\,dp} \tag{6-6}$$

which is probably a more helpful way of evaluating the usefulness of the concept.

The cost function is usually more easily determined from historical data if the firm is a single-product producer. If, however, the firm is a multiproduct operation and a monopolist on some or all of the products, the determination of average cost curves becomes quite complex owing to the difficulty of allocating overhead or fixed costs jointly incurred by different members of the product line. Regardless of whether the overhead costs are closely associated with production, such as janitorial work, or much more indirectly related, such as institutional advertising, the basis for allocation must always be open to question. Various rationales may be developed about why particular bases are the most appropriate for allocation, but no matter what method is utilized, the end pro rata allocated cost is nothing more than serious guesswork. The estimation procedure can be further complicated if one is trying to establish functions for an item not yet in production and expectations, both of consumers and of the production and engineering departments, are being dealt with.

Given the difficulties outlined above, it is entirely possible for the monopolist not to find the profit-maximizing price. For example, Robinson points out that if the marginal revenue or marginal cost curves are complex, the monopolist may find only a local equilibrium point, because of insufficient knowledge.[5] Monopolists have their problems too.

Competition

Although very few industries are monopolistic, the number that can be characterized as completely competitive environments is also small. The best examples are the various agricultural industries. Some other, less perfect, examples can be found in consumer goods industries, such as manufacture of inexpensive men's clothing, shoes, and the like. The necessary conditions for perfect competition are (1) the number of competitors must be large and each one of relatively small size so that no one can affect the market very strongly; (2) a firm must be able to sell all it wishes to produce at the industry price but *almost* none of its output above the industry price; (3) the products must be essentially homogeneous, even though coming from different sources; and (4) purchasers must exhibit no preference for one manufacturer's output over another's. In such circumstances, the firm has relatively little control over price decisions. Although the industry demand and supply curves exhibit substantial slope, as shown in Figure 6-3, indicating the possibility of changes in both price and output, the firm does not have equivalent flexibility, as seen in Figure 6-4.[6] The marginal cost curve for the firm is the supply curve; that is, the amount the firm will produce at any price can be read from the marginal cost curve. In Figure 6-4, the marginal revenue curve is identical with the demand curve, so to maxi-

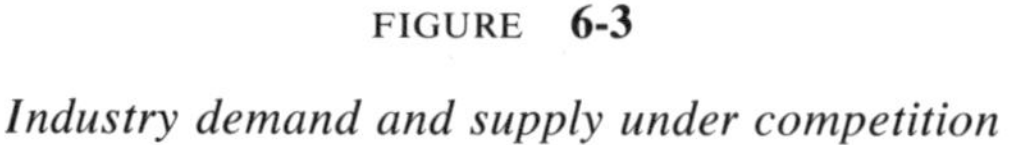

FIGURE **6-3**

Industry demand and supply under competition

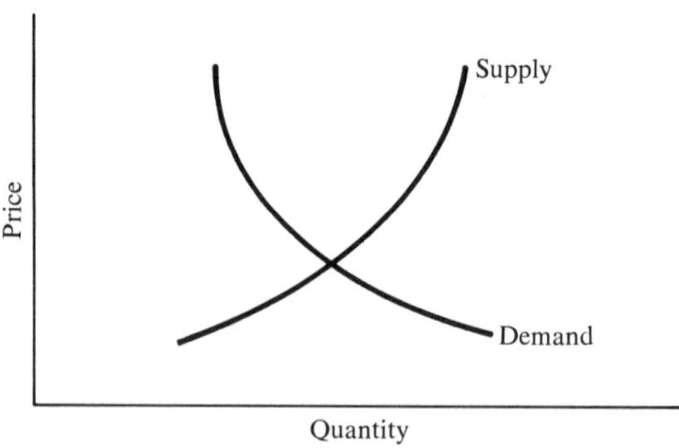

[5] Joan Robinson, *The Economics of Imperfect Competition*, Macmillan, London, 1933, pp. 56–59.

[6] The price level p shown for the firm in Figures 6-4 and 6-5 is obtained from the intersection of supply and demand for the industry (Figure 6-3).

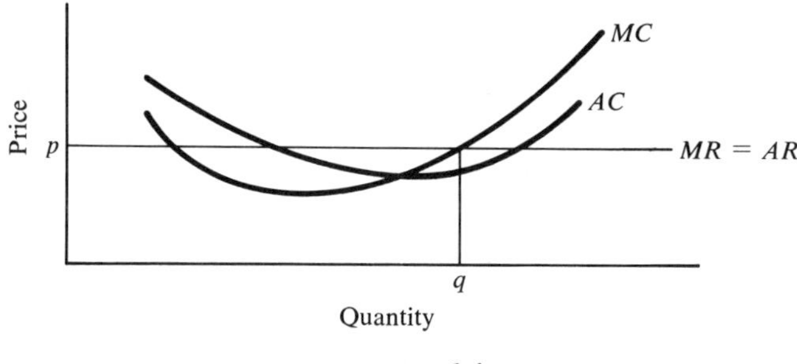

FIGURE **6-4**

Firm demand and supply under competition

mize profits the firm produces the number of units dictated by the intersection of the marginal revenue and marginal cost curves.

In the particular case illustrated, the firm is making a per-unit profit equal to the difference between the price and the average cost. Under such circumstances, there is strong incentive for the firm to expand and/or modernize its production facilities. When many firms face similar situations, a strong impetus for price reduction develops so that each firm can obtain a sufficient quantity of sales to operate at the minimum point on its average cost curve.[7] An adjustment process continues until an equilibrium is reached at which marginal cost, average cost, and price are all equal, as in Figure 6-5. The firm will then be just breaking even; costs are viewed as including some returns to the owners. One other important phenomenon takes place in the long-run adjustment process. Some firms will not be able to achieve the new, more efficient levels of production, and they will be driven out of the industry. Thus, long-run adjustments are brought about not only by changes in price and production but also by changes in the number of firms in the industry.

FIGURE **6-5**

Long-run equilibrium under competition

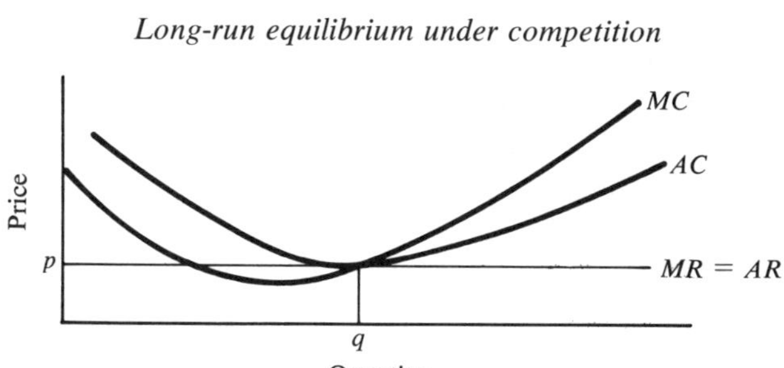

[7] It is easy to show that, in general, the minimum point on the average cost curve coincides with the point at which average and marginal costs are equal.

Neither monopoly nor competition

Obviously, given a choice, most managers would prefer to be monopolists rather than perfect competitors. Thus, managers strive to develop strategies that will move their firms away from completely competitive environments in order to increase the number of controllable factors in the environment, but few can attain monopoly status. The end result is a competitive environment for most American industries that is neither perfect competition nor monopoly but contains strong elements of both. It should be pointed out, however, that certain situations that appear to fall in this in-between grouping can be treated analytically either as monopoly or as competition.[8] For example, in some industries where there are several producers, one firm controls a sufficiently large share of the market that its pricing strategies may be conducted within the framework appropriate for monopolists—the Gillette Safety Razor Company might well have been in this position prior to the introduction of stainless steel blades.

The environments in which most firms operate are usually described as either oligopoly or monopolistic competition.[9] The bases for distinction of these competitive forms focus on the number and size of competitors, and on the degree of homogeneity among the various firms' outputs as reflected particularly in the cross-elasticity of demand (the extent to which a given firm's sales are dependent on the prices competitors are asking for their "similar" outputs). Roughly speaking, in *oligopoly* there are a small number of large firms producing essentially identical products (chemicals, for example), and hence are highly sensitive to each other's prices, whereas in *monopolistic competition* there are more but smaller firms producing "differentiated" products (brand-name foods, for example) and are less sensitive to each other's prices. It is impossible to make the definitions of these intermediate forms of competition as tight as might be desired, and one can find many industries that do not fit neatly into any category.[10] Some other comments about these intermediate forms of industry structure may be offered. Oligopoly is frequently characterized by the extent to which collusion *may* exist among the industry members, but this is a difficult subject to treat because of the effect of the law upon members' activities. A firm's perception

---

[8] There are some economists who maintain that these intermediate forms of competition do not add to the understanding of the firm's behavior and that almost all situations can be treated, with reasonable adjustments, as monopoly or competition. For example, see George Stigler, *Five Lectures on Economic Problems*, Macmillan, New York, Lecture 2, 1950, pp. 12–24.

[9] The principal expositions on these subjects are Joan Robinson, *op. cit.*, and Edward Chamberlin, *The Theory of Monopolistic Competition*, Harvard University Press, Cambridge, Mass., 1933.

[10] The automobile industry is one example. At this point it is tempting to define new categories, such as *differentiated oligopoly* with few firms and differentiated products, but we resist.

of its environment may be more important than the actual character of the environment; for example, a firm in an industry that could be reasonably described as monopolistic competition might make pricing decisions using analysis more appropriate to an oligopolist because of a stronger belief about its interdependency with rivals' actions than the rivals hold with respect to it and to each other. The meaning of competitive equilibrium is not at all clear for industries in which the products are not substantially homogeneous, because different products (and thus, perhaps, different industries) are really being dealt with. Finally, the structure of any industry is not permanently fixed; new firms may enter it and shifts may occur in individual firms' positions, both of which could alter the characterization of the industry.

Follow the leader

In oligopoly and to some extent in monopolistic competition, the actions of the industry members are strongly linked because of the relatively high cross-elasticity of demand. The firm may then reason that if it cuts its own price, competitors will follow suit because of their beliefs that prices must be equal owing to the completely substitutable nature of the product. If there were a general price reduction, in the short run all firms would be selling somewhat larger quantities at somewhat lower prices unless industry demand were highly elastic, which management seldom thinks to be the case. The net effect might well be that the profits of the firm would be reduced. Therefore, when the product is judged highly substitutable, most firms will be extremely reluctant to reduce price, because this action would be thought of as destructive rather than demand expanding. On the other hand, it can be seen that a firm might also be highly reluctant to raise its price unless there were a strong belief that competitors would follow suit. If the others did not follow the price rise, the demand for the firm raising its price might fall substantially, again because of the existence of high product substitutability. In a fully substitutable situation, the only constraint upon how far demand fell for the firm raising price would be other firms' capacities to fill their new demand. It is thus to the advantage of firms in such industrial situations to have their prices move together. Examples of this kind of behavior are to be found in the automotive, oil, and chemical industries.

Usually the largest member of the industry is the chief price setter. *Largest* in this case may be defined by total asset structure or by the percentage of the market share held. This firm usually initiates upward price movements, and other industry members follow along. The behavior is not illegal because it is a form of tacit consent rather than planned or formal agreement. The other firms acquiesce in the leader's moves because of the interdependency of price and to a lesser degree because the leader is thought to (1) have greater skill at analyzing economic conditions; (2) take greater initiative in changing the character of the industry through new product development and new technology; and (3) take any actions in the best interest of the group as a whole, since whatever he does that affects the industry will affect him the most. There is no evidence favoring this last point, however, and it may well be that the situation can be so structured that the leader can take actions that benefit him more than proportionately.

Price leadership may be segmented geographically. Although there may be national leaders, in areas where a particular firm dominates the local market it may be the price leader. An example of this kind of situation can be found in President Kennedy's 1962 dispute with the steel industry. The national price leader, U.S. Steel, was forced to rescind its price increase because Inland Steel, a company that was only eighth in the industry nationally but very strong in the Chicago market, chose not to follow the price increase. U.S. Steel could not afford to have a different price for the Chicago market because of the shifting of demand to the Chicago market that would follow; consequently, the national price rise fell away.

The steel dispute interestingly brings to light the important belief held by many businessmen, that a price is competitive only when it matches competitors' prices. This would, of course, result under pure competition, but as the preceding material indicates, the same situation may arise in oligopoly for quite different reasons.

The leader's dominant role is primarily in the area of price increases, and a leader may actually be a follower when it comes to price decreases. Since this dominant firm usually has the largest share of the market, any price cut without a sufficient attendant increase in the quantity demanded from the industry as a whole will affect it more detrimentally than other members of the industry. Thus, the leader is usually far more reluctant to introduce a price decrease than are smaller members of the industry. However, one may speculate that a smaller member probably does not initiate a price decrease without some belief that the leader will acquiesce and follow with a corresponding price decrease. (Occasionally, price increases will be initiated by other than the leader under a similar set of expectations about the leader's following behavior. In fact, it may be speculated that the leader may encourage this belief on the part of smaller industry members.) If the industry does not move together in this fashion, one can only assume that the initiator of the price cut should benefit since the quantity demanded from him will increase.

In most industries, there are also marginal firms who usually maintain their prices at a specified percentage or number of dollars below that of the remainder of the industry. Their price movements then correspond to those of the industry, but they maintain the price difference. One example would be service stations selling gasoline a few cents per gallon below the major brands. Usually the capacity of these marginal firms is sufficiently limited that they are not considered a factor to be reckoned with in the establishment of price.

These smaller firms bring to light another important fact about oligopoly, namely, that industry structure is oligopolistic only over some price range. To illustrate, if the twelve or so major firms in the steel industry raised price and the marginal firms did not in the long run follow (a possibly unrealistic assumption since the factors that affect costs and exert other influences resulting in price increases may well affect all industry members), the major firms would suffer substantially because of the price competition that would ensue. As a corollary, one can argue that if this hypothetical situation did occur, the response of some big firms would be to reduce price, thereby introducing price competition in another sense; that is, even if the other large firms followed, competition would be established between the major and minor firm groupings.

The question of what price to charge in oligopoly is fairly well decided, then, except for the industry leader—the other members of the industry follow approximately what the leader does.[11] However, this does not mean that these other members need not analyze the market themselves. An assessment of the leader's "wisdom" is always in order. For another thing, the followers would do well to try to anticipate the leader's actions in order to prepare the appropriate responses on their parts. Further, some firms are followers on particular products but leaders on others and must therefore always be concerned with the kind of analysis necessary to establish price.

In monopolistic competition the pricing situation is somewhat different, because it is more difficult for consumers to ascertain the direct substitutability of one product for another. For example, a Ford and a Chevrolet both provide automotive transportation, but ascertaining which one's mechanical performance is superior, or which is quieter, or which has more inherent status tends to be a highly individualistic affair. The likelihood is that the consumer envisions the Ford and the Chevrolet as relatively less substitutable commodities than General Electric and Sylvania light bulbs. On the other hand, although prices of industry members in monopolistic competition are not identical, they do move together, because (1) the members are responding to industry-wide demand determinants, and (2) there is significant cross-elasticity of demand for other than very moderate price differences.

Cost-plus

Having discussed some of the general implications of economic price theory, we now turn to specific procedures available to the individual firm.

One basis for the establishment of price is the cost to produce or purchase the merchandise or service to be sold.[12] If the firm doing the pricing

---

[11] And the leader's analysis is essentially the subject of this chapter.

[12] The concept is less applicable to the case of certain professional services, such as legal or medical services, where the primary cost is for labor whose market value on a per-unit basis by different types of services is not readily identifiable.

is a reseller of merchandise, a percentage is commonly added to the cost that is large enough to cover all overhead plus a desired level of profit. A manufacturer usually behaves slightly differently. In this case, the basic cost is the direct cost of producing the good and several percentages are added. First, a percentage of the direct cost is added to reflect factory and other manufacturing overhead, resulting in the total cost of producing the good. Next, another percentage is added to cover sales and administrative overhead.[13] Finally, the desired profit, a percentage of the total costs to this point, is added. This process is obviously flexible, and any or all of the several percentages could be combined to reduce the number of steps. The various possible combinations are all in fairly widespread use by firms of quite varying size and sophistication.[14]

The price determined by the cost-plus method is frequently adjusted to reflect market conditions. For example, a retailer might alter the price to take advantage of the psychological value of odd-numbered pricing, or a manufacturer may find that the percentage added on for desired profits puts his price above the market level, and so he accepts a smaller percentage for profit while searching for means of reducing production costs.

There are two key internal problems in the use of the cost-plus method: the determination of the various percentages and the relevance of various costs to the decisions. As an illustration of the former, consider the percentage of direct costs used to obtain total cost to manufacture. The justification for any particular percentage is not clear. For example, if the ratio of all overhead to all direct costs for the factory is used, it may be highly inappropriate for specific products. More important, the percentage assigned at this point reflects itself in the magnitude of the ultimate price. This is the essence of the problem: A firm may or may not believe that the price it would like to obtain is competitive more because of the system used for assignment of overhead than because of real differences between its costs and the competitors'. Of course, the same argument may be made for any of the percentages used.

Regarding the relevance of costs, the second problem in cost-plus methodology, it is not always clear what cost concepts should be applied. In any given decision, one may be concerned with many different kinds of cost, such as opportunity costs, incremental costs, and escapable costs. Identifying which of these are appropriate to a pricing decision may be very difficult.[15] For example, some firms fail to take advantage of unusual business

---

[13] This may also be a two-step process, assigning the directly traceable sales costs first.

[14] Not only small retailers but giant firms, too; see A. D. H. Kaplan et al., *Pricing in Big Business*, The Brookings Institution, Washington, D.C., 1958.

[15] A description of different cost concepts and their applicability to various situations may be found in Joel Dean, *Managerial Economics*, Prentice-Hall, Englewood Cliffs, N.J., 1951, pp. 257–272.

opportunities because of adherence only to average cost concepts. Suppose the firm has an opportunity to accept an additional quantity of business that it did not expect and did not plan for in the course of its regular analysis. The only costs relevant to this decision are the incremental costs; as far as production is concerned, the marginal costs, not the average costs, are the correct ones to use. Assume further that the purchaser is fairly sophisticated and is offering to buy these units of output at considerably below their usual market price. If the management elects to treat the units on a fully allocated cost basis, the asking price will probably be too high to secure the additional business. On the other hand, a price that covers marginal costs and provides some contribution to overhead and profit could make the undertaking worthwhile. This reasoning may be explained by the fact that all the units of the product normally budgeted for, if sold, would readily cover overhead. A price determined via marginal analysis would then provide pure profits above the additional costs. If a number of the units budgeted for were not sold, then the incremental units would help cover the overhead that would have been absorbed by the regularly budgeted units. Obviously, though, the firm cannot sell all its output at prices determined on the basis of marginal costs or it would be put out of business because it would not be covering all the overhead costs. Since cost-plus is based on reasoning in terms of averages rather than increments, there will be situations in which business will be declined although it might really be worth accepting. Thus, the choice of appropriate costs is crucial in price determination. But no matter what concepts are utilized, the firm's cost structure serves as the foundation for the process by which price is established.

Price discrimination

We have just seen that flexibility in the establishment of price may reflect itself not only in firms within an industry offering their products at different prices but also in the individual firm charging different prices to different customers for the same product. This last practice is known as *price discrimination* (as used by economists, the term is not intended to have ethical overtones).[16] In effect, price discrimination enables the producer to sell at many different prices the identical quantities of output and services. Common examples of this type of pricing are (1) the medical profession, in which doctors may charge prices based on estimated ability to pay and estimated relative value of the service to the patient, as well as on

[16] If the notion is accepted that the price decision is really reached at the margin—that is, where the buyer is giving up the last dollar he is willing to give up and the seller is accepting the least number of dollars that he is willing to accept from that particular buyer—then price discrimination may be said to be beneficial in that it results in efficient resource allocation.

the type of service rendered,[17] and (2) the various "special" fares of the scheduled airlines. It can be demonstrated that price discrimination yields substantially higher profits to the firm, principally by inducing purchase of units of production at an array of prices on the demand schedule rather than solely at the equilibrium price.[18]

In order for price discrimination to be effective, however, two conditions must exist: (1) The various buyers must be fairly well insulated from each other, in the sense that information exchange must be difficult, and (2) the buyers must not be able to resell their purchases to others who might have bought from the manufacturer in the first place. If the first condition does not hold, buyers will demand lower prices based on those prices received by others and, insofar as their bargaining power commands it, they will be able to obtain those prices. For example, the wealthy but sick person is in a sense a quantity buyer, and the doctor might rather reduce price than suffer the total loss of the patient's business. Also, buyers may begin purchasing from other than their present sources to obtain more favorable prices – if they are treated on a marginal basis by the firms approached, they should certainly succeed – and the general price level will probably fall. If the second condition does not hold, then the economically powerful buyers will purchase in large quantities at lower prices and obtain additional profits by reselling the merchandise.

These drawbacks are also found in incremental sales, for, clearly, the acceptance of business on the basis of covering somewhat more than marginal costs is a form of price discrimination. The implicit danger to the firm stems from the potential demand for the marginally determined price on a regular basis by some sizable number of customers. On the other hand, examples of situations in which buyers might be willing to accept price discrimination that favored other buyers might be the closeout of a particular style in the product line of a clothing manufacturer, a special production run when otherwise the supplying firm is faced with large unused capacity, and so on. Thus, depending on the circumstances, price discrimination can lead either to a price that is somewhat in excess of marginal cost or to one that includes fully allocated costs plus a substantial profit.

In fact, it is probably true that price flexibility is a far more common policy among companies in the United States than price rigidity (the distinction being the willingness to set differing prices for the many customers, that is, to practice price discrimination). For industrial companies with relatively few customers, price discrimination is a more feasible policy than for the individual retail enterprise that cannot easily establish a separate price,

[17] An excellent discussion of the general conditions necessary to the practice of price discrimination, and the means for developing them, may be found in Reuben A. Kessel, "Price Discrimination in Medicine," *Journal of Law and Economics*, Vol. I, October 1958, pp. 20–53.

[18] A simple illustration of such may be found in Armen A. Alchian and William R. Allen, *University Economics*, Wadsworth, Belmont, Calif., 1964, pp. 143–148.

negotiated prior to each sale, for each individual; the retailer, however, can set prices for large groups of customers just as the airlines do. But, in effect, almost all firms practice price discrimination from the standpoint that they give varying kinds of price trade-offs in the form of non-price competition, such as special delivery terms, financiing, or service. Therefore, one may really view non-price competition as a means of creating price discrimination. To illustrate, a department store may be unusually lenient about applying interest charges to the outstanding balances of highly prized customers or even give them a different type of account. Generally speaking, then, if one considers both the situations in which actual prices are different and those in which the effective prices are different because of various forms of non-price competition, price discrimination is very widespread.[19]

An example of non-price competition: industrial reciprocity

Most activities in the economic sphere can be translated into an effect upon price even though they may not be presented in this form. For example, advertising and certain other forms of promotion are thought of as efforts to shift the classical demand curve to the right. This strategy of holding price constant and manipulating other factors is usually referred to as *non-price competition.* In some situations, non-price competition is the principal competitive mechanism for an industry. Service of various types, special delivery considerations, or special financing considerations are all examples of the kinds of trade-offs that can be made in non-price competition.

We now offer a somewhat detailed example that demonstrates the intricate forms non-price competition can take, and its advantages.[20]

Industrial reciprocity, the practice of purchasing from firms to which one is also selling, is a fairly widespread industrial practice. Reciprocity is not necessarily confined to the two-party relationship implied in our definition. The practice can include three, four, or more companies. For example, A may sell to B; B also sells to C; C would like to sell to A but has so far been unsuccessful; so C puts pressure on B, who in turn puts pressure on A to buy from C. When more than two companies are involved, a business

[19] Certain federal and state legislation regulates the ability of the producer to employ price discrimination, that is, the Robinson–Patman Act and state fair-trade laws. Further, a focal point of much antitrust activity is the firm's actual pricing policies and potential competitive effects of changes in the firm's pricing strategies. These subjects, however, are outside the scope of this book. For one appraisal of the effect of governmental policy, see E. T. Groether, "Public Policy Affecting the Competitive Market System in the United States," in *Marketing and Economic Development, Proceedings*, Peter D. Bennett, Ed., American Marketing Association, Chicago, 1965, pp. 533–557.

[20] The material on reciprocity that follows has been adapted from Leonard S. Simon, "Industrial Reciprocity as a Business Stratagem," *Industrial Management Review*, Vol. 7, No. 2, 1966, pp. 27–39, by permission of the copyright owner.

relationship between each pair of the parties is not required. To illustrate, a manufacturer of chemical dyes may solicit the business of a yard goods house for a dyeing and finishing plant on the basis that his dyes will then be purchased by the dyeing and finishing plant. The condition most conducive to the use of reciprocity is diversification as achieved through merger, acquisition, or expansion of the product line. But this condition and some others that have been offered as being conducive to the practice of reciprocity[21] fail to explain adequately why firms utilize the practice.

Stocking and Mueller, in speaking of non-price competition, state that "Reciprocal buying, by shifting a firm's demand curve to the right, may enable a firm to expand its sales and, if it can work out long-term reciprocal arrangements, to grow at the expense of rivals."[22] If marginal cost was then relatively constant, reciprocity would lead to increased profits. The crux of the matter, however, lies in the behavior of the rivals; if they can also exert reciprocal pressure, the market will assume some new equilibrium position, but it is not clear that the firm initially attempting to use reciprocity will have other than a short-term benefit.[23] It may be that the rivals either have more reciprocal power or are capable of foreclosing that part of the market to which the initiator of reciprocity now sells and with which he does not have reciprocal potential. Thus, there is a real question of whether reciprocity can result in a long-term shift of the buyer's demand curve to the right. Rather, if seen from the viewpoint of the firm to whom reciprocal persuasion is being applied, reciprocity appears as a means of preventing its own demand curve from being shifted to the left.

Assume a situation in which companies A and B are reciprocators, A selling product x to B, and B selling product y to A in a ratio of (dollars of x): (dollars of y) = 3:1. B informs A that he has just been offered a somewhat lower price on x by C, a nonreciprocator who cannot possibly be turned into a reciprocator. B inquires of A what he proposes to do. A has essentially four courses of action open to him: (1) He may do nothing and suffer a reduction in B's business or, perhaps, receive none of it; (2) he may reduce his own price; (3) he may accept a price increase on y; or (4) he may buy more y. In each of the last three cases, A is attempting to hold B as a customer by developing an offer that will yield B a dollar amount equivalent to the savings he would incur by accepting C's lower price.

A's analysis would be as follows (see Figure 6-6): At present, B's demand curve for x[24], d_x, is such that quantity q_x at price p_x is being sold to

[21] These are thoroughly discussed in George W. Stocking and Willard F. Mueller, "Business Reciprocity and the Size of Firms," *Journal of Business*, Vol. 30, April 1957, pp. 75–77; and Leonard S. Simon, *op. cit.*, pp. 28–29.

[22] Stocking and Mueller, *op. cit.*, p. 76.

[23] And unlike certain other competitive practices, the firm cannot freely move in and out of reciprocity.

[24] B's demand curve for x is shown as a continuous function, but it may well be a step function; however, the analysis is substantially aided if the former case is assumed.

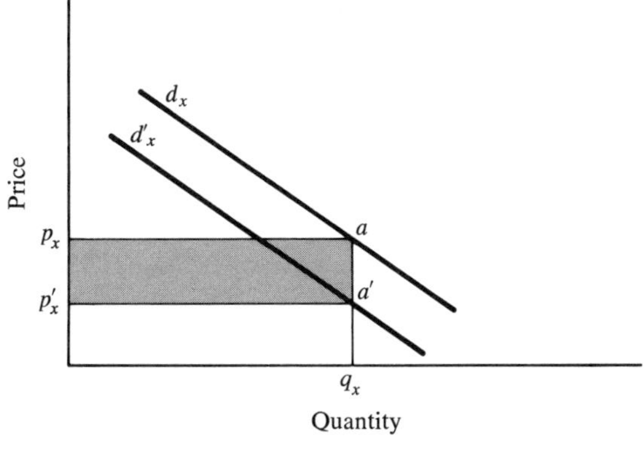

FIGURE **6-6**

Demand for product x *by firm B*

him. C's price cut has shifted B's demand curve to the left, as represented by the line d'_x, resulting in a potential saving to B—if he is able to buy the total quantity originally purchased from A, or q_x, from C—represented by the area $p_x p'_x a'a$. What A must do is find some way to create equivalent savings for B while not exceeding the contribution to overhead and profit associated with sales now being made to B.

The desirability of matching C's price depends very much on the characteristics of the industry containing A and C. By definition, there must be some price competition (or C would not have cut price), and A's decision about reducing price to B will rest on the extent to which he is able to practice price discrimination. If we assume that, for one reason or another, price discrimination is not feasible for A and thus he would like to preserve price p_x and B's business, then he must take one of the two remaining actions. If A elects to accept a price increase on y, resulting in a shift of his demand curve to the right, then the area represented by $p'_y p_y cc'$ (Figure 6-7) will be added to B's revenues. This incremental revenue is not accompanied by any increase in B's costs, so A's objective should be to offer a price high enough to make area $p'_y p_y cc'$ equal to area $p_x p'_x a'a$, subject to the constraint that $p'_y p_y cc'$ is less than the contribution margin of the sales now being made to B. On the other hand, if A elects to buy more of y at the same price, which would also result in a shift of the demand curve to the right, he must increase his purchases so that the revenues to B will equal B's variable cost in producing additional y plus his savings on the proposed price cut from C. Again, this is subject to the same contribution constraint, $q_y q'_y c''c = V_B + p_x p'_x a'a$, where V_B is B's total variable cost in producing the additional quantity of y. This latter action is likely to mean a shift of the demand curve further to the right than in the preceding case, due to the additional requirement of covering the variable costs. Of course, combinations of price and quantity increases can be arranged to achieve the same end.

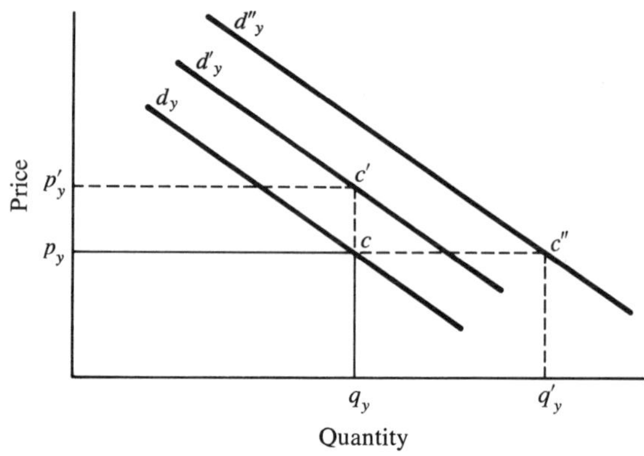

FIGURE 6-7

Demand for product y *by firm A*

Under what conditions would A opt for the various alternatives suggested? He can increase the quantity of *y* purchased from B only under two sets of circumstances: (1) If demand for the end product, of which *y* is a part, is expected to expand, or (2) if a reduction can be made in purchases from other suppliers.[25] The first circumstance is not too probable in the short run; and the long-term implications of a commitment to purchase a greater quantity of *y* are equally dangerous because of the reduced accuracy of forecasts as one moves further into the future.

The ability to follow the second course of action depends on the inherent reciprocal power of A's other suppliers of product *y*; if reciprocity is generally practiced on an industry-wide basis (C being one of the few exceptions), A may not be able to take business away from some other supplier without correspondingly losing sales. If reciprocal relationships are extensive, A's purchase of a greater amount of *y* from B will result in a readjustment of these relationships and in a new equilibrium of questionable benefit to A. Further, it may be that, although A does benefit, the administrative and computational costs of estimating and then establishing the new equilibrium exceed the benefit achieved. In practice, the costs of upsetting a reciprocal equilibrium may be very high, and these costs may act as a strong force for conservation of existing reciprocal systems. If reciprocal relationships are not extensive, a nonreciprocator can be sacrificed so that A may increase the quantity of product *y* purchased from B.

Paying a premium for *y* is a very difficult position to defend. This action would be in direct contradiction to sound purchasing principles and would make the evaluation of the purchasing department's effectiveness highly

[25] It is assumed that whatever changes are contemplated take into account the inventory and order quantity effects A may experience.

complex. In addition, most firms would probably be reluctant to receive a premium over current market price, because one effect of such behavior might be to provide ammunition for Justice Department and F.T.C. contentions that reciprocity gives rise to effects that may be considered "anti-competitive." In spite of these arguments against the practice, companies occasionally do pay premiums to keep reciprocators' business.[26]

A reduction of price on product x by A is a feasible alternative only if A is able to practice price discrimination. If demand is relatively inelastic, as would be the case for most industries in which reciprocity is currently practiced, a general price reduction would not improve A's profit position. Thus, the key to offering a price reduction to B would lie in insularity between the customers and geographic markets of A. Again, price discrimination is relatively more difficult to obtain in the more sophisticated industrial markets. By and large, this alternative is of dubious merit.

There is, of course, still another alternative: A may threaten to discontinue or reduce the present level of purchases of y from B. This now shifts the problem to B, who must make an analysis regarding the equality of the potential savings on x as against the lost profit and overhead contribution of sales of y to A; this is essentially the converse of A's reasoning process as described above. This alternative also clearly illustrates the highly dynamic nature of reciprocal bargaining.

Aside from accepting a reduction in sales of product x to B, all the possible actions center upon preventing a shift to the left in reciprocator A's demand curve for product x. Viewed from the standpoint of the firm upon whom reciprocal pressure is being applied initially, reciprocity is a defensive rather than an offensive form of behavior. Reciprocal buying is a means of preventing sales from declining in situations where price competition is extremely limited, and from the standpoint of the initiator of a relationship it may be considered an offensive move to achieve the equivalent of a price cut.[27] If this argument is accepted, then the primary condition necessary for reciprocity is diversification and a secondary condition is the desire, or need, to eschew price competition as a competitive stratagem. It would seem logical that if price competition existed, a purchaser would be much better off obtaining savings in the form of reduced prices since those dollars can be used wherever they will bring the highest return, as opposed to the commitment to buy from a particular supplier to retain his reciprocal business.

The preceding analysis does not mean that all or even the majority of firms consciously consider reciprocity a means of obtaining a price cut.

---

[26] See, for example, *Sales Management*, May 20, 1960, p. 40.

[27] The firm initiating the reciprocal relationship may view itself as expanding sales, but after most competitors and suppliers have responded by also adopting reciprocity, the use of reciprocity even by the initiating firm is of defensive character. In this respect, reciprocity is like advertising in that no one firm is sure of its own or competitors' benefits, but all believe that reciprocity accomplishes something for them.

However, in at least two instances, firms specifically diversified their operations in order to force the railroads to make purchases from them. Armour and Company[28] and Swift and Company[29] were among the nation's major users of rail transportation in the 1920s. Officials in these meat-packing companies purchased very small companies manufacturing railway equipment and then built them into major factors in their respective industries. Since railroad rates are I.C.C.-controlled, one way of effectively reducing the price paid for transportation services is through the use of reciprocal dealings—precisely the pattern in the meat-packing company situations, although the profits from the railroad equipment sales went to the officials involved.[30]

Price competition in the steel industry is rare. In fact, steel executives consider their prices to be competitive only when they are equal to those of other firms,[31] a condition that is generally true where products are highly standardized. Other evidence of the steel industry's predilection for identical prices is found in the basing point pricing system, developed to eliminate geographical advantages that might reflect themselves in the price offering of given firms.[32] The preceding does not mean, however, that there are not "unreported" attempts to make concessions from list price. These concessions may take the form of actual price reductions, but a much safer alternative is to use methods such as reciprocity, in which the information as to the value of the concession is extremely difficult for competitors to uncover. This form of price reduction also probably gives rise to less criticism of the management by other industry members.

As in the steel and meat-packing industries, in the rubber and paper industries most customers are faced with identical prices.[33] The industry

---

[28] Waugh Equipment Company 15 F.T.C. 232 (1931).

[29] Mechanical Manufacturing Company 16 F.T.C. 67 (1932).

[30] The Swift and Armour Companies did not own the equipment factories; the officials and, in part, the Swift Estate did, but this does not change the analysis.

[31] For an interesting account of the meaning of identical prices presented by Roger M. Blough, Chairman of the Board of U.S. Steel Corporation, see Gardiner C. Means, *Pricing Power and the Public Interest*, Harper & Row, New York, 1962, pp. 25–29. Other descriptions of the nature of the pricing mechanism in the steel industry can be found in Henry W. Broude, *Steel Decisions and the National Economy*, Yale University Press, New Haven, Conn., 1963 (especially the section "Factors in Entrepreneurial Decisions") and the Temporary National Economic Committee Investigation of Concentration of Economic Power, Monographs 41 and 42, U.S. Government Printing Office, Washington, D.C., 1941.

[32] See George W. Stocking, *Basing Point Pricing and Regional Development*, University of North Carolina Press, Chapel Hill, 1954.

[33] See Charles F. Phillips, Jr., *Competition in the Synthetic Rubber Industry*, University of North Carolina Press, Chapel Hill, 1963, particularly pages 181–198; and John A. Guthrie, *The Economics of Pulp and Paper*, Washington State University Press, Pullman, Wash., 1950, pp. 100–121.

structure for both rubber and paper is oligopolistic with the usual patterns of downward sloping demand curves, excess capacity, price leadership, identical prices (or constant differences for those few firms that do not sell at the "market" price), and administered price policies. In fact, these conditions are characteristic of almost all the industries in which reciprocity is known to operate.[34] Thus, reciprocity arises where price competition is extremely limited. And as pointed out before, reciprocity's value lies in competitors' increased difficulty in finding out the extent of the concession in terms of a price equivalent (as opposed to some other forms of non-price concessions, such as technical services, in which estimates of research time necessary to solve a particular customer problem can be made with reasonable accuracy).

Effects of the time dimension

In our discussion thus far of various methods for the establishment of price, we have left implicit a very important consideration, the character of demand over time. For example, in the chapter on product development, we noted some of the problems associated with the introduction of a new product and the changing character of the price of the product as the market for it matures. What is actually happening is that the firm is operating on a series of different demand curves over the product's life. With the passage of time, the price of a product frequently becomes more and more dependent on the actions of competitors. For example, the price of a new product may fall as more firms seek entrance into a given industry, or product class, and the prices of the industry members may become more strongly tied and move up and down together. The producer's evaluation of how quickly his new product will be imitated influences his choice of which of two broad pricing strategies he might utilize: (1) following some type of regularly decreasing price pattern over time, a policy known as *skimming*; or (2) pricing initially at a level that is ultimately expected to be near market equilibrium, usually referred to as *penetration*. In the skimming strategy, for example, the manufacturer is able to take advantage of the satisfaction some potential customers derive from being early adopters of a new idea and extract a premium for fulfilling this need. On the other hand, even if such a need exists, the manufacturer may not be able to take advantage of it because the product idea is not particularly unique and competitors will be quickly attracted by

[34] Gardiner C. Means states that these are conditions that can be expected in any particular market dominated by a few producers: *op. cit.*, p. 20. The theory of competition in oligopolistic industries is well laid out in William Fellner, *Competition Among the Few*, Knopf, New York, 1949. Additional insights into pricing in industries of this character are provided by A. D. H. Kaplan et al., *Pricing in Big Business*, The Brookings Institution, Washington, D.C., 1958.

the apparently high rate of return; in this case, a penetration policy and a lower rate of return may be a better strategy. Other advantages exist for both skimming and penetration.[35]

In speaking of the establishment of a price for an incremental opportunity, an important consideration was whether or not other uninsulated segments in the market would demand the marginal price in the future. In addition to this effect, a price established on the basis of marginal analysis may only shift demand from one time to another. Consider the example of a retail store that sells its own brand of merchandise: If it offers these items for sale at a given time at a price less than fully allocated cost, the demand from people who are loyal customers and would have bought the items in the future may be shifted to the present and new business may also result. The extent to which these kinds of shifts occur through time and the potential associated loss of income as opposed to the new business originating through this type of loss-leader mechanism are very difficult to ascertain.

There are also time effects that are the results of changes in the consumers' perception of the product. When a product is new and unfamiliar and in short supply, the consumer may be willing to pay a relatively high price in order to have this innovation. As the consumer becomes more familiar with the product through repeated purchases, for example, there may be a change in the character of the consumer's utility function with respect to the product; that is, the consumer receives satisfaction that varies from the expectations he previously held about the product's performance. This, in turn, affects his willingness to pay specific prices for the item in the future.

So far, the various time-oriented effects we have discussed have centered on the customer. Another characteristic, however, that can lead to price changes is shifting of the firm's objectives with time. For example, if the initial objective of the marketing group was penetration of a particular market within a given time, a particular price policy might have been dictated. After the penetration has been achieved, the appropriate price or price policy may differ substantially. This illustration should also serve to remind us that the objective under which a particular price is established need not be the obtaining of maximum profits.

Finally, we may consider the intended duration for which a price is established. Some prices change even within the course of a day and the management has no expectation that they will endure for long periods; examples are commodities such as copper, organized exchanges such as for agricultural products, and special sales in department stores. Other prices are ex-

---

[35] For a fuller description of these approaches and the factors that may influence new product pricing, see Joel Dean, "Pricing Policies for New Products," *Harvard Business Review*, Vol. 28, 1950, pp. 45–53.

pected to hold for relatively long periods[36]; examples are list prices of consumer durables, various processed or packaged foodstuffs, and primary metals. Clearly, then, the frequency with which price is changed may be a very important influence on the type and depth of analysis the management is able to undertake prior to each price change. It is evident that pricing takes place in many different dynamic contexts that affect the way price is established.

Competitive bidding

In speaking of price determination, one does not normally think of competitive bidding. However, much pricing follows such a form. The obvious cases concern awards of government contracts and contracts for substantial plant construction by businesses. In addition, each of the subcontractors involved faces the same pricing problems as the prime contractor. The form of bidding followed in these cases, known as closed, or sealed, bidding, gives the bidder only one opportunity to make his offer. No adjustment of price based on new information is possible after submission, and the award is given to the lowest offer from a qualified bidder, one who can be expected to meet his commitments.

Much other business has substantially the same character except that there may be several rounds of negotiation between the buyer and the bidder; that is, the bidding is open rather than closed. For example, when an industrial purchaser calls for quotations he is essentially asking for bids on some quantity of business. But in this case, the purchaser may return to one of the bidders and ask him if he wants to resubmit his bid based on new information the purchaser is providing about the character of other bids. In such a situation, the bidder carries out much the same type of analysis as in preparing his original submission and as would take place in closed bidding.

A price based on marginal costs that is offered in the hope of obtaining incremental business is also a good example of the bidding character of much "regular" business.

To prepare a bid, we must first develop an estimated cost of fulfilling the contract under consideration. This is not so easy as it may appear, for there are several complicating factors. First, failure to win the award may result in losses to the company. For example, if the utilization of production facilities declines, workers may have to be laid off who may be more expensive to rehire, new equipment purchases that were contemplated may no longer be feasible, and so on. Then, too, factory overhead may have to be spread

[36] Oxenfeldt suggests that anything over two months is equivalent to establishing a price for an indefinitely long period. *Models of Markets*, Alfred R. Oxenfeldt, Ed., Columbia University Press, New York, 1963, p. 66 ff.

over a smaller number of units, perhaps necessitating a price increase with a possibility of a further loss of business. Basically, the firm should establish the marginal losses, if any, if the award is lost.[37] Simmonds[38] divides expenditures into stages that may be helpful in estimating the cost of fulfilling the contract. These are preinvitation, invitation, bid preparation, and influence expenditures. The first category encompasses expenditures over the long term directed at building a relationship with purchasers who might offer bidding opportunities. The second category includes expenditures directed at obtaining a specific opportunity to bid. The third category is design, engineering, and other, similar costs. The final category includes expenditures designed to increase the probability of the specific bid being awarded to the firm; as such these costs can be readily incorporated into the model discussed in the next section. Depending on the stage of analysis, certain of the costs just described may or may not be relevant; for example, if the firm is already at the bid preparation stage, any invitation costs incurred are sunk and should not be included in the analysis that follows. On the other hand, if the firm is trying to decide what price to bid, preparation costs, if important, should be a separate term subtracted from the expected profit in equation (6-7) (see below).

A model for competitive bidding

After all the appropriate adjustments have been made to place all costs on equivalent bases, we arrive at C, the estimated cost of fulfilling a particular contract. The true cost is at this point unknown, so we must treat it as a random variable. We choose to write this in the form Cz, where z is the ratio of the true cost to the estimated cost. We should have a good deal of information about the distribution of z, both from past experience and from our judgment of the current situation.

Let S be the bid, or sales price, and let $P(S)$ be the probability that it will win. Then the expected profit is

$$E(S - Cz)P(S) = (S - CE(z))P(S) \tag{6-7}$$

A curve of expected profit against bid price can be plotted and the maximum expected profit determined. The specific shape of the curve, of course, cannot be determined at this point, but in general its form should be as in Figure 6-8.

A principal component of our analysis thus far is the probability of win-

[37] An extensive discussion of these considerations can be found in Franz Edelman, "Art and Science of Competitive Bidding," *Harvard Business Review*, Vol. 43, July–August 1965, pp. 53–66.

[38] Kenneth Simmonds, "Measuring the Effectiveness of Marketing Expenditures in Bidding for Defense Contracts," *New Ideas for Successful Marketing*, American Marketing Association, Chicago, 1966, pp. S-149–S-167.

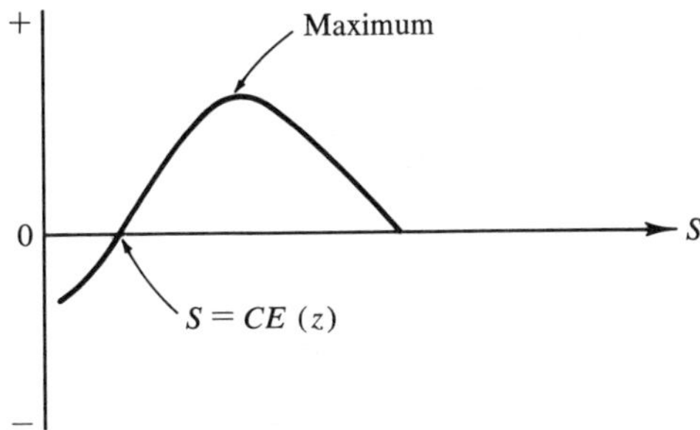

FIGURE 6-8

Expected profit

ning the contract. This, of course, reflects some judgment about the bids of competitors. Let us now investigate this aspect of the model. Assume that because of special intelligence efforts or because results of all previous contract competitions are announced we can obtain information on competitors' past bids. For each competitor we can develop a distribution of the ratio of his bid S_c to our estimated cost C based on the percentage of times particular ratios have occurred. Figure 6-9 is an illustration of such a distribution.

The probability of our being lower than the competitor and winning is the area to the right of S/C, the ratio of our bid price to our estimated cost, that is,

$$P(S) = \int_{S/C}^{\infty} f(x)\ dx \tag{6-8}$$

This formula is appropriate for the case of a single competitor. It is also appropriate if we have combined all competitors into a single composite and have in each previous contract recorded the lowest competing bid. On the other hand, if there are several (k) competitors and we do not wish to combine them, then we can calculate the joint probability of all of their bids exceeding ours as the product

$$P(S) = \prod_{i=1}^{k} \int_{S/C}^{\infty} f_i(x)\ dx \tag{6-9}$$

This formula does not assume that the competitors' bids are absolutely independent, which would be silly, but rather that they are conditionally independent given our estimated cost C. Obviously, the more competitors there are, the slimmer the chances of being the low bidder. Further, the above analysis is based on the assumption that competitors will behave about as they have in the past.

If the number of bidders is unknown and/or assumptions about consistency in their behavior are weak, we can take another approach. A distribution is developed for the "average" bidder based on all previous history.

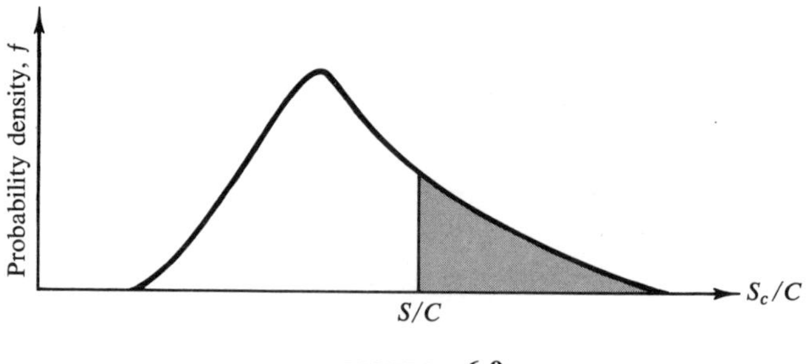

FIGURE 6-9

Probability distribution of competitor's bid

We can assume that Figure 6-9 represents this distribution also. In addition, the distribution of the number of potential bidders should also be developed, $g(k)$ being the probability of k opposing bidders. Now

$$P(S) = \sum_{k=0}^{\infty} g(k)\left[\int_{S/C}^{\infty} f(x)\, dx\right]^k \tag{6-10}$$

and the expected profit is

$$[S - CE(z)] \sum_{k=0}^{\infty} g(k)\left[\int_{S/C}^{\infty} f(x)\, dx\right]^k$$

If we let $y = S/C$, the ratio of our bid to our estimated cost, then the expected profit is

$$C[y - E(z)] \sum_{k=0}^{\infty} g(k)\left[\int_{y}^{\infty} f(x)\, dx\right]^k \tag{6-11}$$

We shall obtain the maximum expected profit for two quite different models for the probability function $g(k)$.

1. Assume that $g(k) = 1$ for some k; this is, essentially, the case of k specific competitors mentioned above. Expected profit is

$$C[y - E(z)]\left[\int_{y}^{\infty} f(x)\, dx\right]^k \tag{6-12}$$

and its derivative with respect to the decision variable y is

$$C\left[\int_{y}^{\infty} f(x)\, dx\right]^k + C[y - E(z)]k\left[\int_{y}^{\infty} f(x)\, dx\right]^{k-1}[-f(y)]$$

$$= Cf(y)\left[\int_{y}^{\infty} f(x)\, dx\right]^{k-1}\left\{\frac{\int_{y}^{\infty} f(x)\, dx}{f(y)} - k[y - E(z)]\right\} \tag{6-13}$$

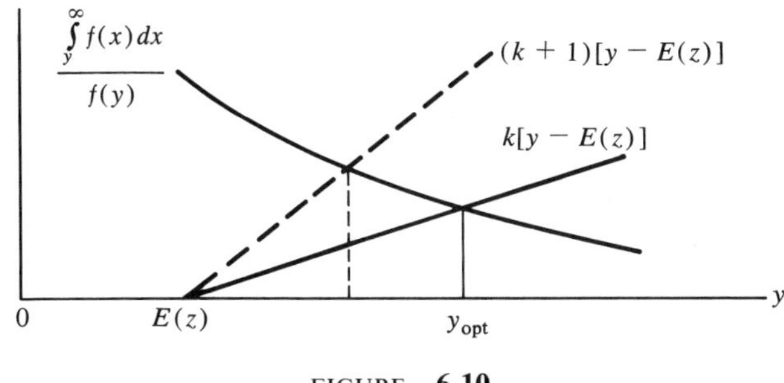

FIGURE **6-10**

Optimum bid for a specified number of competitors

The lowest bid we might make is the break-even value[39] $y = E(z)$. At this value the derivative is positive. For any reasonable probability density, f, the ratio of the right tail to the density is a decreasing function, so, as shown in Figure 6-10, there will be a unique point y_{opt} at which the derivative equals 0. Under these circumstances, a larger number of competitors will lead to a smaller optimum bid (see the dashed lines in Figure 6-10).

The results of this model hold, more generally, if the number of competitors is uncertain but the range of uncertainty is small. For example, we might have $g(k) + g(k+1) = 1$ for some value k. The analysis under these circumstances is considerably more complicated, but it is possible to show that the solution lies between the y_{opt} values for k and $k+1$ shown in Figure 6-10.

2. Assume $g(k) = \lambda^k e^{-\lambda}/k!$, a Poisson distribution for the number of competitors.[40] This allows for any number of competitors, from 0 to ∞, and so is in extreme contrast to the previous model. Expected profit is

$$C[y - E(z)] \sum_{k=0}^{\infty} \frac{\lambda^k e^{-\lambda}}{k!} \left[\int_y^\infty f(x)\,dx\right]^k$$

$$= C[y - E(z)]e^{-\lambda} \exp\left[\lambda \int_y^\infty f(x)\,dx\right]$$

$$= C[y - E(z)] \exp\left[-\lambda \int_0^y f(x)\,dx\right] \qquad (6\text{-}14)$$

[39] The objective of the bidding model as we have structured it is maximization of expected profit. It is possible to construct similar models with other objectives, such as to utilize excess capacity (relative to what is demanded in a particular time period); to increase market share; to minimize competitors' profits in the belief that such a goal might keep them from becoming stronger competitors; to minimize expected losses if the situation is such that the firm is forced to bid, and so on.

[40] This model, which first appeared in Lawrence Friedman, "A Competitive Bidding Strategy," *Operations Research*, Vol. 4, No. 1, February 1956, pp. 104–112, is presented here as an example of how a seemingly innocent mathematical model can provide unpleasant surprises.

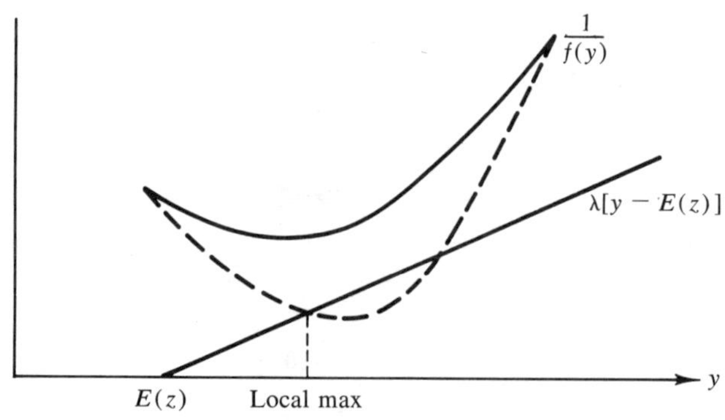

FIGURE 6-11

Collapse of the Poisson model

The derivative of the expected profit with respect to y is

$$C \exp\left[-\lambda \int_0^y f(x)\, dx\right] + C[y - E(z)] \exp\left[-\lambda \int_0^y f(x)\, dx\right][-\lambda f(y)]$$

$$= Cf(y) \exp\left[-\lambda \int_0^y f(x)\, dx\right]\left\{\frac{1}{f(y)} - \lambda[y - E(z)]\right\} \qquad (6\text{-}15)$$

Once again the derivative is positive at $y = E(z)$. Now, however, since any reasonable probability density f will fall off at least exponentially, the derivative will be very positive for large values of y and is likely to be positive for all values of y, as shown by the solid line in Figure 6-11. The dashed line in Figure 6-11 shows the possibility of a value of y at which the derivative of the expected profit is zero; this, however, is only a local maximum. What is happening is that, because of the positive probability $e^{-\lambda}$ of having no competitors, we can make an arbitrarily large profit from a sufficiently large bid. We can correct this defect by using the truncated Poisson distribution,

$$g(k) = \frac{e^{-\lambda}}{1 - e^{-\lambda}} \frac{\lambda^k}{k!} \qquad k = 1, 2, \ldots \qquad (6\text{-}16)$$

The expected profit is

$$C[y - E(z)] \sum_{k=1}^{\infty} \frac{e^{-\lambda}}{1 - e^{-\lambda}} \frac{\lambda^k}{k!} \left[\int_y^\infty f(x)\, dx\right]^k$$

$$= C[y - E(z)] \frac{e^{-\lambda}}{1 - e^{-\lambda}} \left\{\exp\left[\lambda \int_y^\infty f(x)\, dx\right] - 1\right\}$$

$$= C[y - E(z)] \frac{\exp\left[-\lambda \int_0^y f(x)\, dx\right] - e^{-\lambda}}{1 - e^{-\lambda}} \qquad (6\text{-}17)$$

The derivative of the expected profit is

$$C\frac{\exp\left[-\lambda\int_0^y f(x)\,dx\right]-e^{-\lambda}}{1-e^{-\lambda}}+C[y-E(z)]\frac{-\lambda f(y)\exp\left[-\lambda\int_0^y f(x)\,dx\right]}{1-e^{-\lambda}}$$

$$=\frac{Cf(y)\exp\left[-\lambda\int_0^y f(x)\,dx\right]}{1-e^{-\lambda}}\left\{\frac{1-\exp\left[-\lambda\int_y^\infty f(x)\,dx\right]}{f(y)}-\lambda[y-E(z)]\right\} \tag{6-18}$$

The analysis of this derivative is very complicated, but we can show that the expression

$$\frac{1-\exp\left[-\lambda\int_y^\infty f(x)\,dx\right]}{f(y)}$$

should approach a limit as $y\to\infty$. Thus, although we cannot show that there is a unique root, we have avoided the arbitrarily large expected profits produced by sufficiently large bids.

A pricing model for competitors with undifferentiated product[41]

Suppose that we offer to sell a product at a price S, and thereby obtain a probability $P(S)$ of making a sale to any individual customer. As in the previous section, we may conceive of $P(S)$ as the probability that our price, S, is the lowest price offered to the customer. Alternatively, since out of n potential customers the expected number of sales is $nP(S)$, we may interpret $P(S)$ as our expected market share at the price S. In this model, both market share and expected profit depend on the one decision variable, price, so it is not possible to manipulate them independently; this manipulation will have to wait until the richer model discussed in the next section.

If the potential customers decide on their purchases independently of one another, then the actual number of sales is a binomially distributed random variable, with probability

$$p_b(r|n,P(S))=\binom{n}{r}P(S)^r(1-P(S))^{n-r} \tag{6-19}$$

of exactly r sales to n potential customers. The expected revenue from these customers is

$$R=nSP(S) \tag{6-20}$$

We would expect the revenue function to behave as shown in Figure 6-12,

[41] The models in this and the following section are adapted from S. Sankar Sengupta, *Operations Research in Sellers' Competition*, Wiley, New York, 1967, chs. 4 and 7.

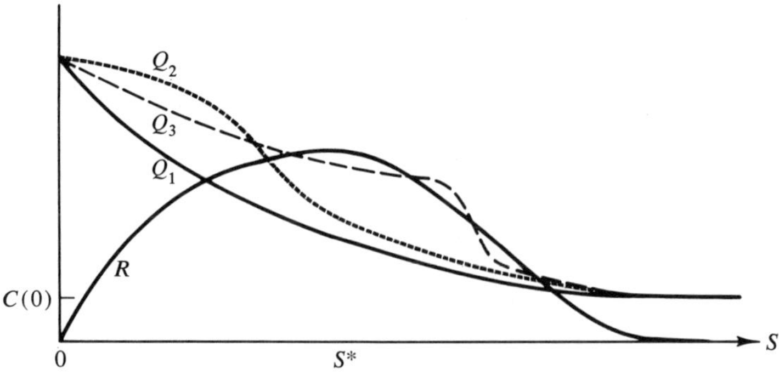

FIGURE 6-12

Expected cost and revenue as functions of sales price

having a unique positive maximum at S^* and falling off to zero as price becomes too large. One set of assumptions that will achieve this is

(i) $0 < P(0) \leq 1$

(ii) $\dfrac{dP}{dS} < 0$

(iii) $\lim_{S \to \infty} SP(S) = 0$

(iv) $S\dfrac{dP}{dS} + P(S) = 0$ has a unique root S^*

As an example of a function satisfying this assumption we have

$$P(S) = P(0)e^{-\alpha S}$$

for which $S^* = 1/\alpha$. This function also satisfies

(v) $\dfrac{d^2P}{dS^2} > 0$

which we will need later.

The cost of producing the r units that are actually sold will be some function $C(r)$, and all we can say in general about this is that it is an increasing function of r. The expected cost is

$$Q = \sum_{r=0}^{n} C(r)\binom{n}{r}P(S)^r(1 - P(S))^{n-r} \tag{6-21}$$

If the cost is proportional to the quantity produced, say $C(r) = Cr$, then $Q = nCP(S)$ and the expected profit is $R - Q = n(S - C)P(S)$. The analysis of this case is similar to that in the previous section. In the case of general increasing costs, further analysis is needed.

By straightforward calculation we can show that

$$\frac{dQ}{dP} = n \sum_{r=0}^{n-1} [C(r+1) - C(r)] \binom{n-1}{r} P(S)^r (1 - P(S))^{n-1-r} \tag{6-22}$$

$$\frac{d^2Q}{dP^2} = n(n-1) \sum_{r=0}^{n-2} [C(r+2) - 2C(r+1) + C(r)] \times \binom{n-2}{r} P(S)^r (1 - P(S))^{n-2-r} \tag{6-23}$$

In equation (6-22), the factor $C(r+1) - C(r) = \Delta C(r)$ is the marginal cost of the $(r+1)$st item; since the marginal costs are positive, so is dQ/dP. In equation (6-23), the factor $C(r+2) - 2C(r+1) + C(r) = \Delta C(r+1) - \Delta C(r)$ is the change in the marginal cost; we then have

$$\frac{d^2Q}{dP^2} \begin{Bmatrix} >0 \\ =0 \\ <0 \end{Bmatrix} \quad \text{if marginal costs} \begin{Bmatrix} \text{increase} \\ \text{are constant} \\ \text{decrease} \end{Bmatrix}$$

Since S, not P, is the decision variable, we must also calculate

$$\begin{aligned} \frac{dQ}{dS} &= \frac{dQ}{dP} \cdot \frac{dP}{dS} \\ \frac{d^2Q}{dS^2} &= \frac{d^2Q}{dP^2} \cdot \left(\frac{dP}{dS}\right)^2 + \frac{dQ}{dP} \cdot \frac{d^2P}{dS^2} \end{aligned} \tag{6-24}$$

By the above analysis and assumption (ii), $dQ/dS < 0$ always holds. We would also like to assert that $d^2Q/dS^2 > 0$, but, even after bringing in assumption (v), we see that this can be proved only if marginal costs increase or are constant; curve Q_1 in Figure 6-12 is typical of this case. If marginal costs decrease, then nothing definite can be proved about the sign of d^2Q/dS^2. Some simple examples show that it is likely that d^2Q/dS^2 is first negative, then positive; curve Q_2 in Figure 6-12 illustrates this case. Finally, if marginal costs change irregularly, then so may d^2Q/dS^2; curve Q_3 in Figure 6-12 is only one of many such possibilities.

In Figure 6-13 we show the expected profit curves corresponding to the revenue and cost curves of Figure 6-12. In each case, the maximum expected profit occurs for $S > S^*$. This happens because

$$\begin{aligned} \frac{d}{dS}(R - Q)\bigg|_{S^*} &= \frac{dR}{dS}\bigg|_{S^*} - \frac{dQ}{dS}\bigg|_{S^*} \\ &= -\frac{dQ}{dS}\bigg|_{S^*} > 0 \end{aligned} \tag{6-25}$$

where we have used the facts that dR/dS is zero at S^* and dQ/dS is always negative. Note also that since sales go to zero with increasing price, expected costs must go to $C(0)$ and expected profit to $-C(0)$.

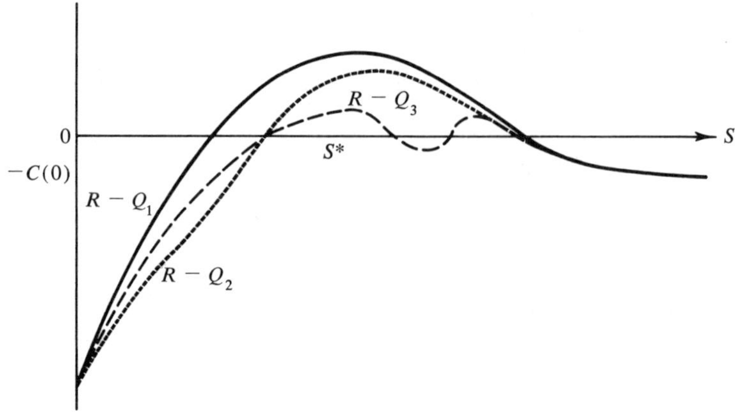

FIGURE **6-13**

Expected profit as a function of sales price

In conclusion, if the character of the cost function were known exactly, the optimal price would be readily identified; even if this is not the case, the foregoing should be quite helpful in establishing price. Specifically, the model demonstrates the existence of a unique profit-maximizing price greater than the revenue-maximizing price S^* in the cases of constant or increasing marginal costs, and where there is only this one maximum, standard search techniques should aid in determining the optimal price. In the case of regularly decreasing marginal costs, the model's usefulness is more limited because there may be several maxima, but the model does show that the region for search lies to the right of S^*. Finally, in the case of irregular marginal costs, little can be said.

A pricing–advertising model for competitors with undifferentiated product

We shall now assume that the number of inquiries,[42] n, is not predetermined but depends on our advertising and promotional activities. It seems reasonable to assume that inquiries satisfy the requirements for a Poisson process, so the number of inquiries is a random variable with a Poisson distribution

$$P_p\ (n|N(A)) = e^{-N(A)}\frac{[N(A)^n]}{n!} \tag{6-26}$$

$N(A)$ is the average number of inquiries generated by an expenditure A on

[42] In the previous section, these were called potential customers. With an undifferentiated product, advertising will affect this number but not the probability of making a sale.

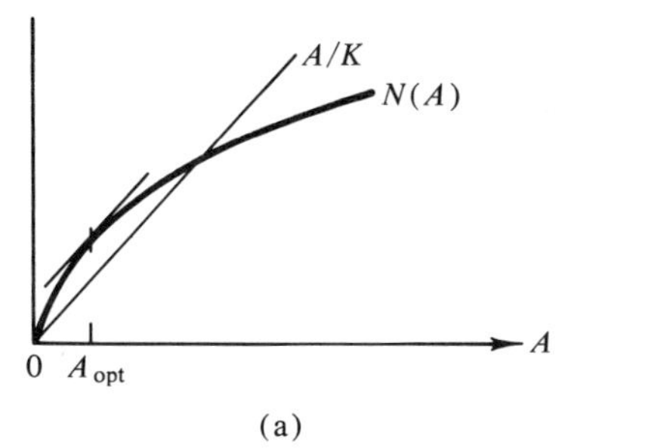

(a)

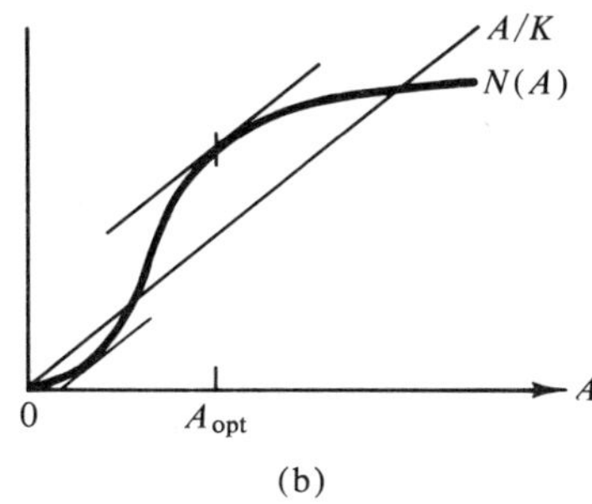

(b)

FIGURE **6-14**

Solving for the optimum level of advertising. (a) *N(A) concave.* (b) *N(A) convex–concave.*

advertising and promotion. Since the binomial distribution of sales given in the previous section was for predetermined n, we now have as the probability of selling exactly r units

$$\sum_{n=r}^{\infty} e^{-N(A)} \frac{[N(A)]^n}{n!} \cdot \binom{n}{r} P(S)^r (1-P(S))^{n-r} = e^{-N(A)P(S)} \frac{[N(A)P(S)]^r}{r!}$$

$$= P_\rho\ (r|M(A, S)) \qquad \text{(6-27)}$$

where $M(A, S) = N(A)P(S)$ is the expected number of sales. Expected revenue is simply

$$R = SM(A, S) \qquad \text{(6-28)}$$

Expected cost of production is

$$Q = \sum_{r=0}^{\infty} C(r) P_\rho (r|M(A, S)) \qquad \text{(6-29)}$$

Expected profit is $R - Q - A = SM - Q - A$.

If $C(r) = Cr$, then $Q = CM(A, S)$, and expected profit is

$$(S - C)M(A, S) - A = N(A)(S - C)P(S) - A \qquad \text{(6-30)}$$

Independently of A, we can choose $S = S_{\text{opt}}$ to maximize $(S - C)P(S)$. Denoting this maximum by $K = (S_{\text{opt}} - C)P(S_{\text{opt}})$, we must now maximize $KN(A) - A = K[N(A) - A/K]$. This is accomplished by setting $N'(A)$ equal to $1/K$. Figure 6-14 shows the two most likely forms the function $N(A)$ might take. If $N(A)$ is concave, $N'(A) = 1/K$ will determine A_{opt}, but if $N(A)$ is convex–concave we must be wary of the false root (actually a relative minimum) in the convex portion of the curve.

If production costs are not proportional to quantity sold, then the analysis is far more complicated than even that of the previous section. It is still straightforward to calculate the derivatives of expected cost of production with respect to expected sales.

$$\frac{dQ}{dM} = \sum_{r=0}^{\infty} [C(r+1) - C(r)]P_\rho(r|M) \tag{6-31}$$

$$\frac{d^2Q}{dM^2} = \sum_{r=0}^{\infty} [C(r+2) - 2C(r+1) + C(r)]P_\rho(r|M) \tag{6-32}$$

Just as in the previous section, we conclude that $dQ/dM > 0$ always holds and that

$$\frac{d^2Q}{dM^2} \begin{Bmatrix} > 0 \\ = 0 \\ < 0 \end{Bmatrix} \text{ if marginal costs } \begin{Bmatrix} \text{increase} \\ \text{are constant} \\ \text{decrease} \end{Bmatrix}$$

With advertising, A, held fixed, the results of the previous section are still valid. In particular, if marginal costs increase, there is a unique $S > S^*$ that maximizes expected profit. This will be obtained by setting the partial derivative of expected profit with respect to price equal to zero:

$$\frac{\partial}{\partial S}(SM - Q - A) = M + \left(S - \frac{dQ}{dM}\right)\frac{\partial M}{\partial S} = 0 \tag{6-33}$$

On the other hand, if price is held fixed, then we would set the partial derivative of expected profit with respect to advertising equal to zero:

$$\frac{\partial}{\partial A}(SM - Q - A) = \left(S - \frac{dQ}{dM}\right)\frac{\partial M}{\partial A} - 1 = 0 \tag{6-34}$$

and investigate the second derivative:

$$\frac{\partial^2}{\partial A^2}(SM - Q - A) = \left(S - \frac{dQ}{dM}\right)\frac{\partial^2 M}{\partial A^2} - \frac{d^2Q}{dM^2}\left(\frac{\partial M}{\partial A}\right)^2 \tag{6-35}$$

Since $M(A, S) = N(A)P(S)$, $\partial^2M/\partial A^2$ will be negative if $N(A)$ is concave (see Figure 6-14). Since also

$$S - \frac{dQ}{dM} = \frac{1}{\partial M/\partial A} > 0$$

the first term in the second derivative is negative. As shown above, the second term is negative if marginal costs increase. If this is assumed, then, for price held fixed, we have succeeded in maximizing expected profit as a function of advertising.[43]

[43] Even for the case of increasing marginal costs the above analysis is incomplete. In order to be sure that we have obtained the maximum when both price and advertising can be varied simultaneously, we must show that the Hessian matrix of second-order partial derivatives has a positive determinant. Furthermore, we have not indicated how to solve the pair of nonlinear equations for S and A obtained by setting the first partial derivatives equal to zero, (6-33) and (6-34).

Except for the special case of production costs proportional to the quantity sold, the model in this section is still in the process of development. It is not yet at a stage at which it will yield insight into the pricing–advertising decision. It is included in the hope that it is at least a step in the right direction.

Characterization of the pricing process

Initially, we pointed out the divergence between the price theorist's statements on the establishment of price and the apparent practices of businessmen. In this section we offer a rationale to tie together all facets of the pricing problem, the theoretical doctrine, the rule-of-thumb models, such as cost-plus, and the formalized models, such as competitive bidding.

Let us begin with some comments about the demand function. First, it is typically described as continuous. It is more likely, however, that it is a step function or some other discrete form. This notion is implicit in the concept of elasticity, but rarely is a demand curve treated as a series of short, highly inelastic segments. Second, the effects of a price rise and a price decline over the same range of prices may not be identical. That is, if one decreases price, quantity sold increases correspondingly along the demand curve. Theoretically, the process should be precisely reversible, *ceterus paribus*, if one were to increase the price. But in practice the lower price may become institutionalized after its establishment; that is, consumer evaluations of the relative value of the product may change, resulting in a different demand curve, with obviously different elasticities. Third, a change in any of the determinants of demand may not affect the demand function uniformly, as, for example, through a shift to the left or right, but may alter its shape substantially.

Let us now introduce the complication that demand is stochastic, and that the demand curve represents the mean (or expected) values of an infinitude of random variables, one for each point on the curve.[44] The more certain the firm is of the anticipated consumer response, the less the variance of the distributions. Thus, if confidence limits were drawn about the demand curve, they would by no means be parallel, or equidistant from it. A principal limitation of this approach is that in most cases the distributions must be estimated subjectively. In addition, both the stochastic approach and the more classical approach to structuring the demand curve are highly time-dependent; one must then raise the question of the opportunity cost of the effort to be expended in this direction, especially in highly dynamic environments.

Given all these problems with demand estimation, it is quite understandable that the manager is somewhat aghast at the thought of establishing

[44] This is, of course, just the model underlying regression analysis.

a demand function. On the other hand, we can interpret his behavior as indicating that he is seeking to learn about the character of the demand function.[45] Suppose we define demand, q, as a function of price, p, and an error term e:

$$q = f(p) + e \tag{6-36}$$

Suppose we then hypothesize that each time the manager makes a pricing decision he acquires additional information about the relationship between price and demand on the basis of which he makes an adjustment, α, to the perceived character of the demand function; that is,

$$q = \alpha[f(p)] + e \tag{6-37}$$

Such a viewpoint might explain several things: First, we find that the concepts of the price theorist are meaningful to the manager but the issue is beclouded by the demand estimation procedures; second, the adjustments made to reflect competitors' prices, special situations, and the like in the cost-plus pricing methodology are simply the activities of demand estimation; third, most of the formal operations research models that have been developed in any depth take account of those adjustments through factors representing learning and/or the cost of obtaining additional information.[46] This particular rationale appears to tie together, in a fairly satisfactory manner, the various approaches to price setting. Hopefully, these differences may now be viewed as being created by the complexities involved in the demand estimation procedure in a situation in which both the pertinence and the accuracy of the information available is open to question.

Summary

Pricing is an area in which the largest part of the available analytical approaches has been developed by economists whose primary interest was other than marketing. The objective of most economic analysis has been to provide a rationale for competitive behavior in the marketplace. Unfortunately, this by no means yields complete guides as to how the firm should set its prices. On the other hand, the general models of competition do provide useful information on the difficult problem of establishing a price; it is thus important to be familiar with the principal economic characterizations of the marketplace.

The main goal of this chapter has been to develop analytical models useful to the marketer faced with specific pricing situations. The most general

[45] We are indebted to our colleague Donald Gordon for suggesting the rationale that follows.

[46] See, for example, Irving H. Lavalle, "A Rayesian Approach to an Individual Player's Choice of Bid in Competitive Sealed Auctions," *Management Science*, Vol. 13, No. 7, March 1967, pp. 584–597.

pricing procedure we have described is the cost-plus methodology, which, although offering relative simplicity, has many drawbacks. Approaches for establishing price have been offered for several different common problems; among these are oligopolistic industry structure, special opportunities to be analyzed via marginal analysis, the utilization of price discrimination, and a rather detailed example of the character that non-price competition may take. Substantial emphasis was placed on this last problem for two reasons: First, there is a large number of basic industries in which ruinous competition is implied if price is used as the principal competitive factor; second, and more important, emphasis on non-price competition is more consistent with the marketing viewpoint wherein price is seen as only a single element in the total marketing mix. Given such a viewpoint, one is more likely to think in terms of non-price equivalents that might produce the same effect as contemplated price changes.

A significant portion of the chapter was devoted to the development of a competitive bidding model. This approach has applicability to a number of other pricing situations even though the latter do not involve competitive bidding in a formalized sense. Further, although we describe a use of the competitive bidding model in which profit maximization is the principal objective, it can be used to attain other objectives such as minimization of competitors' profits.

Finally, we have explored a model for pricing where product is undifferentiated, to give a feeling for the character of the analysis in situations where price is still of primary importance.

Future developments of analytical techniques for the establishment of price are very likely to remain principally the province of economists. The major exception to this is in work that centers on competitive bidding. In addition, some of the most promising work that is not strictly founded in economic theory involves the use of computer simulations of the decision processes of the human beings who set prices.[47] On the whole, however, the pricing function may well show the least development by marketers in the forseeable future because they have accepted their historical role of relative lack of interest in the pricing process.

[47] See, for example, R. M. Cyert, I. G. March, and C. G. Moore, "A Model of Retail Ordering and Pricing by a Department Store," in *Quantitative Techniques in Marketing Analysis*, by Frank, Kuehn, and Massy, Irwin, Homewood, Ill., 1962, pp. 505–522.

DISTRIBUTION SYSTEMS

CHAPTER SEVEN

Channels of distribution

A distribution system comprises two principal elements: (1) a physical distribution, or logistics, system that is concerned with the transportation and storage of a product from the time production is completed until the product is delivered to the purchaser, and (2) a set of organizational relationships among the manufacturer and the various intermediaries, or agents, who influence the product's passage through the physical distribution system. The total system is sometimes called the channel of distribution, but we shall use this term in a narrower sense only, that is, to designate the manufacturer and the corresponding set of intermediaries.

There are many types of intermediary firms that might be included in a channel, but we shall confine our brief discussion to the two broad, or generic, classes, wholesalers and retailers.[1] Even this delimitation leaves the situation complex because of the overlapping functions and interests of each class; for example, how should a wholesaler selling to other firms but also operating his own retail outlets be classified—or an integrated manufacturer? In spite of such difficulties, the principal distinguishing feature of a retailer is that he sells to ultimate consumers. Thus, most definitions of retailers would be like that of Beckman and Davidson, who state, "Retailers are merchant middlemen [i.e., they take title to the goods] who are engaged

[1] Descriptions of many of these types may be found in Theodore N. Beckman and William R. Davidson, *Marketing*, 7th ed., Ronald Press, New York, 1962, parts III and IV; or Ronald S. Vaile, E. L. Grether, and Reavis Cox, *Marketing in the American Economy*, Ronald Press, New York, 1952, ch. 8.

primarily in selling to ultimate consumers."[2] They also define wholesaling as including ". . . all transactions in which the purchaser is actuated by a profit or business motive in making the purchase, except for transactions that involve a small quantity of goods purchased in a retail store for business use, which transactions are considered as retail."[3] A wholesaler, then, is essentially distinguished by the *motivation* of those purchasing from him, rather than by who the purchasers are or what part of the set of activities the wholesaler himself performs.

Obviously, a channel does not have to contain any intermediaries. Examples of possible channel structures are shown in Table 7-1. The "consumer" in these examples may be either an ultimate consumer or an industrial consumer. No direction of flow is indicated because both goods and information may flow both ways between each pair of entities. These types of channels may be illustrated according to some products that might be expected to use them: The first might be the channel for packaged foodstuffs; the second the channel followed by many industrial products such as small motors or safety clothing; the third the channel for ladies clothing; and the fourth the channel used by cosmetics manufacturers who sell to consumers in their homes. Clearly, this last case represents elimination of any intermediaries and points up the fact that although the manufacturing firm can elect to eliminate the organizational interactions, the functions that must be performed in the channel still remain.

The concept of length is used as a shorthand to summarize the characteristics of a given channel system: The greater the number of types of intermediaries, the longer the channel. Although we have specified only the very broad classes of intermediaries, there are, for example, several types of wholesalers who may appear subsequent to each other in the channel. To illustrate, a manufacturer of glass mixing bowls may sell them to a regional wholesaler who, in turn, sells them to a rack jobber whose function it is to keep supermarket shelves stocked with such items. That is, the rack jobber performs the stocking function even though another intermediary, the retailer, effects the final sale. Channel length is also partly defined by the number of tasks that the manufacturer undertakes for himself; the more of these,

TABLE **7-1**

Some types of channel structures

Manufacturer – Wholesaler – Retailer – Consumer
Manufacturer – Wholesaler – Consumer
Manufacturer – Retailer – Consumer
Manufacturer – Consumer

[2] *op. cit.*, p. 134; emphasis and comment added.

[3] *Ibid.*, p. 275.

the more appropriate it is to define the channel as short. The reason for this definition of length is that the performance of the required channel tasks gives the manufacturer greater control over decisions involving his product and, in a sense, brings him closer to the ultimate consumer. Thus, although channel length cannot be precisely measured, the concept is quite useful in describing the character of a channel.

Product classifications and distribution systems

A key issue in distribution systems is the effort the consumer is willing to expend in searching activity to decide which product he will buy and at which outlet. This searching behavior occurs across the distribution systems of different manufacturers as well as within the distribution system of any one manufacturer. In the search process, the consumer obtains information on which to base his purchase decision from the distribution system itself as well as from promotional materials. Intermediaries and their salesmen, the number of locations at which a product is sold, whether or not the desired product is in stock, and the time of day during which the product can be purchased all strongly influence the consumer's decision. The consumer is usually willing to search in proportion to the price of the item and inversely to the frequency of purchase.

One widely used classification of products,[4] based on the length of time the consumer is willing to spend in search and having obvious implications for the character of the distribution systems, uses the following three categories:

Convenience goods. Least search time. Examples: Bread, milk, cigarettes, foodstuffs, proprietary medicines

Shopping goods. Medium search time. Examples: Clothing, consumer durables, automobiles

Specialty goods. Greatest search time. Examples: High brand preference items, such as a particular gasoline, or items that are harder to come by because of more limited demand for them, such as vintage wines and cheeses or designer dresses

As a general rule, convenience goods are sold at many local stores, shopping goods at a few big regional shopping centers, and specialty goods at unique outlets that the consumer must seek out. This means that long distribution channels will be needed for convenience goods, shorter ones for shopping goods, and still shorter ones for specialty goods.

This classification system, however, has some drawbacks in lack of consistency in categorization. For example, gasoline is a specialty good sold

[4] For a fuller discussion see Beckman and Davidson, *op. cit.*, pp. 35–38.

at many local outlets; it differs from a convenience good, such as milk, in that consumers seek out their brand of gasoline but do not seek out their brand of milk. As another example, a woman may initially expend considerable effort locating the outlets in her community, if any, that carry designer dresses (specialty goods), but on subsequent purchases of designer dresses she may actually engage in less search than when purchasing a pair of shoes (shopping goods). Also, the categories do not remain stable even for the same products; gasoline may be a convenience good in a remote area (especially when the gauge reads almost empty) and a specialty good in an urban center.

A better classification system than the preceding has been developed by Leo Aspinwall,[5] who delineates five characteristics common to all goods, relatively measurable, and related to each other. These are given in Table 7-2. To illustrate, bread and cigarettes have a high replacement rate in a one-year period and would score low on all the other characteristics. Terms such as *high* and *low* must be used relative to other goods. For example, bread receives some adjustment in the distribution channel as it is made available in different sizes, different types, and even different degrees of freshness, but relative to a gas clothes dryer that must be delivered, installed, and perhaps have special credit terms arranged, the amount of adjustment for bread is low. At the other end of the spectrum would be a consumer durable, such as a refrigerator, which would have a low replacement rate but score high with respect to the other characteristics.

Having identified these characteristics and the relationships among them, it is now possible to group goods according to their relative degree of each characteristic. Aspinwall uses three groups (red, orange, and yellow goods,

TABLE **7-2**

*Characteristics of goods**

Replacement rate	The frequency, over some specified time period, with which a good is purchased
Gross margin	The money sum that is the difference between the manufacturer's total production cost and the final realized retail sales price
Adjustment	Cost of services applied to goods to make them meet the exact needs of the individual consumer
Time of consumption	The time during which the good yields its utility
Searching time	The measure of the average time and distance from the retail outlets stocking the product class

* The definitions that follow are not precisely those of Aspinwall but have been altered by the authors to reduce the amount of elaboration required.

[5] Leo V. Aspinwall, "The Characteristics of Goods Theory," in *Managerial Marketing: Perspectives and Viewpoints*, rev. ed., William Lazer and Eugene J. Kelley, Eds. Richard D. Irwin, Homewood, Ill., 1962, pp. 633–643.

possibly to conform to convenience goods, shopping goods, and specialty goods), but he points out that any operationally appropriate number of groups may be used. Table 7-3 reproduces his groupings.[6] The use of color categories implies that the spectrum is continuous and a good may really fall anywhere along it.

It can readily be seen how categorizing goods according to sets of characteristics might help a manufacturer evaluate the effectiveness of his distribution system for specified goods and aggregate his total array of products into consistent sets with similar distribution requirements, but there is an additional benefit to be gained from this theoretical structure. The same set of characteristics that gives rise to the use of a particular distribution system may also indicate the appropriate form of promotion to use. Suppose we define the following general types of promotion:[7]

Broadcast. A situation in which many and diverse people are communicated with simultaneously

Semibroadcast. Communications with many people, but in smaller, more homogeneous groups, for example, a special interest magazine

Closed circuit. Two people carrying on a direct and exclusive conversation, such as a salesman speaking with a purchasing agent

In general, we find that each of these types of promotion is strongly, though not exclusively, related to the type of distribution system. If we think primarily of the channel's length as a means of describing the channel, then we can construct Table 7-4.

Aspinwall's classifications have been found to be quite successful in establishing the appropriate distribution and promotional efforts for a product. On the whole, Aspinwall's work is a very useful verbal model for understanding and constructing distribution systems and appears to have high potential for quantification.

TABLE **7-3**

Classification of goods into groups by characteristics

Characteristic	Red goods	Orange goods	Yellow goods
Replacement rate	High	Medium	Low
Gross margin	Low	Medium	High
Adjustment	Low	Medium	High
Time of consumption	Low	Medium	High
Searching time	Low	Medium	High

[6] *Ibid.*, p. 641.

[7] *Ibid.*, pp. 644–652.

TABLE 7-4

Relationship between goods and marketing systems

Goods:	Red	Orange	Yellow
Distribution:	Long channel	Moderate channel	Short channel
Promotion:	Broadcast	Semibroadcast	Closed circuit

The functions of the distribution system

The distribution system has economic benefits for both the manufacturer and the consumer. One of its important accomplishments is the reduction of the number of contacts—which for the consumer means that less searching is necessary to collect information or engage in an exchange of goods. To illustrate, envision a primitive economy in which there are five producing–consuming families, each raising a different crop.[8] Now suppose that each family would like to introduce some variety into its menu and that each has a surplus over its own needs. For each family to make contact with every one of the others, ten relationships would be necessary, as illustrated below:

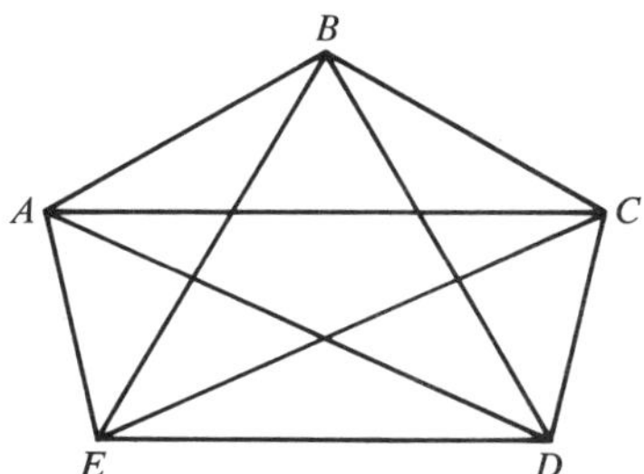

Now, if we inserted a central marketplace or one intermediary, *W*, who bought everyone's surplus and resold it to the other families, only five relationships would be required:

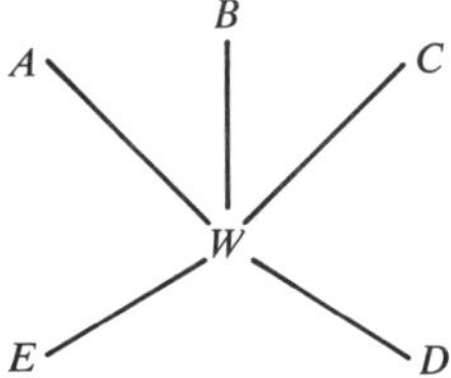

[8] This illustration was originally offered by Wroe Alderson, "Factors Governing the Development of Marketing Channels," in *Marketing Channels*, Richard M. Clewett, Ed., Richard D. Irwin, Homewood, Ill., 1954, pp. 7–9. For further elaboration on the economics of distribution systems, see F. E. Balderston, "Communication Networks in Intermediate Markets," *Management Science*, Vol. 4, No. 2, January 1958, pp. 154–171; and Helmy H. Baligh and Leon E. Richartz, *Vertical Market Structures*, Allyn and Bacon, Boston, 1967.

The number of contacts eliminated by introduction of a central marketplace or an intermediary is $\frac{1}{2}n(n-1) - n = n(n-3)/2$, where n is the number of producer–consumers.

The implications of the introduction of intermediaries into a large economic system with a huge number of producing and consuming points can readily be seen. From an economic standpoint, however, the increase in system efficiency that appears in the form of greater utility for the consumer by reducing his search efforts and as economies of scale for the intermediary is offset by the costs of operating the central marketplace and the profit required by the operator to remain in business. It is conceivable that these costs and profits may be greater than under the more primitive system (although this is probably rarely the case). This last speculation is the basis for the "eliminate the middleman" arguments, which contend that the middleman removes more in profits than he contributes in increased economic efficiency. These arguments are really irrelevant, since, for example, improved time and place utilities produced by an intermediary should be reflected in the gross margin available to move the good – if these utilities are meaningful to the consumer.

Besides benefits produced for the consumer, there are several basic activities that take place in the distribution system and that may involve several manufacturers whose efforts all focus on nearly the same set of intermediaries. The first of these activities is *allocation*, more commonly referred to as "breaking bulk." Because of economies of scale when production occurs in substantial volume, the production process is usually concentrated in one or a limited number of locations. Demand, however, may occur in substantially smaller units and at a much greater number of places. Allocation is the process whereby the two are matched. For example, the cost of moving a single box of a laundry detergent through a distribution system to a housewife would be astronomically high. But large quantities can economically flow through the distribution system well beyond the manufacturer, because a series of intermediaries may successively break bulk at points much closer to the ultimate consumer.

The second principal activity is *assorting*, which is the process of building up a selection of goods that the consumer might expect to purchase from a single supplier.

The third functional activity taking place in the distribution system is *accumulation*. This is the process of building up a supply of nearly homogeneous product; this supply, however, usually cannot be prefectly homogeneous because of branding and minor differences in the product of each manufacturer. A specific manufacturer may, by design, not produce enough of a commodity to fulfill the demand for it in some or all locations, and the function of the intermediary is to accumulate a supply of similar products from different sources. For example, the demand for toothpaste in a large city may be greater than that which could be supplied advantageously by any one producer. Thus, the intermediaries accumulate toothpaste from many sources. An industrial marketing illustration of this phenomenon might be the accumulation of a supply of specialized steel products or a certain article of safety clothing.[9]

Information flow

To this point, our discussion of activities in the distribution system has concerned the flow of goods. The intermediary also facilitates a flow of information in both directions in the channel. For example, he helps in the distribution of promotional material pertinent to the product and may even originate some of this material on his own. At the same time, he collects information about what is happening in the market, which he relays to the manufacturer. Basically, the intermediary is a part of the control system for the flow of information that evidences itself in the form of inventory records, advertisements, purchase orders, and so on. At one extreme the intermediary can expedite the information flow and lend valuable interpretations of the data, and at the other extreme he can act as a substantial block, or feed erroneous information into the system. An example of the latter type of behavior would be a retailer who exaggerates how rapidly the demand for a new product is developing in order to assure himself of obtaining a large inventory for an increase in demand that he expects to materialize considerably later.

Historically, when marketing research was not yet a highly developed field, the manufacturer depended on the intermediary to relay information from the marketplace, but, in many cases, this information flow from market to manufacturer consisted solely of the transmittal of orders. A further complication was the fact that, besides deliberate exaggeration of the type mentioned above, much of the information was distorted unintentionally. Since many intermediaries carry a broad array of products, they frequently cannot devote adequate effort to assuring the accuracy of their reports and expectations of market response for an individual product even if they should want to do so. Then, too, many retail units do not individually service a sufficiently large share of the demand for a product that their interpretations should be given much weight, although collectively these outlets may be significant. Generally, the chief advantage to the use of intermediaries for collection of marketplace information is the relative inexpensiveness of the method; of course, expense must be offset against accuracy.

Adequate alternative sources of information about what was happening in the marketplace began to develop in the post-World War II period. Despite the sizable costs involved, manufacturers are increasingly using

[9] An excellent summary of the activities taking place in a marketing system is given in Vaile, Grether, and Cox, *op. cit.*, pp. 33–43.

these supplemental means of collecting information. Consumer panel data, which provide a host of information – including purchase price, frequency of purchase, whether purchase occurred because of a special deal, place purchased, and so on – are now widely used, and so are retail store inventory auditing services. The information produced by these techniques can be used both to assess the accuracy of the information provided by the intermediaries and to complement it to improve the total analysis.

Service objectives of the distribution system

The objective of the logistics system is to provide the customer with a specified level of service, which may be measured by the time elapsed from when the customer orders the product until the product is delivered to him. This service level, in combination with the marketing appeals of the manufacturer and the intermediaries, influences the demand for the product. Essentially, then, the total distribution system provides more than the possession utilities that the logistics system produces. The objective of an efficient distribution system may be well described by the old saw about providing the right product at the right time, the right place, and the right price. Price is included because the other characteristics are reflected in it. For example, a slow means of transportation, such as a barge, may lower the final price for a good, while on the other hand the customer may be willing to pay a premium for a very high level of service.

The above broadly stated objective, however, is not very useful operationally, since the various utilities resulting from time, place, and product considerations depend on each other and are very difficult, if not impossible, to measure. If we state the level of service concept in another way, we may obtain an objective for the logistics part of the distribution system that clearly reflects customer benefits. Because of deviations from what is normally expected in transportation time, in production time if the good is not in stock or must be produced to order, or in order processing, the delivery date is a random variable. Thus, it would be foolhardy to set the service objective in terms of delivery on the specific date requested. Rather, a realistic service objective should be stated in terms of an obtainable range of days that does not produce great customer dissatisfaction – for example, "95 percent of all orders within n days of the requested date." Delivery substantially before the requested date may be as undesirable as late delivery; for example, a customer may not yet have adequate storage space ready for the shipment. The penalties for early delivery one would put into a model, however, would be less severe than those for late delivery. Correspondingly, the acceptable range about the requested date of delivery does not have to be symmetric.

Finally, the level of service that is established is not only a function of what the firm and the available transportation modes are capable of but also a function of the level of service provided by competitors. Many orders have been won or lost over precisely this issue. This statement also highlights the fact that the level of service does not have to be uniform across the firm's products and in all its markets. In addition, for certain by-products and certain markets, special routines may be developed for handling "Rush" orders so that more than one service objective may exist for a given product or market, depending on the conditions surrounding placement of the order. If competitors' service is generally poor, a firm may not have to perform near the maximum of its capabilities, and, given the price trade-offs that should be available with various levels of service, this firm should be in an excellent competitive position.

Transportation modes and the cost of distribution

A discussion of the various modes of transportation and their relative advantages and disadvantages as reflected in the level of service achieved is not appropriate for this book. However, there are some general characteristics that do influence selection of a mode and the stage in the manufacturing process at which the good should be shipped. The first of these factors is the weight density, or the number of pounds per cubic measure. The second is the dollar density, or the dollar value per cubic measure. The third is the substitutability of other products for the one of interest. The first two factors reflect the amount of money that can be spent on transporting the good; for example, a good with low dollar density and low weight density, such as boxed breakfast cereals, would probably be transported by a relatively slow but inexpensive mode. By contrast, for a good of high dollar density and low weight density, such as women's fashion clothing, the relative cost of transport is such a small part of the final price that a fast mode might be used to provide a high level of service, with scant attention to the cost. In the in-between groupings, such as high dollar density and high weight density, the direction would be toward the fast mode; an example would be a large-scale computer system shipped overseas by air freight. Substitutability clearly affects the service level expected by the customer, and hence the mode of transportation. See Table 7-5.

TABLE **7-5**

Interaction between weight and dollar densities

	High dollar density	Low dollar density
High weight density	Jewelry Computers (fast)	Coal Ores (slowest)
Low weight density	High fashions (fastest)	Breakfast cereal (slow)

If we now consider Aspinwall's concept of gross margin, of which the transportation costs are only a portion, we are able to develop some generalized relationships with the factors that influence transportation mode and with the number of intermediaries. These are summarized in Table 7-6; as one moves across the range of goods from left to right, it may be construed that the shift is really from specialty goods to convenience goods. Table 7-6 indicates that it may be more useful to think of distribution costs as a whole rather than deal with the individual subsets, such as transportation or inventory costs. Further, almost all the identifiable subsets move together with the total costs; for example, the amount of money spent holding inventories increases with the number of intermediaries, the generalized substitutability of the product, and so on.

The storage function and inventory models

Storage of merchandise to meet the prescribed level of service is obviously an integral part of the marketing system. However, the principal advancements in inventory theory have been made in the area of what might be called production-oriented inventories, particularly storage of materials and components for the production process and finished goods at the factory level. People whose primary interest is marketing seem to have relinquished the field. Since an extensive discussion of various inventory models is beyond the scope of this book, and since most production courses contain a discussion of inventory theory sufficient for the needs of the analytically oriented marketing manager, we shall confine our discussion to a description of the principal problems in building *inventory models with a marketing*

TABLE **7-6**

Relationships among distribution costs, number of intermediaries, and transportation-influencing variables

	Heavy machinery Major installations	Automobiles	Appliances Typewriters	Fashion accessories	Clothing	Hardware Packaged foods Cigarettes	
LOW	Distribution costs (total gross margin) as percent of selling price						HIGH
LOW	Number of intermediaries						HIGH
LOW	Substitutability						HIGH
LOW	Dollar density						HIGH
HIGH	Weight density						LOW

Imposing an inverse relationship between dollar and weight densities is an oversimplification. See Table 7-5.

orientation and to some comments on the economic benefits of the storage function.

There are many purposes that the storage function may fulfill. In some cases, this function may even be considered a part of the production process, as in the conditioning of tobacco or wine. But, more basically, inventory holding produces economic benefits in three ways: (1) It stabilizes production where consumption is irregular and permits irregular production of goods that are consumed steadily; (2) it is of economic value to one or several of the members in a distribution system in that it may be undertaken by other members for whom the opportunity cost is lower; (3) it permits economies of scale in the production and transportation of the good by taking advantage of carload rates and of the locales in which specialized labor or other production inputs exist.

The amount of inventory on hand at any point in the distribution system is, of course, determined by the service objective. What is deemed an acceptable level of service, however, depends on the estimate of how much business would be lost for the various alternative levels of service, and this estimate is probably the weakest part of most inventory models. Essentially, what is required is a figure that reflects the present value of all business that would be lost by failure to meet a promised level of service, measured in terms of days late or early and the frequency of this failure. Such a figure is not really obtainable. In the first place, changes in the level of purchases in the future would probably be due to many factors besides dissatisfaction with the supplier's distribution system; for example, prices are bound to fluctuate and the competitive position of the supplier may change. Second, for industrial consumers, it is sound purchasing practice to have more than one supplier, and the purchaser may award future business that results from his own natural growth to the other suppliers; thus, the percentage of business the poor performer receives declines although the actual amount remains relatively constant. Third, since a supplier frequently sells many items to the same purchaser, it is entirely feasible that business opportunities may be lost on products other than the one for which the distribution system has been inadequate. The foregoing should amply illustrate the difficulty of estimating future lost opportunities. Yet almost every inventory model depends on such an estimate, and frequently these models improve the level of service. The success of these models, of course, may be due to the amount of room for improvement of service in some systems prior to the use of the models, and the precision of the estimate of future lost business becomes relatively important only after the gross weaknesses of the inventory system have been corrected.

Location of storage and distribution facilities

In the previous section, some of the main pitfalls in developing inventory models were discussed. We shall soon describe several models for the location of storage and distribution facilities, but first we shall point out some limitations of this class of models.

In most existing location models, a very important variable is the total demand over some specified time period; this figure should allow for peaks in volume due to seasonal effects on sales. The total demand influences selection of sites for the storage of inventory, since both the particular location and the size of the facility are established partly on the basis of the portion of the total demand that can be serviced from that location. However, if the actual service level should be different from expectations, then total demand may be quite far from what was estimated.

Another principal determinant of the favorability of a specific location is the anticipated transportation rate structure under which the firm's products will move from the site in question. Clearly, if two firms have about the same production costs and sales expenses, the one better placed geographically with respect to demand will have an advantage. The advantage, however, is predicated on the assumption that both firms' products are shipped at the same transportation rate, and this is not necessarily the case.[10]

Finally, a market-oriented facility will usually stock an array of the firm's products, and what may be an optimal location for one set of products may not be for other sets. This problem can sometimes be met by having different distribution systems for different product lines (sets).

We are now ready to introduce the location models that we shall study in the next few sections. We shall denote the sources of the goods we are distributing as *plants*, even though these goods may not be coming to us directly from a factory. We assume that the amounts available and the locations of the plants are known. We shall denote the destination of our goods as *consuming centers* and shall assume that their requirements and locations are also known. We shall denote the intermediate storage areas between

[10] All transportation rates are controlled by the Interstate Commerce Commission (ICC), the Civil Aeronautics Board (CAB), or state regulatory agencies. It is estimated that there are on file with the ICC alone some 43 trillion rates (J. L. Heskett, Robert M. Ivie, and Nicholas A. Glashowsky, Jr., *Business Logistics*, Ronald Press, New York, 1964, p. 91), which should give some notion of the complexity of transportation rate structures. This huge number results from the combinations of thousands of destinations, origins, commodities, and types of carriers that are possible. Many of these rates are the result of special efforts to find a way of classifying a product or commodity so that the ICC will let it move at a rate different from the one that would have previously controlled it. In this situation, it is not impossible that competitors might be able to move highly similar goods at different rates. A firm is sometimes able to effect a rate change by changing the packaging or description of the product. The opportunities for such actions probably improve as the character of a good moves from a primary product, such as copper ore, to a finished product, such as a desk lamp. The rate for the latter product will be a function of, among other things, its weight, its packaging, the distance and quantity being moved, and even the materials of which it is composed, illustrating why the rate structure is so complex. At best, however, any advantage gained due to rate differences is only temporary, since the information is likely to spread to competing manufacturers and common carriers who can make appropriate adjustments or, at the least, take advantage of the same rates.

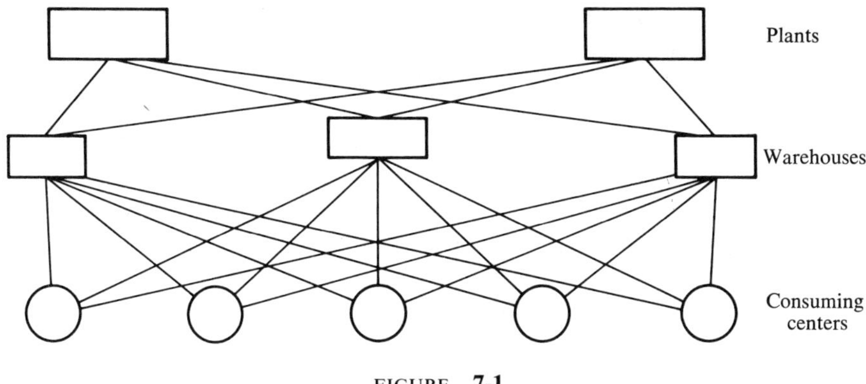

FIGURE 7-1

A logistics network

plants and consuming centers as *warehouses*, even though in a particular application they might actually be retail stores. Our problem is to determine the size and location of the warehouses in order to minimize the costs of transportation from plant to warehouse and from warehouse to consuming center plus the costs of operating the warehouses.

The structure of the logistics network is shown in Figure 7-1. Warehouses can, of course, be located at plants or at consuming centers. Furthermore, it is possible to have warehouses that serve other warehouses, rather than serving consuming centers directly, so that more than one layer would be sandwiched in in Figure 7-1. We will not consider this possibility in our models, nor will we consider multigood distribution networks.[11] Neither of these presents any conceptual or computational difficulties, but they do complicate the notation and explanation.

One final word is needed before turning to the models: Except in the simplest cases, a prohibitive amount of computation is required to obtain optimum solutions. Instead, heuristic methods are presented that attempt to obtain reasonable solutions with reasonable amounts of computation.

Warehouse location model—fixed sites

We shall first consider the problem of where to locate our warehouses if they are restricted to a finite number of fixed sites. We must then minimize the total cost (per time period) of operating the system:

$$\sum_i a_i y_i + \sum_i \sum_j b_{ij} x_{ij} + \sum_i \sum_k d_{ki} z_{ki} \tag{7-1}$$

[11] See V. G. Hurt and T. E. Tramel, "Alternative Formulations of the Transhipment Problem," *Journal of Farm Economics*, Vol. 47, 1965, pp. 763–773, for a "multiregion, multiplant, multiprocessing, multiproduct transhipment formulation."

where a_i = fixed cost of operating a warehouse at location i
y_i = 1 if a warehouse is placed at location i, 0 otherwise
$b_{ij} = c_i + t_{ij}$ = unit cost of operating a warehouse at location i plus unit cost of shipping from location i to consuming center j
d_{ki} = unit cost of shipping from plant k to warehouse at location i
z_{ki} = quantity shipped from plant k to warehouse at location i
x_{ij} = quantity shipped from warehouse i to consuming center j

This is subject to the constraints

$$\sum_k z_{ki} = \sum_j x_{ij} \quad \text{for all locations } i\text{; further restricted to equal 0 if } y_i = 0$$

$$\sum_i z_{ki} = S_k = \text{supply at plant } k \tag{7-2}$$

$$\sum_i x_{ij} = R_j = \text{requirement at consuming center } j$$

Because of the 0–1 variables y_i, the problem we have just formulated cannot be solved by ordinary linear programming methods. However, as we shall now see, once the y_i are all specified, the resulting problem can be treated as a transportation problem[12] (which is, of course, simpler than ordinary linear programming). Suppose that we have the following data:

$a_1 = 70$	$a_2 = 80$	$a_3 = 60$	
$c_1 = 3$	$c_2 = 4$	$c_3 = 2$	
$t_{11} = 3$	$t_{21} = 6$	$t_{31} = 4$	$R_1 = 10$
$t_{12} = 3$	$t_{22} = 6$	$t_{32} = 3$	$R_2 = 6$
$t_{13} = 4$	$t_{23} = 4$	$t_{33} = 1$	$R_3 = 8$
$t_{14} = 5$	$t_{24} = 2$	$t_{34} = 4$	$R_4 = 10$
$t_{15} = 7$	$t_{25} = 3$	$t_{35} = 5$	$R_5 = 6$
$d_{11} = 0$	$d_{12} = 5$	$d_{13} = 3$	$S_1 = 20$
$d_{21} = 5$	$d_{22} = 0$	$d_{23} = 4$	$S_2 = 20$

(2 plants, 3 warehouse locations, 5 consuming centers). Except for the a_i, all these data are used to derive Table 7-7a, which is the cost–requirement–supply tableau for a transportation problem. The cost part of the tableau is divided into four blocks, derived as follows: The upper left block is $((d_{ki}))$; the upper right block is all ∞ or any other number so large as to preclude a plant from directly serving a consuming center in the solution; the lower left block has 0 along the main diagonal and ∞ elsewhere; the lower right block is $((b_{ij}))$. The requirement–supply part of the tableau contains warehouse capacities in addition to the requirements and supplies; since the capacities were not prespecified, they have been set large enough to allow any warehouse to do the entire job. The optimum solution to this transportation prob-

[12] See Hurt and Tramel, *op. cit.*

lem is shown in Table 7-7b, while Table 7-7c shows the optimum solution to the transportation problem if the warehouses all have capacities of 15 units. In each of these solutions, the upper left block is $((z_{ki}))$, the lower right block is $((x_{ij}))$, while the lower left block shows unused warehouse capacity.

Because it was computed ignoring fixed costs, the optimum solution to the transportation problem shown in Table 7-7b need not be the optimum solution to the original problem. In this solution all three warehouses have been allowed to operate, so the fixed cost is the sum $70+80+60=210$. The variable cost is 250, obtained by multiplying the costs in Table 7-7a by the quantities in Table 7-7b and adding. The total cost is then 460.

We must now proceed to study other configurations of warehouse use.

TABLE 7-7

Transportation formulation—all sites available

		Warehouse			Consuming center						
		1	2	3	1	2	3	4	5		
Plant	1	0	5	3	∞	∞	∞	∞	∞	20	supply
	2	5	0	4	∞	∞	∞	∞	∞	20	
Warehouse	1	0	∞	∞	6	6	7	8	10	50	capacity
	2	∞	0	∞	10	10	8	6	7	50	
	3	∞	∞	0	6	5	3	6	7	50	
		50	50	50	10	6	8	10	6		
		capacity			requirement						

(a)

	1	2	3	1	2	3	4	5	
1	16		4						20
2		16	4						20
1	34			10	6				50
2		34					10	6	50
3			42			8			50
	50	50	50	10	6	8	10	6	

(b)

	1	2	3	1	2	3	4	5	
1	15		5						20
2		15	5						20
1				10	5				15
2							10	5	15
3			5		1	8		1	15
	15	15	15	10	6	8	10	6	

(c)

For example, if only warehouses at locations 1 and 3 are open, then the transportation problem, obtained from the previous one by including only the relevant rows and columns, is as shown in Table 7-8a. The optimum solution to this problem is shown in Table 7-8b. The optimum variable cost is 310; fixed cost is $70+60=130$, for a total cost of 440. In Table 7-9 we have presented the results of such calculations for each feasible configuration of warehouses; with limiting capacity constraints, some configurations might not be feasible. In this example two warehouses, at locations 1 and 2, produce the minimum total cost; next best is a single warehouse at location 3.

The procedure just described involves the solution of approximately 2^N transportation problems, where N is the number of available warehouse sites. It has been used successfully for small values of N (a case with $N=12$ was reported by Stollsteimer[13]). However, even though each transportation

TABLE **7-8**

Transportation formulation—limited sites available

		Warehouse 1	Warehouse 3	Consuming center 1	2	3	4	5	
Plant	1	0	3	∞	∞	∞	∞	∞	20 supply
	2	5	4	∞	∞	∞	∞	∞	20 supply
Warehouse	1	0	∞	6	6	7	8	10	50 capacity
	3	∞	0	6	5	3	6	7	50 capacity
		50 capacity	50 capacity	10 requirement	6	8	10	6	

(a)

	1	3	1	2	3	4	5	
1	20							20
2		20						20
1	30		10	6		4		50
3		30			8	6	6	50
	50	50	10	6	8	10	6	

(b)

[13] J. F. Stollsteimer, "A Working Model for Plant Numbers and Locations," *Journal of Farm Economics*, Vol. 45, 1963, pp. 631–645.

problem is solved rapidly, by the time we get to values such as $N = 25$ there are simply too many of them. We shall now consider three attempts to avoid having to solve these problems.

The obvious idea is to use average cost rather than unit cost in the transportation problem. This is done iteratively. To begin, we solve the original transportation problem, in which all locations are allowed (Table 7-7a). We use the solution (Table 7-7b) to calculate average costs

$$c_i' = c_i + \frac{a_i}{\sum_j x_{ij}} \tag{7-3}$$

obtaining

$$c_1' = 3 + 70/16 = 7\tfrac{3}{8}$$

$$c_2' = 4 + 80/16 = 9$$

$$c_3' = 2 + 60/8 \ = 9\tfrac{1}{2}$$

These average cost values are used in place of the variable costs in computing the lower right block in the next transportation problem to be solved, Table 7-10a. The solution, Table 7-10b, makes no use of warehouse location 3. Since the average cost at location 3 is now infinite, the iterative procedure will never make any use of it. An optimum solution has thus been achieved in two iterations in this example.

An obvious property of the above procedure is that any warehouse that has low utilization in the initial solution is likely to be eliminated in the next iteration. In the above example this was desirable, but if all the fixed costs a_i had been 10 units larger this would have meant eliminating the optimum solution (see Table 7-9). King and Logan[14] discuss this and some other

TABLE **7-9**

Cost of location configurations

Locations used	Fixed cost	Minimum variable cost	Total cost
1, 2, 3	210	250	460
1, 2	150	258	408
1, 3	130	310	440
2, 3	140	292	432
1	70	392	462
2	80	426	506
3	60	356	416

[14] G. A. King and S. H. Logan, "Optimum Location, Number and Size of Processing Plants with Raw Product and Final Product Shipments," *Journal of Farm Economics*, Vol. 46, 1964, pp. 94–108.

idiosyncrasies of the procedure and indicate the results of their attempts to deal with them in a rather large-scale problem ($N = 32$).

A second way to cut down the number of transportation problems to be solved is to stay within the unit cost framework but to consider only a small number of feasible configurations of warehouse locations. One way of accomplishing this is presented as a flowchart in Figure 7-2. We might start by solving the all-locations problem (Table 7-7, a and b), and take that as our current best solution. From the current best solution we proceed to the N adjacent problems that consist of those location configurations having all but one location in common with the current configuration (in terms of the y's, all but one y_i is equal to its current value). In our example this would mean solving the $N = 3$ problems indicated on lines 2 through 4 in Table 7-9;

TABLE **7-10**

Transportation formulation—average cost method

		Warehouse 1	Warehouse 2	Warehouse 3	Consuming center 1	Consuming center 2	Consuming center 3	Consuming center 4	Consuming center 5	
Plant	1	0	5	3	∞	∞	∞	∞	∞	20 (supply)
	2	5	0	4	∞	∞	∞	∞	∞	20 (supply)
Warehouse	1	0	∞	∞	$10\frac{3}{8}$	$10\frac{3}{8}$	$11\frac{3}{8}$	$12\frac{3}{8}$	$14\frac{3}{8}$	50 (capacity)
	2	∞	0	∞	15	15	13	11	12	50 (capacity)
	3	∞	∞	0	$13\frac{1}{2}$	$12\frac{1}{2}$	$10\frac{1}{2}$	$13\frac{1}{2}$	$14\frac{1}{2}$	50 (capacity)
		50	50	50	10	6	8	10	6	
		capacity			requirements					

(a)

	1	2	3	1	2	3	4	5	
1	20								20
2		20							20
1	30			10	6	4			50
2		30				4	10	6	50
3			50						50
	50	50	50	10	6	8	10	6	

(b)

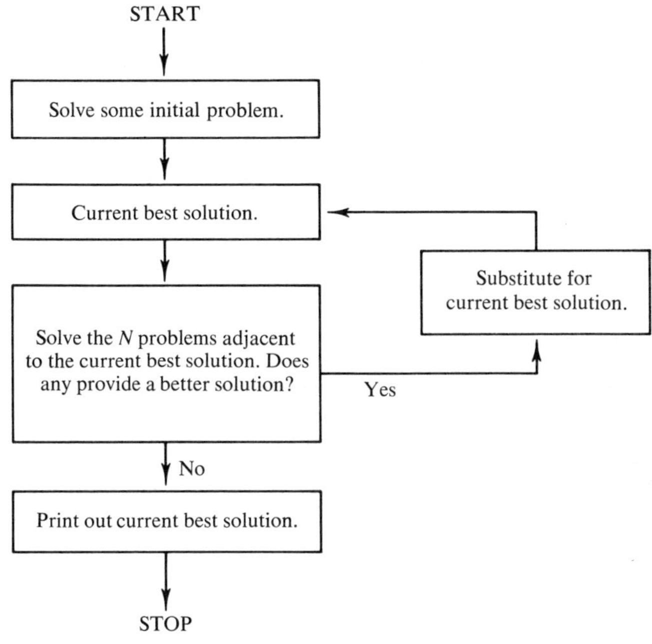

FIGURE **7-2**

Flowchart for adjacent locations method

all three of these happen to be superior to the current solution, so we choose the best of these (locations 1 and 2) for our new current best solution. We again solve the $N = 3$ adjacent problems, lines 1, 5, and 6 in Table 7-9. None of these is superior to the current solution, which we then print out as the best found. Once again our procedure has found the optimum solution for our example, but it would have failed to find the optimum if all fixed costs a_i had been 10 units larger. (Note that the problem on line 7 of Table 7-9 was never considered.) Manne[15] reports considerable computational experience with this procedure. In particular, he finds that it requires the solution of only approximately $N^2/2$ transportation problems.

A third idea for cutting down the amount of computation is to build up a warehouse network one warehouse at a time. In our example (see Table 7-9) this would start with a warehouse at location 3. Because no improvement can be obtained by adding warehouses, this would then be the solution. In a larger problem more warehouses would undoubtedly be added. At the end of the buildup phase, this might result in some of the earlier sites

[15] A. S. Manne, "Plant Location Under Economics-of-Scale—Decentralization and Computation," *Management Science*, Vol. 11, 1964, pp. 213–235.

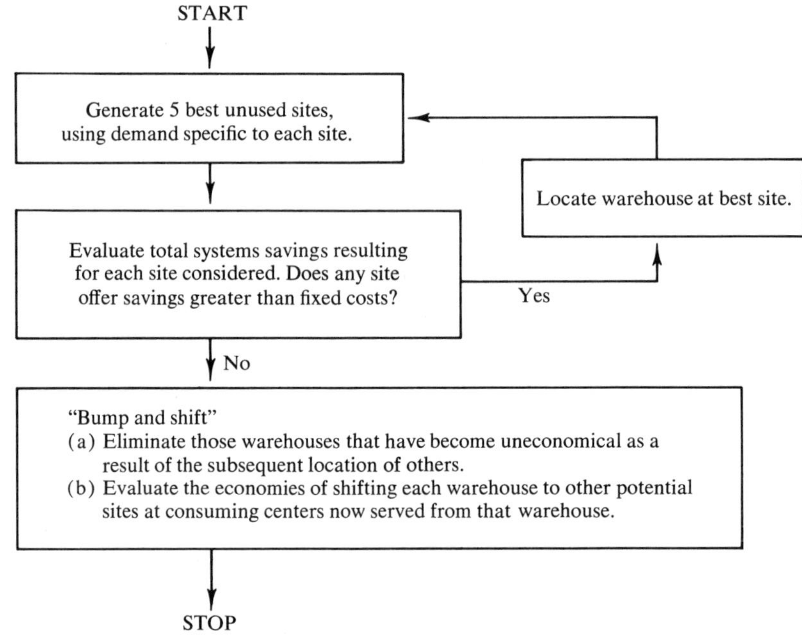

FIGURE **7-3**

Flowchart for network buildup method

selected being badly placed or even superfluous. A second phase would then be necessary to remedy this. Kuehn and Hamburger[16] have investigated such a procedure, which is illustrated as a flowchart in Figure 7-3. They give a number of numerical examples in which the linear cost structure is preserved, but claim that their procedure can also handle nonlinear warehouse operating costs.

Warehouse location model—sites not fixed

We shall now take up the location of a single warehouse with no restrictions on potential sites. We shall consider only transportation costs and shall assume that these are proportional to the distances involved. We can represent this situation graphically by letting

$x, y =$ (variable) coordinates of the warehouse

$x_j, y_j =$ (fixed) coordinates of the jth plant or consuming center, $j = 1, 2, \ldots, n$

[16] A. A. Kuehn and M. J. Hamburger, "A Heuristic Program for Locating Warehouses," *Management Science*, Vol. 9, 1963, pp. 643–666.

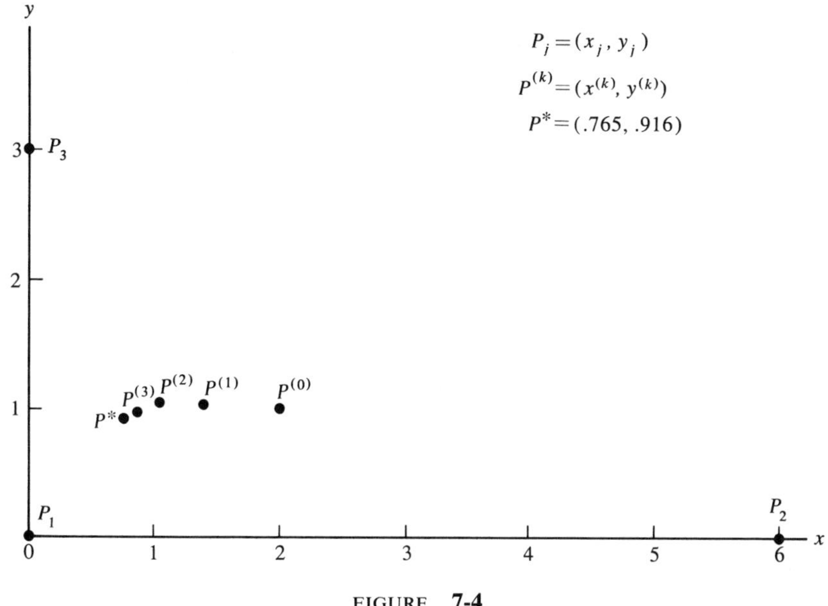

FIGURE 7-4

Optimum one-warehouse location—sites not fixed

Note that because direction of shipment is irrelevant in this model, we need not distinguish between plants and consuming centers. Analytically, we have the problem of choosing x and y to minimize

$$F(x, y) = \sum_{j=1}^{n} w_j [(x - x_j)^2 + (y - y_j)^2]^{1/2} \tag{7-4}$$

where the weight w_j can be interpreted as the unit freight rate times the quantity to be transported to or from the warehouse.

In Figure 7-4 we present a simple example with $n = 3$ plants and consuming centers at locations (0, 0), (6, 0), and (0, 3), and equal weights $w_j = 1$. The locations $P^{(0)}$, $P^{(1)}$, $P^{(2)}$, $P^{(3)}$ are part of a sequence that converges to the optimum location $P = (.765, .916)$. We shall now derive the equations that enabled us to obtain these points.

In order to minimize F, we set its partial derivatives equal to 0:

$$\frac{\partial F}{\partial x} = \sum_{j=1}^{n} \frac{w_j(x - x_j)}{[(x - x_j)^2 + (y - y_j)^2]^{1/2}} = 0 \tag{7-5}$$

$$\frac{\partial F}{\partial y} = \sum_{j=1}^{n} \frac{w_j(y - y_j)}{[(x - x_j)^2 + (y - y_j)^2]^{1/2}} = 0 \tag{7-6}$$

These are two nonlinear equations in the two unknowns, x and y, that cannot be solved explicitly. The difficulty lies in the denominators, which inexorably link x and y. This, however, is also the clue that leads us to an iterative solution. If we can treat the variables in the denominator as if they were known, we can then solve the resulting equations (which are linear in the numerator). Specifically, let $x^{(0)}$ and $y^{(0)}$ be an initial approximation to the solution. For example, we might use the weighted averages

$$x^{(0)} = \frac{\sum_{j=1}^{n} w_j x_j}{\sum_{j=1}^{n} w_j} \qquad y^{(0)} = \frac{\sum_{j=1}^{n} w_j y_j}{\sum_{j=1}^{n} w_j} \tag{7-7}$$

Now suppose that $x^{(k)}$ and $y^{(k)}$ are the kth approximation, and that we wish to determine the $(k+1)$st. First define the distances

$$D_j^{(k)} = [(x^{(k)} - x_j)^2 + (y^{(k)} - y_j)^2]^{1/2} \tag{7-8}$$

The linear equations to be solved are then

$$\begin{aligned} 0 &= \sum_{j=1}^{n} \frac{w_j(x - x_j)}{D_j^{(k)}} \\ 0 &= \sum_{j=1}^{n} \frac{w_j(y - y_j)}{D_j^{(k)}} \end{aligned} \tag{7-9}$$

with solution

$$\begin{aligned} x &= \frac{\sum_{j=1}^{n} \dfrac{w_j x_j}{D_j^{(k)}}}{\sum_{j=1}^{n} \dfrac{w_j}{D_j^{(k)}}} = x^{(k+1)} \\ y &= \frac{\sum_{j=1}^{n} \dfrac{w_j y_j}{D_j^{(k)}}}{\sum_{j=1}^{n} \dfrac{w_j}{D_j^{(k)}}} = y^{(k+1)} \end{aligned} \tag{7-10}$$

These recurrence formulas give the coordinates of the $(k+1)$st approximation in terms of the coordinates of the kth approximation.

In the simple example shown in Figure 7-4, which was chosen to require a minimum of arithmetic, the function to be minimized is

$$F(x, y) = \sqrt{x^2 + y^2} + \sqrt{(x-6)^2 + y^2} + \sqrt{x^2 + (y-3)^2} \tag{7-11}$$

The zeroth and first approximations to the optimum location are

$$x^{(0)} = \frac{0+6+0}{3} = 2 \qquad y^{(0)} = \frac{0+0+3}{3} = 1$$

$$D_i^{(0)} = \sqrt{(2-x_i)^2 + (1-y_i)^2} \qquad D_1^{(0)} = 2.24, \quad D_2^{(0)} = 4.12, \quad D_3^{(0)} = 2.83$$

$$x^{(1)} = \frac{\dfrac{0}{2.24} + \dfrac{6}{4.12} + \dfrac{0}{2.83}}{\dfrac{1}{2.24} + \dfrac{1}{4.12} + \dfrac{1}{2.83}} = 1.40 \qquad y^{(1)} = \frac{\dfrac{0}{2.24} + \dfrac{0}{4.12} + \dfrac{3}{2.83}}{\dfrac{1}{2.24} + \dfrac{1}{4.12} + \dfrac{1}{2.83}} = 1.02$$

Fifteen iterations are needed to obtain the values $x = .765$, $y = .916$, but $F(x, y)$ hardly changes after the third iteration.

So far in this section we have considered only the location of a single warehouse. Now suppose that two warehouses[17] are to be located and that we specify in advance, that is, before the locations are determined, which warehouse will serve each consuming center. Then, if

$x, y =$ (variable) coordinates of first warehouse

$\xi, \eta =$ (variable) coordinates of second warehouse

we must minimize

$$F(x, y, \xi, \eta) = \sum_{j=1}^{n} u_j [(x-x_j)^2 + (y-y_j)^2]^{1/2} + \sum_{j=1}^{n} v_j [(\xi - x_j)^2 + (\eta - y_j)^2]^{1/2} \tag{7-12}$$

where $u_j = w_j$ and $v_j = 0$ if first warehouse serves consuming center j

$u_j = 0$ and $v_j = w_j$ if second warehouse serves consuming center j

Under these circumstances, we can determine x and y independently of ξ and η, each pair of unknowns being obtained in the same way as x and y were in the one-warehouse model. Furthermore, it is not difficult to generalize this result to the location of more than two warehouses.

Difficulty does arise, however, when we consider the problem of specifying which warehouse will serve each consuming center. Even with only two warehouses to be located, such specification can be made in 2^{n-1} distinct ways. It is not efficient to solve the above problem for each of these specifications. On the other hand, once the warehouse locations are determined, the specification problem has a trivial solution: serve each consuming center from the nearest warehouse (keeping in mind the weights w_i). A simple heuristic solution,[18] making use of this fact, is to determine the optimum

[17] In this model we shall omit shipments from plants to warehouses. Including these would not make the theory or the computations any harder but *would* make the notations and the explanations more complicated.

[18] See Leon Cooper, "Location-Allocation Problems," *Operations Research*, Vol. 11, 1963, pp. 331–343; and "Solutions of Generalized Locational Equilibrium Models," *Journal of Regional Science*, Vol. 7, 1967, pp. 1–18.

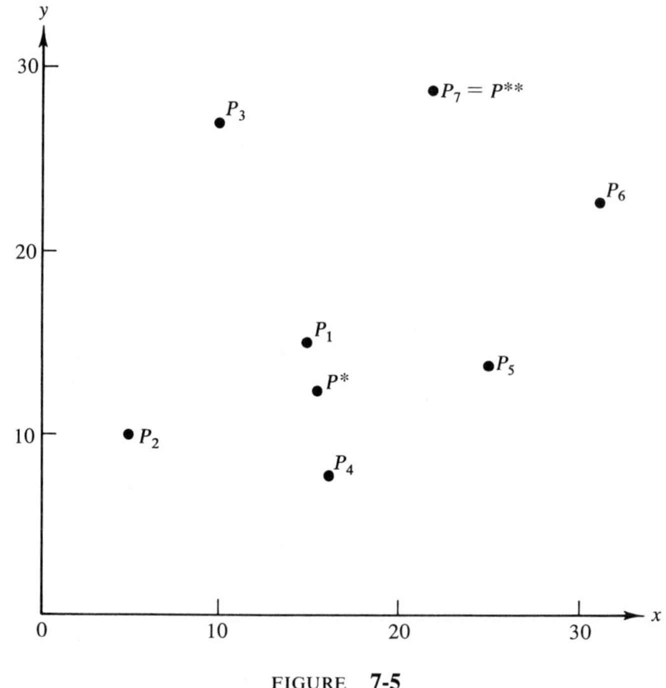

FIGURE 7-5

Heuristic two-warehouse location—sites not fixed

location when the warehouse sites are restricted to the consuming centers. In the example shown in Figure 7-5, the optimum locations for two warehouses restricted to consuming centers are at P_1 and P_7 (all $w_i = 1$). These serve P_1, P_2, P_4, P_5 and P_3, P_6, P_7, respectively. If we then specify that these sets are the consuming centers to be served by $P^* = (x, y)$ and $P^{**} = (\xi, \eta)$, respectively, the best warehouse locations considering each set only are found by proceeding as above and are as shown in Figure 7-5. In this example these happen to be the optimum locations, but in problems with larger numbers of consuming centers and warehouses the heuristic approach will in general not perform so well.

Location model for retail sales facilities

In the previous sections we dealt with the location of physical distribution facilities. The concern was with the minimization of the transportation costs involved in moving the product from the manufacturer to the consumer. In this section we shall consider site selection for retail sales facilities, for an individual store or possibly even for an entire shopping center. Attention will now be focused on the consumer and those things that influence his selection of a place at which to shop.

There are many factors that the consumer takes into account in deciding where to shop. Some of these, such as the satisfaction derived from shopping at a prestigious store or the courtesy of sales personnel, are not readily amenable to quantification. The several models that have been developed for retail site selection usually contain as a key variable the distances of the potential customers from the store sites under consideration. This is sometimes elaborated upon in terms of the cost for the customers of getting to a site, either in terms of dollars or of time expended. Another factor often introduced is a variable that reflects the assortment of a store, that is, the variety in the merchandise carried. The model that follows is built principally around these two factors.

Typically, the shopper patronizing a given outlet hopes to find a particular article that will satisfy the need that induced the shopping trip. The likelihood that such an item will be found is a function of the number of different articles, N, carried by the store. Thus, we can define $p(N)$ as the probability that the consumer will find some collection of items in the store that will make his trip successful.

The consumer's costs in making a shopping trip may be thought of as having three components: the distance the consumer lives from the store, the cost of searching the N different articles in the store to find a satisfactory one, and the opportunity costs of making a particular shopping trip. The total cost of a shopping trip is then[19]

$$C_T = c_d D + c_n \sqrt{N} + c_i \tag{7-13}$$

where C_T = total cost
D = distance of customer from store
c_d = cost per unit of distance
N = number of different articles in store
c_n = unit cost of searching
c_i = opportunity costs

In this model, D is probably best expressed in miles, or some linear measure; however, the approach can be structured to handle D in terms of travel time. The term $c_d D$, representing the cost and trouble of transportation, is taken as proportional to the distance traveled. If the term $c_n \sqrt{N}$, representing the cost of searching through the store, is also to be taken as proportional to the distance traveled, then it must be proportional to the square root of the size of the assortment, since

$$\text{Assortment size} \propto \text{area} \propto \text{distance}^2$$

The term c_i represents those opportunity costs that are independent of the time spent and distance traveled.

[19] This model is fully described in William I. Baumol and Edward A. Ide, "Variety in Retailing," *Management Science*, Vol. III, No. 1, October 1956, pp. 93–101.

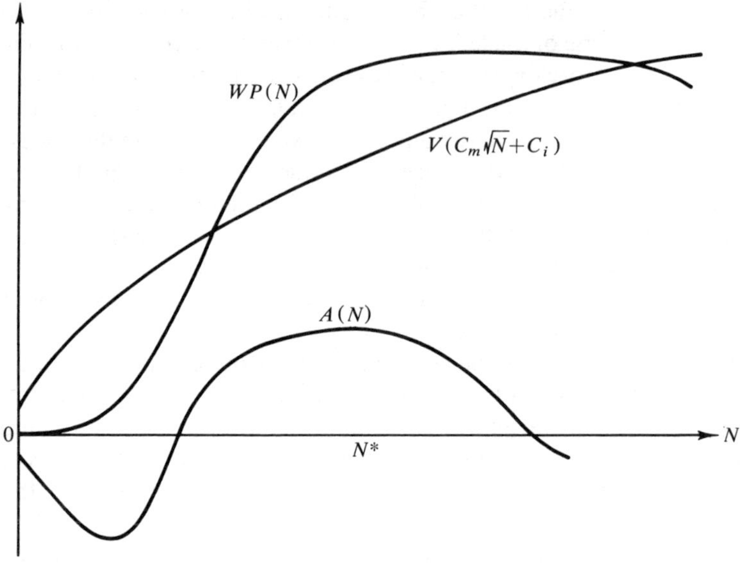

FIGURE 7-6

On the basis of the above formulation, the decision to shop at a particular store becomes an evaluation of the probability of success in finding a desired article against the costs of shopping in that store. In making this decision, the consumer may be thought of as assigning subjective weights w and v to the success and cost terms, respectively, which reflect the utility he would derive from a success or the disutility of the costs. We then have

$$f(N, D) = wP(N) - v(c_dD + c_n\sqrt{N} + c_i) \tag{7-14}$$

Suppose we now assume that the retailer's sales depend principally on the number of people he can induce to shop at his store. We can structure a function, parallel to that for the individual consumer, that represents the retailer's sales as a function of assortment size and distance to consumers:

$$\begin{aligned} F(N, D) &= WP(N) - V(C_dD + C_n\sqrt{N} + C_i) \\ &= A(N) - VC_dD \end{aligned} \tag{7-15}$$

where

$$A(N) = WP(N) - V(C_n\sqrt{N} + C_i) \tag{7-16}$$

consists of those terms that do not vary with distance. For small values of N, $A(N)$ will be negative; in fact, since $P(0) = 0$, $A(0) = -VC_i$. This will also happen for large values of N, since $P(N)$ is bounded by 1 while $\sqrt{N}$ increases without limit. The maximum value of $A(N)$ will occur for some N^* (see Figure 7-6), which, in principle, could be obtained by setting the derivative equal to zero:

$$A'(N^*) = WP'(N^*) - VC_n/2\sqrt{N^*} = 0 \tag{7-17}$$

Since sites are frequently selected with the objective of serving as large a population as possible, one reasonable assumption might be that population density varies inversely with the distance from the site, say K/D^α, where $\alpha \geqq 0$. The total population within some prescribed area about the site, say a circle of radius D_a, is then given by

$$\int_0^{\pi D_a{}^2} \frac{K}{D^\alpha}\, d\,\text{area} = \int_0^{D_a} \frac{K}{D^\alpha} 2\pi D\, dD = \int_0^{D_a} 2\pi K D^{1-\alpha}\, dD = \frac{2\pi K}{2-\alpha} D_a{}^{2-\alpha} \tag{7-18}$$

If $\alpha = 0$, we have constant population density K and total population $\pi K D_a^2$. If $\alpha = 1$, we have high concentration near the site and total population $2\pi K D_a$.

If we define the maximum sales radius, D_{max}, to be the distance at which sales fall to zero, then

$$A(N) = VC_d D_{\text{max}} \tag{7-19}$$

If we now compute total sales to customers within this radius from the site, we have

$$\begin{aligned} S &= \int_0^{\pi D_{\text{max}}^2} [A(N) - VC_d D] \frac{K}{D^\alpha}\, d\,\text{area} \\ &= \int_0^{D_{\text{max}}} [A(N) - VC_d D] 2\pi K D^{1-\alpha}\, dD \\ &= \frac{2\pi K}{2-\alpha} A(N) D_{\text{max}}^{2-\alpha} - \frac{2\pi K}{3-\alpha} VC_d D_{\text{max}}^{3-\alpha} \end{aligned} \tag{7-20}$$

If we use the above formula for $A(N)$, we can combine these two terms to write

$$S = \frac{2\pi K}{(2-\alpha)(3-\alpha)} VC_d D_{\text{max}}^{3-\alpha} \tag{7-21}$$

If $\alpha = 0$, this becomes $S = \frac{1}{3}\pi K VC_d D^3_{\text{max}}$; if $\alpha = 1$, $S = \pi K VC_d D^2_{\text{max}}$.

We could solve for S under other assumptions about how the population is distributed geographically. By itself, any one of these solutions would be difficult to implement because VC_d is not easily estimated empirically. However, if we were attempting to evaluate several sites relatively near each other that are meant to serve about the same population, we could assume VC_d to be constant, in which case the site with highest population density would be chosen.

Since most stores have images among customers that reflect the character of their assortments, the management would have to be planning very different types of stores at each potential site before N became important. Further, because N is a perceived factor, it would not be unreasonable to expect that rather sizable changes must take place in N before the customer becomes conscious of them. These observations are reflected in the fact that

$A(N)$ in Figure 7-6 is relatively flat for a fairly wide range about N^*. On the other hand, if one or more of the sites in question are located in major shopping centers, then significant differences in N might well exist.

The preceding model is actually a more sophisticated variant of Reilly's work on the pulling power of a particular retail location.[20] He hypothesized that persons living in a particular area were attracted to one or the other of two possible sites according to a formula identical to the laws of gravitational attraction. In Reilly's case, the principal variables are population and distance instead of weight and distance. By considering each potential pair of sites, Reilly was able to locate the "breaking point" – that is, the boundary at which the consumer would be indifferent – along major arteries connecting two sites and thus define the trading area of any given site.

A recent model in the tradition of Reilly's work that utilizes essentially the same variables as the model we have given above has the following structure:[21]

$$P_{ij} = \frac{A_j / T_{ij}^{\lambda}}{\sum_{k=1}^{n} A_k / T_{ik}^{\lambda}} \tag{7-22}$$

where P_{ij} = the probability of a consumer at location i traveling to a shopping center j

A_j = the square feet of selling space devoted to the particular class of goods by shopping center j

T_{ij} = the travel time from i to j

λ = an empirically estimated parameter that reflects the effect of travel time on various kinds of shopping trips[22]

n = the number of shopping centers

This approach can be used to establish equiprobability contours about any particular site just as Reilly's laws established breaking points.

Another probabilistic model for site selection that has been used with some success contains an element based on the distance of the buyers from the location and the brand preferences of the buyers.[23] This model was developed for the evaluation of automobile dealerships so that brand preference would be a very real factor in site selection, somewhat analogous to the

[20] For a summary of Reilly's work see David L. Huff, "A Probabilistic Analysis of Shopping Center Track Areas," *Land Economics*, Vol. 39, No. 1, February 1963, pp. 81–90.

[21] *Ibid.*, p. 86.

[22] These have been estimated by Huff for two classes of goods. *Ibid.*, p. 86.

[23] Theodore E. Hlovac, Jr., and John D. C. Little, "A Geographic Model of an Urban Automobile Market," in *Reference Papers on Market Oriented Management Systems*, M.I.T. Industrial Liaison Symposium, M.I.T. Working Paper 225–66, March 29, 1967.

assortment in other types of retail operations. In this formulation, we find

$$P_{ij} = \frac{q_{im_j} a_j \exp\,[-b_j x_{ij}]}{\sum_{k=1}^{D} q_{im_k} a_k \exp\,[-b_k x_{ik}]} \tag{7-23}$$

where P_{ij} = the probability that a customer in market segment i will purchase from dealer j

D = the total number of dealers being considered in the analysis

m = a particular brand or make of automobile

q = the make preference of the buyer: $q \geq 0$ and $\sum_{m=1}^{M} q_{im} = 1$

a_j = the constant that expresses dealer j's strength in his own immediate neighborhood

b_j = a constant indicating how fast sales fall off with distance from dealer j

x_{ij} = the distance of buyer i from dealer j

Note that in the above statement the pull of a dealer on any buyer falls off exponentially with distance. Other assumptions may be used here if their validity can be demonstrated. Dealer sales, S_j, can be estimated from

$$S_j = \sum_{i=1}^{B} N_i P_{ij} \tag{7-24}$$

where N_i is the number of potential buyers in segment i in a given time period, and B is the total number of market segments.

Organizational relationships in the distribution system

In an earlier section we discussed Aspinwall's concept of the gross margin necessary to move a good through the distribution system. This gross margin is composed of both the actual operational costs for the various tasks undertaken in the distribution system and the profits for the various channel members. The fashion in which the profit portion of the gross margin is shared among the channel members is a major determinant of the effort put forth by the individual members. If, for example, a reseller does not believe he is receiving a profit commensurate with his effort, then he will reduce the level of his efforts; in turn, this affects the entire branch of the distribution system linked to the particular intermediary and may result in reduced volume for the branch. A view of the channel that would describe it in terms of independent units cooperating for the common good is essentially erroneous; more appropriately, the channel should be thought of as a series of competitors who cooperate because the expected payoff to each is higher than under noncooperation. A game theoretic framework for the analysis of channels would seem to make sense, but the state of the art is such that the additional insight acquired by this approach is very limited.

In part, an intermediary's decision to handle an item is, at least initially, based on the return he may expect to earn on the particular item in comparison with the other alternatives available to him and the other products he handles. There is a widely held belief that a superior return to the intermediary will therefore evoke much stronger sales effort for the particular product. However, such a reaction is conditional upon many things; for example, even an outstanding return on a good with less than a 5 percent share of market would leave most intermediaries unenthusiastic. Other considerations besides financial returns that may influence an intermediary's decision to sell a particular good would be the reputation of the product among its consumers and potential consumers, the degree to which the product is clearly differentiated from competing items, the familiarity of consumers with the proper use of the product if it is highly innovative, services and advice offered by the product's manufacturer to his intermediaries, the technical service capability of the manufacturer, and so on. The relative importance of the preceding items will vary, of course, depending on whether or not the good is intended for the ultimate consumer market or the industrial market. In either case, a manufacturer would want to emphasize whatever factors assure the stability and quality of his dealer system, and these may include more than superior financial rewards.

In some situations, an intermediary rather than a manufacturer may be the leader of the channel, that is, the developer of policies and the supervisor of activity and total effort. For example, the influence of a large retail store such as Macy's may be great enough to cause a change in the basic character of a product, the way the product is packaged, its advertising, or any other strategic factor. And Macy's influence would vary inversely with the economic strength of the manufacturer. Locating the source of power or its direction in a channel is not always so easy; for example, consider the case of a large, powerful manufacturer negotiating with a large, powerful retail chain. In such situations, the ultimate consumer dictates what will take place in the long run. If a particular outlet, or set of outlets, reaches an important group of consumers, the manufacturer cannot afford to ignore it. Similarly, depending on a product's brand acceptance by the consumer, an intermediary may be forced to carry the product or lose that business and possibly other sales made simultaneously. To structure the situation to his advantage, in the short term the leader may thus not only work hard to obtain the cooperation of other channel members, he may also exert pressure on these others from another direction by approaching the consumer directly through mass communications efforts.

Evaluation of the benefits of a given distribution system becomes even more complex when several channels are used by a manufacturer for the same product or a great many products flow through a single channel. In a multiproduct channel, the problem focuses on getting the intermediary to allocate his efforts in the manner desired by the manufacturer. This is essentially the same problem as that of appropriate allocation of a salesman's efforts across the products in his firm's line, and can be handled in the way suggested for that case.[24]

In the case of several channels for the same product, the issue is one of an additional element of competition. To illustrate, at one time major appliances were sold primarily at list price through many small outlets specializing in sales of this type of merchandise. The advent of the high-volume, low-price discount house created a considerable problem for manufacturers of these durables. The producers did not want to offend the members of the existing distribution structure, but, at the same time, they did not want to miss reaching the segment of the market purchasing through discount houses. The problem was ultimately resolved by adding another channel with discount houses as the principal retail level element. This example highlights the chief problem in multiple channel operations: Namely, the portion of the gross margin received by any intermediary is a function not only of the gross margin a product produces in a given channel but also the success of the given channel in competing with other channel systems. Thus, an intermediary in one channel may be willing to give up a part of his potential profit, not to other intermediaries in his own system but to the consumer, in order to make his channel system as a whole more effective by causing more of the product's total demand to be funneled through his channel.

Clearly, it is very difficult for a manufacturer to evaluate the benefits derived from operating a particular distribution system. The situation is even more complicated for the intermediary who attempts to evaluate his position in a specific distribution system, especially if the manufacturer is a multiple channel operator. The manufacturer is aided in evaluating any single distribution system's effectiveness by the ability to experiment and compare alternative structures. Correspondingly, the intermediary compares the benefits derived by handling a given product or its direct substitutes.

On the whole, too little attention has been paid historically to both the cooperative and competitive aspects of channel systems.[25] The above discussion should indicate why intermediaries normally tend to be hostile to the manufacturer. These differing institutions are, however, bound together

---

[24] See Chapter 8, "Sales Force Management."

[25] An excellent theoretical book on this subject is Helmy H. Baligh and Leon E. Richartz, *Vertical Market Structures*, Allyn and Bacon, Inc., Boston, 1967.

by a community of interests, and their objective should be joint maximization of profits. Overall channel strategies produced with this objective should provide a substantial competitive advantage over noncooperating systems.

Systems analysis of distribution problems

At various points in this text it is possible to treat the material from the point of view of systems analysis. In some instances, we have strong reservations about the benefits that can be derived from such an approach, even though many others have adopted it.[26] But in the case of the logistics of distribution, we believe that a definite, significant contribution can be made.

Various definitions of the term *system* focus on the fact that a system is something that can be broken into smaller parts. Implicit is the notion that each of these parts can somehow be examined and analyzed to gain an understanding of the particular component's behavior. Further, a comprehension of how the various parts interact is necessary to develop any kind of maximizing behavior for the whole system.

A firm's physical distribution system fits nicely within this framework. One may examine the problems of any warehouse, sales center, or other storage point as a component of the total distribution system. For example, it is necessary to determine the optimum inventory level at a given site in terms of the location's role in the total system inventory and not merely in terms of what is best for that site. Similarly, the Kuehn and Hamburger heuristic for warehouse location, which we described earlier in this chapter, examines the system-wide effect of each additional warehouse contemplated. Thus, the systems approach seems quite suitable for analysis of the physical distribution system.

A more important factor, making the systems approach highly valuable, is the dynamic nature of the physical distribution system. If the system were static, the problems of operating it might yield to optimal solutions fairly readily. But because of its dynamic nature, steady-state solutions are only moderately useful in making decisions on the various aspects of the physical distribution system. To illustrate: Several retailers may experience substantial consumer demand for a product. Because the retailers anticipate even further unusual increases in demand, draining their stocks to a dangerous level, they immediately place larger than normal orders with their wholesalers for more of the product. The wholesalers replenish the stock of the retailers but fall prey to the same psychological forces as the retailers and place larger than usual orders with the manufacturer. In fact, the quantity now requested from the manufacturer is some multiple of the quantity originally demanded by the ultimate consumers. If we now assume that in

[26] See, for example, Chapter 11, which discusses marketing information systems.

the time period between the wholesalers' placing their orders and receiving delivery from the manufacturer a second wave of orders can arrive from the retailers, we obtain some notion of how necessary a dynamic systems analysis is.

Although we have whetted the reader's appetite for dynamic systems analysis, we are unable to satisfy it here because the subject is simply too large to be discussed in a few pages. Rather, we refer the reader to Forrester's work on the subject.[27] (Even in context, it takes him fifty oversize pages to develop and discuss a distribution model applicable to problems such as the above.) Some evidence of the magnitude of the dynamic systems problem we have described may be found in the fact that Forrester finds that in his model a permanent 10 percent increase in retail sales leads to a temporary 50 percent increase in orders to the manufacturer before the system finally settles down to its new equilibrium.

System stability and redesign

As the competitive environment and the internal capabilities of the firm change, the strategies and policies that compose the marketing mix are also changed. Changes in elements in the marketing mix other than those that make up the distribution system are more easily effected than changes in the distribution system. For example, a price change can be announced as being effective on a certain date and only a fairly small number of other adjustments will have to be made, such as corresponding changes in published materials and information given to salesmen and intermediaries. On the other hand, a change in the distribution system of equal significance, say an adjustment in the service level, requires far more planning and is probably more difficult to bring about. The service level adjustment may be based on the anticipated performance resulting from a shift in the transportation mode, but the change to a new mode requires analysis of most of the following: differences in packaging that may be required; the desirability or undesirability of new packaging arrangements from the viewpoint of intermediaries; the capability of the physical distribution facilities in terms of handling both the new mode and any packaging changes (this would include any intermediaries' facilities); the optimal warehouse pattern given the new mode; and the effect on intermediaries' inventory requirements and service levels.

Major changes in the distribution system tend to be even more complicated than in our example above. The principal reasons for this com-

[27] Jay W. Forrester, *Industrial Dynamics*, M.I.T. Press, Cambridge, Mass., 1961. See Chapter 15, especially Section 15.7.1. A description of simulation on a much smaller scale, which focuses on retailer ordering patterns, is contained in George Schussel, "Sales Forecasting with the Aid of a Human Behavior Simulator," *Management Science*, Vol. 13, No. 10, June 1967, pp. B-593 to B-611.

plexity are twofold: First, the distribution system must operate in both the physical and verbal aspects of the marketing effort, whereas the other marketing mix elements are almost exclusively verbal; second, where intermediaries exist, they are much more independent in their ability to make decisions about the product than the other organizations, such as advertising agencies, which influence other elements of the marketing mix.

Any distribution system, however, will require periodic evaluation and possibly redesign. The product line, the market targets, and the service levels all change with time, necessitating reevaluation. It is probably most difficult to make changes in the set of intermediaries composing the channel because the channel system is much less amenable to having flexibility designed into it than is the physical distribution system. Consider, for example, the problems involved in dropping a single, somewhat powerful intermediary from the system: This intermediary can wreak havoc in the channel system by immediately adopting and aggressively selling a closely competing product, by attempting to create ill will toward the manufacturer on the part of other intermediaries, and so on. Thus, the decision to drop one or more intermediaries or to add competing ones is a very delicate affair. It is also frequently a decision that cannot be postponed because of the opportunity costs involved. For example, if a particularly desirable intermediary is willing to take on the manufacturer's product at this moment, the likelihood is not great that he will still be available at some convenient moment in the future. In a sense, the channel leader has to think in terms of "stockpiling" intermediaries in the same way that a personnel director in a large corporation may stockpile engineers as an insurance mechanism.

Summary

The models presented in this chapter that deal with the physical distribution system are quite practical and many have received widespread use in industry. If we add to this the substantial theoretical and empirical work completed on modeling inventory systems, physical distribution is clearly one of the most advanced decision areas in marketing. We have described models for each of the following managerial decisions: (1) location of storage and distribution facilities considering both fixed and variable site alternatives, (2) network considerations regarding which distribution facilities should serve which markets and the corollary capacities required for each facility, and (3) location of retail sales facilities. Because these subjects are already so well developed, we should expect that improvements in the technology in the near future will be mainly in the form of refinements in the models—although we do not rule out the possibility of a major innovation. In addition, we have tried to point out the high potential for the application of dynamic systems analysis.

On the other hand, we have been able to present only conceptual models concerning the organizational interrelationships among the intermediaries and the manufacturer in the channel system. Aspinwall's work appears to be particularly useful in structuring channel length, but there is really no way to identify optimal solutions without further quantification of this work. One area in which the amount of research is increasing rapidly concerns the understanding of competition among the institutions in the channel, and significant contributions should be expected here.

SALES FORCE MANAGEMENT

CHAPTER EIGHT

Sales force management is concerned primarily with the establishment and evaluation of territories, determination of the size of the sales force and the sales budgets, and allocation of sales force resources. The last task is in many ways the most important, so we shall treat it first.

Before the allocation problem can be examined, some comments about measurement of sales force effectiveness are appropriate. The problem here is quite similar to the other side of the promotional coin, mass communications, in that much of the success of a given effort is not traceable to that specific effort. However, the sales force situation is somewhat better in the sense that we at least always have an accurate measure of the dependent variable, sales. The interaction between mass communications and personal sales effort is also such that, in many situations, it is almost impossible to assess the role that mass communications played either in gaining the opportunity for the salesman to make a presentation or in effecting the final sale by reinforcing the potential purchaser's evaluation of the firm's products. Measurement of the salesman's effectiveness is further confounded by other types of contributions, such as the advice and analysis of technical personnel.

Identifying that portion of total effect of the marketing mix that is directly attributable to the salesman is often extremely difficult. For some types of products and services, though, the problem is not nearly so great because sales and effort are directly and clearly related. Consider, for example, the route delivery salesman or a salesman for a wholesaler of institutional supplies that are sold only to industrial consumers, where there is little or no use for advertising. Obviously, the way in which the success of sales effort is measured should vary according to the nature of the sales job. The salesman who does pioneering work by opening up a new territory should be evaluated on a somewhat different basis than the salesman who is subsequently assigned to the territory and maintains it. In both instances, however, the primary concern is for the results relative to the effort expended.

Allocation as a key sales force management problem

There are two kinds of allocation problems in sales management: (1) an assignment of resources by management, such as the designation of salesmen to territories; and (2) the development of schemes so that the allocation of time and effort to accounts, products, and the like by the individual salesmen, or the allocation of other types of assigned resources, is close to optimal. Relatively little research has been reported on the first type of allocation problem, and we do not consider it here. The second category should serve to point out that the objective of many sales force management activities is really to achieve a desired allocation of effort, although the activities may not be described in those terms; such items as compensation plans, quotas, sales meetings, budgets, and other motivational techniques aid in reaching this goal.

In the next section we present a model that focuses on allocation of effort among products. The two subsequent sections offer models that deal with allocation of effort among customers.

Allocation of effort among products

Many compensation and motivational schemes have been devised to get the salesman to allocate his selling effort in the fashion desired by the management. The most commonly used methods have been the establishment of control ratios, such as sales vs. sales expenses according to classes of goods and customers, payment of different commissions for different types of business, and reward of appropriately directed effort through special incentives such as vacation trips. For a number of reasons, most of which we shall not go into here, these schemes do not always succeed in allocating effort as desired. One important reason is that they are usually tied to the gross sales attained on a particular product or from a particular customer. But since products have varying rates of profitability, such a system will not usually result in the maximum return to the firm. Of course, gross sales figures are used because of the difficulty of assigning joint sales expenses as well as the usual problems associated with allocation of overhead items.

Since these problems of joint costs cannot be avoided, an approach to allocation of effort based on contribution margin would seem fruitful.[1] Suppose that

[1] See John U. Farley, "An Optimal Plan for Salesmen's Compensation," *Journal of Marketing Research*, Vol. 1, May 1964, pp. 39–43.

π = company gross profit

I = salesman's commission income

B_i = commission rate for product i

t_i = time devoted to selling product i

Q_i = quantity sold of product i

P_i = selling price per unit of product i

K_i = variable nonselling cost per unit of product i

$M_i = P_i - K_i$ = contribution margin for product i

T = total time the salesman devotes to selling in a specified period (week, month, quarter, etc.)

All the variables that concern money are specified in dollars except B, which is a percentage.

Now suppose that Q_i is an increasing function of the amount of time a salesman puts into selling product i. Then,

$$Q_i = f_i(t_i) \tag{8-1}$$

where $df_i(t_i)/dt_i > 0$ over a wide range.[2] Also,

$$T = \sum_{i=1}^{n} t_i \tag{8-2}$$

If we assume T to be fixed, then the salesman attempts to allocate his time to maximize his commissions; this assumption requires that the salesman have some rough notion of his relative effectiveness in selling additional units of each product, which is not unreasonable.

If commissions are based on contribution margin, then company gross profit is

$$\pi = \sum_{i=1}^{n} [Q_i(P_i - K_i) - B_iQ_i(P_i - K_i)] \tag{8-3a}$$

$$= \sum_{i=1}^{n} f_i(t_i)M_i(1 - B_i) \tag{8-3b}$$

which we wish to maximize subject to the constraint on the salesman's total time. By the method of Lagrange multipliers,[3] we get

$$f_i'(t_i)M_i(1 - B_i) = \lambda \qquad \text{for } i = 1, 2, \ldots, n \tag{8-4}$$

For any two products, i and j, we then have

[2] $f_i(t_i)$ is assumed continuous and differentiable for each product, but the model that follows can be adapted to handle the discrete case.

[3] See Chapter 2.

$$f_i'(t_i)M_i(1-B_i) = f_j'(t_j)M_j(1-B_j) \tag{8-5}$$

or

$$\frac{f_i'(t_i)}{f_j'(t_j)} = \frac{M_j(1-B_j)}{M_i(1-B_i)} \tag{8-6}$$

This ratio holds for all pairs of products and maximizes the company's gross profit when the salesman allocates his time as the company wishes. The salesman's commission, given that it is based on contribution margins, is

$$I = \sum_{i=1}^{n} f_i(t_i)M_iB_i \tag{8-7}$$

Following the same procedure as above, we find that the salesman's commission is maximized when

$$\frac{f_i'(t_i)}{f_j'(t_j)} = \frac{M_jB_j}{M_iB_i} \qquad \text{for all } i, j \tag{8-8}$$

To optimize the salesman's commission and the firm's gross profit jointly, we need to establish the set of commissions B_i such that the same set of ratios is desired simultaneously by the firm and the salesman. Thus, we have

$$\frac{f_i'(t_i)}{f_j'(t_j)} = \frac{M_j(1-B_j)}{M_i(1-B_i)} = \frac{M_jB_j}{M_iB_i} \tag{8-9}$$

or

$$B_i = B_j$$

We conclude that the plan that pays equal commissions B on the contribution margin of each product is optimal in terms of satisfying the stated objectives of the firm and the salesman. A specific value of B cannot be determined from the above, however, since this represents a decision in which the interests of company and salesman are diametrically opposed.

Some of the initial assumptions can now be relaxed to demonstrate the fairly broad applicability of this model in achieving allocation of effort. First, the above solution does not require T to be fixed. T can vary over time periods or salesmen without affecting the nature of the solution, although the specific values of some of the variables may change. For the reasons explained in the Markovian call policy model,[4] T is not likely to vary very much, and it can be reassessed periodically, based on reports turned in by the salesmen.

Second, the assumption that sales increase as a function of the amount of time spent, or

$$Q_i = f_i(t_i)$$

guarantees only that $dQ_i/dt_i > 0$ for all values of t. Recall that this argument depends on an assumption made earlier that the salesman can roughly ap-

[4] See below.

proximate his incremental effectiveness on each product. But dQ_i/dt_i will be different for different values of t_i. If for each i we have an increasing first derivative over all values of t_i, the salesman will allocate all his effort to one product, the one with the largest first derivative, a strategy that maximizes his commissions as well as the firm's gross profit. Given that the individual salesmen may devote different amounts of time to selling (have different values of T), leading to somewhat different commission rates (values of B), the overall character of the sales force will be that of specialization of the salesmen by product. The solution for optimality will remain the same, however, despite the different character of the sales force. On the other hand, decreasing first derivatives for all t_i, a more realistic assumption since it means decreasing returns to effort spent in selling a given product, will result in the salesmen dividing their time among several products. These conclusions seem quite plausible and do not depend heavily on the remaining assumption about the salesman's estimation of his incremental effectiveness.

The commission on gross margin model can also be useful in resolving several other problems for which compensation plans are frequently intended. One example is the question of a production capacity limitation. Because unit production costs are likely to first decrease and then increase, a constant contribution margin implies an averaging of costs. One way to adjust for the fluctuation in the actual contribution margin is to vary B, the commission rate, over several wide ranges of output. Thus, the capacity problem may be met by a reduction in the commission rate at the upper end of the output range so that the sales force does not sell more than capacity; of course, the firm may want to stay within a certain percentage of capacity, but a variation in B can achieve this objective too. Obviously, management will need to develop some experience to know how to adjust B for these various situations.

Finally, one other accomplishment of the preceding model should be its effect on loss leader selling. There are some products that the firm might wish to use as a means of attracting customers to its total product line. This is the explanation for the loss leader concept in which the price of an item is reduced well below its "normal" selling price. If the commission on contribution margin model is applied, the salesman is unlikely to allocate much effort to selling such a product, since the returns to him will be smaller than on other products where the contribution margin is higher. The product in question can remain a viable member of the product line, but will be sold mostly at the customer's initiative.

Call policy—new accounts

The probability of obtaining a sale usually increases as more attention is paid to a prospect or an existing account. Each time the salesman visits, he should be able to collect more information on both the prospect's needs and the inadequacies in the supplier's offer with respect to meeting these needs. Over a period of time the salesman strives to induce adjustment in both the set of needs and the offer until a sale is consummated. This adjustment process is obviously facilitated by contacts between the prospect and the salesman.

The salesman, however, has a limited number of selling hours that he can devote to customer contact. Surprisingly, although there may be about 160 hours in a working month, so much of a salesman's time is spent in travel and waiting, clerical duties such as filling out reports, and the like that effective contact hours are usually less than half the total working time. Since actual selling time is a scarce resource, the firm's objective must be to allocate it in the most productive manner possible. There are really two questions here: first, how should a given salesman's time be allocated among the customers and prospects assigned to him, and second, how many salesmen should the firm employ.

One approach to the question of when to call makes use of a Markov chain analysis.[5] Suppose that our problem is to determine how much effort (that is, what number of calls) should be made to convert a prospect into an account. The following assumptions must be made in order to apply Markovian analysis: first, each prospect is of equal value to the firm if converted into a customer; second, each prospect is visited only once during the time period used for analysis; and third, the matrix of transition probabilities, which we shall shortly develop, is independent of the initial age distribution of customers in the state space and is constant over time. Although these assumptions may appear to be in contradiction to an actual marketing situation, certain modifications can make them conform to the real world. For example, customers can be stratified into groups according to their potential and a separate analysis performed on each group; the periods can be defined as relatively short, say one or two weeks, so that a prospect in all likelihood is called upon only once; and some experimentation can test the effect of the assumption of constant transition probabilities.

After some number of calls, a prospect is either converted to a customer or further effort is discontinued because of a decision on the part of the management about the relative ineffectiveness of more than a certain number of calls, n, in producing conversion. We thus have two absorbing states, drop (d), and sold (s), and a number of other states from 0 to n that represent the number of calls a prospect has received. We may thus establish the square matrix G, which is called the *prospect matrix.*

---

[5] This was first described by Abraham Shuchman in "The Planning and Control of Personal Selling Effort Directed at New Account Acquisition: A Markovian Analysis," in *New Research in Marketing*, Institute of Business and Economic Research, Berkeley, Calif., 1966, pp. 45–56, and we have generally followed his formulation of the problem.

$$G = \begin{array}{c} \\ s \\ d \\ 0 \\ 1 \\ 2 \\ \vdots \\ n \end{array} \begin{array}{c} s \quad d \quad 0 \quad 1 \quad 2 \quad \ldots \quad n \\ \left[\begin{array}{ccccccc} & & & & & & \\ & & & & & & \\ & & & & & & \\ & & & & & & \\ & & & & & & \\ & & & & & & \\ & & & & & & \end{array} \right] \end{array}$$

Any individual entry, such as G_{ss} or G_{12}, represents the number of prospects who were in the first subscripted state at time i and have moved to the second subscripted at time $i+1$; for example, G_{12} equals the number of prospects having received one call at time i who at time $i+1$ had received two calls.

We can now transform the prospect matrix, G, into a probability matrix, P. Since s and d are absorbing states, P_{ss} and P_{dd} must equal 1.00. Correspondingly, $P_{sd}, P_{s0}, \ldots, P_{sn}$ and $P_{ds}, P_{d0}, \ldots, P_{dn}$ must all equal 0. All the other probabilities in the P matrix can be found by taking

$$P_{jk} = \frac{G_{jk}}{\sum_{k=s}^{n} G_{jk}} \tag{8-10}$$

where the subscripts j and k represent the states at time i and $i+1$, respectively. Since the prospect cannot jump states—for example, move from a situation of having received two calls to having received four calls in one period—or move to a lower state, all the elements except those in the diagonal represented by an increase of one in the number of calls received must be 0. Thus, if we set $n = 6$ as the maximum number of calls a prospect will receive, the P matrix might look as follows:

$$P = \begin{array}{c} \\ s \\ d \\ 0 \\ 1 \\ 2 \\ 3 \\ 4 \\ 5 \\ 6 \end{array} \begin{array}{c} \begin{array}{ccccccccc} s & d & 0 & 1 & 2 & 3 & 4 & 5 & 6 \end{array} \\ \left[\begin{array}{cc|ccccccc} 1 & 0 & 0 & 0 & 0 & 0 & 0 & 0 & 0 \\ 0 & 1 & 0 & 0 & 0 & 0 & 0 & 0 & 0 \\ \hline 0 & 0 & 0 & 1 & 0 & 0 & 0 & 0 & 0 \\ .05 & .15 & 0 & 0 & .8 & 0 & 0 & 0 & 0 \\ .10 & .10 & 0 & 0 & 0 & .8 & 0 & 0 & 0 \\ .15 & .05 & 0 & 0 & 0 & 0 & .8 & 0 & 0 \\ .20 & .10 & 0 & 0 & 0 & 0 & 0 & .7 & 0 \\ .05 & .35 & 0 & 0 & 0 & 0 & 0 & 0 & .6 \\ .05 & .95 & 0 & 0 & 0 & 0 & 0 & 0 & 0 \end{array} \right] \end{array}$$

This P matrix can be partitioned into four separate matrices, in the fashion shown above, that are necessary for further analysis. We have

$$P = \frac{I \mid 0}{R \mid Q}$$

The matrices have the following dimensions in this specific case and for the general case of n states, respectively:

	Specific case	*General case*
I	2×2	2×2
R	7×2	$n+1 \times 2$
0	2×7	$2 \times n+1$
Q	7×7	$n+1 \times n+1$

For our example,

$$R = \begin{bmatrix} 0 & 0 \\ .05 & .15 \\ .10 & .10 \\ .15 & .05 \\ .20 & .10 \\ .05 & .35 \\ .05 & .95 \end{bmatrix} \quad \text{and} \quad Q = \begin{bmatrix} 0 & 1 & 0 & 0 & 0 & 0 & 0 \\ 0 & 0 & .8 & 0 & 0 & 0 & 0 \\ 0 & 0 & 0 & .8 & 0 & 0 & 0 \\ 0 & 0 & 0 & 0 & .8 & 0 & 0 \\ 0 & 0 & 0 & 0 & 0 & .7 & 0 \\ 0 & 0 & 0 & 0 & 0 & 0 & .6 \\ 0 & 0 & 0 & 0 & 0 & 0 & 0 \end{bmatrix}$$

Next we can obtain the matrix N, which represents the steady-state probabilities of a prospect in a given state surviving a certain number of states (calls) more without being absorbed. We have

$$N = (I - Q)^{-1} = I + Q + Q^2 + Q^3 + \cdots + Q^n \tag{8-11}$$

and, making the appropriate manipulations for the data in our example, we get

$$(I - Q)^{-1} = N = \begin{bmatrix} 1 & 1 & .8 & .64 & .512 & .3584 & .21504 \\ 0 & 1 & .8 & .64 & .512 & .3584 & .21504 \\ 0 & 0 & 1 & .8 & .64 & .448 & .2680 \\ 0 & 0 & 0 & 1 & .8 & .56 & .336 \\ 0 & 0 & 0 & 0 & 1 & .7 & .42 \\ 0 & 0 & 0 & 0 & 0 & 1 & .6 \\ 0 & 0 & 0 & 0 & 0 & 0 & 1 \end{bmatrix} \tag{8-12}$$

Note that each of the terms in equation (8-11) could be read from the diagonals of this last matrix if we were to assume that all other elements but those in the particular diagonal that we are examining are zero. To illustrate, the main diagonal of the N matrix has all ones in it and would be an identity matrix if all other elements were zero, the diagonal to the right of the main one has the probabilities of the original Q matrix, the next diagonal to the right is the Q^2 matrix, the next the Q^3 matrix, and so on. Although they are not obtained in this fashion, these higher order Q matrices may be thought of in terms of taking the original transition probabilities and applying them to each additional step in any row. To illustrate, the probability in the Q matrix of receiving a fourth call after having had a third call is 0.8, so that the fourth column of N is simply each element in the third column times 0.8.

Since the first row of the N matrix gives in each column the steady-state probability that a prospect will survive to the corresponding call, when these probabilities are multiplied by the number of new prospects entering the list we have the number in each state in the steady state. Thus, if we sum the first row of the N matrix and divide this number, 4.52544, into the number of prospects a salesman can see in the relevant time period, here defined as 40 within one week, we obtain the average number of prospects entering the salesman's list each period, 8.84. Multiplying the first row of N by 8.84, we get the number of prospects in each category (number of visits) in the steady state:

$$C = [8.840, 8.840, 7.072, 5.658, 4.526, 3.168, 1.901]$$

We may now multiply the R matrix, which gives the probabilities of being absorbed into either the drop or sold categories from any other state, by the C vector to obtain the number of prospects sold and dropped during each period in the steady state, respectively, or

$$CR = [3.16, 5.68]$$

Thus, on the average, we may expect to gain somewhat more than three customers per period.

The number of conversions per period is, of course, dependent upon several other factors. Some of these factors are not affected very readily by a change in management policy. For example, the number of prospects seen per period cannot be easily altered given that the waiting time to see the prospect, the travel time, the length of time necessary for an adequate sales presentation, and so on, all take such a large proportion of the working day of the salesman, while overtime is effectively precluded by customer unavailability. Similarly, a change in the length of the period of analysis does not really affect the underlying relationships. One variable that we can readily influence, however, is n, the number of calls made on a customer before ceasing further effort. Table 8-1 illustrates the effect of different cutoff policies using the data above and the assumption that P_{ns} remains as originally given in $[R]$ and $P_{nd} = 1 - P_{ns}$ for the cutoff number of calls. Thus,

TABLE **8-1**

Effect of different cutoff policies

Cutoff policy (n)	Number of prospects entering list each period	Expected number of conversions per period	Expected number of drops per period
3 calls	11.63	2.63	9.00
4 calls	10.12	3.32	6.80
5 calls	9.27	3.21	6.06
6 calls	8.84	3.16	5.68

for example, when the cutoff policy is four calls, $P_{ns} = .20$ and $P_{nd} = .80$. For the particular data given, the optimum cutoff point is four calls if the firm's goal is to obtain the maximum number of conversions per period.

One of the chief limitations of the foregoing model lies in the establishment of the transition probability matrix, P, or the underlying prospect matrix, G. The basis for G is historical data. However, there is an interaction effect between the salesman and the prospects in a territory. Even if we assume that the salesman's skill in presentation of his product is relatively constant, his success might vary substantially if he were moved to a different territory, possibly because of regional cultural differences. Further, within any given territory some customers will react more favorably to the particular salesman but over time there will be fewer and fewer prospects to whom this salesman has substantial appeal; consequently, the transition probabilities are probably not stable over a great many periods. By paying careful attention, say through reasonably frequent reevaluation of the P matrix, much of the difficulty can be overcome. In essence, the steady state will never be attained, and the question is whether the elements of P will be stable for a long enough number of periods to use the model just described in planning call policy.[6]

Another characteristic of this model is that it is highly individual-oriented and a separate analysis must be undertaken for each salesman. This should be no great problem on a computer, however, and this individual focus offers another opportunity to the management for sales force control. It is possible to determine the variances as well as the expected values for both the number of prospects in a state and the number of conversions per period,[7] and therefore standard control chart techniques can be applied to each salesman's activities. In fact, when a data point occurs outside a limit, it may be an indication that it is an appropriate time to reevaluate the P matrix. On the whole, this Markovian approach to determining call policy on prospects seems quite useful.

Call policy—regular accounts

The model considered in the previous section can be used for either the sale of a major item or the solicitation of a new account. In either case we might appropriately make several calls on a prospective customer in order to achieve a single sale. On the other hand, once a relationship is established, we would want to visit the customer on a regular basis, say once a month, in order to maintain or increase the quantity sold. Once again

---

[6] Chapter 10, "Models of Consumer Behavior," offers a detailed discussion of the principal problems in the use of Markovian analysis for modeling consumer purchase behavior. Most of these drawbacks appear to exist in the Markov sales call model also but much more weakly.

[7] Shuchman, *op. cit.*, outlines the procedure for this.

we are faced with an allocation problem: With the limited sales force at our disposal, which customers should be visited in a given period? In order to study this question, we shall make use of a model that was formulated by John Magee[8] for retail promotional activities in which a salesman's visit was required to set up point-of-sales advertising and displays.

To begin with, we shall assume that all customers receive sales visits. Suppose that the quantity, n, purchased by such a customer in a single time period is a Poisson random variable

$$P_p(n|c) = \frac{e^{-c}c^n}{n!} \tag{8-13}$$

where c, the expected purchase, is an unknown characteristic of the individual customer. In general, the prior distribution for c would be a gamma distribution, but Magee has found from his data that the simpler exponential distribution

$$f_\gamma(c|1, 1/s) = (1/s)e^{-c/s} \tag{8-14}$$

will do, where s is the expected purchase quantity averaged over all customers. The marginal distribution for n is then

$$P(n) = \int_0^\infty P_p(n|c)f_\gamma(c|1, 1/s)\ dc = \frac{s^n}{(s+1)^{n+1}} \tag{8-15}$$

This is the probability that a customer chosen at random will purchase the quantity n in a single time period. When $P(n)$ is interpreted as a relative frequency, this equation fits Magee's empirical data exceedingly well.

Magee obtained a second empirical check of his model by the following reasoning. Over k time periods a customer would purchase the quantity n_k with probability

$$P_p(n_k|kc) = \frac{e^{-kc}(kc)^{n_k}}{n_k} \tag{8-16}$$

For such a customer the posterior distribution of c would then be the gamma distribution

$$f_\gamma(c|n_k + 1, k + 1/s) = \frac{(k + 1/s)^{n_k+1}c^{n_k}}{n_k!}\, e^{-(k+1/s)c} \tag{8-17}$$

The posterior mean is

$$\frac{n_k + 1}{k + 1/s} = \frac{s}{ks + 1}\, n_k + \frac{s}{ks + 1} \tag{8-18}$$

which can be interpreted as the predicted quantity for the customer's next purchase. This, too, gave Magee a good fit with his data.

---

[8] See John F. Magee, "The Effect of Promotional Effort on Sales," *Journal of the Operations Research Society of America*, Vol. 1, February 1953, pp. 64–74.

Up to this point we have lumped all the customers together into a single distribution. Now, suppose the sales organization has a method of distinguishing a fraction α of the customers[9]; then we can write

$$(1/s)e^{-c/s} = g(c) + h(c) \tag{8-19}$$

where $g(c)$ represents those customers that would be chosen by the sales organization, and $h(c)$ represents those that would not be chosen. To avoid any misunderstanding, we point out that we are still operating under the assumption that all customers actually receive sales visits. What we are trying to determine is how the sales organization's method of choosing customers divides up the total population of customers.

Since only a fraction α of all customers are to be chosen, we require that

$$\int_0^\infty g(c)\ dc = \alpha \quad \text{and} \quad \int_0^\infty h(c)\ dc = 1 - \alpha \tag{8-20}$$

However, if the method of choice is any good at all, the average sales to chosen customers will exceed αs, their proportional share of the overall average sale. Magee found that he could use[10]

$$g(c) = \frac{1}{s}\left[e^{-c/s} - e^{-c/(1-\alpha)s}\right] \tag{8-21}$$

and

$$h(c) = \frac{1}{s}e^{-c/(1-\alpha)s}$$

If we calculate

$$\int_0^\infty cg(c)\ dc = s - (1-\alpha)^2 s = \alpha(2-\alpha)s > \alpha s \tag{8-22}$$

we see that the method of choosing customers was successful in assigning more than a proportionate amount of sales potential to the distinguished group.

In order to show that the formulas for $g(c)$ and $h(c)$ adequately represent the data, we first calculate

$$\int_0^\infty P_p(n|c)g(c)\ dc = \frac{s^n}{(s+1)^{n+1}} - \frac{s^n}{[s+1/(1-\alpha)]^{n+1}} \tag{8-23}$$

$$\int_0^\infty P_p(n|c)h(c)\ dc = \frac{s^n}{[s+1/(1-\alpha)]^{n+1}} \tag{8-24}$$

---

[9] In Magee's example, customers' purchases over the preceding two periods were used as the criterion for distinction.

[10] There is no reason to suppose that those formulas will hold in general. The specific form of $g(c)$ and $h(c)$ will depend on the individual problem being studied. Note that in this example $g(c)$ is not even a gamma function.

Using data obtained when all customers are visited, and dividing up the customers according to the sales organization's method, the relative frequencies of quantity purchased should be given by these formulas. Once again, Magee found good agreement with his data.

So far, as we have been careful to point out, we have developed the model under the assumption that all customers are visited each time period. If we now assume that only the fraction α are visited, what is the effect on sales? We would hope that formula (8-23) is still a valid description for the fraction visited; Magee found this to be the case with his data. On the other hand, we would not want formula (8-24) to still hold for the unvisited customers, since this would indicate that visitation had no effect on sales. Magee found that[11]

$$\frac{(.7)(.71s)^n}{[.71s + 1/(1-\alpha)]^{n+1}} \tag{8-25}$$

was a very accurate formula for the relative frequency of quantity purchased by the unchosen, unvisited customers. This can be interpreted as meaning that 30 percent of the unvisited customers made no purchase at all, while the 70 percent who did make purchases bought, on the average, only 71 percent as much as an average customer. The net result of not visiting, then, was to cut the average sales in half.

Having determined that the effect of not visiting a customer is to cut expected sales in half, we are now prepared to answer two questions about the effectiveness of sales force deployment.

1. What is the efficiency of the sales organization's method of choosing customers to be visited? They achieved an average of

$$S = \int_0^\infty cg(c)\,dc + \frac{1}{2}\int_0^\infty ch(c)\,dc = \frac{1+2\alpha-\alpha^2}{2}\,s \tag{8-26}$$

sales per customer per period. A completely random choice of customers to be visited would yield an average sale of

$$S_{\min} = \left(\alpha + \frac{1-\alpha}{2}\right)s = \frac{1+\alpha}{2}\,s \tag{8-27}$$

which may be taken as the worst possible choice. The best choice would be to visit the fraction α having the largest values of c; since

$$\int_{-s\ln\alpha}^{\infty} \frac{1}{s}e^{-c/s}\,dc = \alpha \tag{8-28}$$

this means visiting all customers for whom $c \geq -s \ln \alpha$. Of course, since c is unknown, this cannot be done, but it does give us an upper bound to the attainable average sale

[11] Once again there is no reason to suppose that this formula, or even its form, is at all general.

$$S_{\max} = \int_{-s \ln \alpha}^{\infty} \frac{c}{s} e^{-c/s}\, dc + \frac{1}{2} \int_{0}^{-s \ln \alpha} \frac{c}{s} e^{-c/s}\, dc = \frac{1 + \alpha - \alpha \ln \alpha}{2} s \tag{8-29}$$

One measure of the efficiency of the sales organization's method is

$$\frac{S - S_{\min}}{S_{\max} - S_{\min}} = \frac{1 - \alpha}{-\ln \alpha} \tag{8-30}$$

This expression is highly dependent on the fraction visited, α.

2. Given the sales organization's method of choice, what fraction α of customers should be visited? If N is the total number of customers, m is the gross margin per unit sold excluding sales visits and C is the average cost of a sales visit, then α must be chosen to maximize

$$\frac{1 + 2\alpha - \alpha^2}{2} smN - \alpha CN \tag{8-31}$$

The derivative of this expression with respect to α is

$$[(sm - C) - \alpha sm]N \tag{8-32}$$

which is zero when $\alpha = (sm - C)/sm$. Taking care to set α equal to zero if this last expression is negative, we obtain

$$\alpha^* = \begin{cases} 1 - \dfrac{C}{sm} & \text{if } C < sm \\ 0 & \text{if } C > sm \end{cases}$$

It is not very surprising that we make no sales visits if the cost of a visit exceeds the average gross profit obtained.

The value of additional salesmen

In the call policy model for regular accounts discussed in the previous section, the level at which α is set is directly related to the number of salesmen. Turning this around, the number of salesmen employed will determine the feasible levels of α. In this way we are able to evaluate such things as the contributions of additional salesmen. Similarly, in the Markovian call policy model for new accounts, the value of additional salesmen can be calculated if we know the cost of making a call and the profit or contribution margin obtained from a conversion. For an unlimited number of available prospects the optimum cutoff policy $n = 4$ would hold regardless of what the number of salesmen was, and each additional salesman would achieve 3.32 additional conversions per period. Given that the value of the incremental conversions exceeds the costs of the additional salesman, we might opt for the larger number of salesmen. An important corollary effect, however, is that we consume prospects at a much higher rate. Thus, some knowledge of the size of the prospect pool is also essential to making a

TABLE **8-2**

Relation of cutoff to number of prospects and salesmen

Cutoff policy	Prospects per period per salesman	Total prospects per period	Number of salesmen	Conversions per period per salesman	Total conversions per period
3	11.63	90	7.74	2.63	20.3
4	10.12	90	8.89	3.32	29.5
5	9.27	90	9.71	3.21	31.2
6	8.84	90	10.17	3.16	32.2
7	8.63	90	10.42	3.09	32.2

decision with regard to how many salesmen to employ. On the other hand, if the number of available prospects per period is fixed, then the cutoff policy and the number of salesmen are related, as can be seen from Table 8-2.[12] Because the total number of prospects is kept fixed and the cutoff policy is an integer, the number of salesmen turns out to be nonintegral. Nevertheless, we can see the relationship between number of salesmen and total conversions per period. Once again a comparison of the value of the incremental conversions with the costs of the additional salesmen would guide us in making our decision. Obviously, the situation in this Markovian call policy model could be more complicated than the preceding in that the probability transition matrix might be very different for each salesman.

One interesting application of queuing theory to sales work, which essentially focuses on evaluating the worth of additional salesmen, attempted to determine the number of retail sales clerks who should be assigned to a floor.[13] The technique used was a Monte Carlo simulation based on the following five variables: the number of potential customers arriving and requesting service per five-minute period; the number of minutes the clerk spends waiting on the customer; the number of items purchased per customer, per transaction; the contribution margin per item sold; and the number of minutes a customer is willing to wait for service before leaving when all clerks on the floor are busy. The resultant measures of clerk idle time and lost sales obtained by examining the distribution of the clerks' work loads as calculated by the simulation enabled the management to assign clerks by evaluating the marginal worth of each one. This analysis can be altered to take account of peak load problems resulting from special promotions or lunch hour trade, and so on. This method is a quite reasonable

---

[12] In calculating Table 8-2 we have used $P_{78} = .01$; if P_{ns} were to remain at .05 for large values of n, then total conversions per period would continue to increase as cutoff policy increased.

[13] Charles J. Stokean and Philip Mintz, "How Many Clerks on a Floor?" *Journal of Marketing Research*, Vol. 2, November 1965, pp. 388–393.

approach and can be applied to a number of other production-type problems where there is strong customer involvement, such as the number of check-out counters in a supermarket.[14]

The addition of sales outlets (or salesmen)

In the previous section we discussed the question of whether or not to take on additional salesmen. For some classes of products, particularly those that have short channels of distribution in which the product is sold by the manufacturer directly to the consumer, the opening of another sales outlet is very much analogous to the addition of a salesman in a specified territory. Hartung and Fisher[15] have examined this question in a particularly interesting context; their model was developed for sales outlets but is equally applicable to salesmen.[16] For certain types of products, sales at a particular outlet are a function not only of factors affecting the particular site but also of more general environmental conditions. An example would be a particular gasoline service station in an area where there are many outlets for the same brand. The total amount of the given brand sold is also affected by the interaction of the outlets; too many outlets in a specific geographical area may introduce substantial diseconomies, but, more important, total sales may increase in the older outlets when a new one is established. This last effect may be due to the increased familiarization and acceptance of the brand by consumers as more outlets are added, and would be one of the broader environmental factors affecting success at particular sites.

This sales interaction effect is not limited to situations in which the outlet sells a single brand or a very limited set of products. If the geographic market area is reasonably delimited, any chain type of operation will experience the interaction effect described in the service station example. Thus, the determination of whether or not to add another outlet involves more than just evaluating the economic factors associated with particular sites.

We can use the model below to evaluate the sales interaction effect. We employ the following variables:

---

[14] As in other chapters, we have refrained from discussing in detail problems that are within the framework of production technology. Occasionally, however, as above, we feel it necessary to offer examples that demonstrate the applicability of this technology to problems that are normally thought to be marketing oriented.

[15] Philip H. Hartung and James L. Fisher, "Brand Switching and Mathematical Programming in Market Expansion," *Management Science*, Vol. 11, No. 10, August 1965, pp. B-231 to B-243.

[16] Our example is described in terms of outlets, but the reader can easily translate the statements to the situation for addition of salesmen.

X = steady-state market share of product A

P = number of outlets carrying product A

O = number of outlets carrying competing brands

S_A = sales of product A

S_T = total sales of all brands

$\bar{S}_A$ = average sales per outlet of product A

$\bar{S}_T$ = average sales per outlet for the industry

The industry purchase pattern can be described by the following two-state Markov chain[17]:

$$\begin{array}{lcc} & \text{Product A} & \text{All other brands} \\ \text{Product A} & \alpha & 1-\alpha \\ \text{All other brands} & \beta & 1-\beta \end{array}$$

We hypothesize the following relationships:

$$\alpha = k_1\left(\frac{P}{O+P}\right) \quad \text{and} \quad \beta = k_2\left(\frac{P}{O+P}\right)$$

where k_1 and k_2 are to be empirically determined. Then,

$$\frac{S_A}{S_T} = X = \frac{\beta}{1-\alpha+\beta} = \frac{k_2 P}{O+P+(k_2-k_1)P} \tag{8-33}$$

or

$$\left(\frac{O+P}{P}\right)\frac{S_A}{S_T} = k_2 + (k_1-k_2)\frac{S_A}{S_T} \tag{8-34}$$

Since $\bar{S}_A = S_A/P$ and $\bar{S}_T = S_T/(O+P)$,

$$\bar{S}_A/\bar{S}_T = k_2 + (k_1-k_2)S_A/S_T \tag{8-35}$$

This relationship is illustrated in Figure 8-1.

Hartung and Fisher found $k_1 = 4.44$ and $k_2 = .64$, respectively, for the situation they studied.[18] Given these figures, we find that $\alpha > 1$ if the ratio $P/(O+P) > .225$. This is, in effect, a result of the assumption of a linear relationship in Figure 8-1 and means that the model will hold only over relatively narrow limits. Further, since α represents the rate of repeat purchases for brand A per period and β the rate of customers switching to brand

[17] See Chapter 3, pp. 30–34, particularly (3-36), which in the current notation would be $X = X\alpha + (1-X)\beta$.

[18] Hartung and Fisher, *op. cit.*, p. B-238.

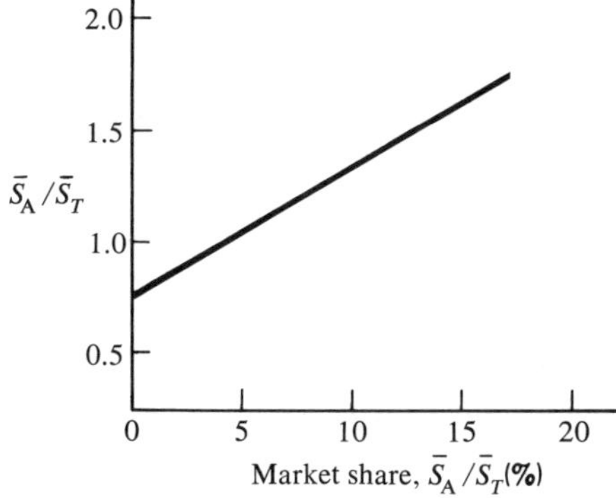

FIGURE **8-1**

Ratio of brand A average sales per output, $\bar{S}_A$, to industry average sales per outlet, $\bar{S}_T$, as a function of market share

A per period, we are also confronted with all the arguments that surround the assumption of stationarity in a Markov process.[19]

Despite the preceding limitations, there are several more things we can learn from the model. We find from equation (8-33) that

$$\frac{d}{dP}\left(\frac{S_A}{S_T}\right)=\frac{(O+P)k_2}{[O+P+(k_2-k_1)P]^2}>0 \tag{8-36}$$

while from equation (8-35)

$$\frac{d}{dP}\left(\frac{\bar{S}_A}{\bar{S}_T}\right)=(k_1-k_2)\frac{d}{dP}\left(\frac{S_A}{S_T}\right)>0 \qquad \text{if } k_1-k_2>0$$

Thus, opening another outlet increases not only the market share but also the average sales per outlet relative to the industry.

The principal drawback of the preceding model, besides those usually stemming from the use of Markov processes, lies in the availability of data. Knowledge of competitors' total sales or average sales per outlet is probably not very accurate – not to mention the problems of identifying the relevant competitors. (Sometimes it is even difficult to determine what the industry of interest is.) On the other hand, if the geographic area is broad enough, government or industrial trade association figures may be applicable. In addition, some competitors are probably entirely regional in character – for example, a drug or grocery chain – and data on these operations should be more accessible.

The principal limitation of the outlet model, availability of accurate data, is especially pertinent to the question of adding salesmen. Data on per-

---

[19] See Chapter 10, "Consumer Purchase Behavior."

formance of competitors' salesmen are probably quite scarce, and the situation may be further complicated by a lack of coincidence of sales territories among the various competitors. On the other hand, this model may be very relevant for certain types of selling situations, such as the cases where salesmen are assigned as specialists to particular industrial groups or all salesmen sell a very limited product line on a national basis.

Establishment of sales territories

The preceding models have spoken to the question of allocation of effort to or within sales territories. We shall now turn our attention to the problem of establishing these territories.

One very reasonable definition of a sales territory is "a number of present and potential customers located within a geographical area and assigned to a salesman, branch, dealer, or distributor."[20] This definition points out a complication in the establishment of territories: The salesman must be easily able to identify the boundaries of his territory or there may be considerable confusion as to whom present or potential customers are assigned. This is why the most usual definition of a territory is based on rather large, easily identifiable political subdivisions of the nation, such as states or counties.

The general goal in territorial design is to have the various territories about equal in potential and work load for the salesmen. Obviously, if such a goal is met, certain kinds of morale problems are obviated and comparison and evaluation of individual salesmen's performance is easier.

But this objective is rather impeded by a large number of factors that might affect the equality of territories. There exist differences in transportation facilities, the intensity of competition, the extent to which the market for the product has already developed, and so on. In addition, the whole matter is further complicated by the quality, or capabilities, of the individual salesmen. A superior salesman might perform well despite severe competition even with a large number of products in his line, whereas the average salesman might not be so successful.

The most widely used method for establishing sales territories is founded upon market data on the geographic distribution of sales for the general product class. Some problems with this procedure are immediately apparent. First, depending on how new or innovative the product is, data may not exist on anything comparable. Second, the impact of the firm itself entering the region may change the sales level in that area; for example, the addition of another salesman may somehow result in expanding both the demand for the product generically and the selective demand for the firm's own product. Third, the precision of the data may be questionable due to

[20] William J. Stanton and Richard H. Busbirk, *Management of the Sales Force*, rev. ed., Richard D. Irwin, Homewood, Ill., 1964, p. 593.

the accuracy with which figures are reported and recorded. Despite these drawbacks, the procedure is still used—possibly because better alternatives are not available and fairly gross estimates of territorial potential are operationally satisfactory. The latter may be especially true where sales potential is dynamic and changes more rapidly than the sales force structure can be revised.

Once we have the distribution of sales according to some geographic designation, we attempt to build territories of equal potential. This is usually done by combining or dividing the geographic regions to get equal potentials and then adjusting the resultant territorial set to allow for the differences mentioned earlier, such as competitive intensity.

Another, somewhat more useful, way to structure territories is to examine the interaction between a territory's size, the number of calls the salesman is expected to make, and the salesman's routing through the territory. First, customers are separated into classes based on the frequency with which they are to receive calls. The call frequency is determined as a function of past business, potential, and so on. Then territories can be made equal based on the expected number of calls per annum, as in Table 8-3. Note how the different distributions of customer types in Table 8-3 all result in about the same call load. The call load per diem is figured at about six, which is reasonable when allowances are made for travel time, waiting time, and the like.

The possibilities for a heuristic or algorithmic approach to territorial design should be obvious. In fact, several authors have used some of the heuristics for warehouse location as a basis from which to develop a territorial model for assigning legislative districts.[21] An improvement on the foregoing heuristics is an algorithm developed by Garfinkel for accomplish-

TABLE **8-3**

Equivalency of territories by number of calls

		Territory X		Territory Y		Territory Z	
Customer class	Call frequency	Number of accounts	Number of calls per year	Number of accounts	Number of calls per year	Number of accounts	Number of calls per year
A	Once per week	10	520	25	1300	10	520
B	Once every two weeks	20	520	5	130	10	260
C	Once every month	30	360	10	120	25	300
D	Once every two months	50	300	30	180	100	600
	Total	110	1700	70	1730	145	1680

[21] S. W. Hess et al., "Nonpartisan Redistricting by Computer," *Operations Research*, Vol. 13, No. 6, November–December 1965, pp. 998–1006.

ing the same job.[22] This work is almost directly applicable to the question of territorial design. Some of the criteria used for evaluating the worth of a particular design for districting would apply equally to establishment of sales territories. For example, one of the criteria is near equality of the districts in terms of population, which can be quickly translated into equal potential or work loads for sales territories. Another criterion is compactness, which may be either geographical compactness or population (potential) compactness, the latter being a function of the distance of the population from the center of the district. Obviously, compactness has significant implications for the utilization of salesmen's time. Other criteria may be readily programmed into the algorithm.

Summary

In this chapter we have intentionally avoided many of the "behavioral" considerations one ordinarily finds in material dealing with sales force management, because we view these factors as being stimuli used to achieve appropriate allocation of the salesman's efforts. Insofar as these motivating factors can be measured, we should be able to handle them in a format similar to the model in this chapter that deals with compensation via commission. As an illustration, sales contests are devices frequently used to influence salesmen's performance, and there is no reason why they cannot be studied analytically to optimize their use. Even in the case of almost exclusively behavioral stimuli, such as training sessions intended to "psych" salesmen into selling hard, if the sales results and the intensity of the behavioral techniques utilized can be measured, then we should be able to model the situation.

The models in this chapter have focused on commission rates in the multiproduct case, allocation of effort to secure new accounts, allocation of efforts among existing accounts, consideration of the appropriate number of salesmen in the sales force, and, finally, some discussion of territorial design techniques. The last area is the one in which the most significant advances in sales force management can be expected. With the exception of the Magee model, which deals with allocation of effort to existing accounts, the models are quite straightforward, and there should be no great difficulties in applying them. There are some minor problems in application, such as classification of customers into groups based on their "value" to the selling firm, but most of the techniques are consistent with already existing practices. On the whole, because of the greater measurability of the models' outputs, significant innovations are to be expected in the modeling of sales force management problems.

---

[22] Robert S. Garfinkel, "Optimal Political Districting," working paper No. 6812, College of Business Administration, University of Rochester, Rochester, N.Y., October 1968.

MASS COMMUNICATIONS

CHAPTER NINE

Communications with the customer may be divided into those forms that are directed to a mass audience and those that are personalized. The former, with which we will deal in this chapter, roughly comprise advertising, sales promotion, public relations, and publicity, whereas the latter focus on the salesman. Salesman-oriented forms of communication have been discussed in Chapter 8. It will be useful, however, to consider the relative emphasis to be given each class of communications in the marketing mix.

Advertising vs. personal sales

The relative emphasis to be placed on advertising and personal sales efforts is primarily a function of the nature of the product or service sold and the character of the market to which it is sold. Certain goods or services are clearly more amenable to mass efforts than others. Table 9-1 presents a list of the factors that should be considered in determining the relative use of advertising and personal sales efforts. Some of these factors are readily quantifiable from data usually available within the firm. However, the nature of the relationships between changes in the enumerated factors and the advertisability of the product is not known. To illustrate, it can be hypothesized that the advertisability of a product will clearly increase as the number of customers in the target group is increased, but it is difficult to say whether this relationship is linear, exponential, logistic, or of some other form. Furthermore, it is even more difficult to speculate on the nature of the interrelationships among the variables that reflect advertisability.

The most essential feature for efficient use of advertising is a perceived difference between the product of concern and its competitors on the part of the consumer. For advertising to be effective, it must convey an image of a difference about the product being advertised. From the standpoint of developing copy for advertisements, actual physical differentiation provides a somewhat stronger and more understandable basis for the selling arguments, but a product or service is not excluded from advertising by the lack of physical differentiation. Both cigarette manufacturers and beer manufacturers have been able to convince consumers of differences in their products. Yet evidence indicates that consumers participating in blindfold tests frequently cannot distinguish one beer from another or one cigarette from another, including their own brands.[1] Cigarette manufacturers establish strong personality characteristics for their products and then attempt to appeal to people who believe they possess these characteristics. In the case of beer, the advertising focuses on differences in the product that are certainly not actual differences—for example, one firm advertises its beer as "the beer with the barrel of flavor." Even if a product does not seem readily differentiable or identifiable, there are means of overcoming such a problem. Advertising a single nut and bolt would be extremely difficult; however, if the nut and bolt are placed with many others and packaged, the package can then carry the manufacturer's brand, and the consumer will be able to identify the product. With appropriate ingenuity, almost any product can be differentiated, but the important question is whether or not this is a profitable strategy.

The size of the market target group is also significant in determining advertisability. If there are only a few potential customers in the group, then personal sales efforts will likely be more effective and efficient (in the sense of cost per customer reached) than mass advertising. To illustrate, a manufacturer of industrial products such as jet engines or air frames would find the use of mass media far too inefficient for his needs; or simi-

TABLE **9-1**

Factors influencing the relative use of advertising effort as contrasted to personal sales effort

Feasibility of product differentiation (physical or imagined)
Size of market target group
Geographic dispersion of customers
Distribution of average order sizes
Frequency with which item is purchased
Dollar value of single unit

[1] See, for example, Ralph I. Allison and Kenneth P. Uhl, "Influence of Beer Brand Identification on Taste Perception," *Journal of Marketing Research*, Vol. 1, August 1964, pp. 36–39.

larly, in the ultimate consumer market, a producer of expensive, high-quality furniture would depend far less on mass media than one producing furniture for a very broad market. Of course, the notion of "mass media" is relative; there are many journals with very focused circulations – directed to certain classes of industrial buyers, for example.

The number of customers in the target group is related to two other factors that affect advertisability: the geographic dispersion of these customers and the distribution of the dollar value of purchases among them. If the market is widely dispersed geographically, although the total number of potential customers may be large, generalized use of mass media will be less effective than for a market target group of the same size that is highly concentrated. Not all mass media are ruled out, though, because the manufacturer may be able to reach some areas at reasonable cost through media with limited audiences, such as newspapers and local radio stations. As for the dollar value distribution, although the number of customers purchasing high dollar amounts may be very small, their purchases may account for the majority of sales. Thus, although the total number of customers may be large, there may be only a few who are really important, and personal sales effort directed toward these customers would be more effective than the use of mass media.

Another factor that influences advertisability is the frequency of purchase. The more frequently an individual purchases a good, the greater the number of opportunities available for advertising to alter his brand preferences. If a good were purchased many, many times in the course of a year, the cost of attempting to reach the individual prior to each purchase through personal sales effort would be enormous – consider, for example, what this would mean in terms of selling foodstuffs. Mass media, on the other hand, make it possible to expose the individual to the manufacturer's chief arguments relatively near to each purchase experience. Some goods that are purchased relatively infrequently, such as automobiles, major appliances, and other consumer durables, are also advertised heavily; this is partially a result of the high price tag attached to these items, which provides a large number of dollars for communicating with the customer. Some support for this position is given by Bucklin, who has found that shoppers purchasing items that are not convenience goods rely on advertising information more for high-priced items, less familiar items, and less frequently purchased items.[2]

Emphasis on advertising does not exclude significant use of personal sales effort, or vice versa. For example, a producer of detergents may spend substantial sums on advertising but must still allocate reasonable effort to building and maintaining dealer relationships through personal sales work; were he to do otherwise, he might find himself with a large consumer de-

[2] Louis P. Bucklin, "The Informative Role of Advertising," *Journal of Advertising Research*, Vol. 5, September 1965, pp. 11–15.

mand and insufficient product available in the distribution system. A similar example is the combination of mass communication and personal sales work used in the selling of automobiles.

Although each of the factors just discussed provides useful information about whether or not the product can or should be advertised, the manner in which successful advertising affects the company's sales and profits has not yet been mentioned. Essentially, advertising is a form of non-price competition and thus shifts the demand curve to the right—that is, greater quantities are demanded at each price. The worthwhileness of an advertising program may thus be judged via marginal economic analysis: The contribution margin on the additional units sold because of advertising would be determined and compared to the cost of the advertising program. Unfortunately, it is easier to state the underlying theory than to make an actual assessment. In order to estimate the gain from advertising, the firm would have to know what sales would be in the absence of advertising; in an ongoing operation this is a difficult figure to determine, though not impossible, as we shall subsequently discuss. Furthermore, there are interaction effects between advertising and the other elements of the marketing mix that complicate evaluation of the contribution margin. In sum, the factors in Table 9-1 may be thought of as somehow affecting the promotional elasticity of demand; that is, the relative effectiveness of an advertising dollar in changing the quantity sold depends on the inherent advertisability of the product.

Objectives of an advertising program

A necessary condition for success in any advertising program is a clear definition of the objectives of that program. This statement strongly influences not only the techniques that will be used but also the size of the appropriation and the ability to measure whether or not the objective has been achieved. This means that the objective should be structured in such a way that it induces assessment of the advertising program and at the same time facilitates the task of evaluation.

Broadly speaking, there are two classifications into which all advertising falls: The first is selective demand stimulation and the second, primary demand stimulation. When a company attempts to persuade consumers to purchase a specific item from its product line through use of mass communications, it is undertaking selective advertising. The major portion of advertising undertaken in this country is of the selective type. Primary demand stimulation, on the other hand, is an attempt to persuade the consumer to buy the generic product classification. The individual manufacturer reasons that if demand for the whole product—that is, the output of all manufacturers—can be increased, he will in some way share in that increase, yielding higher profits than he might otherwise have experienced.

Primary demand stimulation can occur under several different circumstances. For example, when a new product departs considerably from existing products, the innovating manufacturer may attempt primary demand stimulation to familiarize the public with this product. As a case in point, the first manufacturer of electric blankets advocated electric blankets per se rather than his own particular brand; such an action may have been necessary because consumers were wary of the safety of such a product, its actual warmth, etc.

A second kind of primary demand stimulation is that undertaken by trade associations. Frequently, trade associations attempt to expand the generic product's demand through vigorous advertising campaigns undertaken as a result of inroads by other kinds of products or, perhaps, an assessment that the industry is not keeping up with the general rate of growth in the economy. One widely known example of this type of advertising is the American Dairy Association's campaign to induce people to drink more milk.

A third type of primary demand stimulation is institutional advertising, which attempts to feature the firm or organization as opposed to its product or services. Two chief purposes are usually (1) to make the consumer aware of the company's brands so that he will transfer his loyalties across product line members, and (2) to create a favorable image for the company in case it should face government prosecution or any other adverse public exposure. Generally speaking, institutional advertising attempts to create good will for the company as a whole.

Obviously, such considerations are too broad to lead to any kind of reasonably measurable performance. The advertiser must specify his objectives on a narrower basis. Each time an advertsing objective is selected, the corresponding measure that will be utilized to ascertain whether or not that objective has been achieved should also be specified. Therefore, some common objectives, such as increasing the firm's share of market, should not be accepted as viable objectives for the advertising program; too many other variables affect market share, and it would be almost impossible to isolate the effect of advertising.

At this point, some examples of objectives that are considered feasible for the advertising program may be helpful. Suppose analysis has shown that it is advisable for the company to attempt to raise the size of the average purchase, that is, to increase the unit or units of purchase. This is a readily measurable goal, and if advertising is the primary means utilized to achieve this goal, then we have a measure of whether or not the advertising program has been successful.[3] At the same time, the goal is so specific that it facilitates the selection of appropriate copy themes and possibly the selection of media. In addition, other kinds of promotional aids, such as point-of-pur-

[3] Obviously, the problem of evaluation becomes more complicated in inverse proportion to the importance of advertising in the marketing mix, but measurement is still far from impossible.

chase displays, could readily complement the mass advertising effort. Some other objectives that might be specific enough to yield assessable advertising programs might be to educate the consumer in the proper use of products, to introduce a new package design, to induce changes in the level of consumer awareness, and so on.

In addition to specifying how attainment of objectives shall be measured, each proposed advertising effort should be evaluated in terms of whether or not it contributes to profit as well as alternative expenditures might. For example, a company might undertake an advertising program aimed at bringing new customers to the company, and in terms of the number of new customers who were induced to purchase from the company the program would be termed a great success. However, a careful assessment prior to beginning this program might have shown that the present value of the expected profits per customer from additional customers was not sufficiently high to merit the effort expended in getting them. That is, the opportunity costs indicate that the money could have been spent more profitably on some other effort. In this case, it is not the advertising program that is at fault, because its objective was achieved. It is the earlier analysis that underlay the decision to get new customers that is at fault.

It might be argued that many legitimate advertising goals cannot be put into such a specific framework as we have advocated. This is not really the point at issue; rather, it is that when insufficient effort is put into carefully delineating advertising objectives, failure of the advertising program or disenchantment with it is usually the principal result. If advertising is to be utilized properly, its effect must be assessed as strenuously as that of all the alternative elements in the marketing mix—one would never undertake a price reduction without having some clear idea of how its effect on sales was to be measured after the action was taken. This same rigor must be applied to advertising decisions.

The measurement of effectiveness

Advertising effectiveness is presently evaluated by (1) measuring the audience size and characteristics of media alternatives, and (2) measuring specific characteristics of individual advertisements. Obviously, the link between the stimulus provided by an advertisement and the achievement of a sale is extremely complex. Thus, the tendency is to identify variables that look as if they are closely related to the advertisement's or medium's effectiveness and to assess the value of the ad or medium in terms of how high a score it achieves on these surrogates. For example, one widely used criterion of effectiveness in measuring media value is audience size—readership of printed media, which includes both initial circulation and those who see a medium subsequently as a result of a pass-along, can, for practical purposes, be considered synonymous with audience size. The value of an audience is determined by the proportion of its members who possess the demographic, socioeconomic, and other characteristics held by the market target group. The uses to which measurements of audience size are put, such as in preparing a schedule of advertisements to be placed in the diverse media, will be discussed in several subsequent sections of this chapter. At that time we will also consider the problem of precision in measuring audience size and characteristics.

The most commonly used means for evaluating printed individual advertisements are recognition and recall methods[4] and various attempts to measure attitudinal change after exposure to the advertisement. In addition, certain types of advertising yield highly measurable results in and of themselves—for instance, direct mail advertising and couponing, either for ordering purposes or requests for information. Correspondingly, various copy ideas can be tested by use of split runs[5] in printed media, which yield pertinent data on the effectiveness of the ads in creating sales or requests. Measurement of attitudinal change is also widely used for visual, nonprinted media, such as television. To illustrate, a sample of persons is given free tickets to a showing of a special film program that includes several potential television commercials; information on the viewers' preferences between some of the products featured in the program and other products is collected before and after the showing, and changes occurring with respect to the advertised products are assumed to have been induced by the advertisements.[6]

It is not always possible to identify directly the effect of the thematic content of advertisements on sales, although, theoretically, it should not be difficult with an appropriate experimental design.[7] Experimentation in the marketplace has been particularly useful in this connection. For example, in one experiment, sales differences resulting from differences in two campaign themes and several other factors were assessed.[8]

---

[4] These focus on questioning a person about whether or not he remembers having seen a particular advertisement and asking him to detail as much of the ad as he can recall. For a full description of this technique, see Darrell B. Lucas and Stuart H. Britt, *Measuring Advertising Effectiveness*, McGraw-Hill, New York, 1963, pp. 46–101.

[5] In a split run, different issues of a catalog, or the like, carry different advertisements for a particular company. The usual practice is to run two differing ads, each one in half the copies. The practice is widely used by mail-order houses in their catalogs and is also sometimes employed by advertisers in general magazines, but the measurement of effectiveness in this latter case is based on recognition and recall and not directly tied to sales.

[6] Of course, appropriate controls are used to assess how much shifting occurs anyway without the particular stimuli, and so on.

[7] Peter L. Henderson, James F. Hind, and Sidney E. Brown, "Sales Effects of Two Campaign Themes," *Journal of Advertising Research*, Vol. 1, December 1961, pp. 2–11.

[8] A generally excellent reference on the subject of experimental designs for studying marketing is Seymour Banks, *Experimentation in Marketing*, McGraw-Hill, New York, 1965.

We have chosen, however, not to concern ourselves with the problem of measuring the effectiveness of the creative aspects of advertising, such as layout and copy. That is not to say that the problem is unimportant, but rather that we believe that (1) it is more in the domain of the technical specialist than of the manager, and (2) many of the techniques used in such work would carry us into behavioral research and considerations outside the scope of this book—for example, some of the research in this area is based on physiological responses to advertising stimuli.[9] Despite this omission, much of the subsequent discussion does depend on "reliable" work in assessing the creative element. To illustrate, when we discuss response, we are interested principally in the exposure of an individual to part of an advertising campaign; but obviously, if an advertisement is particularly powerful in the creative sense, one exposure may impress itself upon the viewer's memory as strongly as five exposures to a more ordinary advertisement.

Another managerial problem related to creativity is how much to spend in creating an advertisement, or advertising campaign, versus how much to spend in publishing it. This question has been thoroughly studied by Gross, and he concludes that, generally, too little is spent on creation relative to publication.[10] As far as what we can obtain for the sum we have decided to spend on creation is concerned, it is feasible to have some notion of the relationship between effort, as reflected in the talent costs, and creative result. In fact, if one is willing to accept the precision of the proxy variables used by some marketing research services (for example, the Schwerin scores on television advertisements or the Starch scores on magazine readership), it is possible to define a relationship between creative effort and the scores attained on selected proxy variables. Then, given this relationship, objectives can be established for advertisements and the corollary cost of the creative effort can be determined.

Determination of the appropriation

In the previous section we spoke of measuring advertising effectiveness from two standpoints, the measurement of the effectiveness of the advertisements themselves and of the vehicles utilized. Now we shall deal with another aspect of effectiveness, namely, how much money to spend on an advertising program, *in toto*, either for a budgetary period or for a

---

[9] An illustration of how unusual these measurement techniques may be is the work of Eckhard Hess on the development of pupillometrics. See, for example, Eckhard H. Hess, "Pupillometrics," *Applications of the Sciences in Marketing Management*, Frank M. Bass et al., Eds., Wiley, New York, 1968, ch. 15.

[10] See Irwin M. Gross, "An Analytical Approach to the Creative Aspects of Advertising Operations," Case Institute of Technology, Cleveland, Ohio, November 1967, unpublished Ph.D. thesis.

campaign comprising specific advertisements and vehicles. That is, whereas before we gave our attention to the question of getting maximum use from the number of dollars we had available, we now address ourselves to the evaluation of what number of dollars to spend. The general problem we shall be dealing with is that of modeling sales response to advertising expenditures.

It is frequently argued that the gross margin on an article must be large enough to support an advertising program. These arguments have little basis, because the important consideration should be the effectiveness of using advertising in the marketing mix relative to emphasizing other elements of the mix. If advertising is more efficient than whatever other means are being considered, funds can be reallocated to advertising without demanding an increase in the gross margin. Of course, it may be that with an increased gross margin, advertising in combination with the other factors may produce greater net benefits, but this is a matter of a budgetary constraint rather than ability to afford advertising.

Much research has been directed at measuring advertising effectiveness in the ways described in the previous section. Unfortunately, there have been far fewer analytical attempts to deal with the size of the total advertising budget. Essentially, the existing methods for establishing budget size are (1) to take a percentage of past or forecast sales, (2) to spend as much as the company can afford in terms of its marketing operations, (3) competitive parity—that is, to spend amounts equal or proportional to what competitors are spending, (4) the "objective and task approach," and (5) mathematical modeling.

The first three methods are self-evident. The fourth approach is similar to that described in the section dealing with objectives of advertising. A fuller description of this approach would be: (a) specific objectives are established, (b) the various markets, the different media, the thematic approaches, and so on, to be used are derived from the goal, and (c) the attendant cost is tabulated. A principal argument against this method is that the cost to reach all objectives may be a greater sum than management wants to expend on advertising or that the company can afford. The counter argument is that another method, such as percentage of expected sales, can be used as a control, thus forcing the advertising executives to justify expenditures beyond some normal percentage amount. This method also has the advantage of causing management to rank the objectives in order of importance, since the available amount of money will always be too little for the number of objectives and supporting tasks that the advertising department could undertake. However, as Alfred Kuehn has pointed out, the biggest drawback to widespread use of the task method ". . . lies in our inability to evaluate with acceptable accuracy the effectiveness of the budgets proposed under the task method. The objective specified in the task method is seldom, if ever, stated in terms of profitability."[11] Thus, the objectives must be ranked on less desirable bases than profit.

Strictly speaking, although we have been addressing ourselves to the effect of advertising on profits, management may have other objectives that can affect the size of the advertising appropriation. Little and Ackoff report on a situation where such a goal was programmed into their analysis to determine the budget size. They report that

> In the case at hand the results indicated that a large planned increase in advertising expenditures by the company was not justified on the basis of profits alone. The company, however, placed a value on growth as well as on profits. Management was willing to place a dollar value on each million dollars of additional sales. An adjustment was then made in the determination of the annual budget to take into account the value of growth to the company's management. This led to a substantial increase in the estimate of optimal annual advertising expenditures.[12]

Another approach to establishment of total budget size, developed by Robert Weinberg,[13] is based on forecasting of sales for the industry and the company and the relative position of the company in the industry. First, a relation between industry sales and the economic environment is developed for use as a predictor of sales; the technique used is interesting but of no great concern here. Next, the relationship between industry sales and the sales of the particular company is expressed as

$$S_c(t) = M_c(t)S_i(t) \tag{9-1}$$

where the subscripts c and i refer to the company and the industry, $S =$ sales, $t =$ the time period, and $M_c =$ company share of the market. With this equation it is possible to establish the historical pattern and determine the extent to which changes in S_c have been a function of changes in industry sales or an expansion or reduction of market share.

The market share factor, M_c, is obviously the result of a series of strategy interactions among the company and its competitors. These exchanges are really nothing more than attempts of the company to improve its position, and at a more microcosmic level they can be examined with respect to the type of marketing activity involved—advertising, new product development, sales force efforts, etc. The formula for determining the advertising rate of exchange for the company in period t is defined as

---

[11] A. A. Kuehn, "Models for the Budgeting of Advertising," in *Models, Measurement and Marketing*, Peter Langhoff et al., Eds., Prentice-Hall, Englewood Cliffs, N. J., 1965, p. 127.

[12] John D. C. Little and Russell L. Ackoff, "How Techniques of Mathematical Analysis Have Been Used to Determine Advertising Budgets and Strategy," in *Proceedings of the Advertising Research Foundation*, 4th annual conference, New York, N.Y., October 1958. Advertising Research Foundation, New York, 1958, p. 21.

[13] Robert S. Weinberg, *An Analytical Approach to Advertising Expenditure Strategy*, Association of National Advertisers, New York, 1960.

$$E(t)_c = \text{exchange rate} = \frac{R_c}{R_i} \times 100 \tag{9-2}$$

where R_c and R_i are dollars of advertising per sales dollar for the company and for the rest of the industry.

The exchange rate is given as a percentage. Therefore, if the firm is below the industry as a whole, we can determine if its efforts are stronger or weaker than those of the industry. In addition, if the company's share of the market improves while its exchange rate is 100 or less, we can reasonably surmise that its advertising dollars must be more productive than those of its competitors.

Since advertising expenditures will affect market share, according to their relative effectiveness, we compute the change in market share, ΔM_c, and plot it against E or ln E. In the latter instance, a very good fit has been obtained in several studies made by Weinberg.[14] Thus, we have an equation of the general form

$$M_c(t_1) - M_c(t_0) = a \ln E(t_1)_c + b \tag{9-3}$$

A point of clarification about the time periods would be useful; the market share evaluations are really point estimates taken at the beginning or end of each year, whereas the exchange rate is for the entire period (year). In words, equation (9-3) reads (market share at end) − (market share at beginning) = function of exchange rate over entire period. Obviously, we could test for the appropriateness of other equational forms; the procedures would not change substantively if we were to use a different form.

We can now use equation (9-3) to determine the total size of the advertising budget as follows: If the firm's management wishes to increase its sales by a certain amount, we ascertain the required change in market share, if any, based on forecast industry sales. Residual industry advertising expenditures R_i are also forecast. We then compute the E necessary to yield the desired ΔM_c from equation (9-3), the corresponding R_c in equation (9-2), and, finally, the required advertising expenditure, since we already know the desired company sales, S_c. Note that we are able to find the dollars of advertising necessary to maintain the company's position in the industry relative to anticipated changes in general industry sales or competitive tactics.

What difficulties might be encountered in the use of the foregoing model for establishing budget size? First, one of the difficulties of this approach lies in the validity of the data inputs in the exchange ratio—the values for industry advertising expenditures are often merely best guesses. Second,

[14] For example, in one study the explained variation was $r^2 = 0.996$, the standard error of estimate was .03 percent, and n was seven years.

what is an appropriate definition of an industry?[15] Finally, it may well be that changes in market share and the advertising exchange rate are correlated because of an operating rule of thumb that is widely employed but not obvious; an analogy is the high correlation between sales and advertising when the budget amount is based on a percentage of forecast sales. One tends to be somewhat suspicious of such high values of explained variation, especially when the direction of causality may be the opposite of what is suggested.

Another model that attempts to get at the question of total budget size is that of Vidale and Wolfe.[16] After extensive experimentation they found that they could characterize the interaction of sales, S, and advertising, A, by the differential equation

$$\frac{dS}{dt} = rA(t)\,\frac{M - S(t)}{M} - \lambda S(t) \tag{9-4}$$

There are three parameters in this model, all of which can be determined either historically or through controlled experimentation. The saturation level, M, is "the practical limit of sales that can be generated" in response to a specific advertising effort. This is a function of the media used as well as of the character of the product. The response constant, r, is defined as "the sales generated per advertising dollar when sales equal zero."[17] It is assumed that advertising affects only sales to noncustomers and not the retention of current customers. The difference between the saturation level of sales and the current level represents potential customers. Finally, the decay rate, λ, is the rate at which sales decline in the absence of promotion and under relatively stable market conditions. In one situation, Vidale and Wolfe found that favorable publicity caused sales to rise markedly, but that without sustained promotion the original decay rate was soon resumed.

In the steady state—that is, when we wish to advertise enough to maintain sales at some level—we would set dS/dt equal to 0 and obtain

$$A = \frac{(\lambda/r)SM}{(M - S)} \tag{9-5}$$

which offers the conclusion that the larger the ratio λ/r and the nearer the sales to the saturation level, the more expensive it is to maintain the required sales rate.

If we wish to expend a constant amount on advertising for a time period T, the rate of sales is found, by integrating the differential equation, to be

---

[15] This question is discussed in more detail in Chapter 10, pp. 247–248.

[16] M. L. Vidale and H. B. Wolfe, "An Operations-Research Study of Sales Response to Advertising," *Operations Research*, Vol. V, No. 3, June 1957, pp. 370–381.

[17] *Ibid.*

$$S(t)=\frac{M}{1+\lambda M/rA}+\left\{S_0-\frac{M}{1+\lambda M/rA}\right\}\exp\left[-\left(\frac{rA}{M}+\lambda\right)t\right] \qquad t<T \tag{9-6}$$

When advertising ceases, sales decrease exponentially:

$$S(t)=S(T)\exp\left[-\lambda(t-T)\right] \qquad t>T \tag{9-7}$$

The solution conforms with the accepted notion of diminishing marginal returns; that is, the earlier dollars spent on advertising are more effective than the later ones, which are spent closer to the saturation level.

This model permits us to make some interesting comparisons. For example, if we have a fixed sum X to spend on advertising for the firm's fiscal year, we can compare the effects of spending it in many different ways. We might hypothetically spend a constant amount each month, $X/12$, the whole sum at once at the beginning of the year, half the sum now and half six months later, and so on. Under each alternative we would be able to compute the net gain for the whole fiscal period and determine which approach produced the greatest sales.

Generally, this model is quite instructive. The ability to compare the effects of different expenditure strategies over time is certainly valuable. In addition, the three parameters on which the model is based are highly useful conceptually in understanding the effects of advertising. On the other hand, the feasibility of determining such parameters in practice is a serious drawback (but one that could probably be overcome by controlled experimentation on a limited basis, say, in a few markets). Some other limitations of the model have been pointed out: (1) lack of recognition of the effects of different thematic content used in the same media and with the same size budget, (2) a failure to allow for competitor's actions where they may be important in determining the advertising budget level, and (3) the notion that advertising only affects noncustomers. However, these drawbacks can be refined out of the model by introducing additional complexity. One might, for example, substitute a more complex function for r. The decision as to whether there is sufficient payoff to warrant the additional complexity is one that must be made in the context of a specific situation.

Benjamin and Maitland[18] have made some simple empirical studies of four other functional forms of the relationship between advertising and sales. These are as follows.

(1) A logarithmic response curve,

$$S=B\ln A+C \tag{9-8}$$

This is Weber's law of psychological response to stimuli.

[18] B. Benjamin and J. Maitland, "Operational Research and Advertising: Some Experiments in the Use of Analogies," *Operational Research Quarterly*, Vol. 9, March–April 1958, pp. 207–217.

(2) The cumulative normal curve,

$$\frac{S}{S'} = \int_0^A \exp\,[-Kx^2]\,dx \tag{9-9}$$

where S' is the limiting value of S as A becomes infinitely large. This is the curve used in probit analysis.

(3) An exponential response curve,

$$\frac{S}{S'} = 1 - e^{-A} \tag{9-10}$$

(4) Another law of diminishing returns,

$$\frac{S}{S'} = \frac{(A/b)^2}{1 + (A/b) + (A/b)^2} \tag{9-11}$$

Note that each of the four functional forms has one or more parameters to be fitted but that, with the exception of S', these parameters have little to contribute conceptually.

Benjamin and Maitland have tested the models against data obtained by dropping leaflets at different concentrations and measuring response by field surveys of the level of knowledge of the message dropped. Their conclusion was that over the entire range of responses the logarithmic curve was the most suitable (the probit analysis actually had a slightly better fit, but it is more cumbersome to use because it requires a greater amount of computation). Benjamin[19] subsequently applied the logarithmic model to two direct mail campaigns with very good results.

Just as experimental designs have been widely used in attempts to measure the sales due to individual advertisements, they have also been applied to the correlation of sales response to the level of spending on advertising. There is ample literature on this subject; for example, Henderson[20] and Jessen[21] report studies that utilized experimental designs. We shall not explore these techniques in depth because they involve fundamentally little more than the classical statistical procedures and are by no means unique to advertising decision problems.

The principal difficulty in measuring sales response to advertising is sim-

---

[19] B. Benjamin, "The Measurement of Advertising," *Applied Statistics*, Vol. 15, June 1966, pp. 65–73.

[20] Peter L. Henderson, "Measuring Effects of Varying Levels of Advertising Investments on Sales of Third Mills," in *Proceedings: Annual Meeting of Business and Economic Statistics Section of the American Statistical Association*, Philadelphia, Pa., 1965. American Statistical Association, Washington, D.C., 1965, pp. 218–226.

[21] R. I. Jessen, "A Switch-Over Experimental Design to Measure Advertising Effect," *Journal of Advertising Research*, Vol. 1, March 1961, pp. 15–22.

ilar to that of measuring the effect of individual advertisements, identification of the causal relationship by way of which advertising ultimately results in sales. Somehow, one is inherently distrustful of a process that cannot be specified. In this connection, Palda[22] has reviewed the literature on the hierarchy of effects that move the individual from perception of an advertising message to ultimate purchase.[23] The evidence he cites leaves considerable doubt about the existence of this hierarchy. Moreover, Nakanishi has definitively demonstrated that such a hierarchy does not exist for at least two grocery items and that evaluation is a post-purchase phenomenon.[24] Nakanishi speculates that his findings may hold for most packaged convenience goods. Perhaps, however, Palda has asked the truly pragmatic question: "Is it, on balance, really more difficult and expensive to investigate the direct link between advertising expenditure and sales, than it is to undertake research into each step of the hierarchy—*even if the existence of a hierarchy of effects were actually established*?"[25]

Selection of advertising media: the CAM model

Regardless of how the firm establishes total budget size, at some point it must decide how the monies are to be allocated among the different vehicles that might carry its advertising. Should all the money be spent on television? Or newspapers? Or billboards?[26] If not, what combinations of these should be used? Having decided upon vehicles, how often should they be used and, if relevant, at what time of the day or night? This process is usually referred to as *media scheduling*.

Two important problems in selection of media are (1) making comparisons among different vehicles where the proxy variables used to measure effectiveness are only weakly related to sales and may not even be expressed in similar terms, and (2) determining the "effectiveness" of a total schedule. An example of the first type of problem is found in trying to relate audience size for a television program to a magazine's circulation. There may be several opportunities to expose a reader to a magazine advertisement inasmuch

[22] Kristian S. Palda, "The Hypothesis of a Hierarchy of Effects: A Partial Evaluation," *Journal of Marketing Research*, Vol. III, No. 1, February 1966, pp. 13–24.

[23] One widely referenced formulation of this flow is Attention → Interest → Desire → Action.

[24] Masao Nakanishi, "A Model of Market Reactions to New Products," Graduate School of Business Administration, University of California at Los Angeles, June 1968, unpublished Ph.D thesis.

[25] Palda, *op. cit.*, p. 23; emphasis in original.

[26] Most media scheduling work concerns itself only with press, radio, and television. It is important, however, to recognize that the problem can be cast in a wider setting to include less common vehicles, such as billboards, handbills, direct mail literature, and so on.

as the magazine's "life" is fairly long, whereas there is only one opportunity on a specific television show. In addition, the problem is further complicated by attempting to define *reader*; certainly, the number of readers is larger than the number of subscribers, but does it include a person who occasionally thumbs through a particular magazine in a doctor's office? Similarly, does a person have to see all of a particular television show to qualify as a viewer?

The measurement of schedule effectiveness is really a matter of determining the marginal rates of return for specific vehicles and specific frequencies. Until recently, the right mix of media was determined by a person who was similar to a master brewer, blending the ingredients until the schedule seemed right for achieving the desired objectives. More recently, mathematical programming and simulation procedures have been developed that are intended either to substitute for the brewer altogether, at least in some aspects, or to improve the decision-making process by allowing very rapid examination of a much greater number of alternatives. The simulation we describe in the following is of the latter type. Our purpose in presenting it is twofold: (1) to provide a basis for discussing many of the key problems in measuring advertising effectiveness that are incorporated into this model, and (2) to demonstrate how a modern tool, such as simulation, can be used on what is really nothing more than an institutional checklist and yet produce a substantial increase in the sophistication of the methodology.

The media scheduling simulation presented here is that developed by the *London Press Exchange*.[27] At several points in their description of their work, the developers emphasize that optimization as regards the media scheduling problem is probably impossible while retaining the richness of the simulation model. Rather, what they hope to do is to give the media planner more information about the character of the response surface so that he can learn more about the underlying structure of the problem.

Figures 9-1 and 9-2 are flowcharts of the Computer Assessment of Media (CAM) model.[28] A study of these charts will show that there are many inputs that are entirely qualitative in nature. These are the areas in which the skilled media planner contributes significantly to the model. This need not be considered a drawback of the model, for previous methods were almost entirely dependent on the planner, so CAM must be at least as good if the level of skill is held constant. On the other hand, an actual drawback of the model is its failure to assess the varying results of advertisements, depending on how they are spaced over time. For example, the model might

---

[27] E. M. L. Beale, P. A. B. Hughes, and S. R. Broadbent, "A Computer Assessment of Media Schedules," *Operational Research Quarterly*, Vol. 17, December 1966, pp. 381–411.

[28] The symbols in the flowcharts are those suggested by the American Standards Association Committee on Computers and Information Processing as described in Gordon B. Davis, *An Introduction to Electronic Computers*, McGraw-Hill, New York, 1965, pp. 97–104.

suggest 20 advertisements in a particular daily newspaper, but one should expect quite different results if they were all scheduled within a single month as compared with their being spread out over an entire year.[29]

The flowcharts are quite complex, so let us spend some time developing an overview of the model before delving into its structure in detail. A sample audience of possibly as many as several thousand adults is established, based on studies of the television viewing and printed media readership habits of the population in Great Britain. These studies contain data that provide the probability of an adult viewing at a particular time by quarter-hour segments for the week and the probability of seeing a particular advertisement in a printed medium. This latter probability is based not only on knowledge of which media are read but also on examination of how people proceed through the contents of a newspaper or magazine and their ability to recall the matter on a given page.

Certain demographic and socioeconomic information is also gathered about the sample audience. The advertiser specifies the importance of various demographic and socioeconomic characteristics of his market target group, and a subsample is selected in weighted proportion to these charac-

---

[29] In all fairness to Beale et al., we must report that no model of which we are aware does very much with dynamic campaigns. On the other hand, timing is a sufficiently important subject that we feel it appropriate to reference the literature here and let the reader decide the worthwhileness of the available literature for himself. Lee has attempted to treat dynamic campaigns, but he has done little more than lend formal structure to the problem. See Alec M. Lee, "Decision Rules for Media Scheduling: Dynamic Campaigns," *Operational Research Quarterly*, Vol. 14, December 1963, pp. 365–372. Similarly, Stasch has indicated that the basic linear programming approach (see below, pages 229–233) can be modified to handle the time at which an advertisement appears by means of a series of static constraints and objectives, but he does not come to grips with the dynamic nature of the problem. See Stanley F. Stasch, "Linear Programming and Space–Time Considerations in Media Selection," *Journal of Advertising Research*, Vol. 5, December 1965, pp. 40–46. Another topic related to timing is the carryover effect of advertising, which considers how long the effect of a campaign lasts on an individual. Tull has summarized some of the literature on the subject and has conducted an experiment that purports to show the existence of such an effect. See Donald S. Tull, "The Carry-over Effect of Advertising," *Journal of Marketing*, Vol. 29, April 1965, pp. 46–53. Palda has examined this question for a particular company and concluded that the duration (in years) of the cumulative effects of advertising expenditures can be described by a distributed lag model. See Kristian S. Palda, "The Measurement of Cumulative Advertising Effects," *Journal of Business*, Vol. 38, April 1965, pp. 162–179, and *The Measurement of Cumulative Advertising Effects*, Prentice-Hall, Englewood Cliffs, N.J., 1964. Telser has shown that advertising builds a fund of goodwill that depreciates at a rate of 15–20 percent per annum, and he has calculated marginal rate of return on advertising capital. See Lester G. Telser, "Advertising and Cigarettes," *Journal of Political Economy*, Vol. 70, October 1962, pp. 471–499. Finally, Kuehn has suggested that a better way of measuring advertising effectiveness might be to compute the distribution of time periods between exposures rather than the distribution of exposures. See A. A. Kuehn, "A Model for Budgeting Advertising," in *Mathematical Models and Methods in Marketing*, Frank M. Bass et al., Eds., Richard D. Irwin, Homewood, Ill., 1961, pp. 315–348.

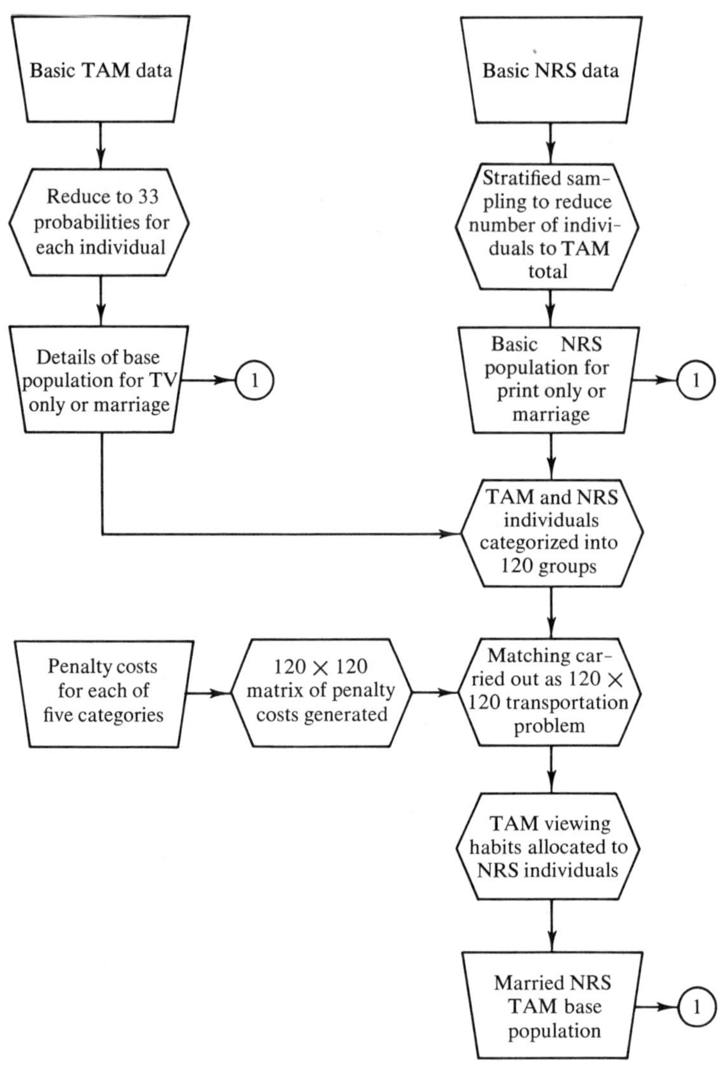

FIGURE **9-1**

CAM simulation: quarterly update program

teristics. A potential media schedule is chosen. The "value" of each medium in terms of its match with the desired target group characteristics and the "impact" of each advertisement in a specific vehicle is estimated by the advertiser and the agency. These data along with the aforementioned probabilities of viewing or reading are used to obtain the number of impressions each advertisement will produce in each vehicle. This number of impressions is divided by the cost of the particular vehicle to provide the valued impressions per pound (£) that is later used in planning additions and deletions to the proposed schedule. At the same time, the impressions for all items in the originally proposed base schedule are cumulated over all individuals and the resulting distribution of the number of individuals receiving one, two, three, . . . , n impressions is weighted by a response function that reflects the estimated worth of an additional impression given that a certain number have already been received. This produces a single figure of effectiveness for the base schedule. Potential media additions to and deletions from the schedule are then evaluated in terms of the change in effectiveness they produce divided by the changes in cost, which yields the marginal rate of return for the addition or deletion. The final output provided by the simulation is the effectiveness of the base schedule plus the marginal rates of return for contemplated changes in the schedule, and the planner makes his substitutions according to this latter information.

We shall now proceed to use the CAM model as a means of introducing some of the important topics in measurement of advertising. In order to aid our discussion, we have prepared Table 9-2 (see page 216), which summarizes the principal variables in the CAM model and the data sources underlying these variables. Again, with regard to the qualitative variables, that is, those based on judgments, the developers indicate that sensitivity analyses and several other tests of their procedures do not alter results to the point where the model no longer conforms with existing evidence or with what the present media planner thinks is an appropriate schedule for a given objective. For example, a comparison of the number of TV ads seen in specific time periods as given by the Television Audience Measurement survey data versus CAM estimates showed very little discrepancy.

Let us now begin a detailed examination of the CAM model. The question of who is exposed to an advertisement is a deceptively simple one. A quick answer would be the audience that observes or hears a particular program or the people who purchase a specific printed medium. But in actuality these groups are only starting points in the estimation process, and even they are not that easily estimated.

First, consider how we may determine the audience for a television or radio program. The two most widely practiced methods are (1) the coincidental telephone method, in which homes are called and the person answering is asked what program he is watching or listening to; and (2) use of a mechanical device that records the program to which the set is tuned. In this pure form, both have notable drawbacks. The person answering the phone may report other than what is actually the case,[30] and those families

[30] Several studies have shown that people report magazine readership or television viewing habits that lend status to themselves—for example, reporting readership of the *Atlantic Monthly* or viewing of educational television programs.

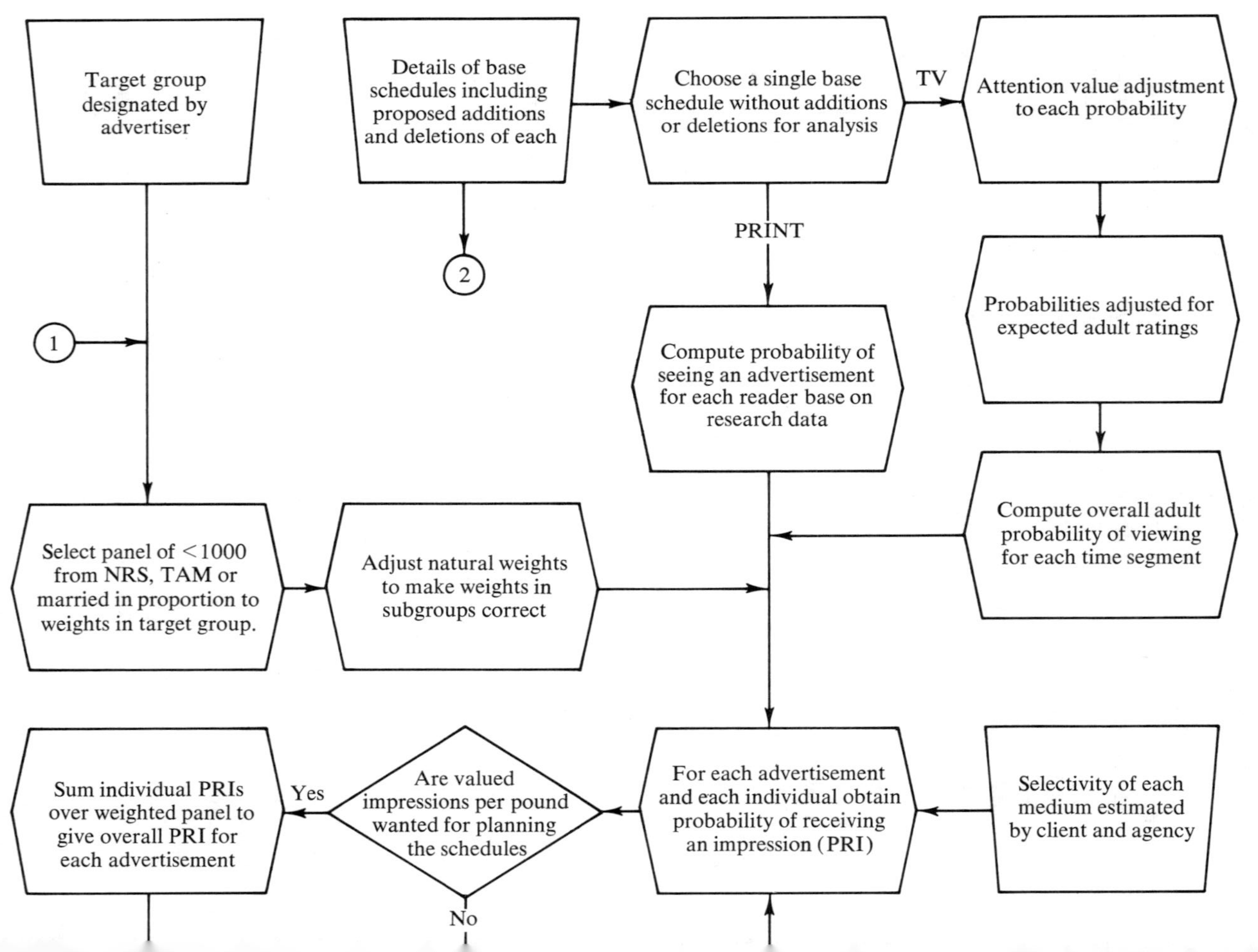
Target group designated by advertiser
Details of base schedules including proposed additions and deletions of each
Choose a single base schedule without additions or deletions for analysis
TV
Attention value adjustment to each probability
2
PRINT
1
Probabilities adjusted for expected adult ratings
Compute probability of seeing an advertisement for each reader base on research data
Compute overall adult probability of viewing for each time segment
Select panel of <1000 from NRS, TAM or married in proportion to weights in target group.
Adjust natural weights to make weights in subgroups correct
Sum individual PRIs over weighted panel to give overall PRI for each advertisement
Yes
Are valued impressions per pound wanted for planning the schedules
No
For each advertisement and each individual obtain probability of receiving an impression (PRI)
Selectivity of each medium estimated by client and agency

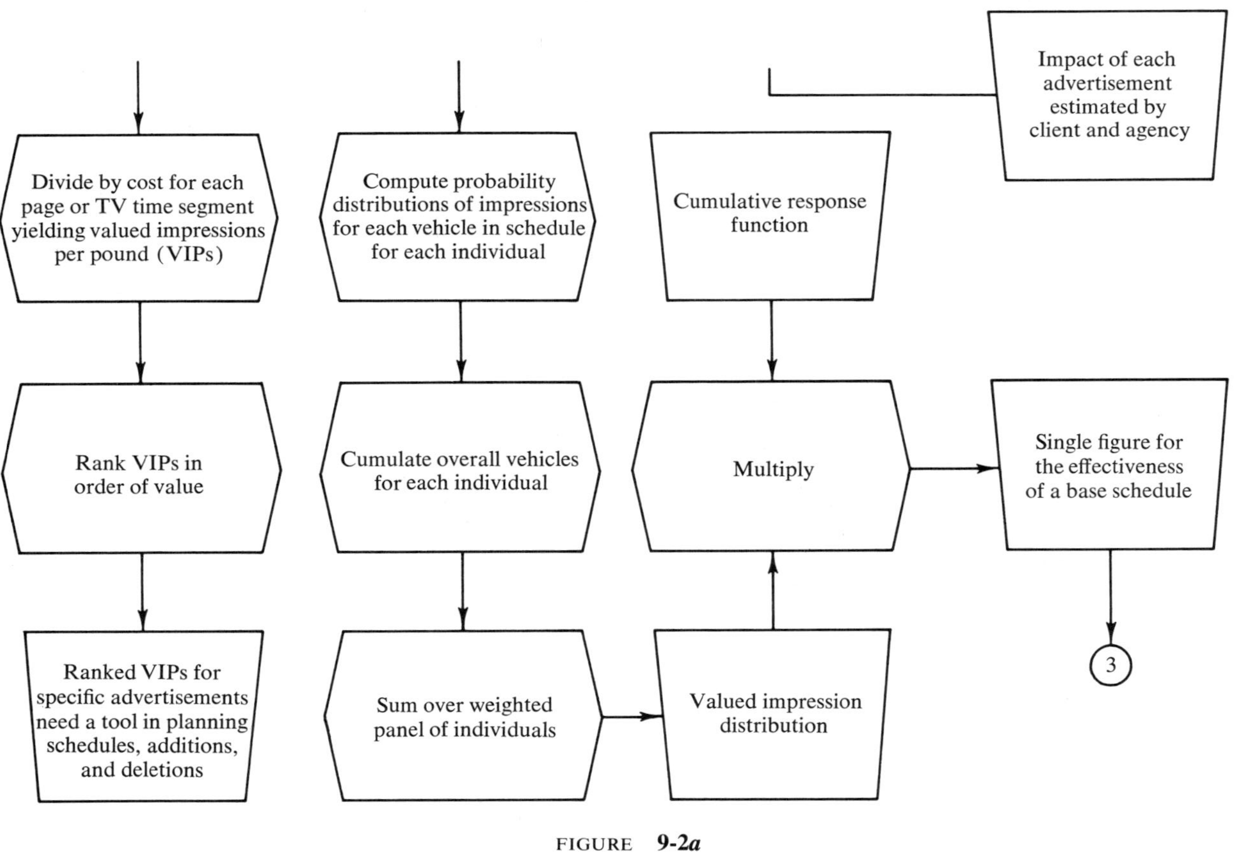

FIGURE **9-2*a***

CAM simulation: evaluation of base schedules

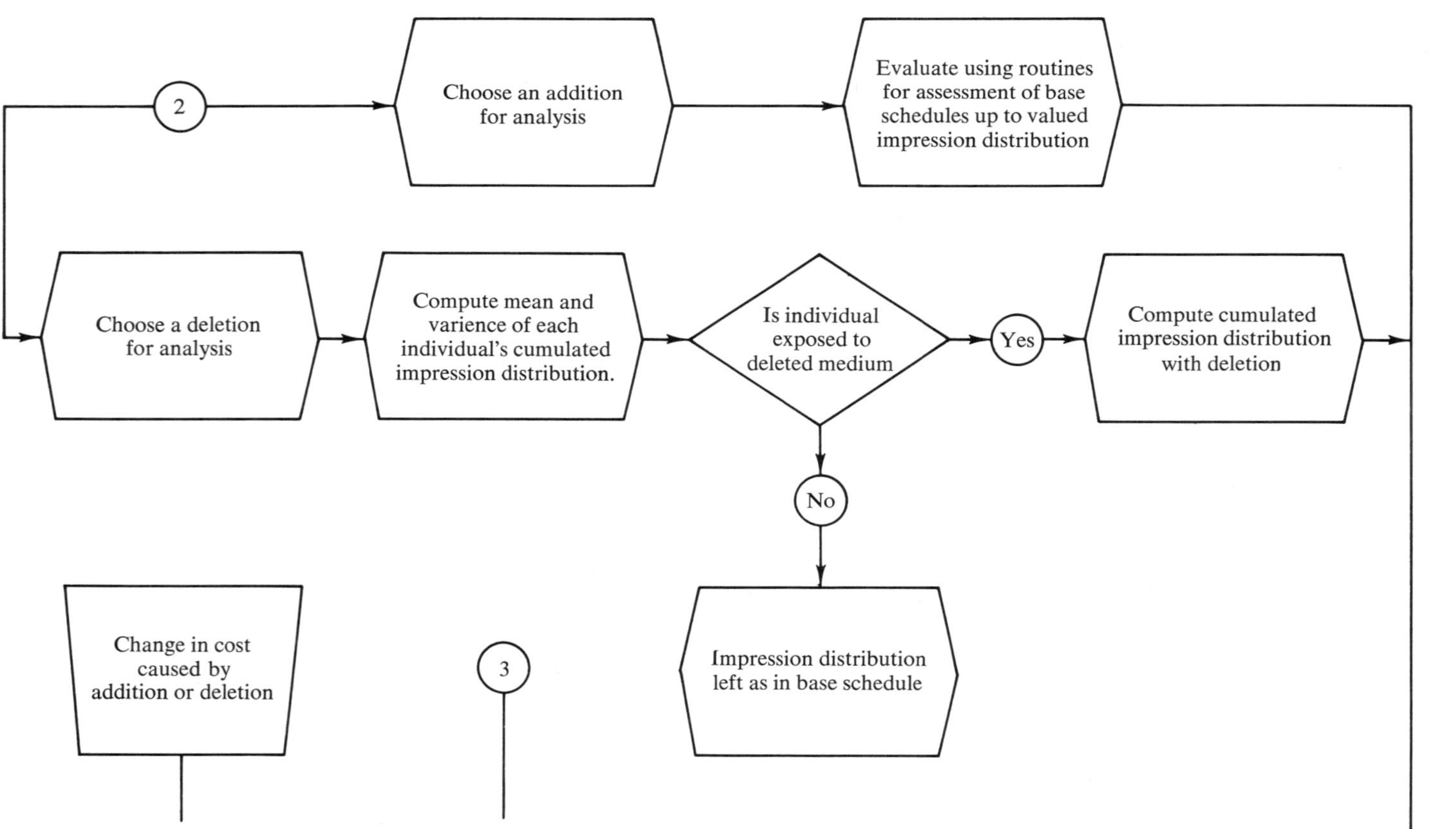
2
Choose an addition for analysis
Evaluate using routines for assessment of base schedules up to valued impression distribution
Choose a deletion for analysis
Compute mean and varience of each individual's cumulated impression distribution.
Is individual exposed to deleted medium
Yes
Compute cumulated impression distribution with deletion
No
Impression distribution left as in base schedule
Change in cost caused by addition or deletion
3

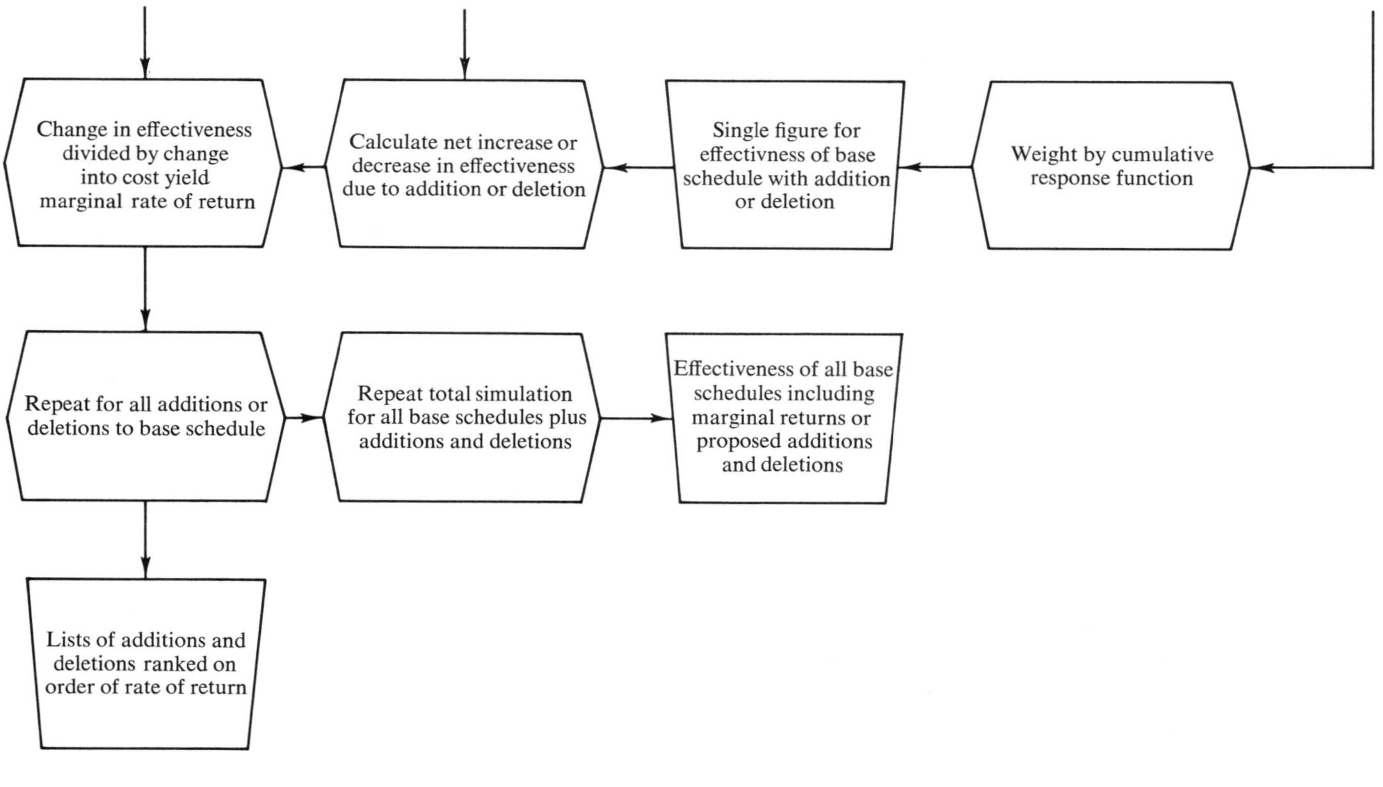

FIGURE **9-2*b***

CAM simulation: investigation of additions and deletions

TABLE 9-2

Variables in the CAM program

Variable	Data input
Viewing habits of individuals	Television Audience Measurement (TAM) panel, including demographic information.
Reading habits of individuals	National Readership Survey (NRS), including demographic and TV viewing index.
Attention value of TV time segment	Proportion of TV viewers in a specific time interval who actually see a commercial, as opposed to going out for a beer, etc. This is similar to perception.
Percentage of adults viewing TV in a time segment	*Buyer's forecast based on unusual ratings due to special program content, or the like.
Adjusted probability	Mathematical adjustment of individual's viewing habits to yield the buyer's forecast of percentage of adults viewing TV time segment.
Perception	Research on page traffic and attention paid to advertising, yielding probability of a reader seeing an advertisement.
Penalty costs	*Estimated by buyer and management.
Target group	*Socioeconomic characteristics designated by firm's management as describing people they want to see the advertisement.
Weights on population characteristics	*Designated by management on scale of 0 to 100 (most important).
Base schedule	*Selections of media planner among available alternatives.
Selectivity	*Buyer's or management's rating on scale of 0 to 100 (best editorial context) of the value of an individual's seeing an advertisement in a particular medium, in addition to considering match of viewership with target population, cost, probability of seeing an advertisement, and so on.
Impact	*Buyer's or management's estimate on scale of 0 to 100 (best creative effort).
Probability of Receiving Impression (PRI)	*$\underbrace{\text{Adjusted probability} \times \text{Attention value}}_{\text{or Perception}}$ × Selectivity × Impact
Response	*Cumulative function based on buyer's estimate of additional response for each impression added.
Valued impressions per pound	*PRI divided by cost in pounds (£).
Impression distribution	Cumulation of individual probabilities of receiving a specific number of impressions from a single vehicle.
Effectiveness	*Impression distribution weighted by cumulative response function.

* Variables that are subjective in nature or derived from variables that are subjective.

without telephones must necessarily be excluded from the sample.[31] Similarly, a mechanical device notes only whether the set is on, but not whether anyone is in the immediate area listening to or observing the program.[32] These drawbacks can be overcome, though—for the coincidental method by means of questioning about program content and for the mechanical by the keeping of a diary.

Second, others besides the purchaser of a printed vehicle read it. The daily newspaper is read by several but not necessarily all family members and not necessarily every day for each of them. Of course, the same would be true of any magazine. However, given an appropriate definition of *reader*, the question of total number of readers can be answered for almost any vehicle by fairly straightforward marketing research. Such information is available from several services and frequently from the medium itself.

Another matter of great importance is the structuring of a representative sample for estimating the number of readers and viewers.[33] The sampling problem in television and radio is further complicated by the potential variation of audience size within a specified time period. For example, the size of the audience in any half-hour segment changes as a function of the number of people who become dissatisfied with the program and switch to others or vice versa, who shut off or turn on the set, who enter and leave the listening and viewing area (say, while completing other household activities), and so on. By and large, however, the audience estimation and readership problem is fairly well handled with existing technology. The preceding issues have been introduced to illustrate the potential complexity of the situation before raising the question of what proportion of the readers or viewers see the advertisement.

Determining whether or not an advertisement has actually been seen or heard involves a somewhat more tenuous process than measurement of the number of people who may have been exposed. The most common way to determine if someone has been exposed to an advertisement is to question

---

[31] There is substantial debate about the merit of methods that exclude parts of the population (another one frequently cited is consumer panel data, which may exclude the income extremes of the population—that is, the very poor, whose education may be such that they cannot keep diaries carefully enough and the wealthy who do not wish to be bothered and to whom the proffered rewards are insignificant). One rationale is that most products using mass media are intended for the middle socioeconomic groupings, broadly defined, where the mass market is anyway.

[32] This issue was one of the most widely discussed in the Congressional hearings on measurement of audience size as it is reported by various television rating services.

[33] An excellent treatment of the theory of sampling at an advanced level is that of William G. Cochran, in *Sampling Techniques*, 2nd ed., Wiley, New York, 1963. A somewhat more applied approach is Leslie Kish, *Survey Sampling*, Wiley, New York, 1965. This topic was also a subject in the Congressional hearings on television rating systems.

him about it. But this procedure fails to separate the physical aspect of noticing the advertisement from the one of remembering it because of the creative effects. To illustrate, a person watching a television program may have been exposed to a particular commercial for an analgesic, but he cannot remember having seen that particular commercial at the specified time slot; on the other hand, if the commercial was unlike any other he had ever seen before in a way that was highly attractive, he would be more likely to remember the situation. A similar analogy can, of course, be made for printed media.

The most widely used methods for determining exposure to an advertisement are, however, still based on memory; that is, quite soon after the potential exposure the person is questioned with respect to whether or not he recalls having seen the particular advertisement. This may be done by showing the respondent part or all of the advertisement (obviously, this is readily feasible only for printed media), giving various clues to help him recall what advertisements he may have seen; or by general questioning about what advertisements he recalls having seen recently, with no clues. These methods are generally referred to as *recognition* and *recall.* Their drawback is that they succeed more in determining the creative effects of an advertisement than in assessing pure physical noting.[34] In the case of printed media, however, there have been several studies directed solely at determining page exposure that enable one to make some reasonable speculations about exposure,[35] and it is this information that the CAM model utilizes.

An examination of the CAM model shows that the foregoing problems have been handled as follows: For printed media, each person's reading habits are adjusted by available information on page traffic and exposure to advertisements specifically, resulting in an estimate of the proportion of the population who will see the advertisements in a publication being considered. Adjustment is also made for regularity of readership of a publication.[36] For visual media there is some research on the proportion of viewers seeing a commercial, and these data are used to determine the attention value for a particular time segment.

Besides the attention value adjustment, another very important adjustment is made to the viewing data. The number of individuals observing a program can vary quite widely over the average for the time segment as a whole for the reasons already discussed. Thus, a commercial shown at dif-

---

[34] The value of these methods in measuring creativity is taken up at a later point in our discussion of the CAM model.

[35] Lucas and Britt, *op. cit.*, ch. 12.

[36] Techniques that might be suitable for making adjustments are similar in character to those discussed later in the section on audience duplication. For a specific discussion see S. R. Broadbent, "Regularity of Reading," *Journal of Marketing Research*, Vol. 1, No. 3, August 1964, pp. 50–58.

ferent times on a program or in different weeks within a series can have audiences of very different sizes. In the CAM model, the media buyer should ". . . have a good idea what adult rating he expects to obtain for each of the spots he is considering"; that is, he must be able to anticipate significant departures from the average audience size in various time slots. These adult rating estimates are then used to adjust the individual viewing probabilities by use of the process we now describe.

The choice of an appropriate adjustment to the probability, p, that an individual views in a particular quarter-hour is constrained by the fact that p must vary only between 0 and 1. Thus, the addition or subtraction of a constant from p would not be a suitable means of adjustment. The developers of the CAM model contend that the most logical approach is to use a logistic transformation that will permit the adjustment factor to vary from plus infinity to minus infinity and still leave p between 0 and 1. That is, we shall be adding or subtracting a constant from $\ln \{p/(1-p)\}$.

To obtain an overall adult rating of P, the buyer's estimate of the percentage of adults viewing a TV time segment, we must have

$$P = Q(1 - p_a - p_n) + p_a \tag{9-12}$$

where Q = the average adjusted probability of viewing

p_a = the proportion of adults who always view at this time

p_n = the proportion of adults who never view at this time

The right-hand side of equation (9-12) is composed of two elements: those who always watch in that particular quarter-hour, p_a, and who we are therefore sure will be in our audience, and another group composed of those who sometimes watch. Since the latter is the variable component of the audience, it is upon this group that we need to make our adjustment to obtain a specified P. The average adjusted value Q is not used directly but, rather, becomes part of an adjustment factor x, which is obtained as a polynomial in $y = \ln [Q/(1-Q)]$:

$$x = a_0 + a_1 y + a_2 y^2 + a_3 y^3 \tag{9-13}$$

The individual adjusted probability of viewing, p', is then defined by

$$\ln \frac{p'}{1-p'} = \ln \frac{p}{1-p} + x \tag{9-14}$$

which can be rewritten as

$$p' = \frac{pe^x}{1 + p(e^x - 1)} \tag{9-15}$$

The values of the coefficients a_0, a_1, a_2, a_3 are chosen by least squares to make the overall adult rating as equal to the desired value P as possible. If

p' is plotted against p, a bow-shaped curve results, passing through (0, 0) and (1, 1). If x is positive, the curve lies above the diagonal, and if negative, below. When $x = 0$, the curve coincides with the diagonal.

At this point in the CAM model, the developers review their assumptions and treatment of the data and attempt to demonstrate their validity. They do this by comparing the frequency distributions of television advertisements (seen) based on predictions by the CAM model to actual data collected by TAM for several regions and several weekday and weekend combinations. The data for the predicted distributions are extremely close to the actual case.

The next step in the CAM simulation is to combine the two groups of sample data, one containing the television viewing habits of a representative group of persons and the other the reading habits of a different representative group. The matching is done on the basis of similar demographic and socioeconomic characteristics of the individuals and some limited amount of information about the viewing habits of NRS individuals, particularly the number of days in a week in which television is viewed.

Matching of individuals is a very widely used procedure, but not necessarily carried out in the above fashion. In marketing research it is a common procedure to attempt to develop two groups of individuals whose characteristics are very much alike in order to use one as a control group in an experimental design.

The actual matching in the CAM model is carried out by taking a stratified sample from the NRS data, which contain many more individuals than TAM, and marrying each of these to a TAM individual. Numerical measures of the discrepancy between the demographic and viewing characteristics of potential pairings of TAM and NRS data are defined on a judgmental basis; these are called *penalty costs*. For each of the five characteristics on which matching is done—sex, age, with or without children, social grade, and television viewing intensity—separate penalty cost submatrices are prepared; these have 0's in the diagonal elements, to indicate perfect matching, and positive elements elsewhere. These penalties for individual characteristics are added together when the submatrices are amalgamated into a 120×120 square matrix of overall penalties. The problem of matching may then be viewed as an assignment problem in linear programming, and the transportation method is used to resolve it.

With the matching complete, we now have a sample of persons with their total viewing and reading habits. In addition, the program can also make separately available an NRS sample for testing printed-media-only schedules or a TAM sample of persons with adjusted viewing probabilities for testing TV-only schedules. The programs that produce the samples are updated quarterly to reflect changes in the basic TAM and NRS data.

The program assessing various schedules has two starting points: (1) designation of the market target group toward whom the product is aimed, and (2) selection of several possible base schedules with possible additions and deletions of vehicles, time slots, or the like by the media planner. For the former, the advertiser specifies which demographic and socioeconomic characteristics are important in influencing the purchase of his product, and these are weighted on a scale of 1 to 100. The weights are taken as being multiplicative and may be assigned wherever there are data on the population; for example, in some cases information on product usage is available. The weights for each category are then applied to the sample selected, after first correcting for the fact that only a proportion of those with the desired characteristics are selected. These operations result in what the developers call *natural weights* for the target population. In turn, the program allows for these natural weights to be adjusted to their correct known values for selected subgroups; for example, the weighted readership of a particular publication may not be correct after the previous weighting manipulation, so a correction is now made. We shall discuss the base schedule inputs later.

Next, two variables are introduced into the CAM model that are based entirely upon judgment. These are *selectivity* and *impact*; the former refers to the environment in which the advertiser's message may appear, whereas the latter is concerned with the creativity of the advertisement itself. These can be very influential in the selection of vehicles. For example, an advertiser might not wish to advertise in *Playboy* even though the audience coincided highly with a part of his product's target group because of a fear that the general image of his product will be affected adversely. Also, supermarket and other food advertising in newspapers is mostly run later in the week (Wednesday, Thursday, and Friday) in order to reach its audience just before marketing day. Similarly, some advertisements are probably more effective than others because of the character of the creative effort; that is, the advertisement may be thought to be more likely to evoke response in the form of purchase or to be remembered longer, etc. Impact, as used herein, is also taken to reflect differences in size of the advertisement and the use of color if printed, in the length of the commercial if on TV, and so on.[37] The developers of CAM do not make the distinction, but it is important to remember that an advertisement does not have to be clever, witty, sophisticated, urbane, or the like to have substantial impact; in fact, some advertisements that seem esthetically reprehensible may have great favorable impact for the advertiser—obviously, there is the possibility of negative impact, too. Selectivity and impact are assigned values on the same

[37] Diamond has demonstrated the relationship between various factors such as color, size of advertisement, number of words, headline prominence, etc., and advertising effectiveness in printed media as measured by a proxy variable, the Starch Readership score. See Daniel S. Diamond, "A Quantitative Approach to Magazine Advertisement Format Selection," working paper 277–67, Alfred P. Sloan School of Management, Massachusetts Institute of Technology, Cambridge, Mass., 1967.

basis. The best environment for the firm's advertisements is defined to have a value of 100 and other contexts are assigned values relative to this one. Correspondingly, the best advertisement is assigned a value of 100 and others defined relative to it. For both factors, "best" is operationally defined on the basis of experience. The advertiser, however, might consciously select not to use the best advertisement and best vehicle because of the cost or the number of persons reached.

Impact and selectivity can now be combined with perception or attention value and the adjusted probability of viewing to form a new and very important variable, the Probability of Receiving an Impression. Thus, for any individual:

$$\text{PRI(visual)} = \text{adjusted probability} \times \text{attention value} \times \text{selectivity} \times \text{impact}$$

$$\text{PRI(print)} = \text{perception} \times \text{selectivity} \times \text{impact}$$

The concept of the PRI is essential to the CAM model: It is the basic unit of measure of effectiveness. For example, for each TV advertisement that may be used in the campaign under consideration, we can sum the PRI's over the entire weighted panel for any geographic region on any day of the week in any time segment of interest. We can perform a similar operation for printed media. If these totals are now divided by the cost in pounds for the appropriate time segment or page, a new figure, called Valued Impression per Pound (VIP), is obtained. These VIP figures may now be ranked, and the media planner can use them to develop his base schedules and potential additions and deletions. The VIP is similar to another widely used yardstick for evaluating a medium, cost per thousand persons reached, but it is much richer because of the various other factors it encompasses. For example, a frequent criticism of the cost-per-thousand approach is that it does not reflect the coincidence of the audience with the target group of the advertisers; on the other hand, the VIP measure does. The same advantages also exist regarding the other factors composing the VIP. Therefore, despite the inclusion of some highly qualitative factors, such as selectivity and perception, we expect the VIP to be a much more valuable measure.[38]

Although useful for evaluating single insertions, the VIP does not apply to entire campaigns. The problem now is to accumulate impressions (the PRI's) upon the individual and assess the value of different numbers of impressions by means of the response function. In the CAM model, response is defined as the usefulness of an additional impression. The developers recognize that the data that can be used to define response functions are quite limited. They do believe, however, that persons within the agency and

---

[38] Several advertising agencies have developed formal models for media selection that are fundamentally based on marginal analysis similar to ranked VIP's. See, for example, William T. Moran, "Practical Media Decisions and the Computer," *Journal of Marketing*, Vol. 27, July 1963, pp. 26–30.

the advertiser's firm should be able to indicate their feelings about whether additional impressions will be of value relative to the objective of the current campaign. This response function is not defined to have any particular mathematical form, but examination of the data obtained from agency and advertisers' personnel shows the following to be extremely common:[39]

(i) Step functions: These state that at one or two or three impressions the job of the campaign is done and further impressions are unnecessary.

(ii) Linear functions: These state that response rises steadily, each successive impression being equally valuable. There may be a limit, after which there is no further increase in response, or the increase may be unlimited.

(iii) S-shaped functions: These are popular in the literature and correspond to the notion that a few impressions do little good, while after a certain number there is little additional response; in the middle range response increases more rapidly.

(iv) Geometric functions: These state that each additional impression adds to response a constant fraction of the amount added by the previous impression.[40]

Schedule evaluations may use different response functions for different schedules or for different parts of a single schedule. Or the same schedule can be evaluated under different assumptions about the character of the response function(s), in effect providing a sensitivity test of the schedule's overall effectiveness. Finally, response is not dimensional, since it is solely a vehicle to facilitate comparison of alternatives, and the response function is used in the cumulative form for computational convenience. The response function is also useful in formulating a base schedule. For example, if the media planner wished to reach as many people as possible at least once, he would strongly limit the repetitive use of each vehicle. If many impressions per individual were wanted, he would use the VIP as his principal planning tool, resulting in a much shorter schedule of vehicles. With the aid of the ranked VIP's and the response function, the media planner can now prepare several base schedules, including potential additions and deletions, for evaluation.

Assessment of a given schedule proceeds by taking the weighted viewers and computing the PRI for each individual for each advertisement, printed

---

[39] In a subsequent paper, one of the CAM developers quite thoroughly surveyed existing knowledge about response functions and concluded that most of the evidence indicates that the linear function is the most satisfactory fit of available data and the geometric function the second most satisfactory. Interestingly, the logistic function is found to be quite unsuitable. See S. R. Broadbent and Susanna Segnit, "Response Functions in Media Planning," *London Press Exchange*, October 1967. Another critique of the character of response functions may be found in M. H. J. Webb, "Advertising Response Functions and Media Planning," *Operational Research Quarterly*, Vol. 19, No. 1, March 1968, pp. 43–59.

[40] E. M. L. Beale, P. A. B. Hughes, and S. R. Broadbent, "A Computer Assessment of Media Schedules," *Operational Research Quarterly*, Vol. 17, December 1966, p. 399.

or viewed. Duplication—that is, exposure of one individual to several vehicles—does not have to be accounted for in the CAM model because the data are at the individual level and no approximation of this effect is required.[41] Next, we must cumulate the impressions received by each individual across all the vehicles to obtain the distribution of impressions that result from the schedule under evaluation, that is, his probability of receiving no impressions, one, two, . . . , etc. Cumulation of impressions is handled in the CAM model as follows: The probability of receiving a given number of impressions from a single vehicle may be expressed by use of the binomial formula:

$$p_i = \binom{n_r}{i} P_r^i \, (1 - P_r)^{n_r - i} \tag{9-16}$$

where r = a vehicle such as a publication or TV time segment

p_i = the probability of receiving i impressions from the rth vehicle

n_r = the number of insertions in vehicle r

P_r = the individual's PRI for a specific advertisement in vehicle r

To cumulate over several vehicles from which impressions might be received, we would convolute

$$C_j' = \sum_{i=0}^{j} C_{j-i} P_i \tag{9-17}$$

where C_j = the probability of receiving j impressions from vehicles $1, \ldots, r-1$

C_j' = the probability of receiving j impressions from vehicles $1, \ldots, r$

Since use of the above formula is quite laborious and time consuming, even on a computer, the CAM developers use the device of grouping the probabilities around discrete points and linearly interpolating for probabilities between these points.

The final step is to calculate the expected response, using the individual frequency distributions of impressions given above. Obviously, some distributions will be more valuable to us than others, and this fact is reflected in the character of the response functions utilized.

Thus, to obtain our final measure of the schedule's effectiveness, we weight each frequency distribution of impressions by the individual's weight in the panel, sum across all individuals, and then weight this overall impression distribution multiplicatively by the response function. This procedure is very similar to that which we describe in discussing mathematical programming approaches to media scheduling, so we do not repeat it here.

---

[41] In some models that work with total audience size for a particular vehicle, this is a very important correction that must be attempted. See section on Audience duplication.

The remaining tasks for the CAM model are the evaluation of additions and deletions. Additions are handled in the same way as the main program, each one or each group being treated as if it were another element in the original program; that is, a PRI is calculated for each individual and each advertisement and then the impressions are accumulated. The marginal rate of return, defined as the percentage improvement in effectiveness as given by the change in the total number of impressions obtained for a 1-percent increase in cost, is calculated. All or some of the additions may be used or a decision may be delayed until the potential deletions are evaluated and the percentage gain in effectiveness, if any, is ascertained for a set of deletions and a set of additions with equal costs.

Deletions cannot be computed by reversing the cumulation process because the procedure is numerically unstable. The basis for the deletion method used is that the probability distribution for the number of impressions produced on an individual by a particular schedule is approximately binomial, having mean $\Sigma n_r P_r$ and variance $\Sigma n_r P_r(1 - P_r)$, where n_r and P_r are as previously defined. Examination is first made of whether an individual has been exposed to the medium deleted; if not, the mean and variance remain as before. If the individual has been exposed, the mean, m, and variance, v, of the impression distribution after the deletion are computed exactly, and parameters n and p for the distribution after deletion are chosen in such a way as to make the mean and variance of this distribution as nearly equal to m and v as possible, subject to the restriction that n must be a whole number.

Thus,

$$n = \frac{m}{1 - v/m}, \quad \text{rounded to the nearest whole number}$$

$$p = m/n \tag{9-18}$$

Beale et al. provide detailed descriptions of examples of the use of CAM that highlight its sensitivity and demonstrate its general utility in media planning. Before reporting these examples, a few comments about the scope, or capability, of the CAM model are in order. In Table 9-3 we summarize the

TABLE **9-3**

Variants per run of principal factors in the CAM model

Factor	Number of variants
Schedules	9
Number of insertions per vehicle	72
Response functions	11
Key groups (market target)*	8
Additions or deletions	300

* These are special subgroups for whom we have deemed a separate assessment of the planned schedule worthwhile.

number of variations that can be processed per computer run for each of the principal components of the CAM model.

Clearly, a great deal of information is available in a single run, revealing much about the response surface. In fact, the case may now be that digestion and interpretation of the results of a run become a more significant problem than estimation of response.

The material that follows is an operational description of how the CAM model is used.[42]

We first give an example of an ordinary, typical job. The product concerned is sold to motorists and motorcyclists. A budget of about £350,000 was available for a national advertising campaign for which both television and press are considered suitable.

The target population

The following sets of weighting factors were decided upon to define the target group weights.

Definition	Weighting factor
Motorist	100
Nonmotorist	10
Male	100
Female	25
Aged 16–24	85
Aged 25–44	100
Aged 45+	65

The schedules

The media planner considered that a television schedule supplemented by press was likely to be the best approach. He was uncertain how large the press share should be. He wrote one schedule in which press takes 13 percent of the appropriation and another in which it takes 21 percent; we called these Schedules 1 and 2. He also wished to check his opinion that this emphasis on television is correct. He wrote a press-only schedule costing £306,000 which we called Schedule 4. Schedule 3 was the television portion of Schedule 1 and had the same cost as Schedule 4.

Additions and deletions

The media planner prepared a list of 35 publications for consideration as possible additions to schedules basically involving television. He used 9 of these publications in Schedule 1. He wished to know if any of those he had included should be omitted, or, alternatively, whether more advertisements should be taken in them. He also wished to know if any of the other 26 publications should be substituted. He required similar evaluations for Schedule 2 and for the television portions of both these schedules. In all 283 possible additions and deletions were to be assessed.

[42] Beale, Hughes, and Broadbent, *op. cit.*, pp. 405–408. Reprinted by permission of Operational Research Society Ltd.

Judgement factors

Three different response functions were specified. Each of these attached less value to the first few impressions received compared with those received subsequently. The accent in the campaign was on obtaining a large number of impacts rather than a high cover.

The impact of a 45-second spot (the only length considered) was considered to be 100; a half-page press insertion was considered to be 50. Different publications had different selectivities; Friday and Saturday on television had higher selectivities than other days of the week.

The computer run

As the main schedules that we wished to assess were mixed television and press, the married tape was used as the source population. The tape contained 2295 individuals; the panel selected contained 564 individuals. Forty-five separate characteristic groups were used.

Conclusions

We give an outline of the main conclusions drawn from this run.

1. *Was emphasis on television correct?* We compared Schedule 3 (television only) with Schedule 4 (press only). The effectiveness figures with the "best" response function were 12.0 and 7.8 respectively. This indicated that with the judgement factors as chosen, television appeared to be the better medium for the campaign. This conclusion was the same with all three response functions tried. The two media produced quite different shapes of impression distribution. If the response function had given greater emphasis to impression cover, i.e. the percentage of the target receiving one impression, then press would have been chosen as the following table shows.

TABLE 5

	No. impressions (%)	1–20 impressions (%)	At least 24 impressions (%)
Television	15	58	27
Press	3	92	5

2. *How much press should be added to the television schedule?* Schedule 1 had an effectiveness of 14.1 compared with 14.0 for Schedule 2. The difference was hardly significant, but it indicated that if anything the press element should be small as in Schedule 1.

3. *Improvement of Schedule* 1. The program prints out for each base schedule full lists of the additions and deletions that have been evaluated, sorted in order of their marginal rate of return.

Consideration of the table of deletions indicated that the late Saturday spots in Region 6 (South Wales and West and the Northeast) and Region 5 (Scotland, Northeast Scotland and Border) could be dropped with least loss in effectiveness.

The next television spots on this table all had about the same marginal rate of return; we picked one in Region 2 (Midlands) as the table of additions shows there is a good segment here in which to reinvest: we deleted some of the 8:0–8:30 p.m. Friday spots.

In press, the *Daily Express, TV Times* and *Reader's Digest* could be dropped with least harm to effectiveness. Thus we arrived at the list of deletions shown in Table 6. They removed about £46,000 from the schedule and dropped effectiveness by only 10 percent.

TABLE 6

Deletions

Description	No. of spots or advertisements		Marginal rate of return	Saving (£)	Percentage loss in effectiveness
	Original	Deleted			
Region 2, Friday, 8:0–8:30 p.m.	18	8	0.8	8800	2.1
Region 5, Saturday, 11:0–11:30 p.m.	12	12	0.7	3948	0.8
Region 6, Saturday, 11:0–11:30 p.m.	12	12	0.5	4860	0.7
Daily Express, ½ page	6	6	0.8	18,000	4.0
TV Times, full page	3	3	0.8	5400	1.2
Reader's Digest, full page, 4-colour	4	4	0.9	4900	1.2
			Totals	45,908	10.0

TABLE 7

Additions

Description	No. of spots or advertisements		Marginal rate of return	Cost of change (£)	Percentage gain in effectiveness
	Original	Added			
Region 1, Saturday to 3:45 p.m.	27	7	2.7	2100	1.6
Region 1, Saturday, 11:0–11:30 p.m.	12	3	2.1	2025	1.2
Region 1, Friday, 6:30–7:0 p.m.	–	2	1.6	1950	0.9
Region 2, Saturday, 11:0–11:30 p.m.	12	15	1.7	6975	3.3
Region 4, Saturday, 11:0–11:30 p.m.	12	14	2.1	2395	1.5
Region 5, Saturday, 5:15–5:45 p.m.	–	16	1.8	3072	1.5
Daily Mirror, ½ page	6	10	1.5	16,240	7.1
Daily Sketch, ½ page	6	10	1.4	4250	1.7
Reveille, ½ page	3	7	1.3	4130	1.5
Do-it-Yourself, full page, face matter	4	4	1.6	1012	0.5
Car Mechanics, full page, face matter	4	4	4.3	960	1.2
Practical Motorist, full page, face matter	4	4	6.2	840	1.5
			Totals	45,949	23.5

We reinvested the £46,000 where it did most good as indicated by the table of additions. We noticed that *Practical Motorist* and *Car Mechanics* are outstanding and we added here up to the maximum (8, since this is an 8-month schedule). We increased the number of insertions in four other publications, particularly the *Daily Mirror*. We also added some of the best television spots. We arrived at the list of additions shown in Table 7 which increased effectiveness by about 23 percent.

Because the marginal rates of return for the additions we made were higher than for the deletions, the net result of all these changes was an increase in schedule effectiveness. The increase was approximately 13 percent. While there is no exact cash equivalent, as a proportion of the appropriation this was over £40,000.

Assumptions

In making these calculations we have assumed that the effect of the additions or deletions in individual media as calculated in the program can be added together. How justified is this assumption in practice? Obviously in pathological cases we could not do this. There is, of course, an easy test: we can rerun the program to reassess the amended schedule. We have done this for various early trial runs and this gave us sufficient confidence in our assumptions. The total change, as calculated by summing the separate effects (applying in effect a series of partial derivates of effectiveness with respect to the various media in turn, all measured at the same point on the response surface), turned out to be close to the exact change.

We have also calculated the effects of adding (or deleting) a varying number of insertions in a particular medium. In most cases the change in total response was very nearly proportional to the change in the number of insertions, within a sensible range.

Linear programming approaches to media selection

Whereas the approach to media scheduling in the previous section stressed simulation as a means of enrichment wherein more variables could be introduced, the models in this section seek optimal solutions but cannot handle as many variables. Linear programming is frequently one of the first quantitative models applied to an allocation problem such as media scheduling, because of (1) its demonstrated value, (2) a formulation that is fairly easily understood without extensive mathematical training, and (3) the provision of an "optimum" solution within the definition of the particular problem. At first glance, the linear programming approach seems to be tractable for media scheduling, but as one develops the approach its shortcomings become more apparent and the need for other, more complex approaches arises.

To begin with, let us define a *vehicle* consistent with the way in which we use it in the CAM model: a particular space that the advertiser may reserve for himself. Thus, two separate quarter-hours on the same television station are different vehicles and the inside front cover of a magazine is a different vehicle from one of the inside pages. Of course, the fineness of the definition is a function of the extent to which the advertiser has control over selection of the space. For example, most magazines do not sell specific inside pages, so the entire group of inside pages is considered only one vehicle.

The selection of vehicles gives rise to some of the constraints in the linear programming format. A weekly publication cannot receive more than 52 insertions so long as the firm does not want to use multiple insertions in the same issue. Moreover, the management may choose to constrain the number of insertions to many fewer than 52. This is not an unreasonable action, since it implies that the management feels a need to reach more than just the audience of the single magazine, and might happen even if the number of persons seeing insertions in the particular magazine were the highest among the media available. On the other hand, if the solution were not "arbitrarily" constrained and required 52 insertions in a specific vehicle, one could argue that this is the path the management should follow. It is difficult, however, to believe that the entire target group for a product would be exposed to only one vehicle, or that diseconomies in terms of the efficiency with which prospects are reached would not appear, since there would be fewer and fewer unexposed after each insertion. A discussion on the evidence for economies of scale in advertising may be found in an article by Simon.[43] Another example of a so-called natural constraint would be the total number of 9:00 a.m. radio news broadcasts in a fixed time period.

In addition to the foregoing natural, or institutional, constraints, the advertiser may wish to impose other constraints on use of the various media based upon past experience or, more generally, upon managerial judgments about the character of the vehicle.[44] An example of this type of constraint would be elimination of a particular vehicle from consideration or limiting expenditures on a particular vehicle to a specified amount.

Finally, an overall budget constraint is imposed on the system.

The establishment of an objective function is probably the most difficult part of structuring the linear programming model for this problem. As pointed out earlier, the measurement of response to advertising is quite a difficult task. Thus, none of the preferred linear programming formulations to date have attempted to relate the media schedule to sales results but have rather followed the simulation models in maximizing proxy variables that are somehow related to sales response. The objective function is then usually developed in terms of a series of desirable characteristics possessed by the market target group and how closely each vehicle comes to approximating these. For example, Brown and Warshaw[45] use the following factors as indications of the value of a vehicle: (1) audience size or total readership,

---

[43] Julian L. Simon, "Are There Economies of Scale in Advertising?" *Journal of Advertising Research*, Vol. 5, No. 2, June 1965, pp. 15–20.

[44] See Douglas B. Brown and Martin R. Warshaw, "Media Selection by Linear Programming," *Journal of Marketing Research*, Vol. 2, 1965, p. 84.

[45] *Ibid.*

r_i; (2) an array of demographic characteristics weighted for their adjusted importance in influencing the purchase decision,[46] e_i; (3) editorial climate and an evaluation of the vehicle's past performance in producing successfull advertising readership, q_i; (4) the effectiveness of color as opposed to black and white (obviously, this factor is not applicable to radio), c_i; and, finally, (5) the size or duration of the advertisement, s_i. The objective function then has the form

$$\text{Maximize } Z = s_1c_1q_1e_1r_1n_1 + \cdots + s_nc_nq_ne_nr_nn_n \tag{9-19}$$

where n_i is the number of times the ith vehicle is used, or the number of units.

The subjective constraints could take the form

$$n_1 \leqslant 52, \quad n_2 \leqslant 7, \quad \text{etc.}$$

and the budget constraint would be

$$x_1n_1 + x_2n_2 + \cdots + x_nn_n \leqslant M$$

where x_i is the cost of vehicle i per unit, and M is the total budget dollars available.

From here on, the problem is fairly straightforward; the solution is readily obtained through use of an appropriate algorithm, such as the simplex method. But this approach to media selection has ignored or assumed away several major difficulties. First, the response function is usually not purely linear, although some argue that this may be the case for certain vehicles or media.[47] Second, besides the nonlinearity in response, there are certainly nonlinearities in costs due to purchase discounts for large quantities, specific spaces, and so on. Third, the linear programming approach as formulated above may produce results that recommend purchase of infeasible units, such as half a television quarter-hour.[48] Fourth, there are dynamic

[46] The value of individual geographic markets can also be handled in this fashion or by including the geographic factor as one more characteristic needed to define the individual vehicles —see, for example, Stanley F. Stasch, "Linear Programming and Space–Time Considerations in Media Selection," *Journal of Advertising Research*, Vol. 5, December 1965, pp. 40–46.

[47] One advertising executive argues that, since so little is known about the nature of the nonlinearities, the linear assumption is not unreasonable until more definite proof is uncovered. See Clark L. Wilson, "Use of Linear Programming to Optimize Media Schedules in Advertising," in *Innovation Key to Marketing Progress*, Proceedings of the American Marketing Association, 46th National Conference, Washington, D.C., June 1963. American Marketing Association, Chicago, 1963, p. 105.

[48] This might actually be feasible if the advertisements in the quarter-hour are viewed as spots and the firm buys half of them. But since this has a very different vehicular connotation, it might be better to reprogram considering the potential times at which the ads may appear as different vehicles.

effects that should be accounted for. The time at which the response is achieved may be extremely important for the advertiser; Lee mentions as an example an airline advertising for winter Caribbean vacations, which would find it quite useless if the messages affected people during the summer months.[49] Fifth, members of the target group are probably exposed to many of the vehicles, and the value of the combined audiences for two vehicles is less than the sum of the individual values for the vehicles because of this audience overlap. This complication is usually referred to as the *audience duplication problem.* Each of the preceding difficulties has been attacked by various researchers in an effort to improve the "realism" of the linear programming model.

Bass and Lonsdale have used sensitivity analysis to examine the influence of various subjective constraints and weighing systems used to adjust the value of the response produced by a particular vehicle in a schedule composed entirely of printed media.[50] One of the important features of their work is that the analysis was performed using data for an actual product as opposed to some of the more theoretical descriptions of linear programming formulations. Three types of weights were applied to the audience data: (1) adjusted audience, or the proportion of total circulation thought to be customers for the product, (2) weighted audience, which is the adjusted audience multiplied by the fraction of the audience expected to be exposed to the advertisement (obtained from Nielsen or Starch ratings) and by a subjective evaluation factor scored on a 0–1 scale that reflects the appropriateness of the editorial content, etc., and (3) weighted exposure units that further weight the audience figures to give greater weight to vehicles where the audience profile is most similar to specific demographic characteristics of the market target group. Separate solutions were obtained using each set of weights, first by introducing the institutional constraints sequentially and then by imposing all the constraints at once. Bass and Lonsdale reached the following conclusion regarding these weighting schemes:

> . . . *the weighting system has very little influence on the solution* . . . [which] is significant since it suggests that sophisticated weighting systems tend to be "washed out" in linear models. This suggests that cruder models such as cost per thousand will produce media schedules not very different from those produced by linear models.[51]

---

[49] See Alec M. Lee, "Decision Rules for Media Scheduling: Dynamic Campaigns," *Operational Research Quarterly*, Vol. 14, 1963, pp. 365–372. Stasch again includes the time effect as part of the definition of the vehicle. *Op. cit.*

[50] See: Frank M. Bass and Ronald T. Lonsdale, "An Exploration of Linear Programming in Media Selection," *Journal of Marketing Research*, Vol. 3, May 1966, pp. 179–188.

[51] *Ibid.*, pp. 180–181.

Our discussion has thus far treated audience characteristics or, more generally, the proxy variables that form our objective function, as deterministic. However, it is clear that the figures that we use for these proxy variables are actually stochastic. Massy has pointed out that we may restructure the problem of advertising coverage to put it in a decision theoretic framework.[52] This is a very logical step, since the character of an audience is highly dynamic regarding both the quality of the audience in relationship to the firm's market target group and the total size of the audience.

Bass and Lonsdale also find that subjective constraints do not contribute to an improvement in the solution and speak to the question of the rationale for subjective constraints. They state:

> Ordinarily, in linear programming applications the restraints are imposed by the physical environment. In applying linear programming to media selection problems, however, restraints are imposed by the decision maker, essentially *because he lacks faith in the linearity assumptions* [emphasis added] in linear models. The peculiar result is that the attempt to improve efficiency of programs by adding restraints necessarily reduces the value of the objective function.[53]

The principal reservation one might have about the Bass and Lonsdale experiment is that its generality has not been demonstrated by applying the techniques to other bodies of data and other products. Further, they point out that a nonlinear model might reduce most of the difficulties resulting from the imposition of judgmental constraints on the system.

How may the problem of nonlinear response be treated? Several researchers offer the suggestion of approximating any curvilinear function by a series of linear segments, a constraint being added to the system of equations that forces sequential use of each linear segment as one moves along the curve away from the origin.[54] This tack, of course, does not really resolve the question of the shape of the response function.

The second and third reservations raised with respect to the use of linear programming—those of nonlinearity in costs and the requirement of integral units—can be resolved by use of integer programming.[55] Thus, these are not highly significant drawbacks in utilizing mathematical programming as an approach to media scheduling. A much more serious problem is that of audience duplication.

---

[52] William F. Massy, "Costs of Uncertainty in Advertising Media Selection," working paper No. 2, Graduate School of Industrial Administration, Carnegie Institute of Technology, Pittsburgh, Pa., 1966.

[53] Bass and Lonsdale, *op. cit.*, p. 181.

[54] See, for example, Brown and Warshaw, *op. cit.*, pp. 86–88; and Wilson, *op. cit.*, p. 105.

[55] See Willard I. Zangwill, "Media Selection by Decision Programming," *Journal of Advertising Research*, Vol. 5, September 1965, pp. 30–36.

Audience duplication

The most widely known of the attempts to resolve the problem of audience duplication is the work of Agostini. He has examined the question in two different contexts: first, the case in which several different media are used,[56] and second, the case in which there is use of multiple issues of a single medium.[57] In either case, the objective is to determine how many different individuals are exposed at least once to the advertising campaign; the technical terms used for this variable are *reach* or *coverage*. The Agostini model is developed as follows:

Let $A_1, A_2, \cdots, A_n$ be the individual audiences of the n vehicles, and let C be the unduplicated audience. Define

$$A = \sum_{i=1}^{n} A_i \tag{9-20}$$

and

$$z = C/A \qquad 0 \leqslant z \leqslant 1 \tag{9-21}$$

Next we define an $n \times n$ matrix $((D_{ij}))$ in which each element is the number of people in the total audience covered by each pair of vehicles. For example, D_{ij} would be the number of people simultaneously covered by media i and j (the matrix is obviously symmetric).

Now define D as the sum of the duplicated readership; that is,

$$D = \sum_{i<j} D_{ij} \tag{9-22}$$

and let

$$x = D/A \tag{9-23}$$

Our objective is to define a curve that gives z for any x. Since when $D = 0$, $x = 0$, $C = A$, and $z = 1$, we have one point on the curve. By definition, one would expect that the higher D is, the lower C will be, so that the curve should decrease as x increases.

In Agostini's work, C, D, and A were obtained from a study of the readership of 30 French magazines. These values were then used to determine x and z, and a relationship of the following form resulted:

---

[56] J. M. Agostini, "How to Estimate Unduplicated Audiences," *Journal of Advertising Research*, Vol. 1, March 1961, pp. 11–14.

[57] J. M. Agostini, "Analysis of Magazine Accumulative Audience," *Journal of Advertising Research*, Vol. 2, December 1962, pp. 24–27.

$$z = \frac{1}{Kx + 1} \tag{9-24}$$

When K equaled 1.125, there were only small discrepancies between the observed and estimated values for z up to $x = 1.7$, the highest observed value of x in the French data. The chief drawback in the Agostini method is that it is based on the assumption of similarity in character among the groups of vehicles; newspapers, magazines, and trade papers, for example, must all be treated separately with no effort to assess duplication among these major groups.

Several other investigators have attempted to verify Agostini's work.[58] Generally speaking, they have found that the constant, K, varies according to the character of the specific magazines included in any type of group as well as across groups. In the judgment of these researchers, the variation is sufficient to question the general applicability of Agostini's formula. On the other hand, the general form of the curve is always downward sloping and convex to the origin. K may also be a function of the number, n, of magazines in the combination as well as the duplication. In this last case, the relationship has been hypothesized as exponential and of the form[59]

$$z = \exp\,[-K_n x] \tag{9-25}$$

where K_n varies from approximately 1 for $n = 3$ down to .627 for $n = 10$. Tests of the preceding equation show a somewhat better fit to a limited set of data than does the Agostini form.

The other principal approach to audience duplication builds on the proportion of the target population not covered by any single magazine. If readerships of different magazines were independent random events, then the fraction of the population comprising the unduplicated audience would be

$$U = 1 - q_1 q_2 \cdots q_n \tag{9-26}$$

where $q_i = 1 - p_i$ is the fraction of the relevant population not reached by the ith magazine. Even though readerships are not independent, if no information is available about duplications, then the above formula is the only one to use.

A feasible variation on this method occurs when the pairwise duplica-

---

[58] See, for example, John Bower, "Net Audiences of U.S. and Canadian Magazines: Seven Tests of Agostini's Formula," *Journal of Advertising Research*, Vol. 3, March 1963, pp. 13–20; and Marcel Marc, "Net Audiences of French Businesspapers: Agostini's Formula Applied to Special Markets," *Journal of Advertising Research*, Vol. 3, March 1963, pp. 26–29.

[59] See Walther Kuhn, "Net Audiences of German Magazines: A New Formula," *Journal of Advertising Research*, Vol. 3, March 1963, pp. 30–33.

tion is known. If magazine 1, say, has the largest audience, we adjust the other figures to it by the conditional probability formula

$$q_j' = q_{1j}/q_1 \qquad j = 2, \cdots, n \tag{9-27}$$

where $q_{ij} = 1 - (p_i + p_j) + p_{ij}$ is the fraction reached by neither the ith nor the jth magazine. The new, or modified, value for the unduplicated audience is then

$$U = 1 - q_1 q_2' \cdots q_n' \tag{9-28}$$

It is reported that this procedure tends to give better estimates of the true cover than the unmodified one and smaller error than the Agostini model.[60]

Still another way in which the concept of non-cover has been used to assess the unduplicated audience was developed by Metheringham.[61] Let

$$k_i = \frac{\sum_i q_i}{n} = \text{average non-cover of single publications} \tag{9-29}$$

$$k_2 = \frac{\sum_{i<j} q_{ij}}{\binom{n}{2}} = \text{average non-cover of pairs of publications} \tag{9-30}$$

$$k_3 = \frac{\sum_{i<j<k} q_{ijk}}{\binom{n}{3}} = \text{average non-cover of triads of publications} \tag{9-31}$$

$$\vdots$$

$$k_n = q_{1,2,\cdots,n} = \text{non-cover of the whole set of } n \text{ publications} \tag{9-32}$$

Then

$$U = 1 - k_n \tag{9-33}$$

so that what is needed is a way of calculating k_n knowing only k_1 and k_2. If we hypothesize that

$$k_r = \frac{s(s+1)(s+2)\cdots(s+r-1)}{t(t+1)(t+2)\cdots(t+r-1)} \qquad r = 1, 2, \cdots, n \tag{9-34}$$

then

$$k_1 = \frac{s}{t} \quad \text{and} \quad k_2 = \frac{s(s+1)}{t(t+1)} \tag{9-35}$$

---

[60] See J. M. Caffyn and M. Sagovsky, "Net Audiences of British Newspapers: A Comparison of the Agostini and Sainsbury Methods," *Journal of Advertising Research*, Vol. 3, March 1963, pp. 21–25.

[61] Richard A. Metheringham, "Measuring the New Cumulative Coverage of a Print Campaign," *Journal of Advertising Research*, Vol. 4, December 1964, pp. 23–28.

so we can calculate

$$s = \frac{k_1^2 - k_1 k_2}{k_2 - k_1^2} \quad \text{and} \quad t = \frac{s}{k_1} \tag{9-36}$$

The last term of the series is

$$k_n = \frac{s(s+1)(s+2)\cdots(s+n-1)}{t(t+1)(t+2)\cdots(t+n-1)} \tag{9-37}$$

This procedure appears to yield very good estimates for both printed media and radio and television.

Other methods besides those offered herein have been developed to assess audience duplication, but in our judgment they are essentially variants on the Agostini and non-cover approaches. Before we attempt evaluation of the question of the importance of assessing duplication, we shall first discuss two approaches to estimating duplication for multiple issues or telecasts of the same "general" vehicle.

The non-cover approach of Metheringham can be used for multiple issues if the procedure is appropriately modified to identify the different pairings between and within publications. For instance, if four publications are to be used – A, B, C, D – and three specific issues each of the last two – say C_1, C_4, C_6, D_1, D_3, D_5 – then $q_{C_1D_1} = q_{C_1D_3} = q_{C_1D_5} = q_{C_3D_1} = q_{C_3D_3}$, and so on. This effect holds because we assume that the fraction of the population reading a publication is the same for any issue (p_i = a constant). Also, $q_{C_1C_4} = q_{C_1C_6} = q_{C_4C_6}$, and so on. Thus, we have to identify a representative of each set of different pairs and need work only with these.[62]

Agostini also developed a model for several issues of one publication based on the non-cover.[63] Essentially, if P = proportion of adult population reached by one issue and P_i = accumulated audience of i issues, then

$$\begin{aligned} P_1 &= P \\ P_2 &= P_1 + P(1 - P_1) \end{aligned} \tag{9-38}$$

and, in general,

$$P_n = P_{n-1} + P(1 - P_{n-1}) \tag{9-39}$$

that is, each new issue adds a constant fraction $P = P_1$ of the population not already covered.

By subtracting both sides of equation (9-39) from 1, we obtain

$$\begin{aligned} 1 - P_n &= 1 - P_{n-1} - P(1 - P_{n-1}) \\ &= (1 - P)(1 - P_{n-1}) \end{aligned} \tag{9-40}$$

Since $P = P_1$, if we set $n = 2$ in (9-40) we get

---

[62] *Ibid.*, pp. 25, 26.

[63] Agostini, *Journal of Advertising Research*, Vol. 2, December 1962, pp. 24–27.

$$1 - P_2 = (1 - P_1)^2 \tag{9-41}$$

More generally, we see that

$$1 - P_n = (1 - P_1)^n \tag{9-42}$$

Agostini claims good results for this estimation formula as compared to actual data.[64]

Although we have not discussed the various empirical tests made on the different models for measurement of audience duplication, two things are worth noting: (1) Some of the methods appear to work fairly well with both printed and nonprinted media, and (2) none of the researchers tested his work against the body of data used by any of the others.[65] The testing procedure usually involved applying the several different approaches to a data body the specific researcher had been able to secure himself; there is no mention of any attempts to obtain the data base other experimenters used. Thus, the case may really be that no generalizations can be made and each specific instance has to be attacked separately. It is not unreasonable to believe that English viewing and reading habits are somehow basically different from French, which are different from American, and so on. In addition, the various media may have institutional characteristics, which, when taken in combination, make each set unique. In this case, we have offered the reader a number of approaches from which he can begin to construct his own individualized approaches to measurement of audience duplication and, implicitly, net coverage. It should also be apparent that one of the principal comparative advantages of the simulation approach to media scheduling is that the problems inherent in assessing audience duplication can be avoided altogether.

A different approach to media scheduling

We have already pointed out that the CAM model attempts to solve a very complex problem through simulation, which allows many factors to be represented properly but does not guarantee an optimum solution. On the other hand, linear programming, which does produce an optimum solution, does not model the problem very well. Several researchers have attempted to solve the media scheduling problem optimally through use of nonlinear mathematical programming.[66] This work provides another useful

---

[64] Note that this is the same form as the unmodified non-cover model discussed on page 235.

[65] There is very, very limited comparability between small segments of some of the experiments.

[66] D. M. Ellis, "Building Up a Sequence of Optimum Media Schedules," *Operational Research Quarterly*, Vol. 17, December 1966, pp. 413–424; Alec M. Lee, "Decision Rules for Media Scheduling in Static Campaigns," *Operational Research Quarterly*, Vol. 13, September 1962, pp. 229–242; and C. J. Taylor, "Some Developments in the Theory and Application of Media Scheduling Methods," *Operational Research Quarterly*, Vol. 14, September 1963, pp. 291–305.

way of looking at the problem. In the following discussion we shall attempt, wherever possible, to make the terminology conform with that we have used in discussing CAM.

Every campaign results in a frequency distribution of persons who have "seen" no advertisement, one advertisement, two advertisements, and so on. Let I_r be the fraction of the target population who see exactly r advertisements. The *reach* or *cover* is the number of persons who have been exposed to at least one advertisement. This is simply the sum of the frequencies of receiving one or more impressions, $\Sigma_{r=1}^{\infty} I_r$. Cover is important because for certain types of campaigns the widest possible exposure may be a valid objective, but it ignores the value of repeated exposure. Another factor of considerable interest to the advertiser is the *average* number of impressions seen by a member of the target population. This is, of course, just the mean of the frequency distribution $\Sigma_{r=1}^{\infty} rI_r$. Finally, although people will have different levels of awareness due to a campaign depending on the number of impressions they have received, it is not true that the marginal effectiveness of additional exposures is constant. We will therefore define the level of awareness in the population to be $\Sigma_{r=1}^{\infty} W_rI_r$, where W_r is a value lying between 1 and r (which will be further explained when we get to it). For now it suffices to point out that this yields a measure intermediate to the previous two.

We shall consider an advertising campaign of long enough duration so that there is a possibility of placing advertisements in more than one issue of a medium. To begin our analysis, we define the following:

M_i = a medium in which any advertisement can appear, $i = 1, 2, \cdots, k$

a_i = the proportion of the target population who read medium M_i

z_i = the proportion of readers of M_i who will see a specific advertisement (of fixed size)

c_i = the cost of inserting the advertisement

n_i = the number of issues of M_i carrying single insertions of the advertisement

For the ith medium we can calculate

$$F = \text{average number of impressions} = n_i a_i z_i \tag{9-43}$$

$$G = \text{cover} = a_i[1 - (1 - z_i)^{n_i}] \tag{9-44}$$

$$C = \text{cost} = n_i c_i \tag{9-45}$$

provided we assume that the readership is constant, that a reader's viewings of advertisements in different issues are independent events, and that there are no quantity discounts.

In order to derive the formulas for K media, the above assumptions would be given their natural extensions. For example, we would assume that the events of viewing are independent between issues of different (as well as the same) media. At this point we shall also assume that the readership of one medium is independent of the readership of any other medium. For example, for two media we assume that the proportion of the target population who read both M_i and M_j, a_{ij}, is equal to the product of the individual proportions, or $a_{ij} = a_i a_j$. Having just been through the section on audience duplication, the reader may feel that this assumption is unrealistic. We can attempt to justify it by the simplicity of the model to which it leads, both in data requirements and computation of solution. Furthermore, there has been some experience in Great Britain that indicates that the assumption is a good enough approximation to reality.[67]

We can now calculate

$$F(z_i, n_i; k) = \sum_{i=1}^{k} n_i a_i z_i \tag{9-46}$$

$$G(z_i, n_i; k) = 1 - \prod_{i=1}^{k} [1 - a_i + a_i(1 - z_i)^{n_i}] \tag{9-47}$$

$$C(z_i, n_i; k) = \sum_{i=1}^{k} n_i c_i \tag{9-48}$$

where the notation is meant to indicate that F, G, and C are functions of the $2k$ variables $(z_1, n_1; z_2, n_2; \cdots; z_k, n_k)$.[68]

As we have noted above, when we calculate the average we give each impression equal weight, whereas the cover gives zero weight to each impression beyond the first. Suppose, instead, that we give the first impression unit weight but that each additional impression receives only q times the weight of its predecessor,[69] where q is some number between 0 and 1. The rth impression is given weight q^{r-1}, so the value of an individual who has received exactly r impressions is

$$W_r = 1 + q + q^2 + \cdots + q^{r-1} = \frac{1 - q^r}{1 - q} \qquad r \geqslant 1 \tag{9-49}$$

This is, as previously stated, a value between 1 and r. We then have (with $W_0 = 0$)

---

[67] Alec M. Lee and A. J. Burkhart, "Some Optimization Problems in Advertising," *Operational Research Quarterly*, Vol. 11, September 1960, pp. 113–122.

[68] Kolesar has demonstrated how Ellis' statement of the problem may be transformed into an integer linear programming problem in zero–one variables. See Peter J. Kolesar, "A Remark on the Computation of Optimum Media Schedules," *Operational Research Quarterly*, Vol. 19, 1968, pp. 73–75.

[69] This is, of course, just a geometric response function as described in the CAM section. The average is a linear response function, whereas the cover is a step function (at $r = 1$).

$$R = \text{response} = \sum_{r=0}^{\infty} W_r I_r = \frac{1 - \sum_{r=0}^{\infty} q^r I_r}{1-q} \tag{9-50}$$

Although the expressions for the individual I_r are complicated, we can easily obtain the generating function

$$\sum_{r=0}^{\infty} s^r I_r = \prod_{i=1}^{k} [1 - a_i + a_i(1 - z_i + sz_i)^{n_i}] \tag{9-51}$$

which is just what we need to evaluate R. We then have

$$R(z_i, n_i; k) = \frac{1 - \prod_{i=1}^{k} [1 - a_i + a_i(1 - z_i + qz_i)^{n_i}]}{1-q} \tag{9-52}$$

The choice of q is a subjective managerial input. The extreme values, 1 and 0, correspond to choosing average impressions and cover, respectively. The choice of an intermediate value can be guided either by the rule that r impressions on an individual are $(1 - q^r)/(1 - q)$ times as valuable as one impression on that individual, or the inverse rule that r impressions on a fraction $(1 - q)/(1 - q^r)$ of a group of individuals are as valuable as one impression on the whole group.

For computational purposes, it is convenient to set $p = 1 - q$ and to rewrite the response function as

$$\Pi = 1 - pR = \prod_{i=1}^{k} [1 - a_i + a_i(1 - pz_i)^{n_i}] \tag{9-53}$$

Maximization of response is then equivalent to minimization of the product, Π. If all the other factors are held constant, then for medium M_i it is desirable to make $(1 - pz_i)^{n_i}$ as small as possible.

We can now answer the question of what insertion size is optimal in each medium. Suppose that insertions are available in M_i with either seeing probability z_i and cost c_i or seeing probability z_i' and cost c_i'. For a fixed cost we could buy n_i of the former or n_i' of the latter, provided $c_i n_i = c_i' n_i'$. The former will be more effective if $(1 - pz_i)^{n_i} < (1 - pz_i)^{n_i'}$, which is equivalent to

$$\frac{1}{-n_i \ln (1 - pz_i)} < \frac{1}{-n_i' \ln (1 - pz_i')}$$

Multiplying on the left by $c_i n_i$ and the right by $c_i' n_i'$, we obtain the criterion

$$\frac{c_i}{-\ln (1 - pz_i)} < \frac{c_i'}{-\ln (1 - pz_i')}$$

We thus see that the optimal size insertion in medium M_i is the one that minimizes

$$\frac{c_i}{-\ln(1-pz_i)} \approx \frac{c_i}{pz_i + \frac{1}{2}(pz_i)^2}$$

for that medium. If p is small, then the exact criterion is approximately equal to $(1/p)(c_i/z_i)$, so the simple criterion of cost per viewer is useful. If p is large, however, then this simple criterion is biased toward small insertions; that is, it tends to understate optimal insertion size.

The following data on seeing probabilities and costs are taken from Taylor's paper.[70] These are average data, based on *London Press Exchange* studies.

Insertion size	Seeing probability	Relative cost	c/z	$c/-\ln(1-z)$
4 in. × 2 cols.	0.052	0.05	.962	.936
6 in. × 2 cols.	0.057	0.075	1.316	1.278
8 in. × 2 cols.	0.059	0.10	1.695	1.644
11 in. × 3 cols.	0.11	0.23	2.091	1.974
13 in. × 5 cols.	0.20	0.46	2.300	2.061
half-page	0.32	0.60	1.875	1.556
full page	0.61	1.04	1.705	1.104

If p is near 0 (maximization of the average number of impressions), then a large number of very small advertisements is most effective. If p is near 1 (cover maximization the objective), then, except for the "bargain" smallest size, which may be too small to present the message, a small number of full-page advertisements is best.

We are now ready to determine the optimum media schedule. We must choose the n_i in such a way as to minimize

$$\Pi = \prod_{i=1}^{k} [1 - a_i + a_i(1 - pz_i)^{n_i}] \tag{9-54a}$$

$$= \prod_{i=1}^{k} \prod_{r=1}^{n_i} \frac{1 - a_i + a_i(1 - pz_i)^r}{1 - a_i + a_i(1 - pz_i)^{r-1}} \tag{9-54b}$$

In this form the quotient

$$Q_i(r) = \frac{1 - a_i + a_i(1 - pz_i)^r}{1 - a_i + a_i(1 - pz_i)^{r-1}} \tag{9-55}$$

explicitly shows the reduction in Π produced by the rth insertion in M_i. Note that $Q_i(r) < Q_i(r+1)$; that is, the insertions follow a law of diminishing marginal effectiveness in reducing Π.

It is more convenient to deal with sums than with products, so we shall write

[70] Taylor, *op. cit.*, p. 298.

$$-\ln \Pi = \sum_{i=1}^{k} \sum_{r=1}^{n_i} [-\ln Q_i(r)] \tag{9-56}$$

the minus signs being introduced because the logarithms are negative. We are required to maximize the double sum, subject to a budgetary constraint:

$$C = \sum_{i=1}^{k} n_i c_i = \sum_{i=1}^{k} \sum_{r=1}^{n_i} c_i \tag{9-57}$$

To achieve this, all we need do is tabulate the cost-effectiveness ratios

$$T_i(r) = \frac{c_i}{-\ln Q_i(r)} \tag{9-58}$$

and choose the insertions having the smallest values of $T_i(r)$ until we exhaust our budget.

The diminishing marginal effectiveness of additional insertions in a medium, combined with the constant marginal cost, assures us of an increasing cost-effectiveness ratio $T_i(r)$. Thus, we will never want to use the $(r+1)$st insertion in a medium if the rth has not already been used. If there are quantity discounts, so that c_1 is not a constant but a decreasing function of r, then it is quite possible for $T_i(r+1)$ to be smaller than $T_i(r)$ if the $(r+1)$st insertion is one at which a discount becomes effective.

The optimization method we have just presented is due to Ellis, and we adapt an example in his paper to illustrate it. He presents data on four daily and six weekly publications, as shown in Table 9-4. For the moment the last column should be ignored; it presents the solution we are about to calculate. If it is judged that each additional impression received by an indi-

TABLE **9-4**

Ellis data

Medium	Cost	Readership	Seeing probability	Optimum number of insertions
Daily Mirror	3225	.41	.50	6
Daily Express	3000	.34	.40	5
Daily Mail	2480	.17	.40	2
Daily Telegraph	1930	.09	.45	1
News of the World	4224	.44	.30	5
People	3750	.41	.30	5
Sunday Express	3750	.27	.30	1
Sunday Times	2277	.09	.45	1
ITV publications	3003	.35	.40	5
Radio Times	3600	.33	.50	4

SOURCE: D. M. Ellis, *Operational Research Quarterly*, Vol. 17, Dec. 1966, p. 422.

vidual is only half as valuable as its predecessor, $q=\frac{1}{2}$, then we can calculate the cost-effectiveness ratios $T_i(r)$. By choosing the insertions in the order of increasing ratios, we build up a schedule giving the best response for each given cost, as demonstrated in Table 9-5. Because the *Sunday Times* did not appear among the first 35 insertions on the list, we have calculated the result of using it rather than another insertion in ITV publications. Even so, we end up using three of the weekly publications five times each and another one four times. If it is judged that this would result in the campaign's

TABLE **9-5**

Optimum schedule based on Ellis data

Insertion	Cost-effectiveness ratio (thousands)	Cumulative cost	Cumulative response
Daily Mirror	30	3,225	.205
Daily Mirror	36	6,450	.359
ITV publications	41	9,453	.474
Radio Times	42	13,053	.600
Daily Express	43	16,053	.695
Daily Mirror	44	19,278	.787
ITV publications	48	22,281	.860
Daily Express	50	25,281	.926
Radio Times	52	28,881	.999
Daily Mirror	55	32,106	1.055
ITV publications	57	35,109	1.104
Daily Express	59	38,109	1.148
People	59	41,859	1.201
News of the World	62	46,083	1.253
Radio Times	65	49,683	1.294
People	65	53,433	1.333
ITV publications	68	56,436	1.362
News of the World	68	60,660	1.400
Daily Mirror	70	63,885	1.427
Daily Express	70	66,885	1.451
Daily Mail	72	69,365	1.470
People	73	73,115	1.496
News of the World	76	77,339	1.524
People	82	81,089	1.545
ITV publications	82	84,092	1.562
Radio Times	82	87,692	1.580
News of the World	84	91,916	1.601
Daily Express	84	94,916	1.615
Daily Mail	87	97,396	1.626
Daily Mirror	89	100,621	1.639
Sunday Express	91	104,371	1.654
People	92	108,121	1.667
Daily Telegraph	95	110,051	1.674
News of the World	95	114,275	1.688
ITV publications	99	117,278	1.698
Sunday Times	111	116,552	1.695

being stretched out over too long a time span, then these media can be restricted to some smaller number of insertions. Of course, this will result in the use of insertions with higher cost-effectiveness ratios and hence a smaller response per given cost.

Summary

In this chapter we have discussed analytical approaches to determining the advertising appropriation and how this money should be allocated among the various media alternatives. Questions having to do with the creativity and effectiveness of individual advertisements have not been considered because the former is beyond the scope of this text and measurement of the latter involves principally the well-known techniques of experimental design. Even for those subjects included here, it was difficult to decide on the depth to which we should explore each one. There is, for example, a fair amount of additional material on the nature, or character, of response functions that we could have covered, but, as the reader has probably observed, this chapter is already the longest in the book.

This chapter has also highlighted, more strongly than any of the preceding chapters, the differences, difficulties, and benefits of simulation as opposed to optimizing models. In addition, the effect of introducing managerial judgments into both types of models has been explicitly considered, with quite diverse conclusions about the value of such judgments.

Actually, for two of the most important aspects of advertising we are unable to offer any quantitative models; both the setting of objectives and the development of measures to assess progress toward achievement of these objectives are highly situation specific. Despite this inability, we speculate that the payoffs from giving substantial attention to these considerations may well be as great as those from any of the models designed to achieve efficient use of media and monies.

The models in this chapter are, on the whole, more complex than in any other chapter except the next one, Chapter 10, "Consumer Purchase Behavior." Essentially, both chapters have as their prime topic the analysis and influencing of consumer behavior. Since simple models seem to fail to "explain" consumer behavior adequately, particularly as they deal with response to advertising, the obvious tendency is to build more and more complicated models. This is, then, the direction in which future work on the construction of models for decision making in advertising will probably go. In any event, there is a strong likelihood that further quantification of most management decisions in advertising will take place, especially considering the fact that work is now going on to measure creative output.

CONSUMER PURCHASE BEHAVIOR

CHAPTER TEN

It is difficult enough to understand the decision process behind a given act. The marketing manager, despite the conflicting theoretical explanations of behavior, must go one step further and predict how the consumer will respond to his strategies. It is not surprising, then, that a vast amount of effort has been directed at developing models of consumer behavior, including many that are quantitative. The various approaches to this analysis are probably as diverse as the number of researchers.

Obviously, we could not hope to discuss the extremely large number of approaches to the analysis of purchase behavior that have been posited. Instead, the plan of this chapter shall be: (1) to describe briefly the classical psychological and neoclassical economic models in limited mathematical form, and (2) to discuss the principal quantitative approaches. Since the latter are quite numerous, we shall limit ourselves to a set that appears to describe adequately the variety of these models and the frequency with which they appear to have been applied. As one proceeds through these models, it is very important to keep in mind the assumptions underlying each one, because these are the points about which arguments concerning the relative merits of each model turn—much more so than the correctness of the mathematical techniques employed.

The reason why so many more models of purchase behavior have been developed than models for other managerial areas in marketing may also have to do with the data base for these models. There is a richness and abundance of data that can be overwhelming, the sources for which are the several consumer purchase panels run by different marketing research agencies.

Usually, to form a panel, a representative sample of families is selected and then the individual families keep diaries of their purchases.[1] Typical information included in a purchase diary might be the quantity purchased and the unit sizes, the price, whether or not the item was on sale or purchased under a deal, the brand, the type of store in which the purchase was made (discount, chain drug, department, etc.), which member of the family made the purchase, and so on. Almost all foodstuffs and other items bought in supermarkets or drug stores are included, as well as certain clothing and hardware items. The choice of the particular items to be included is based on those items about which manufacturers now want information, or are thought likely to want information in the near future. This does not bias the data but it does imply that the specific set of models cannot be applied to some products about which data are unavailable, and may indicate weakness in the generality of the models.

The neoclassical economic model

The neoclassical economic model of purchase behavior concentrates on the changes in quantity purchased of a particular product or class of goods that will result from a change in real income, also allowing for changes in the quality of the item purchased. The fundamental estimating relationship is frequently derived via regression and might have the following form:

$$q = ay - bp \tag{10-1}$$

where q, y, and p are the percentage changes in quantity bought, real income, and price of the good, respectively, and a and b are elasticities derived from the data. Actually, the situation is more complex in that changes in the price of substitute and complementary goods must also be allowed for: That is, if the price of a substitute good decreases relative to the good we are examining, less of the good with which we are concerned will be bought; the effect is the opposite for complementary goods. Thus, the estimating equation may be rewritten as

$$q = ay - bp_1 + cp_2 + dp_3 - ep_4 \tag{10-2}$$

where p_2 and p_3 represent percentage price changes in substitute goods (note the positive coefficients, implying an increase in q for an increase in p_2 or p_3) and p_4 corresponds to a complementary good.

The foregoing types of relationships are usually derived from budget studies or records of consumer expenditures for various commodities over long periods of time. A frequent difficulty with such relationships is that the

[1] Several authors have examined the validity of the sample selection procedures and the accuracy of family reporting and have found panels, on the whole, to be quite reliable. See for example, Donald G. Morrison, Ronald E. Frank, and William F. Massy, "A Note on Panel Bias," *Journal of Marketing Research*, Vol. 3, February 1966, pp. 85–88; and Seymour Sudman, "On the Accuracy of Recording of Consumer Panels: I," *Journal of Marketing Research*, Vol. 1, May 1964, pp. 14–20.

definition of the product classes is usually made so broad for purposes of assuring adequate data that the operational usefulness of the relationships for the marketing manager is limited. This lumping of data to derive estimates for a generic product usually obscures the differences in behavioral patterns resulting from purchases of different brands over time.

There is another problem that makes use of this model difficult. One is hard put to define the sets of substitute and complementary goods. Surely, in some sense, a trip to Europe and the purchase of a yacht are substitutes; imagine, however, the problems involved in gathering data on the relationship between the two expenditures, let alone identifying other alternative expenditures for "luxury" consumption. These problems may explain why the purchase relationships have most commonly been derived for staples, such as foodstuffs. As a means of narrowing the set of alternative expenditures to a feasible collection, current practice is to concentrate on technical substitutes. But even this approach has great limitations. For example, technical substitutes for a bar of soap may be readily defined, but what is the set of technical substitutes for a television set?

Finally, the purchase relationship in the neoclassical economic model is not directed at the types of things over which the manager has control, with the exception of price, and thus provides the manager with few guidelines on how to market the good appropriately. Most of the models to be described subsequently do imply what strategies may be appropriate for given types of results. On the whole, the economic model seems most useful for estimating aggregate demand for a product or product class.[2]

The classical psychological model

Studies of buyer behavior are usually based on one form or another of the psychological learning model. In brief, the sequence of events is as diagrammed in Figure 10-1. The diagram is sufficiently generalized that it may apply to most learning situations, but we shall illustrate it in terms of a purchase. Let us start with the assumption that the consumer has a need. The cause may be as simple as the fact that the household has run out of laundry detergent or as complex as the consumer's unconscious desire to maintain his status with the next-door neighbors who have just purchased a pleasure boat. The consumer then goes through a period in which he shifts and analyzes the various means by which he can satisfy this need; this may include a large variety of activities: from comparison shopping and extensive analysis of alternative brands to determining where the nearest supermarket is, or the most convenient marina. The consumer now selects one of the available alternative reactions, which becomes his response, for ex-

---

[2] Some of the other factors in the neoclassical economic model, such as elasticity, are discussed under pricing in Chapter 6.

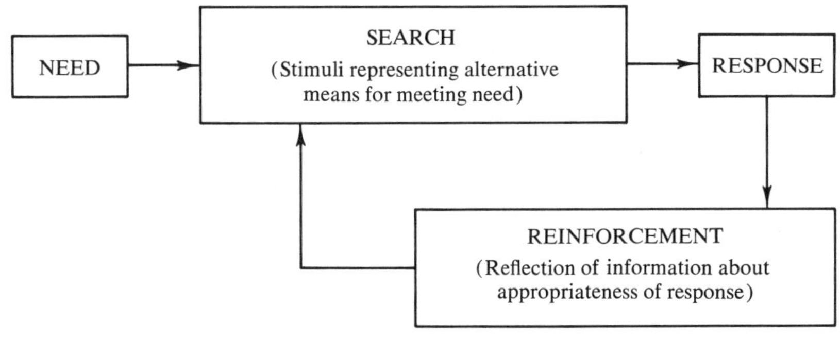

FIGURE **10-1**

Learning model of human behavior

ample, the purchase of a particular brand of detergent. The consumer is then positively or negatively reinforced that he made the correct response (chose the best detergent for his needs) according to his satisfaction or dissatisfaction with the product relative to his expectations about the product's performance – that is, the consumer has learned. This information about satisfaction is then utilized the next time a similar need arises, and the probability of a specific response is increased or decreased in accordance with how well the response met the consumer's needs on the previous purchase occasion. As some one response or set of responses becomes more and more likely, the search time – that is, the cognitive process – is reduced. This increase in the likelihood of a specific response, which we may recast in the form of the probability of purchase of a particular brand, is the basis for the quantitative models of learning behavior that we shall discuss subsequently.

Another aspect of this process is selective attention. The consumer does not constantly evaluate all possible products. Rather, consumers engage in learning selectivity. Thus, in the above example, once a satisfactory group of detergents is known, the consumer will habitually purchase from this group for a while. Then, after some time, the consumer once again decides to engage in learning about detergents. Such a decision may be cued by the appearance of new products, special sales, out-of-stock situations, or simply the realization that the product class has not been "looked at" recently. By organizing learning in this fashion, the consumer is able to cope with the evaluation of the large number of products available.

The psychological process that gives rise to a need is beyond the scope of this book, so we shall not indulge in discussion of motivations, attitudes, beliefs, drives, and other terms that relate to need arousal and developmer There are two reasons for taking this stance: First, there is still much con troversy over the proper application of these concepts to consumer purchase decisions, and second, the problems of measurement are very large. Most of the quantitative models subsequently discussed do not explore any phenomena that precede the searching process, but they do rely heavily on hypothesized effects of the information feedback resulting from the character of the reinforcement. It is certainly true that the relationships among variables that reflect activities subsequent to the searching process are not necessarily well defined either; however, this starting point is usually selected because of the relatively easier conceptualization and idealization of the elements in the system and their interactions and the much greater measurability of events due to the availability of data on purchase transactions.

Attempts have been made to put the whole of the learning process, including events preceding search, into a quantitative framework. The abovementioned problems with the study of the psychological activities still hold, but useful insights are sometimes gained. In the appendix to this chapter we describe one effort at quantification of some behavior preceding search.

Before preceding with our discussion of some of the quantitative models of purchase behavior, a comment on the organization of the material is necessary. There are certain problems common to all the following models, such as whether to treat individual families separately or work with more aggregate forms of the data. We have chosen to delay summarization of these common factors until the last section of the chapter, because we believe that the student will be better able to evaluate their implications for all present and future models of consumer purchase behavior after he has examined their influence in specific instances. For the same reason, categorization of the models into broad types will be facilitated by delaying discussion until the last section of this chapter.

Markovian analyses

In the Markovian model of purchase behavior, we derive a probability transition matrix $[P]$, which provides information on the likelihood that a consumer who bought a particular brand i at time t will buy brand j at time $t + 1$. We also have information on the share of market held by each brand at time t, which we shall call the market share vector, M. Clearly, we now have all we need to determine[3] the steady-state market shares or the division of the market at any other time n periods hence, if time t brand shares are taken as the starting point.

The principal use of such an approach would be to compare alternative strategies. That is, the manager may evaluate different marketing strategies in terms of how they are believed to affect $[P]$ and the corresponding steady-state implications, although he is cognizant that the steady state may never be attained. Another factor of interest to the manager is the mean run length of a brand, that is, the number of periods it will stay in a state. If our interest were in brand i, this would be

[3] See Chapter 3, especially equations (3-32) and (3-36).

$$\bar{n}_i = 1/(1 - p_{ii}) \tag{10-3}$$

Thus, the manager is able to obtain some feeling for how long, on the average, customers will remain loyal to his brand. Strategies may also be devised on the basis of assessment of what brands customers are being won from and lost to and the size of the group that remains loyal to a given brand. On the whole, the usefulness of the Markovian model appears to lie more in comparison of implications than in determination of the long-term values of important variables.

Use of the Markovian approach embodies several assumptions, which we shall now discuss in detail. One assumption of the Markovian model is that of the stationarity of the transition matrix. If this transition matrix were not fixed through time, we would be unable to make any statements about future market shares of the various brands or ascertain the equilibrium conditions. Few researchers maintain that the assumption of stationarity is absolutely realistic. Rather, the question usually asked is: Are the transition probabilities invariant over a sufficiently long period that we could act as if they were stationary? If a principal use of the Markovian model is for comparison of alternative strategies, this implicitly suggests that those utilizing the model do not expect long-run stationarity.

Recent evidence on the assumption of stationarity is not very conclusive. Styan and Smith found in their work that the null hypothesis of stationarity could not be rejected, but, as with many of the empirical studies that deal with the assumptions of the Markovian model, the sample size is relatively small, 100 families.[4] Massy, on the other hand, found that the stationarity hypothesis was not tenable for family purchase patterns for coffee; however, this study was family specific (which has implications for another assumption we shall discuss shortly, homogeneity) and of limited size, 39 families.[5] Patric and Haines found in a recent study that the null hypothesis of stationarity could not be rejected at the .05 level for any of eight brands or for the total product class.[6]

The statistical procedures that have been used by most researchers in testing hypotheses of order and stationarity are those developed by Anderson and Goodman.[7] These procedures (chi-square or likelihood ratio) are tests for "goodness of fit" and are both easily understood and applied.

---

[4] George P. H. Styan and Harry Smith, Jr., "Markov Chains Applied to Marketing," *Journal of Marketing Research*, Vol. 1, February 1964, pp. 50–55.

[5] William F. Massy, "Order and Homogeneity of Family Specific Brand-Switching Processes," *Journal of Marketing Research*, Vol. 3, February 1966, pp. 48–54.

[6] Lowell C. Patric and George H. Haines, Jr., "A Test of a First Order Markov Chain Theory of Consumer Behavior," College of Business Administration, University of Rochester, Rochester, N.Y., 1968, unpublished manuscript.

[7] T. W. Anderson and L. A. Goodman, "Statistical Inference About Markov Chains," *Annals of Mathematical Statistics*, Vol. 28, 1957, pp. 89–110.

One of the most important and difficult assumptions to deal with concerns the order of the Markov process. Traditional analysis requires that only the last purchase influence the next purchase, in other words, that the process be of first order. Correspondingly, a zero-order process would exist if past purchase behavior were irrelevant insofar as the present purchase was concerned; this is the basic assumption of traditional economic analysis. The critical question is: How far into the past should we go to establish the effect, if any, of past purchase behavior on the consumer's present purchases? Argument on this question has frequently focused on the consumer's memory span, but nothing definitive has resulted. The limited evidence has supported both the zero-order and first-order hypotheses. Massy found that for his small sample of coffee users, a zero-order process seemed to be adequate.[8] He also suggested caution in analyzing aggregate data (recall that his work was family specific) because of the substantial dependence of the order of the process on the assumptions of stationarity and homogeneity. Styan and Smith, on the other hand, found that their data rejected the hypothesis of a zero-order process and suggested a higher order process, but they did not test the null hypothesis of first order versus higher order.[9] Patric and Haines, on the basis of their data, concluded that both zero-order and first-order hypotheses must be rejected.[10] The evidence is not so strong as one would wish with regard to the "true" order of the Markov process in analysis of purchases by brands.

Markov chains of higher than first order are not particularly easy to deal with. For a second-order chain, each transition probability is a function of the two previous states. Notationally, we would use p_{ijk} instead of p_{ij}, and graphically we would use three axes representing times $t-1$, t, and $t+1$. Obviously, a process of any order can be represented in n-dimensional space, but as the order gets higher the number of cells increases to the point where the entries per cell may be so few as to render the analysis meaningless. For example, if there were five brands in some situation, a second-order process would have 125 cells. Given that the largest consumer panels rarely contain more than 5000 families, any order higher than second might conceivably divide the data too finely to permit generalizations. Similarly, on a family-specific basis, the number of purchase occasions would be small relative to the number of cells and, possibly, widely diffused among them.

Another problem encountered in the use of Markovian models is a requirement of discrete time periods, which are necessary for analysis. In order for the model to be mathematically tractable, each consumer must purchase only once in each time period. Consider the alternatives in meeting this requirement: (1) The time period can be made long enough so that every

---

[8] Massy, *op. cit.*

[9] Styan and Smith, *op. cit.*

[10] Patric and Haines, *op. cit.*

consumer in the sample will have purchased once, or (2) a "no purchase" state can be established. In the first case, because of differing purchase frequencies, some consumers will have purchased several times, thereby violating a requirement of the model. In the second case, although the tactic of a "no purchase" brand eliminates the problem, its realism is open to serious question. How much is the consumer's true brand loyalty obscured if he purchases only in every other period, but always the same brand? On the other hand, it is certainly true that for many categories of products, "no purchase" may be equivalent to having shopped in a particular week, passed by the displays of the particular product in the store, and consciously decided not to purchase (which decision may be either a reconfirmation or a reversal of an earlier decision planned at home before the shopping trip was begun). This kind of behavior would truly reflect a "no purchase" decision, but the question of interpretation of the "no purchase" state is still unresolved.

A means of dealing with unequal time intervals in a Markovian framework is outlined by Howard.[11] He suggests use of a semi-Markov process in which interpurchase time is a random variable, τ_{ij}, selected from a density function $h_{ij}(t)$, where a separate time density function may exist for each potential transition. The Markovian model is then seen as just a special case of the semi-Markovian, where all τ_{ij} are impulses at one time unit. An element of this new matrix, $\phi_{ij}(t)$, that is, the probability that a person in state i at time zero will be in state j at time t, is given by

$$\phi_{ij}(t) = \delta_{ij}\left[1 - \sum_{k=1}^{N} p_{ik}\int_0^t h_{ik}(\tau)\, d\tau\right] + \sum_{k=1}^{N} p_{ik}\int_0^t h_{ik}(\tau)\phi_{kj}(t-\tau)\, d\tau \qquad (10\text{-}4)$$

where $t \geq 0$, $1 \leq i, j \leq N$, and

$$\delta_{ij} = \begin{cases} 1 & \text{for} \quad i = j \\ 0 & \text{for} \quad i \neq j \end{cases}$$

The above equation assumes that $p_{ii} = 0$, since only actual transitions are recorded. The first term on the right only appears when $j = i$ and accounts for the probability of never leaving state i in time t. The second term on the right expresses the probability of going from state i to state j, allowing for the possibility of intermediate states k as well as a direct transition.

Calculation of the preceding probabilities is difficult though by no means impossible. In attempting to utilize the semi-Markov process, we would specify two matrices, the transition probability matrix, $[P]$, and the holding time matrix, $[H]$, the latter of which has elements $h_{ij}(t)$. The elements of

[11] Ronald A. Howard, "Stochastic Process Models of Consumer Behavior," *Journal of Advertising Research*, Vol. 3, September 1963, p. 39.

$[P]$ are determined by noting the number of times the purchase of brand j follows a purchase of brand i without regard to time intervals. Then a histogram of the time between purchases is prepared for each of the possible transitions, and this becomes the estimate of each $h_{ij}(t)$, which in turn is an element of $[H]$.

Unfortunately, the literature contains no reports of the application of the semi-Markov process to purchase data despite the superiority of the process. As Kuehn and Rohloff point out, this may be due to the difficulties faced in transforming processes indexed on real time, that is, the consumer's actual behavior pattern, to purchase-to-purchase time.[12]

Although Howard's approach eliminates the problem of multiple purchases per period, there still remains a complication that even the semi-Markov process cannot account for. There are some product categories for which individual household members may have different preferences—for example, breakfast cereals, toothpaste, or toilet soap. The effects on the Markovian model may be quite different, depending on how the housewife shops for these items. She could purchase each different brand for each family member at regular intervals of once every several weeks but with none of the brands being bought together—the pattern for three brands, A, B, C, over a nine-week period might be A, B, C, A, B, C, A, B, C,—or she could buy all brands once every three weeks. In the first case, the data would look as if there were substantial brand switching, whereas there may actually be very high loyalty on the part of the individual household members. If a semi-Markov process were not being used, the all-at-once purchase pattern would result in considerable movement in and out of the "No purchase" state, provided that a way could be found to handle the multiple brand purchases—which does not seem too likely. Thus, another requirement of the Markovian model that is frequently imposed on the data is the purchase of a single brand per shopping trip; the realism of this requirement is obviously open to question.

The final assumption of the Markovian model that requires discussion is that of homogeneity. This means essentially that all families of one type (for example, income category or social class) who bought brand i have a probability of exactly p_{ij} of buying brand j next time. If this assumption is not made, the problem of how to aggregate the individual family purchase patterns arises. Obviously, the assumption is somewhat unreal; p_{ij} should be viewed as a random variable resulting from cumulative individual behavior patterns.

Howard, in addition to treating the problem of interpurchase times, describes a means for aggregating individual family purchase patterns and thereby introducing heterogeneity. Suppose we state that a customer is pur-

---

[12] A. A. Kuehn and Albert C. Rohloff, "Consumer Response Functions," in *Promotional Decisions Using Mathematical Models*, Patrick J. Robinson, Ed., Allyn and Bacon, Boston, 1967, p. 60.

chasing brand i at time zero. Now we ask ourselves the question: What is the probability that he will purchase brand j at time n? It is the multistep transition probability $p_{ij}(n)$, which is readily derived from the transition matrix: $((p_{ij}(n))) = P^n$. Now *each* customer of brand i at time zero has probability $p_{ij}(n)$ of purchasing brand j after n periods. If we assume that each customer acts independently of the others, the process is a Bernoulli process, and the resultant number of purchasers of j at n is given by the binomial distribution with probability of success $p_{ij}(n)$ and number of trials c_i equal to the number of customers in the original state.

Following the same argument, for each brand that exists at time zero we would have a separate probability distribution that describes the number of customers originally buying that brand who would purchase brand j at time n. The total number of customers who would purchase brand j at time n, then, is the distribution that results from the convolution of all the separate binomial distributions, or

$$p\ \{c_j(n) = m\} = \underset{i=1}{\overset{N}{*}}\ p_b[m_i|c_i,\ p_{ij}(n)] \qquad (10\text{-}5)$$

where $N=$ the number of brands at time zero, $m=$ the number of successes, where $\Sigma m_i = m$, and $*$ is a symbol for manifold convolution.

More generally, we would have to obtain similar distributions for each and every brand. However, we can still draw several more conclusions from the above formulation. The expected number of customers of brand j at time n, $\bar{c}_j(n)$, is the sum of the means of the appropriate binomial distributions,

$$\bar{c}_j(n) = \sum_{i=1}^{N} c_i p_{ij}(n) \qquad (10\text{-}6)$$

or, in the more usual vector notation,

$$\bar{c}(n) = c(0)p^n \qquad (10\text{-}7)$$

Similarly, the variance, $\sigma^2_{c_j(n)}$, would be

$$\sigma^2_{c_j(n)} = \sum_{i=1}^{N} c_i p_{ij}(n)[1 - p_{ij}(n)] \qquad (10\text{-}8)$$

which could also be expressed in vector-matrix notation.

The above arguments demonstrate several important characteristics of the Markovian model. First, even in the steady state the c_j (the number of consumers purchasing a particular brand) will fluctuate, since $\bar{c}_j$ is an expected value with corresponding variance $\sigma^2_{c_j}$. Second, the assumption of homogeneity is by no means necessary if one is willing to use a more complicated model, and, further, it disguises some of the potential richness of the Markov process. Third, even if the problem of homogeneity is eliminated, the requirement of stationarity is still necessary, since $p_{ij}(n)$ is found by determining the nth power of the transition matrix.

Morrison has offered and tested another means of introducing heterogeneity.[13] Suppose we describe the state space as containing only two brands, a family's most frequently purchased (favorite) brand and all others. We denote the purchase of one of the other brands as a 0 and the favorite brand as a 1. If the process were zero order, or Bernoulli, the probability transition matrix would look as follows:

$$\begin{array}{cc} & \begin{array}{cc} & t+1 \\ 1 & 0 \end{array} \\ t \begin{array}{c} 1 \\ 0 \end{array} & \begin{bmatrix} p & 1-p \\ p & 1-p \end{bmatrix} \end{array}$$

The parameter p is assumed to have some distribution across the population; heterogeneity is therefore introduced into the system. Morrison then introduces a constant k, lying between 0 and 1 and having the same value for all families, into the second row:

$$\begin{array}{cc} & \begin{array}{cc} & t+1 \\ 1 & 0 \end{array} \\ t \begin{array}{c} 1 \\ 0 \end{array} & \begin{bmatrix} p & 1-p \\ kp & 1-kp \end{bmatrix} \end{array}$$

He terms this the Brand Loyal model, because an individual with a high value of p is more likely to purchase brand 1 on the next trial regardless of his current state than an individual with a low p. If the terms in the second row of the preceding matrix are reversed, we obtain what Morrison terms the Last Purchase Loyal model, which is obviously the case in which the consumer with a high p is most likely to purchase again the brand he last purchased. Of course, the magnitude of these effects depends upon the value that k is found to have in the relevant population; the independent case is simply $k = 1$ in the Brand Loyal model.

Linear learning models

The Linear Learning model has its foundation in the work of Bush and Mosteller on learning theory.[14] Kuehn was the first to recognize and explore the possibility of applying their work to consumer purchase behavior.[15] The Linear Learning model is based on the classical psychological learning model discussed previously and holds that the purchase of a brand

---

[13] Donald G. Morrison, *Stochastic Models for Time Series with Application in Marketing*, technical report No. 8, Program in Operations Research, Stanford University, Stanford, Calif., August 1965.

[14] Robert R. Bush and Frederick Mosteller, *Stochastic Models for Learning*, Wiley, New York, 1955.

[15] The most recent statement of this work is found in Kuehn and Rohloff, *op. cit.*

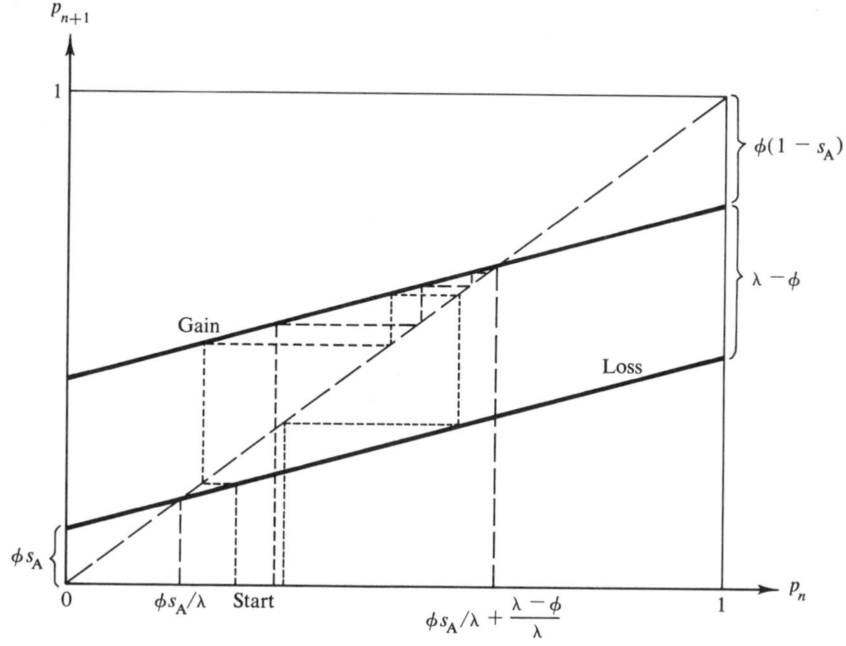

FIGURE **10-2**

Linear learning model for brand A

increases its probability of purchase (or the nonpurchase decreases the probability of purchase) on the next shopping trip.

The Linear Learning model is based on a binary choice system, the same as Morrison's models, in which the brands are "ours" and "others." Since on a given purchase occasion (trial) either our brand is purchased or some other brand is purchased, if we define the probability of purchase of our brand on trial n as p_n, then $1 - p_n$ is the probability of purchasing another brand. Next, we specify two equations that describe how p_n is modified according to whether or not purchase of our brand took place. If our brand was purchased, we have:

$$\text{Gain} \qquad p_{n+1} = (1 - \lambda)p_n + \phi s + (\lambda - \phi) \tag{10-9}$$

and the following equation if our brand was not purchased:

$$\text{Loss} \qquad p_{n+1} = (1 - \lambda)p_n + \phi s \tag{10-10}$$

where λ and ϕ are constants depending on the product class, but independent of a particular brand, and s is the projected market share of our brand at equilibrium.[16] Also $\lambda > \phi$, and obviously $\Sigma s = 1$ over all brands. Figure 10-2 is a graphic representation of the model.

---

[16] Since $Ep_{n+1} = (1 - \lambda)p_n + \phi s + (\lambda - \phi)p_n = p_n + \phi(s - p_n)$, we see that $Ep_{n+1} = p_n$ if and only if $p_n = s$. See equation (10-11) and the subsequent discussion.

Two new quantities, $\phi s_A/\lambda$ and $\phi s_A/\lambda + (\lambda - \phi)/\lambda$, are introduced in Figure 10-2. These are, respectively, the lower, L, and upper, U, boundaries that the probability of purchase of brand A may attain.[17] In other words, p_n may never be 1 or 0 but lies between the above-defined boundaries. The dotted and short dashed lines in Figure 10-2 illustrate two possible purchase sequences of four trials each. In the dotted line case, the consumer purchase pattern is ZAAZ, whereas for the short dashed line it is AAAA, where Z indicates a purchase other than brand A, our brand. Note that in the latter case the consumer has become increasingly brand loyal and is almost at the upper boundary.

We offer below a simple numerical illustration of the model for both of the four-run purchase sequences illustrated in Figure 10-2. Assume a four-brand market in which the probabilities of purchasing each brand at time n and the projected market shares at equilibrium are:

Brand	p_n	s_i	L	U
A	.50	.40	.20	.70
1	.15	.20	.10	.60
2	.30	.30	.15	.65
3	.05	.10	.05	.55
	1.00	1.00		

We have used $\lambda = .4$ and $\phi = .2$ in computing L and U. If the consumer purchases brand A, we would obtain

Brand		p_{n+1}
A	$(1 - .4)(.50) + (.2)(.40) + (.4 - .2) =$	.58
1	$(1 - .4)(.15) + (.2)(.20) =$	.13
2	$(1 - .4)(.30) + (.2)(.30) =$	.24
3	$(1 - .4)(.05) + (.2)(.10) =$	.05
		1.00

If the consumer purchases in the AAAA pattern, we can now calculate the market shares at the end of each of the four trials, and we find:

Brand	p_n	p_{n+1}	p_{n+2}	p_{n+3}	p_{n+4}
A	.50	.58	.63	.66	.67
1	.15	.13	.12	.11	.11
2	.30	.24	.20	.18	.17
3	.05	.05	.05	.05	.05

For the ZAAZ case (assuming purchase of brand 3, a new brand, when A is not purchased), the results would be as follows:

Brand	p_n	p_{n+1}	p_{n+2}	p_{n+3}	p_{n+4}
A	.50	.38	.51	.59	.43
1	.15	.13	.12	.11	.11
2	.30	.24	.20	.18	.17
3	.05	.25	.17	.12	.29

What is happening above is that the consumer is learning or "dislearning"

[17] U and L are the solutions to $p_{n+1} = p_n$ if equations (10-9) and (10-10), respectively, are used.

about A at some rate, and each trial provides an additional opportunity for him to evaluate his satisfaction with A.

There are several additional important characteristics of the Linear Learning model. If the slopes of both the rejection (loss) and acceptance (gain) operators are equal, the influence of past purchases on the next purchase decreases exponentially. There are other important reasons for assuming the slopes to be equal: First, this means that the learning rate for all products is equal, permitting combination of all brands except ours (A) into one group and comparison of ours to others at the same time; second, the mathematics of the model becomes much more complicated if the slopes are unequal and the available evidence seems to indicate that greater sophistication is not required. Differences in buying rate are reflected in the perpendicular distance separating the gain and loss operators and the slope of these operators[18]; for both light and heavy buyers (frequent and infrequent purchasers) the lines are close together, but the latter pair has much greater slope, approaching 1 in the limit, with the slope of the other pair approaching 0 in the limit. For "average" buyers the operators are further apart.

The discussion to this point has viewed the model as family specific, but Kuehn suggests that the model would be more realistic if p_n were interpreted as an expected value over a population of families. Given such an interpretation, U and L are not binding limits on a specific family but rather on the expected value of p_n. Thus, the model quite readily admits a family who is totally brand loyal or disloyal. The expected value, $\bar{p}_n$, would satisfy

$$\begin{aligned}\bar{p}_{n+1} &= \bar{p}_n[(1-\lambda)\bar{p}_n + \phi s + \lambda - \phi] + (1-\bar{p}_n)[(1-\lambda)\bar{p}_n + \phi s] \\ &= (1-\phi)\bar{p}_n + \phi s\end{aligned} \tag{10-11}$$

Note that the rate at which $\bar{p}_n$ approaches the equilibrium brand share s depends only on ϕ. We graph $\bar{p}_{n+1}$ in Figure 10-3, and we also show that $\bar{p}_n = s$ at the point where the line $\bar{p}_{n+1} = (1-\phi)\bar{p}_n + \phi s$ intersects $\bar{p}_{n+1} = \bar{p}_n$.

The preceding model does not take account of time effects. However, they can be included by means of the following formulation:

$$p_T - s = (p_0 - s) \exp[-T(\alpha + \sigma/N)] \tag{10-12}$$

where T = elapsed time

p_0 = probability of purchase at initial time

p_T = probability of purchase at time T given that the brand was purchased at time 0

N = number of purchases in the elapsed time

α, σ = parameters for the product class

q = T/N = average time between purchases

---

[18] See the discussion following equation (10-13).

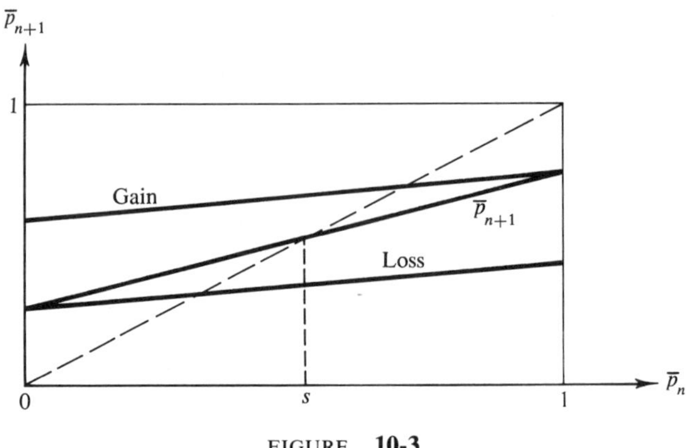

FIGURE 10-3

Expected value $\bar{p}_{n+1}$

If $p_0 > s$, we can rewrite equation (10-12) as

$$\ln(p_T - s) = \ln(p_0 - s) - \alpha T - \sigma q \tag{10-13}$$

We can make the following observations from equation (10-13). First, if T is fixed and q increases, then p_T decreases to the equilibrium brand share s; that is, heavy buyers remain more loyal to the brand in a fixed period of time. Second, in the gain and loss equations presented originally, ϕ and λ were not made time dependent, which they actually are. For example, as T and q become larger, p_T decreases to s no matter what p_0 is. Examination of the gain equation shows that both λ and ϕ must approach 1 to make this possible. Thus, if a family purchases very infrequently, no matter what the value of p_n, p_{n+1} will be near to s. This is the character of the narrow separation and shallow slope described earlier for gain and loss equations for light buyers. Similar analysis will lead to the descriptions given previously of the characteristics of the Linear Learning model for heavy and average buyers. Estimation of $\lambda(t)$ and $\phi(t)$ is very difficult because of the same problem we found in Markovian analysis: In equation (10-12) the parameters are indexed on real time, whereas the gain and loss equations are based on purchase-to-purchase time. A typical relationship between $\lambda(t)$ and $\phi(t)$ for a specific product class is given in Figure 10-4.

The available empirical evidence on the Linear Learning model as a useful tool for normative decision making is not great. Some of what has been uncovered is contradictory in nature, and the sum total of reported research on this model is relatively small. In one of the more widely circulated studies, Carman finds that repurchase probability does not decay in the fashion predicted by Kuehn as interpurchase time increases. On the other hand, Carman's results also show that the Linear Learning model seems to characterize well the purchase behavior of those whom he classified as brand

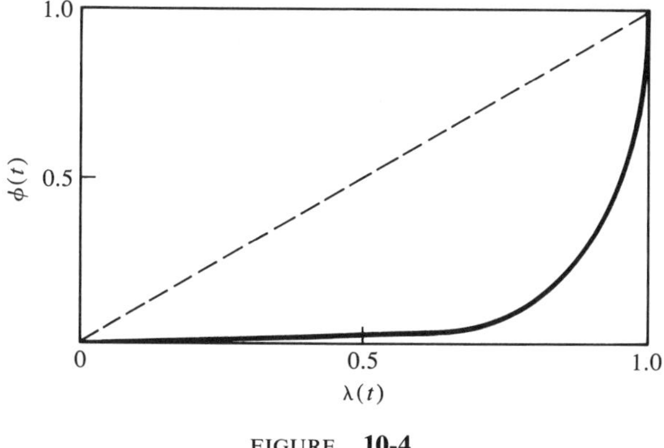

FIGURE **10-4**

The relationship of λ and φ over time

switchers.[19] In a different vein, Massy has demonstrated a means for distributing the initial response probability across the population; previous versions of the model assumed that all members of the population have the same probability of purchasing "our" brand or the "others'" brand or that the aggregate average probability could be used as a base starting point.[20] In effect, this procedure introduces heterogeneity.

What of the relative advantages of the two approaches to the analysis of purchase behavior discussed so far? The learning model has more appeal intuitively because it has an apparent psychological explanation, whereas the Markovian model whose states are brands bought only describes the phenomena without producing any insight into why they occur. In addition, Kuehn has developed the Linear Learning model beyond the description provided above in order to incorporate the effects of the firm's marketing strategies upon consumer choice.[21] In fact, in Kuehn's formulation the long-run probability of purchase is determined by the factors in the marketing mix. Since, clearly, consumer behavior is not something that operates in a

[19] See James M. Carman, "Brand Switching and Linear Learning Models," *Journal of Advertising Research*, Vol. 6, No. 2, June 1966, pp. 23–31.

[20] William F. Massy, "Estimation of Parameters for Linear Learning Models," working paper No. 78, Graduate School of Business, Stanford University, Stanford, Calif., October 1965.

[21] See: A. A. Kuehn, "A Model for Budgeting Advertising," in *Mathematical Models and Methods in Marketing*, Frank M. Bass et al., Eds., Irwin, Homewood, Ill., 1961, pp. 315–348; and "An Analysis of the Dynamics of Consumer Behavior and Its Implications for Marketing Management," Carnegie Institute of Technology, Pittsburgh, Pa., November 1958, unpublished Ph.D. thesis. Telser has undertaken similar work using a Markovian model in which the transition probabilities are a function of the price charged (this could possibly be generalized to other elements in the marketing mix); see Lester G. Telser, "Least-Squares Estimates of Transition Probabilities," in *Measurement in Economics*, Carl F. Christ et al., Eds., Stanford University Press, Stanford, Calif., 1963.

vacuum but rather is affected by the actions of the firm and its competitors, incorporation of the marketing mix may yet prove to be the most valuable feature of the Linear Learning model. On the other hand, the mathematical manipulation is somewhat easier in the Markovian class of models, which may, in part, explain why there has been relatively much more work on these—this observation is probably less true as the Markovian models become more sophisticated, taking account of heterogeneity, for example.

A penetration model

In the Markovian and Linear Learning models, the analytical emphasis has been placed on purchase occasions and some difficulty was experienced in realistically taking account of the time horizon. In the models that follow, the analytical focus is on the time dimension and, correspondingly, on the assessment of the implication of particular purchase patterns through periods of time (as opposed to a sequence of n purchase occasions). In their pioneering work, Fourt and Woodlock[22] suggested that an appropriate way to measure consumer acceptance of a new product could be developed by concentrating on the time interval between purchases for repeat customers. Obviously, this implies careful attention to identifying the initial purchase in the data pertaining to an individual customer. For example, in current practice, a first purchase as the result of a deal (say, a cents-off coupon) is not considered the initial purchase; rather, the usual definition is based on the first full-price purchase. Penetration is here defined as the number of households that have tried the product, that is, who have made the initial purchase. The first repeat ratio is the fraction of initial buyers who make a second purchase, the second repeat ratio is the fraction of those who made a second purchase who make a third purchase, and so on.

We proceed by utilizing knowledge gained from experience with similar products previously marketed and estimate the general shape of the penetration curve. Based on the data, we then estimate[23] the specific parameters for the product of concern. A common form of this curve that seems quite generally applicable is

$$I_i = rx_0(1 - r)^{i-1} + k \qquad (10\text{-}14)$$

where I_i = the increment in penetration for the ith time period and the parameters are roughly describable as follows:

---

[22] Louis A. Fourt and Joseph W. Woodlock, "Early Prediction of Market Success for New Grocery Products," *Journal of Marketing*, Vol. 25, No. 2, October 1960, pp. 31–38.

[23] See Francis J. Anscombe, "Estimating a Mixed-Exponential Response Law," *Journal of the American Statistical Association*, Vol. 56, 1961, pp. 493–502, for a theoretical discussion of estimating the parameters in equations (10-14) and (10-15).

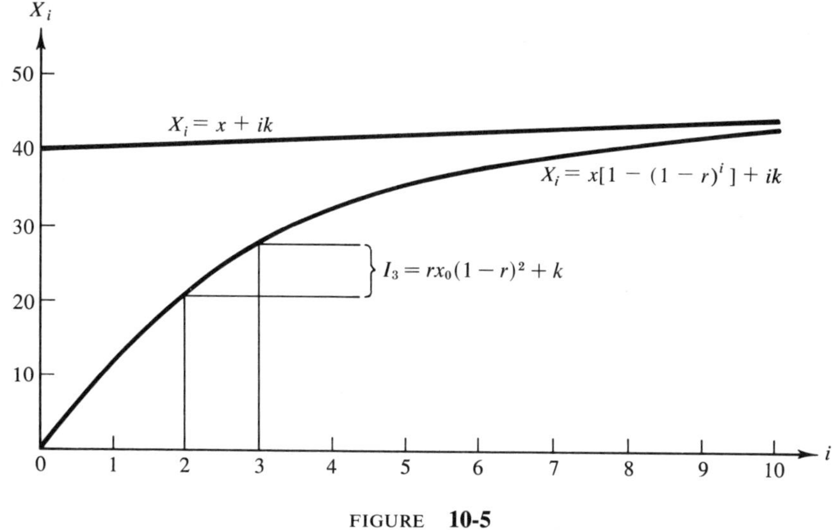

FIGURE **10-5**

Depth of penetration over time

r = constant of proportionality

x = the maximum level of penetration of the product, analogous to ultimate market share

k = a small positive constant

The cumulative penetration curve, as opposed to the incremental one, is given by

$$X_i = \sum_{j=1}^{i} I_j = x[1 - (1 - r)^i] + ik \tag{10-15}$$

In the limiting case as i approaches ∞, $I_i = k$ and the boundary line that the cumulative penetration curve approaches asymptotically is defined by $X_i = x + ik$. This formulation is illustrated in Figure 10-5 with $r = .3$, $x = 40\%$, and $k = .004$.

The first step in use of the model will be to derive the repeat ratios. Several things must be considered before this can be undertaken. The model is valid only under the assumption that there have been no significant changes in the environment, either in those factors controlled by the manufacturer, such as price and product design, or in the particular character of competitive activity. Obviously, the validity of this assumption is very difficult to establish (as is true whenever it is utilized), but the model's predictions have been good except for those instances where it is known that the assumptions have been significantly violated.

Another consideration is a complication introduced by "heavy" buyers of a product class. In a fixed time period, the number of repeat buyers is an underestimate of those who will ever repeat because the "lighter" buyers may not yet have had an opportunity to repeat. Accordingly, adjustments have to be made in the data to reflect these buying differences, based in part on whether the product class is bought relatively frequently or infrequently and on an estimate of the average time interval until the next purchase for each level of repurchase.[24] This problem and that of the imposition of a ceiling are better handled by converting to more sophisticated continuous forms of the model.[25]

The repeat ratios are calculated using the revised number of purchasers at the end of the first period of analysis obtained by means of the corrections just described. The estimated number of new buyers at the end of the second period of analysis is obtained by using equation (10-14) with whatever values of r, x, and k apply to the product class. The repeat ratios are then applied successively to the estimated number of buyers at the end of the second period to obtain the number of purchasers at each repeat level. The original (uncorrected) numbers of buyers at each repeat level in the first period are then subtracted from the estimates of those at the corresponding levels at the end of the second period to obtain the net estimated gain at each level. This net estimated gain is then finally compared to the actual gain. Table 10-1 will help illustrate the procedure. The repeat ratios are calculated by dividing the ith row of column 1 by row $i-1$ of column 2. The estimated number of buyers at the end of the second period is obtained by multiplying the ith row of column 4 by row $i+1$ of column 3. The data have been devised for illustrative purposes and the actual gain column is left blank, because any comparison of actual against predicted would be arbitrary. To obtain estimates for a third time period, the entire process would be repeated, beginning by correcting the actual number of repeat purchasers at the end of the second period to reflect the inadequacy of time for the next repeat.

The success in utilizing this model for predictive purposes has been quite respectable. As a result, the manager's ability to make a number of operational decisions is enhanced. For example, the model permits a manufacturer to withdraw a new product at an early stage if success appears unlikely or to pursue the product's marketing more strongly in the opposite situation. Other strategic implications may also be obtained from the model.

---

[24] This adjustment is made by reducing the denominator of the repeat ratio to reflect the number of persons adjudged not to have adequate time to make another purchase prior to the end of the arbitrarily established time period.

[25] See William F. Massy, "Models for Purchase Timing and Market Penetration," working paper No. 3, Graduate School of Industrial Administration, Carnegie-Mellon University, Pittsburgh, Pa., February 1967, pp. 27–35.

TABLE **10-1**

Estimated repeat buyers in the second time period

Buyer type	(1) Number of purchases during observation period	(2) Corrected number of purchasers during observation period*	(3) Repeat ratio	(4) Estimated number of purchasers at end of prediction period	(5) Estimated gain in purchasers at end of prediction period	Actual gain
New buyers	10,000	6,050		13,000†	3,000	
1st repeat	3,500	3,150	.579	7,520	4,020	
2nd repeat	2,100	1,900	.668	5,030	2,930	
3rd repeat	1,200	1,100	.632	3,180	1,980	
4th repeat	800	700	.727	2,320	1,520	
Over 4th repeat	1,200		1.703	3,950	2,750	
Total purchases	18,800			35,000	16,200	

* Correction is for sufficient time to permit or repeat purchase.

† Obtained via use of equation (10-14).

Too few triers may indicate something wrong with advertising or packaging; a low repeat ratio may indicate dissatisfaction on the part of the purchasers when they actually use the product, implying that there is something wrong with the directions, the product itself, or the like; a long interval between purchases suggests that promotional emphasis might best be directed at triers; and so on. The manufacturer would alter his marketing mix accordingly.

An improved penetration model

The work of Fourt and Woodlock has been significantly extended by Massy. Massy calls this extension STEAM (Stochastic Evolutionary Adoption Model), and has described it in the following terms.[26] STEAM consists of: (i) a primary model that links the waiting times between new product purchases (or the time between the product's introduction and the first trial) to the probability that the product will be purchased in any particular interval of time; (ii) a series of secondary models that relate the purchase probabilities to time-varying phenomena and provide for population heterogeneity; (iii) a set of probability distributions for waiting times, based on the above; (iv) parameter estimation methods; and (v) a Monte Carlo simulation procedure that develops forecasts from the waiting time distributions.

The immediate objective in applying a depth-of-trial oriented model (one based on the number of times the brand has been bought) is to predict the time paths of the cumulative proportions of one-time buyers, two-time buyers, and so on. These groups are handled separately because of the probable importance of purchase event feedback in the new product context. Effects of feedback are incorporated into the analysis by estimating the model's parameters separately for each depth-of-trial group. Although this procedure is somewhat unwieldy, it has significant diagnostic advantages and avoids prior assumptions about the form of the crucial feedback relations. All the relations are assumed to hold separately for each depth-of-trial class.

The STEAM model is built around two random variables, which are defined as follows:

t = the time between a household's entry into a given depth of trial group and its conversion to the next level; that is, an interpurchase time

[26] This description is taken directly from William F. Massy, "A Stochastic Evolutionary Model for Evaluating New Products," paper presented at the United States Meeting of the Institute of Management Sciences, Statler Hilton Hotel, Boston, April 4–6, 1967, pp. 3–8. See also Massy's "A Dynamic Model for Monitoring New Product Adoption," working paper No. 95, Graduate School of Business, Stanford University, Stanford, Calif., March 1965.

μ_0 = a household's propensity to purchase the new product,[27] evaluated right after the last purchase (or the product's introduction); this variable provides the starting point for the household's time path of purchase propensities, which we shall denote by $\mu(t)$

For each depth-of-trial class, we assume that the density function of t is given by the following, which is the primary model mentioned above:

$$f(t|\mu(.)) = e^{-m(t)}\mu(t) \tag{10-16}$$

where

$$m(t) = \int_1^t \mu(x)\, dx$$

This is essentially a "nonhomogeneous Poisson" assumption. The time origin is taken as 1 rather than 0 in order to accommodate the secondary models given in equations (10-17) and (10-19).

The cumulative effects of advertising, distribution, word of mouth, and other external factors combine with the effect of forgetting to produce a net change in μ according to

$$\mu(t) = \mu_0 t^\lambda \qquad t \geq 1 \tag{10-17}$$

providing for an upward or downward drift of purchase propensities, depending on the sign of λ.

Different households react differently to exposure and use of the new product. In the absence of any prior segmentation on the basis of descriptor variables, such as attitudes or demographics, heterogeneity is introduced by assuming that the members of our panel are selected at random from a population where μ_0 is distributed according to

$$P(\mu_0 > 0|T) = M_T \tag{10-18}$$

$$f(\mu_0|\mu_0 > 0, T) = \frac{\beta \exp\,[-\beta\mu_0](\beta\mu_0)^{\alpha(T)-1}}{\Gamma\,(\alpha(T))}$$

This assumes that a proportion $1 - M$ of households is not in the market for the new product at all; that is, those households have zero purchase propensity. The μ's of the remainder are distributed according to the gamma density with parameters α and β. The variable T is defined as the time at

[27] Purchase propensity is defined as the limit of the purchase incidence probability as the time increment goes to zero. That is,

$$\mu(t) = \lim_{h\to 0} \frac{1}{h} P\,\{\text{Purchase in } (t, t+h)|\text{past history}\}$$

In a stationary exponential model, μ would be the parameter of the underlying Poisson process.

which the household in question converted to the current depth-of-trial level and affects the distribution of household purchase propensities according to

$$\alpha(T) = \alpha_0 T^{\gamma} \qquad T \geq 1 \tag{10-19}$$

The mean of the prior distribution of μ for households who reach a given trial level early will be larger than for the laggards if γ is negative, and conversely. The weighted average M for each depth-of-trial class, $\bar{M}$, where the weights are the proportion of respondents in each T-value group for that class, is provided by the model.

The version of the STEAM model outlined contains five free parameters (after collapsing the M_T's into $\bar{M}$).[28] They can be interpreted as follows:

λ — The rate at which a household's purchase propensity changes with the time since its last purchase of the new product. If $\lambda < 0$, propensity declines with time; for example, the forgetting effect dominates the cumulative effects of marketing variables and word of mouth. The opposite is true if $\lambda > 0$. The model requires that $\lambda > -1$ in order for $f(t)$ to be defined, and we would expect $\lambda < 1$ to avoid explosive behavior.

α, β — The parameters of the conditional distribution of initial purchase propensities. The model requires that both be positive. Interpretations will often be made in terms of the mean and variance of the conditional distribution:

$$E(\mu_0 | \mu_0 > 0) = \alpha/\beta; \text{ var } (\mu_0 | \mu_0 > 0) = \alpha/\beta^2$$

If $\alpha \leq 1$, the conditional density assumes an exponential-like shape, whereas for $\alpha > 1$ it has a distinct mode. (Recall that α is a function of α_0 and T.)

γ — The rate at which the α parameter given above changes as a function of time of conversion. There are no necessary limits on γ, although we would expect $-1 < \gamma < 1$ to achieve reasonable behavior.

$\bar{M}$ — the average proportion of households who are "in the market" for the new product.

All five parameters apply to each depth-of-trial class separately.

The density and distribution functions for interpurchase times, conditional on the values of the parameters and T, are obtained by substituting equations (10-17), (10-18), and (10-19), which are the secondary models referred to above, into the primary model given in (10-16) and integrating

[28] A free parameter is one estimated directly from the data.

out μ_0. (The initial purchase propensity μ_0 is an unobservable random variable; integration removes the condition on μ_0 and expresses $f(t)$ in terms of the known T value and the parameters.) After performing these operations we have

$$f(t|T) = M_T\alpha_0 T^\gamma \beta^{\alpha_0 T^\gamma} \frac{t^\lambda}{\{(t^{\lambda+1} - 1)/(\lambda + 1) + \beta\}^{\alpha_0 T^\gamma + 1}} \qquad (10\text{-}20)$$

and

$$F(t|T) = M_T - M_T \left\{\frac{\beta(\lambda + 1)}{t^{\lambda+1} + \beta(\lambda + 1) - 1}\right\}^{\alpha_0 T^\gamma} \qquad t \geq 1$$

We will also have occasion to use the distribution of t given T and the knowledge that $\mu_0 > 0$. If we apply the rules of conditional probability, it is easy to see that

$$F(t|T, \mu_0 > 0) = 1 - \left\{\frac{\beta(\lambda + 1)}{t^{\lambda+1} + \beta(\lambda + 1) - 1}\right\}^{\alpha_0 T^\gamma} \qquad (10\text{-}21)$$

Obviously, the STEAM model can be put to use in answering the same kinds of managerial questions as those addressed by the Fourt and Woodlock model, as well as some of the operational questions posed for other models discussed earlier.

The negative binomial distribution

Still another approach to the analysis of consumer purchase behavior is the use of the Negative Binomial Distribution (NBD).[29] The use of the NBD is founded upon several assumptions: (1) The methodology requires integral units, so different package sizes of a product may have to be analyzed separately; (2) a single brand at a time is analyzed; (3) there is no general trend among the quantities of each brand consumed, so the system may be considered stationary[30]; (4) the purchases of any consumer over time may be characterized as though coming from a Poisson distribution and, correspondingly, the time periods are of sufficient length that purchases

---

[29] The chief proponent of this approach is A. S. C. Ehrenberg. See the following examples of his work on the subject: "The Pattern of Consumer Purchases," *Applied Statistics*, Vol. 8, 1959, pp. 26–41; "Estimating the Proportion of Loyal Buyers," *Journal of Marketing Research*, Vol. 1, No. 1, February 1964, pp. 56–59; and C. Chatfield, A. S. C. Ehrenberg, and G. I. Goodhart, "Progress on a Simplified Model of Stationary Purchasing Behavior," *Journal of the Royal Statistical Society*, Vol. 129, 1966, pp. 317–367. Additional empirical work on the negative binomial distribution was done by Gary L. Grahn while he was a graduate student at the University of Rochester, and his exposition of the NBD has helped our own presentation.

[30] This is Ehrenberg's definition of stationarity. However, the authors would suggest that the only criterion for stationarity is that the process not be time dependent; thus, trends or even wild fluctuations are quite permissible. A sine wave is a stationary process.

made in one period do not directly affect those made in the next; and (5) the Poisson parameters for different individuals in the population have a gamma distribution so that the (marginal) purchase distribution for any one individual is a negative binomial.[31]

The negative binomial probability[32] of purchase of r units in a single time period can be written as

$$p_r = \binom{k-1+r}{r}\left(\frac{k}{m+k}\right)^k\left(\frac{m}{m+k}\right)^r \qquad r = 0, 1, 2, \cdots \tag{10-22}$$

where m and k are parameters of the model. In this parametrization the mean and variance are[33]

$$\mu = k\,\frac{m/(m+k)}{k/(m+k)} = m \tag{10-23}$$

$$\sigma^2 = k\,\frac{m/(m+k)}{k^2/(m+k)^2} = \frac{m(m+k)}{k} \tag{10-24}$$

The distribution is always positively skewed and has a single mode at zero for small values of m and k that are typical of consumer purchase data.

Clearly, m, the mean amount of purchase of all consumers, will vary according to the length, T, of the time period. When necessary, we shall make use of the notation

$$m_T = mT \tag{10-25}$$

On the other hand, we expect k to be constant for any single brand and package size irrespective of the length of the time period. We can estimate[34] k_T from the proportion of consumers who buy, b_T, if we use the equation

$$b_T = 1 - p_0 = 1 - \left(1 + \frac{m_T}{k_T}\right)^{-k_T}, \tag{10-26}$$

If we know b_T and m_T for several different periods, we can obtain estimates of k_T that should turn out to be about equal.

Additional understanding of the NBD may be gained by examination of its probability generating function. From equation (3-21) we have

$$P_X(z) = \left[1 + \frac{m}{k}(1-z)\right]^{-k} \tag{10-27}$$

---

[31] See formula (3-54).

[32] See formula (3-18).

[33] See formulas (3-19) and (3-20).

[34] Estimation of this parameter is discussed at length in Francis J. Anscombe, "Sampling Theory of the Negative Binomial and Logarithmic Distributions," *Biometrika*, Vol. 37, December 1950, pp. 358–382.

Using the methods of that chapter we can also obtain the multivariate probability generating function for the quantities[35] $r_1, r_2, \ldots, r_n$ purchased by one customer in nonoverlapping intervals of lengths $T_1, T_2, \ldots, T_n$:

$$P(z_1, \ldots, z_n) = \left[1 + \frac{m}{k} \sum_{i=1}^{n} T_i(1 - z_i)\right]^{-k} \tag{10-28}$$

where we have made use of equation (10-25) for each m_{T_i}. We see that if we have estimated m and k for a single time period, then we have all the information we need to work with the multiperiod model.

If we consider two equal time periods, the predicted standard deviation of the differences in purchases of individual consumers for the two time periods should be distributed over all consumers as $\sqrt{2m}$. These values can then be compared to the observed standard deviation (root mean square), and they are in very close agreement for some 25 brands tested by Chatfield et al.[36]

When NBD is used to predict purchasing behavior within a single time period, a consistent discrepancy appears: The predicted standard deviations are almost always larger than the observed for high values of the observed. (For low values of the observed standard deviation, this discrepancy does not appear.) We might attempt to meet this problem by reasoning that the particular result may be a function of the number of zero purchasers in the population, since the definition of the nonbuyer is somewhat arbitrary anyway. One reasonable tactic might be to truncate the NBD and eliminate the zeros. To obtain the probabilities for the truncated distribution, we divide the probabilities for the NBD by $b = 1 - p_0$. Thus,

$$p_r = \frac{\binom{k-1+r}{r}(1-p)^k p^r}{1-(1-p)^k} \qquad r = 1, 2, \cdots \tag{10-29}$$

for the truncated NBD. The results[37] show that the fit of the NBD to the data is insensitive to how we treat the zeros: If the original fit was good, so is the fit after the number of zeros has been arbitrarily increased or decreased; if the original fit was poor, no such modification appears to improve it.

A second attempt to meet the discrepancy is to use a different, but closely related, distribution, the Logarithmic Series Distribution (LSD) to describe the data; that is, the nonzero part of the NBD can be described by

---

[35] Note that the r's are independent with regard to their (underlying) Poisson distributions but not with regard to their (marginal) negative binomial distributions.

[36] See Chatfield, Ehrenberg, and Goodhart, *op. cit.*, pp. 324–325.

[37] *Ibid.*, pp. 336–339.

the simpler, one-parameter LSD. Mathematically, this is obtained from the truncated NBD by letting k approach zero while holding the ratio

$$p = \frac{m}{m + k} \tag{10-30}$$

constant. Thus, for the LSD,

$$\begin{aligned} p_r &= \lim_{k \to 0} \frac{\binom{k-1+r}{r}(1-p)^k p^r}{1-(1-p)^k} \\ &= \frac{1}{-\ln(1-p)} \frac{p^r}{r} \qquad r = 1, 2, \ldots \end{aligned} \tag{10-31}$$

This approximation is, of course, most valid for cases where the parameter k of the NBD is small.

The mean of the LSD is

$$w = \frac{1}{-\ln(1-p)} \frac{p}{1-p} \tag{10-32}$$

This is approximately equal to m/b as defined for the NBD. The mean, w, is the mean rate of buying per buyer, rather than per customer, and this turns out to be a very fruitful way of analyzing the data. For example, the fraction of all purchases accounted for by purchasers of more than r units is theoretically equal to

$$\frac{1}{w} \sum_{i>r} i p_i = p^r \tag{10-33}$$

which is closely supported by actual data.[38]

Although the LSD model turns out to be useful, it does not overcome the variance discrepancy of the NBD model. In fact, either both models fit well or both fit poorly.[39] As yet, there is no satisfactory explanation for the variance discrepancy and no way of eliminating it.

As noted above, one of the advantages of the NBD is that it can be used to estimate loyalty or other purchasing characteristics over two periods on the basis of a single period's data. The NBD can also be used, given the assumption of stationarity, to signal the beginning of a possibly significant trend on the basis of "abnormal" loyalty levels. Similarly, the LSD model allows us to relate w in a given time period to factors such as the proportion of buyers in a longer time period, the proportion of buyers who will buy again in the following time period, the proportion of total purchases accounted for by these repeat buyers, and so on. Some of the operational alternatives that may result from such information should be fairly obvious.

---

[38] *Ibid.*, pp. 344–345.

[39] *Ibid.*, pp. 342–346.

Summary

From the preceding descriptions of several approaches to modeling consumer purchase behavior, we can separate out the chief problems in such work. The first and most obvious of these is the question of how to take account of the passage of time. Many of the peculiar time difficulties of certain classes of models result from the requirements imposed upon the data to make it conform to the mathematical character of the model. Further, as Nicosia has pointed out, the choice of the period for study and the size of the time interval may have very different behavioral implications and yet these implications have often been ignored.[40] A related, subsidiary part of the time question that has behavioral implications is the assumption of stationarity. This assumption seems reasonable for relatively short periods of time—for example, one period into the future in the case of the NBD—and the empirical evidence does not seem contradictory.

A second important consideration has to do with aggregation and population heterogeneity. On the whole, it would surely be worthwhile to structure a model that reflects individual consumer or family differences. But enriching models in this fashion introduces additional mathematical complexity and makes parameter estimation more difficult. The problem of aggregation of individual differences may also prove to be a principal stumbling block in the development of models more firmly rooted in the psychology of human behavior, because of the fundamental inadditivity of behavioral patterns. How does one, for example, find a means of summarizing drives or motivations across a relevant population?

A third issue in modeling purchase behavior is determining how much past purchase behavior is relevant to future decisions. Each of the models presented has a somewhat different approach to this issue, and no synthesis is readily apparent. The argument ranges, from the NBD and first-order Markovian models, which require purchase history from only one previous period, to the Linear Learning model and STEAM, which attempt to account for all past purchase history but with memory and experience decaying in some fashion. The empirical evidence here is, again, not clear-cut.

We have not attempted to interrelate the models. There are many points at which the different models utilize the same assumptions or the same mathematics, but these points are too numerous to deal with in detail. By way of illustration, however, the reader should note that the Markovian models are actually special cases of the Linear Learning models and that the Poisson distribution is a building block in both the STEAM and NBD models.

What we have basically are two mainstreams in the construction of mod-

---

[40] Francesco M. Nicosia, *Consumer Decision Processes: Marketing and Advertising Implications*, Prentice-Hall, Englewood Cliffs, N.J., 1966, p. 204.

els of consumer purchase behavior, one focusing on purchase occasions, the other on the incidence of purchases during a specified time period. The Markovian and Linear Learning models are examples of the first type of approach, whereas the remainder of the models described illustrate the second. Although much experimental and developmental work is being done in the direction of improving models of purchase behavior, there will probably not be significant improvement in the behavioral foundations of these models in the near future. Rather, what can be hoped for is increased accuracy in the predictions extracted from models based primarily on the observation of the purchase event.

Appendix

Some excellent recent work in the quantification of psychological models of behavior has been done by Nicosia.[41] Although his work is theoretical, one can learn much about the human decision process by studying it. We present here the structure of Nicosia's model primarily to familiarize the reader with this type of work, for we could not hope to discuss all the behavioral ramifications. Nicosia defines the decision process as being composed of the following variables:[42]

B The "final" act. For instance, the act of buying brand X.

M The consumer's motivation. A strong driving force resulting from some underlying process of interaction that specifically leads a consumer toward brand X more than toward any other brand.

A The consumer's attitude. A driving force that is weaker than M and not uniquely crystallized on brand X.

C The communication sent by a business firm. This may be any stimulus: a new package design, or an advertisement of brand X, and so on.

t The calendar time.

For at least one type of consumer the relationships among these variables can be described by the following postulates:

Postulate 1. The time rate of change of the level of buying B of a brand X at time t is some function f_b of the level of a consumer's motivation M toward that brand and the level of buying B of it at time t.

Postulate 2. The level of a consumer's motivation M toward a certain brand X at time t is some function f_m of the level of a consumer's attitude A toward that brand at time t.

Postulate 3. The time rate of change of the level of a consumer's attitude A toward a certain brand X at time t is some function f_a of his level of buying B of that brand, of the level of his attitude A toward that brand, and of the level of the communication (e.g., advertising) C of that brand, all at time t.

---

[41] Nicosia, *op. cit.*, ch. 7.

[42] *Ibid.*, p. 197.

Postulate 4. The level of the communication C at time t is chosen by the experimenter rather than being determined by any of the variables operating in the decision process; that is, C is an exogenous variable.[43]

If we assume that the relationships are linear, we can obtain the following set of differential equations:[44]

$$\frac{dB(t)}{dt} = b[M(t) - \beta B(t)] \tag{10-34}$$

$$M(t) = \dot{m}A(t) \tag{10-35}$$

$$\frac{dA(t)}{dt} = a[B(t) - \alpha A(t)] + cC(t) \tag{10-36}$$

$$C(t) = \bar{C} \tag{10-37}$$

where b, β, m, a, α, and c are coefficients that reflect the type of consumer personality. $\bar{C}$ is a constant and indicates that the stimulus is applied uniformly through time. Equilibrium at time t is obtained when equations (10-34) and (10-36) are set equal to zero after substituting (10-37) into (10-36). Each of the coefficients has a readily comprehensible meaning; for example, if we look at equation (10-36), we can see that, at equilibrium in the absence of advertising ($C = 0$) or where the impact of the influence of advertising is zero ($c = 0$), the coefficient α relates B to A. This coefficient can then be interpreted as summarizing through time "the way the attitude toward the advertised brand is affected by past purchases and consumption."[45] By similar analysis, the meaning of the other coefficients may be defined. The feasible values that the coefficients can take on and still have a meaningful behavioral interpretation are identified and found to be

$$a, b > 0$$

$$0 < m < 1$$

$$\alpha > 0$$

$$\beta \geq 1$$

The coefficient c may assume any value. These conditions hold for the case where $B, M, A, C \geq 0$. B is taken as the dependent variable, M and A are endogenous to the consumer's decision process, and C is the exogenous, independent variable.[46]

The preceding model really has few normative implications at this stage of development. Our objective in presenting it, however, is different from that for most of the other models in this book. Here we are attempting to

---

[43] *Ibid.*, p. 198.

[44] *Ibid.*, p. 209. This model can also be cast in a nonlinear framework, but exposition is more difficult.

[45] *Ibid.*, p. 213.

[46] *Ibid.*, pp. 214–215.

acquaint the reader with a very important area of research that may yield important results in the not too distant future, as opposed to presenting an operational model. Some study of the literature in this area will give the reader a feeling for the direction in which this psychological and sociological research work on decision making is moving, as well as an ability to assess the points at which these models and the quantitative models presented herein will interconnect.[47] Such study now should permit more rapid assimilation of these techniques into the manager's set of analytical tools in the future.

[47] An illustration of a different attack on the problem emphasizing sociological influences may be found in James S. Coleman, *Models of Change and Response Uncertainty*, Prentice-Hall, Englewood Cliffs, N.J., 1964.

INFORMATION FOR MARKETING DECISIONS

CHAPTER ELEVEN

In previous chapters our concern has been with the design and analysis of models for decision making. Emphasis has been placed on demonstration of the interrelationships of various factors in the marketing environment and the construction of normative models based on these relationships. However, few of the models are useful without a sufficient data base, which can be defined as one from which the values of the parameters in a particular situation can be established. Given the established parameters, the ability of the model can be evaluated in terms of given criteria. This chapter examines the ability to design, evaluate, and implement decision-making models as related to the data bases that support them.

Frequently, a mathematical model of some situation is not constructed because of an inability to quantify what are thought to be the relevant factors in the situation. However, marketing managers often have a wealth of data available—much of it only collected and never analyzed and utilized for decision-making purposes. The real problem seems to be selection of the appropriate factors and a definition of the interrelationships among them. The point is that the marketing manager is less often confounded by lack of information than by the need for a precise statement on how to utilize the information. Thus, many more models may be possible in marketing than are actually built.

The type of data we have been speaking of are frequently termed "hard" data as opposed to "soft" data, which are essentially judgmental data. Examples of soft data are the scores a product is assigned by a manager in a product-screening system composed of many different factors, values assigned to the editorial climate of a particular communications vehicle in terms of its effect on the image of the firm or product, subjective estimates of the likelihood of different states of nature occurring, and so on. The methodology for eliciting and combining subjective estimates is beyond the scope of this book.[1] The important point to note, however, is that substantial controversy exists about the implications and validity of models built largely upon soft data. Our view is that if a model is instructive and produces useful insights for the management, the character of the data in terms of "soft" vs. "hard" is not too important.[2]

Information systems

The data base supporting the firm's marketing operations is usually referred to as a *marketing information system.* Closer inspection of most material on this subject reveals that what is being discussed is really little more than the various requisite information flows and is a far cry from generally accepted definitions of a system. A system is a configuration of elements in interaction whose characteristics – economic, physical, biological, etc. – are known. The study of the relationship of the behavior of the system to that of the elements composing it is called *system science*; the properties of particular interest are transient and steady-state behavior, fluctuations, capacity, delay, loss, reliability, efficiency, and cost. Optimization and control of such systems must be based on understanding and quantification of their overall behavior. We are thus reluctant to use the term *information system*, but because of its widespread acceptance we shall adopt the convention; however, our references shall always be in the more limited sense of identifying the data bases and the information flows rather than a concern with questions of quantification and optimality.

From the plethora of articles and books that have appeared since the mid-1960s on the subject of management information systems, one would get the impression that managers previously operated without information or with extremely limited information. Such is not the case, of course. Accounting systems have always provided information on operations, although these data have not been useful for all types of decision problems. Various control reports not directly tied into the accounting system, such as reports of sales activities, are in widespread use. Moreover, it is difficult to imagine how any firm could operate if it did not have, at the minimum, a well-established informal information system composed principally of people. The notion of an information system has been brought to the fore by the use of

---

[1] A description of one procedure for collecting subjective data may be found in C. West Churchman, Russell L. Ackoff, and E. L. Arnoff, *Introduction to Operations Research*, Wiley, New York, 1952, ch. 6.

[2] Nevertheless, there seems to be a greater burden of proof with respect to a model's ability to generate *valid* insights placed on complex models built largely on subjective data.

electronic data processing to supposedly summarize and analyze vast quantities of data. In fact, it may be suspected that one reason for the use of the term *information system* is the common practice of attaching the word *system* to a configuration of electronic data processing equipment and its corresponding software. Many such computer-based systems have been installed whose output no one uses. The basic reason for this situation is that the computer-provided output has little or no value compared to the human information processing organization output. This phenomenon has led the designers of computer-based information-processing systems to realize that the capabilities of computers to process information rapidly and in almost any form desired do not, in themselves, guarantee that a computer-based information system will even be usable, let alone an improvement over the system it replaces. Rather, it has become recognized that certain key questions must be posed and answered before a computer system to provide information for decision making is designed: What information should be collected? How should this information be analyzed? To whom should reports be sent? To what extent is management evaluation necessary? (That is, can some reports result in adjustment and correction of operations without management intervention?) Obviously, numerous other pertinent questions can also be asked. In the succeeding sections of this chapter we shall attempt to delineate the key problems for the marketing manager in utilizing information and then discuss the design of an information system.

Information management problems

The goal of a management information system is a relatively simple one: to provide each decision maker with the information required for him to make his decisions, insofar as it is available and is amenable to analysis. Unfortunately, the statement of the objective is easier than its attainment. Consider, first, the question of what is *relevant* information. In some sense, it could be argued that the more we know the better off we are. There are, however, two flaws in such an argument: (1) Each piece of information is not equally valuable in terms of how much it reduces the uncertainty surrounding a given decision, and (2) information is not a free commodity, in terms of either generation or accumulation. Thus, all the information provided to a manager should be pertinent to his decisions.

Unfortunately, large volumes of irrelevant information are directed at managers. Sometimes this is due to the fact that the information was useful for one or more decisions at an earlier time, and although the character of the decisions has changed, the information flow has not. In other instances, information may be accumulated because someone "felt" that a particular report would be useful and no one bothered to verify its usefulness; for example, a company may have its salesmen file daily sales call reports, which are then aggregated and forwarded daily to high levels in the firm, where they are ignored. The report may be issued too frequently and be too detailed for the level of management to which it is directed.

Regrettably, there is no magic formula for determining the degree of relevancy of information to a particular set of decisions to be made by a manager; in fact, it is usually much easier to discern what is not relevant. The information will also vary somewhat depending on the preferences of the individual making the decisions. This difference in preferences, when related to the rate at which managers pass through various positions, may also help to explain the "leftover" information problem touched upon above. Further, as Ackoff has pointed out, sometimes the problem of selecting and generating relevant information is more aptly viewed as a question of how to screen out irrelevant information from the vast quantities of data that an information system is already generating.[3]

Unlike relevancy, the *reduction* of data is apparently an easily measured phenomenon. After all, in the crudest sense, one can settle for measuring the number of lines or pages a summary report occupies as compared to the original data. But the quality of the summary or of the analysis underlying the summary is ignored when we accept such simple measures. For example, vital information about poor product sales in a given region could be washed out in the summary if no preparations are made when designing the report to pull out and note exceptional circumstances. Another illustration might be the importance of placing in a summary report the assumptions under which a given model of advertising response has been constructed and evaluated.

Reduction of data is also important for removing irrelevant information. For example, panel data that are to be used for analysis of consumer purchase behavior often contain much information that may not be pertinent to a particular problem; and removal of this information markedly lessens the volume of data to be handled.

The discussion to this point may have given the impression that the appropriate action is to pare to the bone the relevant information for each decision. However, this is not quite accurate, since some *redundancy* in the flow of information may be valuable as a check on the accuracy of other information. This desire for confirmation may explain why, for example, a firm will frequently purchase very similar data from two different sources or, in another area, employ an outside consultant to evaluate the same problem as an internal staff group. Again, determining how much redundancy is required in an information network in the firm is at best a highly subjective trial-and-error procedure.

Another question concerns the efficient use of information by managers. The provision of appropriate information does not always lead in the direc-

---

[3] Russell L. Ackoff, "Management Misinformation Systems," *Management Science*, Vol. 14, No. 4, December 1967, pp. 147–156.

tion of "optimal" decisions on the parts of managers. Ackoff cites an example of how additional information that could have been helpful in refining the decisions of two managers actually caused the decisions made to be less beneficial to the firm as a whole; each manager used the additional information to protect his own position from the normal effects of decisions by the other manager.[4] On the other hand, improvement in decisions is usually the result if the information flow inputs into a highly routinized or automated decision system requiring little further evaluation. For instance, the effect of the "correct" information on an inventory system can be directly related to a reduction in inventory costs or an improvement in the level of service.[5]

A final problem concerned with proper utilization of information has to do with management's attitude toward the subject. Several authors have emphasized that a management information system cannot bring to the firm all the benefits of which it is capable unless it has the solid support and enthusiasm of the top management.[6] However, this enthusiasm must be tempered with caution. Frequently, the costs of a computer-based information system and even the revisions in procedures that it will require are not warranted by what management perceives to be its potential benefits. This may be partly due to the natural tendency of any specialist to devise, at first blush, the optimal and most complete plan according to the dictates of his specialty. Given such a tendency, a relatively jaundiced view of the information requirements of the firm will probably serve the management well. A management that too eagerly accepts the suggestions of the information planners may find that there has been a reduction in the efficiency with which important decisions are made due to inadequate understanding of the decision problems on the part of the information analysts and their proclivity to utilize highly sophisticated equipment even though relatively simple tools and techniques may suffice.[7] Clearly, managerial attitude can substantially affect both the design and the success of an information system.

Types of information systems

Thus far we have not directly addressed ourselves to the questions of whom the information system serves and in what fashion it serves them. Dearden has suggested that there are really three main managerial levels that require information: (1) the top level of management, where long-range

---

[4] Ackoff, *op. cit.*, pp. 150–152.

[5] The concept of level of service was discussed in Chapter 7.

[6] See for example, Donald E. Cox and Robert E. Good, "How to Build a Marketing Information System," *Harvard Business Review*, Vol. 46, No. 3, May–June 1967, pp. 145–154.

[7] Again, Ackoff provides an excellent illustration of this result: *op. cit.*, pp. 152, 153.

objectives are determined and broad policies to achieve them are established; (2) a management level just below the top, where broad strategic plans are formulated by functional areas to move the company toward its goals; and (3) an operations level that is responsible for carrying out the plans formulated at the second level.[8] Obviously, the information requirements of each of the levels are different. At the topmost level, questions are frequently evaluated on which the company initially has very little or no information—for example, whether or not to enter a particular industry by pursuing an acquisition opportunity. A system designed to produce information at regular intervals based on the company's own operations cannot be helpful in such circumstances. At the middle level, more detailed information in summary form is required; here, information is fundamental to planning and evaluating the marketing effort—an illustration might be a decision to switch emphasis from personal sales effort to mass communications. Finally, at the third level, the most detailed information is necessary because management must be able, so far as the data base provides, to ferret out the causes of particular problems and make appropriate corrections in the operating system.

The most progress has been made, and is likely to continue to be made, in developing information systems for the third, or operational, level. This is because of the greater facility possible in defining problems that are routine, that is, regularly occurring, and that have limited, well-defined objectives. Examples are order-processing systems, media scheduling, some forecasts, and the like. On the other hand, for problems that are nonroutine and/or poorly defined, the information system has had less impact; examples would be marketing research on desirable characteristics of a new product, and measurement of sales effectiveness of the retailers in a distribution network.

The difficulty in specifying what levels of management will benefit most from an improved information system has led Massy to suggest that these systems might best be categorized by how they aid in problem solution.[9] He identifies three types of information systems: (1) a library-type system with the capability of supplying data on almost any question that may be presented[10]; (2) a system that feeds information into well-specified models that are used to evaluate results given different possible values of the in-

[8] John Dearden, "Can Management Information be Automated?" *Harvard Business Review*, Vol. 42, March–April 1964, pp. 128–135.

[9] See William F. Massy, "Information and the Marketing Manager: A Systems Analysis," paper presented before the Ninth Annual Paul D. Converse Symposium, Robert D. Allerton House, University of Illinois, Urbana, Ill., April 13–14, 1967.

[10] Brief descriptions of two such systems can be found in "Information Systems in Management Science," Harry Stern, Ed., *Management Science*, Vol. 13, No. 12, August 1967, pp. B-848 to B-851.

dependent variables, for example, the data input into short-term sales forecasting models; and (3) a system that produces data for models that help the manager explore feasible solutions to his problem, for example, several heuristic approaches to selecting an advertising media. All three types of systems could, of course, exist in the same environment. The first and second types represent those most useful to the operational level of management, whereas the third type is probably most useful to the second level of management. Massy's classification does not provide for an information system for the top management, although the third type may occasionally be helpful.

In Figure 11-1 we have attempted to show how the operating level for which the information system is designed and the character of the information provided by the system interact. For illustrative purposes, the figure concentrates on information produced by the sales force and by no means includes all the types of reports that may be generated or models that may be evaluated. The models mentioned at the Sales and Product Manager level and the Vice-Presidential level are all discussed elsewhere in this text.

Data inputs

Further reflection on Figure 11-1 may enable us to make some useful generalizations about the characteristics of data in an information system. Consider the sources from which the data may come. Almost all the information listed under the heading "Salesmen" comes from a source *internal* to the firm's operations. On the other hand, models that might be used at higher levels call for information generated from sources *external* to the company's operations—for example, the cost of transporting a good from each distribution center to a specific customer or market.

Information from internal sources can usually be organized on a routine basis so that it is generated at specific time intervals and in a particular fashion. In contrast, external information divides into two distinct groups requiring different treatments. First, there is regularly originated external information, such as reports from federal government sources, which can be planned for in the routine fashion associated with internal information. Second, there is available for decision-making purposes a large body of irregularly generated information, an example of which is information about competitors' bids on a nonrecurrent type of contract. But even more important is information that is both occasional and *unexpected* in nature, such as detailed information about the strategy a competitor plans to follow in marketing a new product. An information system provides for the organized dissemination of all types of external and internal information except the unexpected, yet the unexpected information may be of greater importance than any of the routinely generated information. Because it is nonroutine, there is danger that unexpected information will not be com-

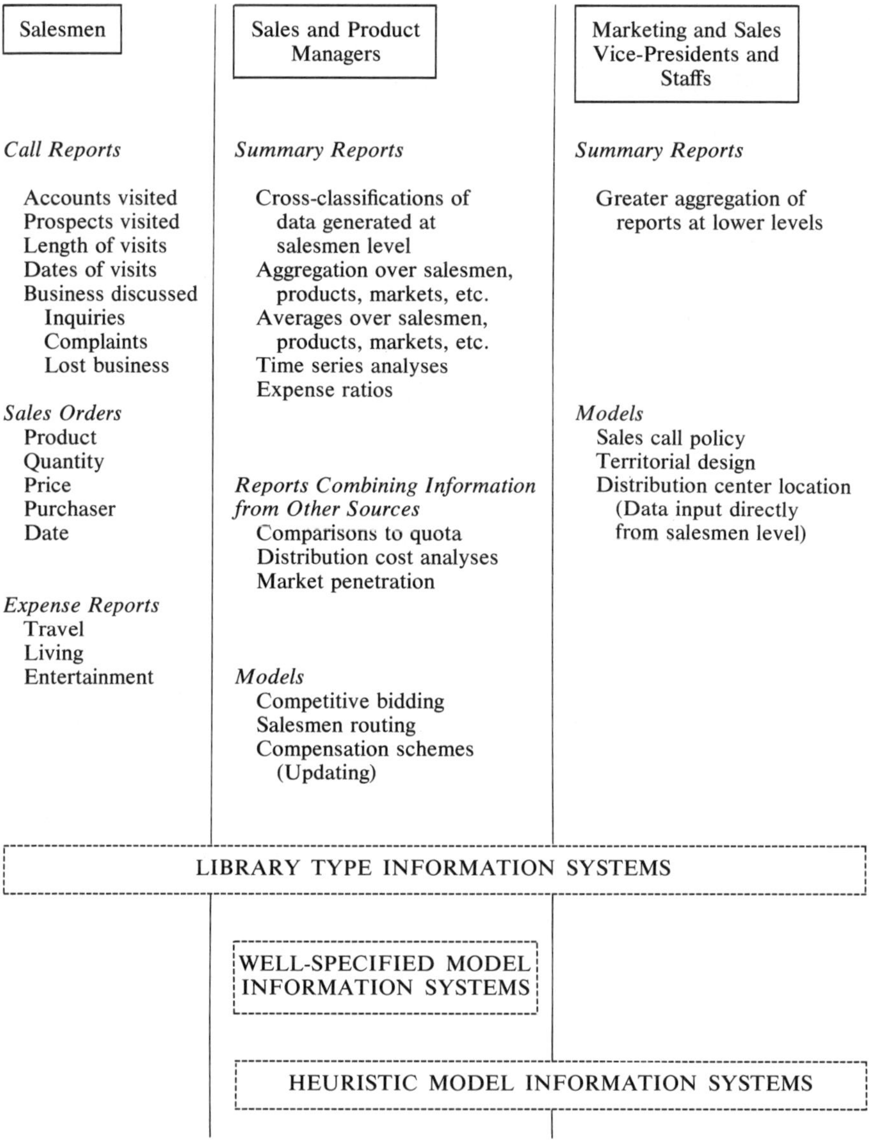

Salesmen	Sales and Product Managers	Marketing and Sales Vice-Presidents and Staffs
Call Reports	*Summary Reports*	*Summary Reports*
Accounts visited Prospects visited Length of visits Dates of visits Business discussed Inquiries Complaints Lost business	Cross-classifications of data generated at salesmen level Aggregation over salesmen, products, markets, etc. Averages over salesmen, products, markets, etc. Time series analyses Expense ratios	Greater aggregation of reports at lower levels
Sales Orders Product Quantity Price Purchaser Date	*Reports Combining Information from Other Sources* Comparisons to quota Distribution cost analyses Market penetration	*Models* Sales call policy Territorial design Distribution center location (Data input directly from salesmen level)
Expense Reports Travel Living Entertainment	*Models* Competitive bidding Salesmen routing Compensation schemes (Updating)	

LIBRARY TYPE INFORMATION SYSTEMS

WELL-SPECIFIED MODEL INFORMATION SYSTEMS

HEURISTIC MODEL INFORMATION SYSTEMS

FIGURE **11-1**

Information flow and operating levels

municated to the decision points where it would be most useful. An effective information system would therefore have structured into it a special procedure for handling unexpected information, regardless of the source from which it arises.

Although there is a tendency for researchers in the marketing area to develop their own data, depending on the character of the problem being examined, there are many external data available from public sources. The term "public" is used here to denote any data that are not generated by the firm itself solely for its own purposes; in this context, consumer panel data are public, although a given firm can purchase some in a proprietary fashion. Sources for these "public" data include government agencies, industry trade associations, chambers of commerce, individual project reports, marketing research agencies, and the like.[11] On the whole, probably too little effort is devoted to utilizing these public sources when searching for relevant data for structuring or evaluating models. Such data are likely to be most useful for decision problems in which the competitive and environmental factors are extremely important, for example, forecasting, sales territory design, selection of advertising media, and so on. The cases in which public data are not useful usually center on problems that are basically internal to the company, such as the influence of a new product on the relevant product line of the company, the setting of pay scales for salesmen to achieve a desired level of effort, and the ability to realize marginal pricing to attract business.

Within the firm, almost any data that are desired can be recorded and collected. However, here the essential problem is evaluating the worth of the data in terms of their potential effect on decision making as against the costs of securing the data. Besides the obvious costs for clerical time and processing, a more important cost may be the effect of the data collection process on individual behavior in the organization. For example, a salesman may be asked to fill out numerous reports not so much for purposes of controlling his activities as to provide data for various attempts at modeling sales behavior; if the salesman perceives these reports solely as a management attempt to check up on him, he may alter the reports to enhance his standing or enter inaccurate data, in both cases causing serious problems for those relying on the data for analytical purposes. More of the problems of the quality of the data and the information flow will be discussed in the next section.

The amount of nonsampling error in the data inputs into an information system is also an important factor for consideration. One problem that can be avoided fairly easily is the introduction of errors into data in the course of preparing the data for analysis. These errors are exemplified by misclassification, mistakes in initial recording and subsequent keypunching, inaccuracies in transcribing from one form to another, and so on. Data that have been carefully worked over to screen out such errors are usually referred

[11] For a discussion of the limitations of "public" data and some clues about sources for such material, see Harper W. Boyd, Jr., and Ralph Westfall, *Marketing Research*, rev. ed., Richard D. Irwin, Homewood, Ill., 1964, ch. 7., or any other basic marketing research text.

to as *clean* data, whereas the original inputs are *raw* data.[12] Obviously, an information system must contain procedures for converting raw data to clean data.

The form in which the data should be retained must also be considered when structuring the information system. There are several advantages to retaining data in *disaggregated* form. For example, only those data required to study a particular problem need be utilized, and no information is lost in the process of aggregating. On the other hand, retention of some data in aggregated form may avoid repetition of calculations and validation of results each time a problem is examined; for example, in exponential smoothing, one would not want to reprocess the entire time series each time new data are gained. An important thing to note is that the top managerial level may need detailed, disaggregated data as well as aggregations such as summary reports. This need is generated by the activity of model construction and evaluation at higher levels; such data are not required if the management objective is principally to evaluate organizational performance—in that case the summary reports will do.[13]

Although it is clear that both aggregated and disaggregated data will be contained in the system, a related question is how long to keep any body of data. This is a difficult question to answer because of the inability to determine when any given data might be pertinent to a future problem. Some guidelines can be offered, however. Most problems for which data are required in completely disaggregated form are very specific and timely; for example, sales have fallen off in a particular territory and management wants to ascertain the cause. Data needed in the analysis of such a question need not be maintained for more than a few years, retention for that time being primarily to provide a base against which to compare current performance. In contrast, aggregated data may be maintained for very long periods in order to be able to examine long-run trends.

The cost of maintaining data in various forms should also be compared to the benefits derived from having it. For example, it is clearly very costly to demand that all data be maintained in the central processing unit of a

---

[12] Although we do not propose to discuss it here, the process of cleaning data may be both very expensive and very time consuming, depending on how error-free the data must be.

[13] We have not included material dealing with control theory because there has been very little actual application of control theory to marketing processes. On the other hand, we do not mean to imply that marketing is a futile area for application of control theory. Basic control theory is discussed in most statistics or production texts. A particularly interesting paper that applies statistical decision theory to control theory and examines the implications of control theory for operations research models is Russell L. Ackoff, "The Concept and Exercise of Control in Operations Research," *Proceedings of the First International Conference in Operations Research*, Operations Research Society of America, Baltimore, Md., December 1957, pp. 26–43.

computer. A curious aspect of many existing information systems based on computer technology is that they are designed without any simple housekeeping routines for determining the costs and benefits of maintaining data in various forms. The result is that decisions about whether to hold data on cards, on tape, on disc, or in main frame memory are all too often made on the basis of intuitive judgment. There is considerable evidence that people and organizations will overinvest in data if the costs of acquiring and maintaining them are hidden rather than made explicit; this fact constitutes an argument for keeping cost-benefit data on data files and periodically reviewing the system to determine if the current formal data storage is the "best" or even if the data should be kept at all.

Some examples using the sales force information structure of Figure 11-1 may help to illustrate the previously discussed points. Almost all the reports generated at the salesmen level contain only raw data, whereas the percentage of such data in a given report or model decreases as one proceeds through the managerial hierarchy. Errors may be introduced by the salesman himself, for instance, by incorrectly totaling a column of figures in an expense report, or by those processing the reports. The data from the salesmen's reports is coded, cleaned, and fed into the information system in disaggregated form. The first aggregations, which are undertaken periodically, are by summing over (1) salesmen in a particular territory, (2) all products sold by a single salesman, (3) all products bought by individual major accounts, and/or a variety of other bases required for decisions that must be made. These results can be compared to other internally generated information that has been cleaned and introduced into the system, such as the individual salesman's actual performance compared to his previously determined quota. Individual performances against quotas may then be aggregated into another report, which is moved up in the managerial hierarchy. Higher level aggregations and combinations of data can obviously occur in innumerable ways throughout the information system. In fact, total company sales for the year is obviously the grandest aggregation of all. The aggregation of salesmen's effort within a territory can also be combined with routinely generated external information, such as competitors' sales in the area, providing an estimate of market share. An example of an unexpected piece of information would be that a supersalesman has become dissatisfied with the competitor for whom he is working and is planning to seek another job.

Obviously, we could continue to create examples of the management and character of the data in the sales force information system almost at will. The fundamental concerns, however, are those stressed earlier, which have to do with deciding what data are necessary for a decision. The data management problems stem from these fundamental concerns; for example, the level at which to aggregate certain data is derived from the decision maker's needs.

Model inputs

The models in an information system may be of many forms, ranging from something as simple as the calculation of a mean to the most complex set of mathematical relationships. Several important questions arise regarding the models structured into the system: (1) the choice of which models should be utilized on a routine basis, (2) the scope or flexibility of individual models, and (3) evaluation of the validity and refinement of the model. Obviously, we are using the term *model* here in a very broad sense. The models that are necessary for the everyday operational control of the marketing effort are the ones that should be programmed for routine use. For example, if an industry is particularly dynamic with respect to price changes, then those models that help the decision maker with respect to price policy must be available on a routine basis; an illustration might be a company requiring copper as a raw material using a model to help decide when, and at what price, to buy copper futures. An analogy from production would be a quality control method. In essence, the keys to whether or not to routinize are frequency and time. If the decision is to be made with great frequency, or if there is not adequate time to explore a large number of alternatives and possibly develop new models and approaches, then the existing appropriate models must be routinely available. With the current state of computer technology, the mechanics of making models easily accessible have become quite simple.

The second question, how flexible should a given model be, is more difficult to answer. Obviously, in the ideal world one would have the model so loosely structured as to admit a problem in any form, require only a minimum of information, and even be so wise as to educate the decision maker on what additional information he needs and how the problem may be looked at in a different way to produce new insight. One researcher has even suggested that models should do the "right" analysis even when the decision maker has requested another; for example, suppose that the decision maker has called a simple linear programming routine and the data could be more correctly explored with an integer programming approach; the first model would have sufficient diagnostics incorporated within it to turn the problem over to the second model. Unfortunately, however, such a general capability is somewhat in the far-off idealistic future.

The most common way to introduce flexibility is to program the model for data processing purposes in as general a fashion as possible. The several disadvantages to this approach are: (1) the man-hours of computer programming effort required may be extremely large; (2) efficiency in the computer program is often lost to achieve generality—for example, much more of the core memory may be utilized by the program, reducing the feasible size of problems; and (3) in the end, many users still require some alterations of the basic model for the particular problem they are exploring.

In general, the amount of flexibility necessary depends on what models are included, since expected usage is probably the fundamental factor in the decision. If the model is likely to be used by only one person or by a very limited number of people for the foreseeable future then it can be tailor-made to the user's specifications.

Obviously, greater flexibility is really a form of refinement of the original model. The other principal form of refinement is the improvement of fundamental underlying relationships, such as by substituting an empirically proven statement for an assumption in a model or, perhaps, by allowing judgmental data that were previously incorporated in the form of a point estimate to be given by a confidence interval or even by the entire judgmental distribution.

Evaluation of validity poses a serious problem. Initially, when the model is structured into the information system, some checks may be made to see that it operates properly. One simple check is to run a problem whose answer is known and see if the correct data are outputted in the desired format. A more difficult problem arises when the model has been in use for a period and then suddenly fails to perform. More than likely, an error was made in the original construction of the model, but finding the error may be no mean task. However, this situation is still preferable to that in which the model makes small, consistent errors from the very beginning that are not observed because the output they affect is considered unimportant compared to a mass of other information produced by the same model. An example might be a report that summarizes salesmen's daily call sheets and provides data on the number and type of customers seen, which would be an item of primary importance, and also data on the number of miles traveled between customer calls. This last item would in all likelihood be ignored unless the efficiency of routing was to be analyzed. Occasional monitoring of the validity of the models is essential to the operation of an information system.

The information system of the future

Management information systems are not really a new concept. Rather, what appears to have happened is that the revolution in computer technology has tremendously heightened the classical problems of dealing with the information flow in an organization. Put another way, high speed computers have offered the possibility of generating an almost limitless number of reports for any purpose, but the principles by which earlier information systems were built are still the basis on which a modern system is constructed. In fact, these principles may be even more important; consider, for example, the increased attention necessary to minimize the effect of the increased amount of redundant information produced by computer use.

Various authors have provided a picture of the future in which the information system serves as a fundamental tool in the decision-making process. For example, Montgomery and Urban describe a situation in which four men using a remote console video display unit, which is part of a general large-scale, real-time computer system, examine the prospects for a new product. The information system retrieves a wide variety of pertinent data, graphs demand curves, estimates the effect of advertising in different marketing mixes, estimates the cost of a marketing research study, and so on.[14] At the present time such scenes are still extremely rare. The example, however, does highlight one important feature of a true managerial information system: the almost incredible amount of data that the system will have to be able to assess. For example, a "true" information system of the future would be able to signal and present the president of an organization with information pertinent to the judicial—say, antitrust—implications of a contemplated move.

Although we do not quarrel with others' descriptions, we do believe that this implementation is much further in the future than many now assume. To date, much of what has been touted as being a marketing or management information system has in reality been little more than a data processing system. However, as the costs of computer technology gradually fall relative to the wage rate, then eventually the benefits from a computer-based marketing information system will become so great that the goal is worth pursuing even given the present limited nature of the prospects.

[14] David B. Montgomery and Glen L. Urban, *Management Science in Marketing*, Prentice-Hall, Englewood Cliffs, N.J., 1969, pp. 1–3.

THE ATLANTIC MONTHLY COMPANY[1]

Atlantic subscribers and prospects

The Atlantic Monthly Company, publishers of the magazine *Atlantic Monthly*, conceives of itself as producing a magazine with selective editorial appeal. It focuses on reaching a highly select market target group rather than a mass audience. In a report in which the publisher of the *Atlantic* attempted to identify the audience of this magazine, the terms "of superior taste, intelligence, education, independence of thought, curiosity of mind" were used to describe the readers. Further, he stated that "such criteria as income, home ownership, geography, etc., while not irrelevant seem to me secondary in the selection of prospects to be solicited." Another colleague of the publisher has defined the *Atlantic* readers as "the highly educated, the sophisticated, the professionally trained, the open-minded."

The *Atlantic* does not seek mass circulation for fear of diluting the quality of the magazine's audience. Larger circulation would, of course, lead to greater advertising revenues as well as whatever profit contribution is obtained from sale of the magazine itself. In spite of this additional profit potential, the *Atlantic*'s management has leaned heavily on selective reader appeal for support of its operations. The publisher has commented,

> Since we do need a certain amount of advertising support we must publish with the advertisers' interests in mind. This we do *not* do by publishing material calculated to make advertisers happy, or by refusing to publish otherwise valid material which

[1] Prepared with the cooperation of the late publisher, Frank M. Herbert, Jr. The material in this case refers to the years 1963 and 1964.

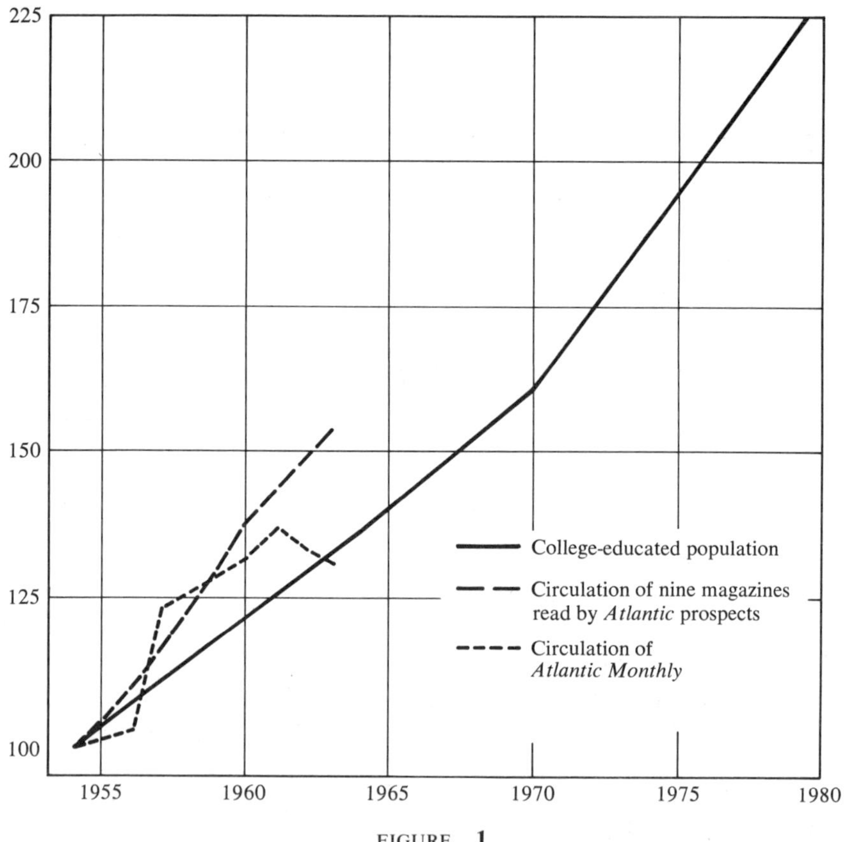

FIGURE 1

Circulation of selected magazines compared with growth in college-educated population

might make an advertiser unhappy. Rather, we publish material which will enable us to present to advertisers a market of sufficient size and influence to constitute a worthwhile audience for the advertisers' messages.[2]

The report went on to presume that as the size of the college-educated population increases, so should the potential audience of the *Atlantic*. Using U.S. Census Bureau figures, the college-educated population over 25 years of age was projected to 1980 (see Figure 1). The graph shows both the circulation of the *Atlantic* and the combined circulation of nine magazines[3] read by people who, in the management's judgment, were also *Atlantic* read-

[2] Quoted from an internal company report, by permission.

[3] These were *Harper's, Esquire, Newsweek, New Yorker, Time, Saturday Review, U.S. News & World Report, The Reporter*, and *Atlantic*.

ers or prospects. These figures, given only through the last year available at the time of the report (1963), are indices with the base year 1954.

On the basis of Figure 1, the publisher of the *Atlantic* projected circulation figures year by year through 1980. These are shown in Table 1, along with projections on the number of living college graduates over 25 years of age at five-year intervals. These projections for the *Atlantic* were regarded as minimum target circulations for two reasons: First, the circulation of magazines aimed at the market target group defined by "the college-educated" has been growing faster than the market itself; and second, the figures were generally thought by management to be somewhat conservative. Table 2 shows the projected income in selected years up to 1980 based on the estimates in Table 1. It is worth noting that newsstand circulation is expected to decrease as a percentage of total circulation but to grow in absolute magnitude.

Several years previously, in an attempt to learn more about the character of the market target group, the publisher had conducted a study of the characteristics of newsstand purchasers. A postage prepaid card was bound into newsstand copies shipped into certain geographically dispersed metropolitan centers. It asked the purchaser to provide the following information: (1) sex; (2) age; (3) buying frequency; (4) reason for buying; (5) previous subscriptions to the *Atlantic*; (6) names of other magazines that were more or less regularly bought on a newsstand. There were 1214 of these newsstand cards returned and analyzed. Some comparison to mail subscribers was also made by collecting information from the monthly opinion ballots that the *Atlantic* regularly obtains. Tables 3 through 5 present the results of the information obtained from the returned cards and the monthly ballots where appropriate.

At one time the management hypothesized that good prospects for the *Atlantic* would be "a person's next-door neighbor." If socioeconomic and demographic influences accounted for the primary influences on people in subscribing to the *Atlantic*, then *Atlantic* subscribers' neighbors should be

TABLE 1

Projection of Atlantic *circulation to 1980*

Year	*Atlantic* circulation	College graduates	Year	*Atlantic* circulation	College graduates
1965	290,000	8,880,000	1973	372,000	
1966	297,500		1974	385,000	
1967	306,000		1975	398,500	12,210,000
1968	313,500		1976	414,000	
1969	322,500		1977	427,500	
1970	330,500	10,123,000	1978	441,000	
1971	343,500		1979	455,000	
1972	358,000		1980	469,500	14,386,000

TABLE 2

Income projections for selected years

Fiscal year	1964 actual	1970	1975	1980
Subscription circulation	217,698	277,500	341,500	404,500
Newsstand circulation	44,273	53,000	57,000	65,000
Total circulation	261,971	330,500	398,500	469,500
Income per subscription year	$4.94	$5.05	$5.10	$5.15
Accrued subscription income	$1,075,692	$1,401,400	$1,741,600	$2,083,200
Accrued sales expense	$ (472,175)	$ (532,500)	$ (644,400)	$ (750,000)
Fulfillment	(123,418)	(161,200)	(200,300)	(239,600)
Manufacturing and shipping	(358,015)	(466,700)	(580,000)	(693,700)
Total subscription costs	$ (953,608)	($1,160,400)	($1,424,700)	($1,683,300)
Subscription balance	$ 122,084	$ 241,000	$ 316,900	$ 399,900
Newsstand income (39¢ per copy)	$ 204,008	$ 248,000	$ 266,800	$ 304,200
Newsstand sales cost	$ (39,805)	$ (37,200)	$ (40,000)	$ (45,600)
Manufacturing and shipping (including unsold copies)	(154,608)	(156,400)	(161,400)	(179,800)
Newsstand balance	$ 9,595	$ 54,400	$ 65,400	$ 78,800
Total circulation balance	$ 131,679	$ 295,400	$ 382,300	$ 478,700

TABLE 3

Sex and age of purchasers of Atlantic Monthly

	Newsstand (percent)*	Mail subscribers (percent)†
Male	60	48
Female	40	52
Age		
Under 25	39.1	12.9
25–34	28.8	21.1
35–44	14.4	18.3
45–54	10.7	17.1
55 and over	7.0	30.6

* Based on analysis of 1214 returns to survey of newsstand readers.

† Based on monthly ballots (cumulation of twelve months with 250–300 returns out of 1000 mailed each month).

good prospects. However, a study of this particular subject indicated that this was not the case. The key difference seemed to rest in character traits. The result of this study described *Atlantic* readers as being primarily experience-oriented (interested in travel, the arts, and so on) and nonreaders, who were frequently neighbors of these *Atlantic* subscribers, as "things"-oriented (material objects—boats, cars, furniture, etc.)

Another effect noted by the publisher has been periods of aging of the target group with the magazine. That is, the history of the *Atlantic* seems to split into eras. Early in a given era a sizable group of young people would be attracted to the *Atlantic*, with many of them remaining faithful subscribers over the course of their lives. Later in the era the attractiveness to new young readers would diminish. Two long-term extreme alternatives were thus open to the management: One was to attract a new group of young readers every 30 to 40 years and mature with them, and the other was to revamp the magazine's editorial stance at much shorter intervals to induce college students to become regular subscribers, recognizing that each sharp change in editorial structure would probably result in the loss of a substantial percentage of those attracted by a previous editorial change. For the moment the management had decided to compromise somewhere between these two extremes and had devoted somewhat less than 20 percent of the present editorial matter to topics of especially strong interest to the current college generation.

TABLE 4

Number of issues purchased per annum by newsstand purchasers of the Atlantic Monthly

Number of issues	Percent of purchasers*
0	9.8†
1	6.3
2	8.4
3	11.7
4	12.4
5	8.1
6	11.0
7	3.5
8	4.7
9	3.7
10	6.6
11	1.6
12	12.2

* 25.3 percent of all respondents were former subscribers, and two-thirds of these had subscriptions that expired during the past five years.

† 5.1 percent of all respondents indicated that they were buying the *Atlantic* for the first time.

TABLE 5

Other magazines also "regularly" purchased on the newsstand by newsstand purchasers of the Atlantic Monthly

Harper's	461	*National Review*	35
Time	336	*McCall's*	37
Saturday Review	273	*Vogue*	35
New Yorker	193	*Holiday*	31
Newsweek	134	*Show*	29
Life	122	*Ladies Home Journal*	27
Saturday Evening Post	121	*Mad*	27
U.S. News & World Report	112	*Fortune*	74
Scientific American	96	*Sports Illustrated*	24
The Reporter	83	*Glamour*	23
Playboy	75	*True*	19
Reader's Digest	65	*Good Housekeeping*	18
New Republic	64	*Mademoiselle*	16
Esquire	62	*Harper's Bazaar*	15
Look	61	*House Beautiful*	15
Nation	40		

Number of respondents: 1214

Circulation

The *Atlantic Monthly* is distributed through two principal mechanisms: sale on newsstands and subscription circulation.[4] The Atlantic Monthly Company considers both segments of its distribution structure important, although, as will be seen in subsequent data, the profitability to the company from each segment varies considerably.

There are approximately 114,000 retail magazine outlets in the United States. The *Atlantic* is sold in approximately 20,000 of these. Currently about 80,000 magazines are distributed, which would be an average of about 4 per outlet. Since monthly sales are between 50,000 and 56,000 copies, the remainder is overdistribution. This is a technique used in the publishing industry to make sure that there is sufficient visibility of any of the firm's magazine publications. Even if an outlet typically sells only one copy, at least two must be distributed. If only one copy is distributed, it tends to get "lost," causing sales to drop to zero. Of course, a key problem is selection of these outlets.

The *Atlantic* is distributed by the Curtis Circulation Company, which distributes many other prominent magazines, such as *Saturday Evening Post, Look*, and the *New Yorker*. Twice a year Curtis performs a comparative distribution analysis for the Atlantic Monthly Company. This describes what magazines are sold by the various outlets, the proportions in which

[4] As discussed later, subscribers may be obtained from several different sources.

they are sold, and other similar characteristics. The *Atlantic*'s management then examines whether the newsstand or other outlet is selling substantial quantities of the *New Yorker, Esquire, Time*, and *Newsweek*. If this is the case, and if the particular stand is not already an outlet, they evaluate the question of whether or not it would pay to put in the *Atlantic Monthly*. The trial for a stand usually involves placing three or four copies for a period of four or five months. If these copies do not move, the particular stand is dropped as a potential location. If, on the other hand, the newsstand is already selling the *Atlantic* as well as substantial quantities of the magazines mentioned before, then an analysis is undertaken to develop a notion of why the *Atlantic* is or is not performing well in the particular location. There are some outlets at which the *Atlantic* sells very large quantities; one example is in Harvard Square, where the *Atlantic* is stacked from the floor up just like *Newsweek* and *Time*.

The majority of the *Atlantic*'s sales are to long-term subscribers. Not only do these sales support an editorial continuity, but they are also financially rewarding, since the costs involved are relatively small. However, about one-third of the long-term subscriptions are lost each year through nonrenewal or cancelation and must be replaced by new subscribers if circulation is not to drop. Even more new subscribers are needed if the projected growth is to be achieved. Circulation data for the years 1961 to 1963 are shown in Table 6.

There are five main sources from which the *Atlantic* obtains new subscribers: (1) direct mail promotional pieces; (2) newsstand copy inserts; (3) classroom copies used in high schools and colleges and promoted directly to the teachers; (4) contract agents who promote the *Atlantic* as one of a group of magazines on which direct mail customers are offered a substantial discount; (5) catalog agents who sell subscriptions on a commission basis.

Trial subscriptions offered by direct mail or newsstand copy inserts are usually at half price.[5] There is some concern that regular subscribers will be unhappy when they are asked to pay full price as compared to this. The *Atlantic* makes a strenuous effort to prevent these trial offers from being sent to current subscribers; in this way it is hoped that the current subscribers will not let their subscriptions lapse and then pick up a trial subscription in order to get the price advantage. The revenue from trial subscriptions just succeeds in covering the costs of obtaining the subscription. However, the payoff lies in converting trials into long-term subscribers. The conversion rate among trial subscribers is about 25 percent (Table 6), which compares extremely well with almost any other magazine.

Of the classroom circulation, about two-thirds are high school seniors and the rest college freshmen. Although these students do not immediately

---

[5] A lower price would preclude inclusion in the ABC figure.

convert to regular subscribers, management's hope is that a habit may be formed to which they will return later in life. Except for classroom sales, efforts directed toward the populations on college campuses have been sporadic. At one time the *Atlantic* ran ads every month for six to eight months in a list of 95 college newspapers. The results of these efforts are very difficult to trace. The best data the *Atlantic* can get is the rise in sales in the cities concerned. Wholesaler records are not very good, and to determine the effect at particular newsstands or outlets the data would have to be obtained directly from these outlets. In isolated situations like Ann Arbor, on the other hand, a rise in circulation may be assumed to have some direct relationship to the effort in the college newspaper. The payoff for all this has been almost negligible. Little effort is now directed at college campuses generally. However, a cover sticker is placed on issues containing articles that refer to particular colleges.

Contract agency renewal is very low. The contract agency is now used primarily to keep circulation up and preserve advertising revenue. The *Atlantic*'s liaison with the contract agency was entered into several years ago, and the management does not now feel they can easily terminate it for fear of adverse effects on the advertising guarantee. On the other hand, the cata-

TABLE **6**

Atlantic Monthly *circulation*

	1961	1962	1963
Subscriptions			
Total longs (Jan. 1)	131,527	123,218	123,208
Renewed	80,626 (61.3%)	77,117 (62.6%)	78,061 (63.4%)
Not renewed	45,865 (34.9%)	40,417 (32.8%)	39,193 (31.8%)
Cancelled	5,036 (3.8%)	5,684 (4.6%)	5,954 (4.8%)
New longs	24,871	24,244	26,211
Total trials	68,659	107,304	70,539
Converted to longs	17,721 (25.8%)	21,847 (20.4%)	18,058 (25.6%)
Not converted	50,938 (74.2%)	85,457 (79.6%)	52,481 (74.4%)
Newstand			
Total shipped (12 months)	1,010,074	975,492	1,300,727
Sold	650,733 (64.4%)	593,571 (60.8%)	578,341 (44.5%)
Returned	359,341 (35.6%)	381,921 (39.2%)	722,386 (55.5%)
*Average ABC**			
Mail delivery	224,136	219,918	217,935
Newsstand sales	54,228	49,464	48,195
Total	278,364	269,382	266,130

* ABC is the acronym for Audit Bureau of Circulation, an independent agency that corroborates circulation figures reported by magazines.

log agents used by the *Atlantic* seem to do a good job of obtaining renewals. In general, they tend to use low pressure methods rather than door-to-door or telephone selling.

Gift subscriptions do not renew of their own accord to any extent; rather, most of the renewals are from the original donors. This phenomenon is not unique to the *Atlantic*. Since most gifts are given at Christmas time, the *Atlantic* sends the donor a total of five letters prior to Thanksgiving asking him if he would not like to continue sending the gift subscription. If the donor does not continue the subscription, the recipients of the original gifts are solicited in January, and approximately 3 or 4 percent of these people renew. About 20,000 magazines are given as gifts at Christmas time as well as some very small number scattered throughout the year. The latter is not large enough to merit a concentrated program of obtaining renewals. Of the 20,000 gift subscriptions, 58 to 60 percent are renewed each year by the donors. Thus, the percentage of gift subscriptions renewed is about the same as that of regular subscriptions.

One of the most effective and least expensive ways of developing trial subscriptions is through the use of direct mail literature. The *Atlantic* does "cold" mailing right after Labor Day and again in January. The offer made on the first mailing is usually a 12-month trial subscription and the later one for 8 months. Since the percentage response is about the same in either case, the fall mailing is usually more profitable. The principal problem faced by the *Atlantic* is selection of prospect names that have high probabilities of subscribing. The more pieces that are mailed, the more likely that the aggregate number of new subscribers will be large although the percentage will be small. Obviously, this is the effect of decreasing selectivity in identifying prospects. Table 7 summarizes the *Atlantic*'s experience for the period 1961 through 1963 with the January mailings.

Table 7 shows a steady increase in the percentage response to the mailings, even in the face of a price increase.[6] Much of this increase must be attributed to the *Atlantic* management's efforts in examining lists to determine their worth. Table 7 breaks down the figures according to top, middle, and bottom thirds of performance of old (previously tested) lists, and a separate category for lists being tested (or retested). Because the classification is according to performance in the current mailing, the same list may appear in different categories in different years. Indeed, some old lists will be dropped and some new lists added in any given year.

Similarly, the mailings are also used as a vehicle to test different pieces of copy in terms of effectiveness in inducing people to accept trial offers. For a new letter—that is, one with a new approach—the *Atlantic* may use four or five lists, select a portion of these, say 20 percent, and mail the new

[6] The offering price was $2.50 for 8 months in 1961 and 1962, and $2.84 for 8 months in 1963.

TABLE 7

Comparative performance of lists used for January "cold" mailings

	Pieces mailed			Orders received			% response			Cost per response		
	1961	1962	1963	1961	1962	1963	1961	1962	1963	1961	1962	1963
Top third	784,416	432,341	526,212	13,511	9,721	14,987	1.72	2.25	2.85	$2.90	$2.22	$1.90
Middle third	766,485	440,443	330,044	8,698	6,977	6,097	1.13	1.58	1.85	5.05	3.23	3.68
Bottom third	393,726	348,702	116,861	2,918	3,678	1,486	.74	1.05	1.27	9.03	5.36	5.73
List tests	110,494	57,128	148,206	926	635	1,545	.84	1.11	1.04	7.64	6.18	6.16
Total	2,055,121	1,278,614	1,121,323	26,053	21,011	24,115	1.27	1.64	2.15	4.47	3.22	2.86

TABLE 8

Atlantic *rate cards*

Rate card	#32	#31	#30	#29	#28
Effective date	Sept. 1963	July 1960	Jan. 1959	May 1958	Jan. 1954
Guaranteed paid circulation	262,500	255,000	240,000	215,000	200,000
Cost of one insertion:					
Black and white page	$2,275	$2,100	$1,950	$1,750	$1,500
Four-color page	3,525	3,250	2,925	2,650	2,200
Cost per thousand circulation for black and white page	$8.67	$8.24	$8.13	$8.14	$7.50

letter only to these. Finally, some lists do much better with 8-month offers and others with 12-month offers.

Advertising and its contribution to *Atlantic* operations

The *Atlantic* has historically not been a vehicle favored by advertisers. Gaining acceptance of the *Atlantic* as a vehicle to reach a small, select audience has been an uphill fight until recently. Despite current success, the management believes that in a serious recession advertising in the *Atlantic* would be severely reduced.

Table 8 presents information with respect to various rate cards of the *Atlantic* over the past 12 years. Actually, the rate structure is more complex in that there are special discounts for use of 12 insertions in any 12-month period, and for certain categories of publishers, such as book publishers, and so on.

Because there is very little readership of both *Harper's* and the *Atlantic* in any one month, the two magazines formed a joint sales company to sell advertising in both magazines. Each company owns 50 percent of the sales company, which is run on a break-even basis. The sales company has realized substantial economies of scale and the selling of much space in both publications at the same time. A special 10 percent discount is offered to advertisers for such a joint appearance in both magazines. Each magazine pays the sales company a commission based on the net revenue produced. The *Atlantic*'s billings were in excess of one million dollars for the first time in 1963.

The philosophy of the *Atlantic*'s management in connection with the interaction between advertising revenue and circulation has been described by the publisher in the following manner:

> The last thing anyone connected with the *Atlantic* would favor would be to play "the numbers game" – assuming that we all agree a proper definition of that expression to be a policy of increasing circulation with little regard to cost or audience quality, for the sole purpose of selling more advertising space. No magazine of selective editorial appeal can ever develop circulation numbers which will, of themselves, impress the advertising fraternity.[7]

Both the present publisher and his predecessor believe "that the reader should pay his own way – reader income should cover the costs of reader procurement, subscription fulfillment, textpaper and printing, text shipping, and editorial costs." This goal has not always been attained. In seven of the 23 years prior to 1964, including the last four consecutively, income from advertising was required to meet the expenses outlined above. Two other expenses that were not charged against reader income and were nor-

---

[7] Quoted from an internal company report, by permission.

mally applied against advertising income were general overhead and the cost of the company pension plan.

The publisher has summarized in Table 9 the *Atlantic*'s experience in meeting the above objectives.

Competition and price

The *Atlantic*'s management views *Harper's* as its chief rival for readers, and vice versa, so both magazines' competitive actions are predicated on expectations of what the other will do. In terms of the *Atlantic*'s demand structure, *Harper's* appears to be the closest substitute available. Some studies have shown that, in fact, the joint readership of both magazines is extremely low. To some extent, there may exist a pattern in which people read *Harper's* for a while, then drop it to read the *Atlantic*, then drop that and possibly read the *Saturday Review*, and so on, but not necessarily in this order or all of these. That is, there is substantial interchange among these magazines, with periodic loyalty. However, the numbers involved are not very significant. Of the 300,000 *Atlantic* subscribers and newsstand purchasers, there are 10 to 11 percent who purchase both *Harper's* and the *Atlantic* almost every month. Each year, 8000 to 9000 new subscriptions are obtained from *Harper's* readers, but it is not easy to tell whether these are the people who are giving up *Harper's* for the *Atlantic* or the joint purchasers. In any event, the numbers are too small to pay much attention to, and the effect is not known to occur substantially with any other magazine.

Other magazines that might be viewed as reasonably close substitutes for the *Atlantic* are the *New Yorker* and the *Saturday Review*. However, there are sufficient differences, such as editorial content, weekly instead of monthly publication, and so on, that the two cannot be placed in the same category as *Harper's*. Mass distribution magazines, of course, do not focus on the select target group the *Atlantic* aims for.

Generally speaking, the *Atlantic* seems to be fairly price inelastic; that is, substantial changes in demand have not been experienced upon price increases.[8] The offering of various trial prices is the only area in which price elasticity appears to exist. A half-price trial offer gets a much better response than any other discount structure that the *Atlantic* has tried. The *Atlantic* cannot sell below half price because of restrictions placed by the Audit

---

[8] Over the last decade, the *Atlantic* has been forced to raise price several times to meet increasing manufacturing and editorial costs, most recently going from $7.50 to $8.50 for a 12-month subscription in 1961. The corresponding increase in newsstand price was from $.60 per issue to $.75. *Harper's* has followed much later each time. The two magazines exchange subscriber lists, so this information was the basis for this analysis as well as the above-mentioned knowledge of switchers.

TABLE 9

Contributions of advertising and reader income

				Obligations to be met from this balance					
	1	2	3	4	5	6	7	8	9
Fiscal year	Balance from reader income plus miscellaneous magazine income	Less: magazine editorial costs	Balance left for overhead, pensions, profit	Overhead and undivided payroll	Pension cost (allowable tax deduction)	Total	Column 3 minus Column 6	Advertising balance to cover Column 7	Magazine balance before dividends, taxes, bonuses, nonoperating expenses
1954	$200,744	($168,108)	$ 32,636	$ 80,093	–	$ 80,093	($ 47,457)	$ 51,464	$ 4,007
1955	194,238	(175,112)	19,126	77,923	–	77,923	(58,797)	40,894	(17,903)
1956	206,270	(174,130)	32,140	81,107	–	81,107	(48,967)	62,786	13,819
1957	213,955	(198,114)	15,841	95,603	–	95,603	(79,762)	54,454	(25,308)
1958	318,841	(250,124)	68,717	108,846	–	108,846	(40,129)	86,473	46,344
1959	376,011	(238,742)	137,269	102,415	–	102,415	(34,854)	110,706	145,560
1960	378,713	(248,984)	129,729	100,611	$51,334	151,945	(22,216)	143,081	120,865
1961	261,320	(275,518)	(14,198)	109,460	53,112	162,572	(176,770)	227,605	50,835
1962	283,154	(289,189)	(6,035)	107,582	55,014	162,596	(168,631)	169,542	911
1963	276,776	(306,646)	(29,870)	102,856	64,613	167,199	(197,069)	275,498	78,429
1964	161,676	(313,491)	(151,815)	111,230	62,925	174,155	(325,970)	328,445	2,475

Bureau of Circulation on what can be considered true circulation. Headlines featuring half-price offers seem to work better than similar offers buried in the middle of the text of the covering letter.

One interesting facet of the price reduction to lure new subscribers is that the higher the total trial price an individual pays, the more likely he is to renew; that is, there is a much higher conversion percentage in this case. Since long-term trials, two years or more, lose money for a longer period, the objective of the management is to convert people as soon as possible. The essential problem here is to equilibrate the costs of getting trial subscribers paying higher prices who will have a better conversion rate against lower priced trial subscriptions with lower conversion rates but with lower solicitation costs.

As far as pricing within the channel system goes, the *Atlantic* policy is to give commissions as low as will still motivate the distributors. Some high pressure distributors given larger amounts of money would push the *Atlantic* sales much harder, but this is not in line with the philosophy of the management. The contract agency is the only case in which the *Atlantic* has had experience with the effect of increasing the commission, and this was rather successful; after some experience with the increase, the agency wanted to sell many more subscriptions, but the *Atlantic*'s management limited the agency due to the poor long-term payoff.

QUESTION

The area of operations that has been described in this case study is generally known in the magazine business as *circulation management*. Develop an approach for the *Atlantic* to the question of circulation management, making sure to comment on what policies the *Atlantic* should follow with regard to trial subscriptions, solicitation of advertising, distribution methods, and target audience, among others, and also the implications of these suggested policies on profits.

COMMUNITY SAVINGS BANK

The Community Savings Bank of Rochester, New York, is one of three mutual savings banks in the city of Rochester. There are also several savings and loan associations and four commercial banks within the city. By 1960, Community was one of the largest of the savings institutions and was considering adding a new branch to its existing locations.

When the Community Savings Bank was founded in 1946, through the merger of two smaller mutual savings banks within Rochester, its assets approximated $50 million. By 1959, its total assets were on the order of $174 million. Exhibit I shows a comparative state of condition for the Community Savings Bank as of January 1, 1960, 1959, and 1958.

The principal philosophy guiding the managerial behavior within the Community Savings Bank had always been that of attaining growth, since the achievement of profits cannot be a primary goal for an organization of this type. The management argued that the quality of service to the members (depositors) of such a mutual association is a function of the asset size. For example, improving the physical convenience of service might require additional branch offices, but, in turn, growth in asset size would generate enough additional money to cover the operating expenses of providing more branches for the depositors. Similarly, growth in asset size and its accompanying connotation of increased aggregate returns upon investment meant that the mutual organization could hire more administrative people of increasingly higher caliber. For example, when a mutual savings bank becomes large enough, it can hire a specialist in securities investment.

The second guiding philosophy of the management of the Community Savings Bank was that of public service – primarily, the provision of encouragement and guidance for members of the Rochester community in learning the habits of thrift. For example, Community had undertaken the establishment of school savings programs, payroll savings accounts, and other similar features that, in terms of their revenues and operating costs, were unprofitable. In the same vein, tours of the bank's facilities and lectures to interested groups were given in order to increase the public understanding of how a mutual savings bank operated. Similarly, active involvement in the affairs of the community at large was considered a necessary part of

EXHIBIT I

Community Savings Bank
COMPARATIVE STATEMENT OF CONDITION
January 1, 1960

	January 1, 1960	January 1, 1959	January 1, 1958
Assets			
Cash	$ 3,478,223	$ 5,090,136	$ 3,017,826
Government bonds	15,629,983	13,133,770	12,446,412
Other bonds	35,472,347	35,444,259	31,694,001
Stocks	6,704,193	6,079,199	6,155,139
Mortgages	108,430,487	100,700,097	93,453,313
Loans	415,739	367,244	300,466
Other investments	663,075	675,375	641,476
Banking houses & equipment	2,046,023	1,967,838	1,392,424
Interest due & accrued	1,042,429	961,726	855,652
Other assets	33,368	32,471	46,413
Total assets	$173,915,872	$164,452,118	$150,003,126
Liabilities and surplus			
Savings deposits	$152,274,158	$144,347,680	$130,750,425
Silver Spoon Endowment	27,802	29,420	28,345
Christmas Club	94,501	93,803	69,977
Payroll Savings deposits	1,762,686	1,781,851	1,838,511
Other deposits	355,915	334,162	331,313
Dividends accrued	408,411	356,386	322,675
Taxes & expenses accrued	74,902	94,946	95,615
Other liabilities	2,271,680	1,866,395	1,737,267
Total liabilities	157,270,058	148,904,646	135,174,132
Reserve			
Mortgages	25,970	0	1,000,000
Stocks	1,585,154	1,399,744	1,159,928
Furniture, fixtures & equipment	0	20,391	249,480
Other	27,734	28,178	22,054
Surplus Fund	11,396,931	10,797,657	9,313,406
Undivided profits	1,486,578	1,517,309	1,480,046
Reserve for bad debts	2,123,443	1,784,189	1,604,077
Total liabilities & surplus	$173,915,872	$164,452,118	$150,003,126
Ratios			
Cash to deposits	2.24%	3.46%	2.26%
Government bonds to deposits	10.09	8.94	9.33
Cash and governments to deposits	12.33	12.40	11.59
Mortgages to total assets	62.35	61.23	62.30
Surplus to deposits	9.69	9.59	9.30

the officers' job descriptions; it was not an infrequent occurrence for officers to chair fund drives in the City of Rochester or to serve on the boards of public institutions.

In New York State, mutual savings banks are limited to certain types of business. They may have no dealings with commerical enterprises, except the financing of real estate; they may not make unsecured personal loans; they may not offer checking accounts; and there are a number of other restrictions. Thus, they are chiefly engaged in securing deposits in savings accounts and in investing this money in the form of mortgages.

Historically, other savings banks and, somewhat later, savings and loan associations were considered to be the chief competitors of any savings bank. However, in the late 1950s, commercial banks began to take much stronger interest in time deposits and the financing of home construction and achieved noticeable penetration of these markets. For this reason, Exhibit II, below, shows the locations of branches of all other banks, regardless of type of institution, that might provide competition in the areas in which Community Savings Bank was considering locating its new branch.

The new branch

Mutual savings banks under New York State charter may operate at a maximum of five locations. In 1955, with a main office and three branch offices in operation, Community Savings Bank began to investigate the possibility of opening a fourth branch and conducted a study of possible branch locations within the County of Monroe, in which Rochester is located. The emphasis at that time was on a branch location that might have regional potential, that is, one that could serve population from 30 to 60 miles distant, as well as Rochester and its immediate suburbs. Because of the planned location of a major shopping center on the south side of Rochester near the existing regional farm market, it was thought that a new branch within this area would have the greatest regional attraction. Other potential locations considered at this time were the suburban town of Brighton, which is on the southeast side of Rochester, and two possibilities on the west side of Rochester. These were rejected because they were not regional in nature. However, in the final analysis, the Community Savings Bank decided to delay the decision on the location of a new branch.

No further action was taken until 1960, when the possibility of a new branch location was again considered. At that time, management thinking had switched from the concept of a regional branch to that of a suburban branch. Three location possibilities were considered at this time: (1) in the village or township of Pittsford, southeast of Rochester; (2) in the township of Greece, to the northwest of Rochester; and (3) in the northern suburb of Irondequoit. Exhibit II is a map of Rochester and nearby regions in Monroe County showing the census tracts from the *1960 Census of Population*.

TABLE 1

General characteristics of the population, by census tracts: 1960

[Asterisk (*) denotes statistics based on 25-percent sample. Population per household not shown where less than 50 persons in households. Median not shown where base is less than 200]

SUBJECT	BALANCE OF MONROE COUNTY													
	TRACT C-0002	TRACT C-0003	TRACT C-0004	TRACT C-0005	TRACT C-0006	TRACT C-0019	TRACT C-0022	TRACT C-0023	TRACT C-0030	TRACT C-0031	TRACT C-0035	TRACT C-0036	TRACT C-0040	TRACT C-0041
RACE AND COUNTRY OF ORIGIN														
TOTAL POPULATION	4 563	4 683	5 688	4 759	5 548	4 011	5 791	4 427	5 268	7 201	5 618	6 734	5 806	5 672
WHITE	4 557	4 683	5 687	4 750	5 539	4 009	5 784	4 418	5 259	7 192	5 605	6 730	5 798	5 664
NEGRO	2	...	1	8	5	1	5	8	9	2	2	2	3	1
OTHER RACES	4	...	...	1	4	1	2	1	...	7	11	2	5	7
BORN IN PUERTO RICO*	...	...	...	...	...	...	4	...	5	...	...	...	...	...
PUERTO RICAN PARENTAGE*	...	...	...	...	...	8	8	...	...	8	...	...	...	...
TOTAL FOREIGN STOCK*	1 215	1 520	2 601	1 216	2 010	963	1 320	995	1 362	1 512	1 417	2 007	1 486	1 527
FOREIGN BORN	217	411	603	223	438	208	300	219	263	271	284	449	344	345
NATIVE, FOR. OR MIXED PARENTAGE	998	1 109	1 998	993	1 572	755	1 020	776	1 099	1 241	1 133	1 558	1 142	1 182
UNITED KINGDOM	193	157	184	131	164	233	239	186	191	160	195	242	196	240
IRELAND (EIRE)	37	67	37	44	43	57	121	53	63	57	58	108	48	42
NORWAY	4	...	...	16	...	...	7	13	10	...	4	8	...	12
SWEDEN	32	24	4	4	13	8	12	16	50	15	9	4	17	8
GERMANY	280	461	380	208	336	189	128	235	256	197	244	345	171	196
POLAND	36	90	249	113	250	12	61	9	90	55	63	75	44	97
CZECHOSLOVAKIA	...	9	...	4	...	9	17	...	6	4	8	43	19	...
AUSTRIA	47	31	62	20	20	12	20	25	36	53	15	16	31	32
HUNGARY	17	8	33	4	20	...	8	...	12	14	...	23	24	...
U.S.S.R.	22	156	575	88	100	20	33	4	88	50	14	21	8	8
ITALY	178	153	673	125	641	156	198	85	194	347	274	468	388	413
CANADA	224	210	181	272	162	215	236	214	212	408	269	439	332	319
MEXICO	...	...	...	...	...	...	4	...	...	...	...	...	...	...
ALL OTHER AND NOT REPORTED	145	154	223	187	261	52	236	155	154	152	264	215	208	160
HOUSEHOLD RELATIONSHIP														
POPULATION IN HOUSEHOLDS	4 541	4 683	5 671	4 759	5 537	3 956	5 324	4 405	5 235	7 184	5 614	6 723	5 790	5 672
HEAD OF HOUSEHOLD	1 223	1 427	1 596	1 277	1 541	1 116	1 510	1 340	1 443	1 752	1 428	1 788	1 477	1 506
HEAD OF PRIMARY FAMILY	1 162	1 329	1 512	1 229	1 457	1 072	1 413	1 204	1 348	1 694	1 366	1 723	1 429	1 434
PRIMARY INDIVIDUAL	61	98	84	48	84	44	97	136	95	58	62	65	48	72
WIFE OF HEAD	1 100	1 226	1 425	1 181	1 368	1 023	1 340	1 090	1 260	1 626	1 300	1 633	1 358	1 362
CHILD UNDER 18 OF HEAD	1 854	1 515	2 010	1 916	2 099	1 535	2 011	1 523	2 112	3 359	2 504	2 781	2 575	2 330
OTHER RELATIVE OF HEAD	336	472	608	356	493	248	365	376	373	381	340	490	336	414
NONRELATIVE OF HEAD	28	43	32	29	36	34	98	76	47	66	42	31	44	60
POPULATION IN GROUP QUARTERS	22	...	17	...	11	55	467	22	33	17	4	11	16	...
INMATE OF INSTITUTION	...	...	...	...	...	51	25	5	...	...	4	...	...	...
OTHER	22	...	17	...	11	4	442	17	33	17	...	11	16	...
POPULATION PER HOUSEHOLD	3.71	3.28	3.55	3.73	3.59	3.54	3.53	3.29	3.63	4.10	3.93	3.76	3.92	3.77

MARRIED COUPLES*	1 133	1 237	1 436	1 208	1 368	1 014	1 336	1 083	1 288	1 693	1 353	1 677	1 359	1 399
WITH OWN HOUSEHOLD	1 114	1 219	1 423	1 196	1 348	991	1 327	1 067	1 269	1 664	1 318	1 662	1 339	1 373
WITH OWN CHILDREN UNDER 6.	329	302	363	341	524	369	425	279	501	968	663	729	652	528
WITH OWN CHILDREN UNDER 18	756	667	917	799	878	630	805	548	865	1 352	972	1 210	1 036	941
WITH HUSBAND UNDER 45.	532	419	594	583	862	593	609	460	771	1 288	877	1 120	995	804
WITH OWN CHILDREN UNDER 18	496	370	569	511	717	512	538	365	674	1 184	778	1 005	896	694
UNRELATED INDIVIDUALS*	88	137	116	86	172	56	636	260	139	99	118	93	98	123
PERSONS UNDER 18 YEARS OLD*.	1 869	1 570	2 009	1 945	2 152	1 564	2 057	1 542	2 175	3 425	2 577	2 851	2 640	2 309
LIVING WITH BOTH PARENTS*.	1 834	1 509	1 944	1 878	2 065	1 522	1 932	1 407	2 020	3 358	2 507	2 757	2 516	2 217
*SCHOOL ENROLLMENT														
TOTAL ENROLLED, 5 TO 34 YEARS OLD.	1 472	1 288	1 627	1 485	1 462	1 062	1 883	1 215	1 359	2 013	1 660	1 856	1 716	1 580
KINDERGARTEN	98	71	121	110	106	111	146	83	161	237	212	144	202	128
PUBLIC	52	63	117	110	106	105	117	55	155	225	204	140	198	124
ELEMENTARY (1 TO 8 YEARS).	972	754	1 043	936	965	717	939	755	907	1 465	1 129	1 270	1 194	1 073
PUBLIC	642	534	756	719	565	636	690	613	671	1 215	808	793	769	762
HIGH SCHOOL (1 TO 4 YEARS)	371	396	394	392	322	194	364	302	248	258	293	362	273	324
PUBLIC	261	327	317	318	264	158	220	252	213	240	265	260	231	276
COLLEGE.	31	67	69	47	69	40	434	75	43	53	26	80	47	55
*YEARS OF SCHOOL COMPLETED														
PERSONS 25 YEARS OLD AND OVER.	2 552	2 908	3 371	2 635	3 134	2 290	3 180	2 646	2 913	3 483	2 837	3 555	2 921	3 016
NO SCHOOL YEARS COMPLETED.	...	22	58	8	73	4	9	16	19	18	12	4	8	8
ELEMENTARY: 1 TO 4 YEARS.	20	36	64	24	78	29	50	24	29	16	20	81	40	30
5 TO 7 YEARS.	122	159	223	101	265	120	91	132	146	169	208	315	189	217
8 YEARS	264	384	475	240	441	233	197	309	332	303	481	411	344	430
HIGH SCHOOL: 1 TO 3 YEARS.	335	648	727	348	687	360	334	435	502	931	755	953	759	708
4 YEARS	617	809	1 067	797	1 022	698	840	664	676	1 230	898	1 094	1 120	918
COLLEGE: 1 TO 3 YEARS.	390	376	334	448	256	378	649	497	430	408	280	368	282	417
4 YEARS OR MORE	804	474	423	669	312	468	1 010	569	779	408	183	329	179	288
MEDIAN SCHOOL YEARS COMPLETED.	12.9	12.3	12.1	12.7	12.0	12.6	13.3	12.6	12.6	12.2	11.8	12.0	12.1	12.1
*RESIDENCE IN 1955														
PERSONS 5 YEARS OLD AND OVER, 1960	4 145	4 315	5 235	4 262	4 813	3 476	5 211	4 063	4 502	5 807	4 733	5 708	4 892	4 926
SAME HOUSE AS IN 1960.	3 021	3 000	3 728	2 811	1 923	1 803	2 226	2 334	1 956	1 515	2 434	2 509	2 502	2 898
DIFFERENT HOUSE IN U.S.	1 101	1 285	1 503	1 405	2 853	1 669	2 905	1 612	2 452	4 068	2 171	3 084	2 330	2 002
CENTRAL CITY OF THIS SMSA.	659	931	1 065	905	2 102	736	1 098	472	1 303	2 393	1 196	1 788	1 524	1 533
OTHER PART OF THIS SMSA.	181	181	161	205	383	547	782	584	476	800	708	677	430	203
OUTSIDE THIS SMSA.	261	173	277	295	368	386	1 025	556	673	875	267	619	376	266
NORTH AND WEST	231	147	209	287	345	354	930	477	550	764	261	560	345	261
SOUTH.	30	26	68	8	23	32	95	79	123	111	6	59	31	5
ABROAD	11	27	4	42	33	4	53	54	30	75	17	46	25	3
MOVED, RESIDENCE IN 1955 NOT REPORTED.	12	3	...	4	4	...	27	63	64	149	111	69	35	23
*FAMILY INCOME IN 1959														
ALL FAMILIES	1 165	1 327	1 526	1 224	1 431	1 073	1 414	1 187	1 376	1 706	1 360	1 728	1 439	1 432
UNDER $1,000	...	13	8	4	7	16	20	14	15	18	32	28	34	15
$1,000 TO $1,999	8	17	23	8	29	22	50	47	19	23	15	31	4	13
$2,000 TO $2,999	12	36	19	32	44	37	46	15	25	16	29	37	38	25
$3,000 TO $3,999	7	53	39	12	49	43	13	49	25	46	42	68	42	41
$4,000 TO $4,999	30	47	91	28	58	61	33	70	16	74	53	74	96	41
$5,000 TO $5,999	47	124	124	56	158	74	93	107	107	159	138	139	203	116
$6,000 TO $6,999	70	122	114	112	117	104	77	115	141	291	160	233	218	163
$7,000 TO $7,999	108	173	169	99	170	138	52	112	177	282	160	290	265	224
$8,000 TO $8,999	103	136	202	163	218	97	74	78	103	207	164	189	170	143
$9,000 TO $9,999	96	131	164	108	109	101	80	42	118	170	178	257	98	119
$10,000 TO $14,999	360	277	378	386	379	261	345	270	380	308	295	317	242	397
$15,000 TO $24,999	263	156	158	135	86	81	314	140	206	108	90	65	29	115
$25,000 AND OVER	61	42	37	81	7	38	217	128	44	4	4	...	...	20
MEDIAN INCOME: FAMILIES	$11 410	$8 577	$8 871	$9 907	$8 383	$8 428	$12 449	$8 827	$9 508	$7 801	$8 311	$7 876	$7 319	$8 545
FAM. & UNREL. INDIV.	$10 854	$8 110	$8 584	$9 580	$8 043	$8 213	$8 392	$7 688	$8 981	$7 645	$7 994	$7 720	$7 172	$8 210

EXHIBIT II

Census tracts—Monroe County towns

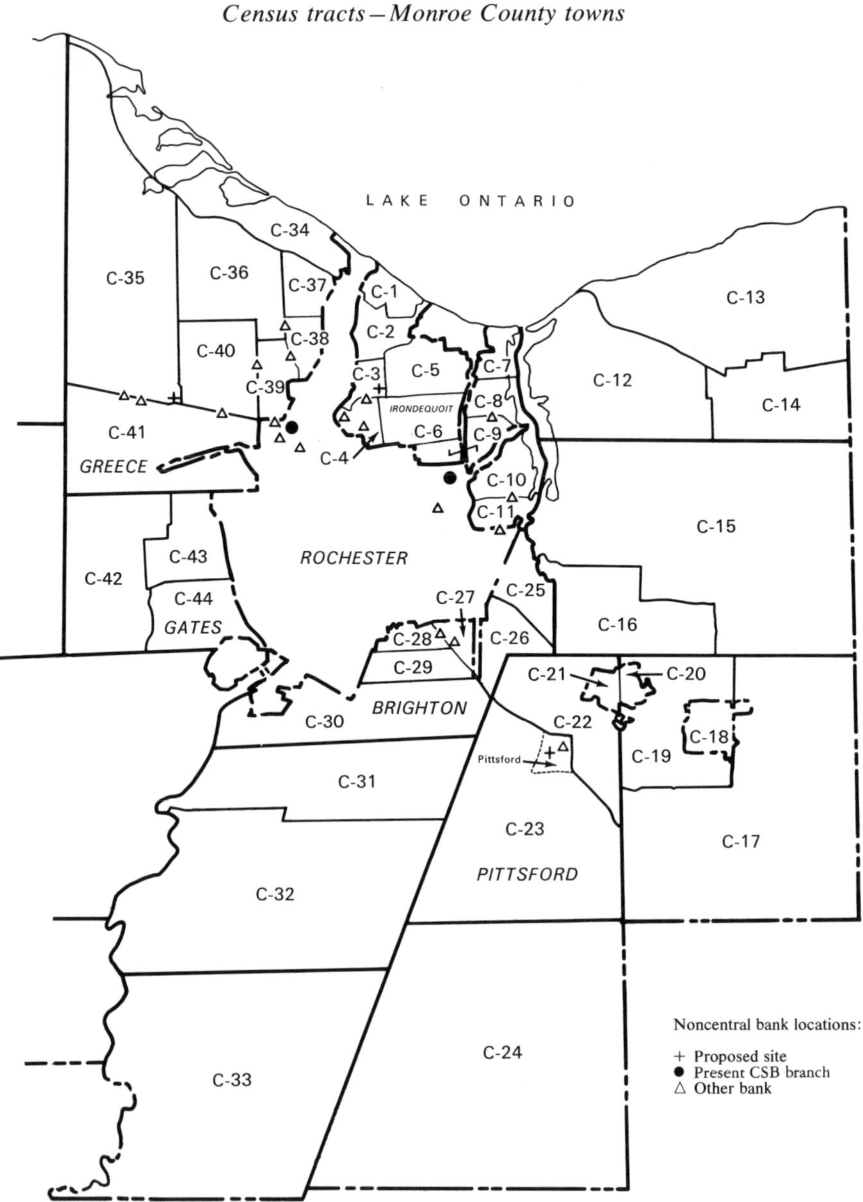

A study was made of each of the possible locations, and the limits of the trading areas were defined on the basis of the sites at which the branch might actually be placed in each case, the highway systems leading to this site, population concentration, natural physical barriers, and the like. The

Pittsford area was then delineated as including census tracts C-19, C-22, C-23, and half each of C-30 and C-31; Irondequoit as C-2, C-3, C-4, C-5, and C-6; and Greece as C-35, C-36, C-40, and C-41. Table 1 presents information about the general characteristics of the population in each of the relevant census tracts taken from the 1960 Census. In addition to the census data, information regarding the number of dwelling units in each of the census tracts for the period from 1952 to 1960 was obtained from the Monroe County Planning Commission; these data are given in Table 2.

The last branch office opened by Community Savings Bank had been the Waring Road office opened in 1950. Table 3 presents information regarding the growth of the Waring Road office since 1950. Table 4 gives data on population and housing in the Waring Road trading area for 1950 and 1960. Traffic patterns were such that the Waring Road branch would probably reduce the potential of the proposed Irondequoit branch in Census tract C-6 by one-half. On the other hand, a similar situation did not exist between the proposed Greece branch and the existing Dewey Ridge office of Community Savings Bank.

The development costs of a new branch office were approximately the same in any one of the three potential locations—about $200,000. The management estimated that deposits of $4.5 million were required for a branch office to break even. A branch bank should reach the break-even point in about three to five years.

The Community Savings Bank management tended to be quite progressive in its policies. In 1959, Community was the first major banking institution in Rochester to open a new main office in thirty years, and now it was about to become the first savings bank in Rochester to extend itself to the full limitation of its branching privileges. Community's management had begun to utilize the tools of marketing research quite some time before they were widely adopted. One finding, for example, resulting from a study of their market target group was that as family income rose, the percentage of

TABLE 2

Total number of dwelling units in selected census tracts, 1952–1960

	Census tract number													
Year	C-2	C-3	C-4	C-5	C-6	C-19	C-22	C-23	C-30	C-31	C-35	C-36	C-40	C-41
1952	1018	1317	1159	828	526	542	834	822	701	450	634	747	876	1012
1953	1085	1343	1219	921	598	627	902	861	745	500	767	783	956	1065
1954	1123	1365	1289	1013	731	675	973	962	796	565	921	817	1090	1168
1955	1153	1387	1375	1099	942	716	1140	996	993	952	1114	880	1260	1260
1956	1170	1390	1407	1155	1082	805	1186	1026	1111	1136	1205	956	1332	1313
1957	1191	1397	1417	1192	1180	823	1301	1044	1217	1246	1262	1008	1381	1359
1958	1203	1404	1437	1208	1299	898	1387	1086	1324	1392	1319	1159	1424	1406
1959	1212	1417	1459	1238	1450	1023	1457	1149	1408	1563	1371	1333	1449	1458
1960	1223	1427	1596	1277	1541	1116	1510	1340	1443	1752	1428	1788	1477	1506

TABLE 3

Selected measures of growth 1950–1960: Waring Road office

Year	New accounts opened	Accounts closed	Deposits: Year end
1950	966	7	$ 344,142
1951	1068	198	956,395
1952	1116	330	1,611,663
1953	1635	412	2,435,525
1954	1457	519	3,161,288
1955	1475	607	4,012,493
1956	1704	791	5,362,574
1957	2114	789	6,583,076
1958	1556	1018	7,767,465
1959	3585	1073	9,593,401
1960	1473	1410	10,995,139

TABLE 4

Population and housing for Waring Road office trading area, 1950–1960

Year	Population	Number of dwelling units
1950	18,211	5130
1951	18,553	5323
1952	18,900	5510
1953	19,239	5728
1954	19,603	5942
1955	19,997	6119
1956	20,362	6337
1957	20,712	6543
1958	21,040	6725
1959	21,388	6922
1960	21,741	7115

income saved in savings accounts also rose: The function was $Y = -2.0 + .0005X$, where Y = percentage of income saved and X = total annual family income.

Community Savings Bank had in its organization a number of competent junior officers who could serve as branch manager for the new location. In addition, no unusual problems were expected in the hiring of personnel, such as tellers, to conduct the operations of the new branch.

The management did not know when the legislature of the State of New York might extend the number of branches permitted a mutual savings bank, but, despite this uncertainty, they felt that a new branch was desirable and that its location should be decided upon without further delay.

QUESTION

Do you agree with Community management's decision to go ahead with the opening of the new branch? If so, where should it be located?

MODERN SHIRT COMPANY[1]

As part of its research to find uses for by-products of meat packing, the Tasty Meat Company, a national manufacturer and distributor of canned and processed meats, discovered a new process for making synthetic fibers. After considerable experimentation it was discovered that this fiber was ideal for use in white dress shirts. Without blending with any other fibers, it made excellent wash-and-wear shirts that were highly spot and crease resistant, exceptionally soft, and static free; it also could be woven so that the shirts would be porous (that is, they would "breathe"). Unfortunately, the cost of producing this material was relatively high, so there was no hope of competing with the large cotton shirt market strictly on a price basis. Cotton shirts sell in the range of $2.00 to $5.00 and enjoy a large market; the total adult male market for shirts is estimated at 50 million. The product was more directly competitive with the synthetic and synthetic blend shirts, which retailed from $7.00 up.

The executives of Tasty Meat Company were quite enthusiastic about their find but felt that they ought to obtain wider distribution for their shirt than would be obtained at the $7.00-or-above price. Their experience with selling meat products in low-margin outlets had convinced them that it was possible to sell almost anything in grocery stores and make a profit on large volume, even though margins were low. Therefore, rather than turn the basic patent for their fiber over to established shirt manufacturers, they set up the Modern Shirt Company to distribute high-quality shirts on a low-margin basis.

[1] Adapted from E. Jerome McCarthy, *Basic Marketing: A Managerial Approach*, Richard D. Irwin, Homewood, Illinois, 1960, pp. 687–691.

The Modern Shirt Company was set up as a sales subsidiary with its own president and vice-president. Both of these men were strongly sales-minded, and this subsidiary was to do no manufacturing, shipping, warehousing, or bookkeeping. Production was to be subcontracted to specialists in shirt manufacturing. All the other physical handling and bookkeeping activities were to be handled by Tasty Meat with a charge made to Modern Shirt Company.

In line with the philosophies of the parent organization, the executives of the Modern Shirt Company set as their goal a $5.00 retail price. Plans were then constructed in a fashion that would aid in achieving distribution of a top-quality synthetic white dress shirt in popular styles at this relatively low price. Order-getting salesmen were to be used to open up new accounts among almost 300,000 grocery and meat markets (including supermarkets). The salesmen would explain the nature of the company's offering and install, at no charge to the retailer, a wire-and-plastic display rack in a suitable place. After the initial placement, Tasty Meat Company salesmen would continue to check the display racks and handle any necessary details. Tasty Meat Company already had salesmen calling regularly on the grocery trade. These men were basically supporting salesmen, because the company sold exclusively through wholesalers. They were necessary, however, because the meat business is exceptionally competitive and the wholesalers did not give any special promotion to Tasty Meat Company's products. All orders for the meat products were filled by these wholesalers, so it was decided that they would also handle the shirts. The grocery retailers were to be allowed a fairly attractive 25 percent discount from the retail list price, whereas wholesalers would be allowed a 35 percent discount.

Modern Shirt Company planned to buy shirts from a shirt producer at $2.80 each; they would be already sealed in a plastic package that would be especially suitable for self-service selling. The plastic covering was transparent but especially heavy so that it would not easily rip or tear under handling, and therefore retailers would not have to be concerned about soiling through handling. In addition to the basic $2.80 per shirt cost, Modern Shirt Company planned an expenditure of $50,000 per year for national magazine, newspaper, and radio advertising tied in with the meat company advertising, and $150,000 for salaries and expenses for eight men and a secretary. In addition, $300,000 was budgeted for the purchase of display racks, which were to be loaned to retailers. Also, an arrangement was made with Tasty Meat Company whereby a charge of 5 percent of the shirt company's selling price (based on a $5 retail price) would be made for the cost of shipping, billing, collection, and sales assistance from the Tasty Meat Company's retail salesmen.

All things considered, the company executives were certain they had a high-quality product and that their usual methods of promotion would enable them to secure good dealer support, especially with good margins on an item that appeared to be attractively priced. Their major concern was the approximate size of the market. There were already a substantial number of well-known manufacturer's brands on the market, including Manhattan, Arrow, and Van Heusen. But the many dealer brands and nondescript brands led the executives to believe that brands were not too significant in the shirt market. Also, although the total shirt market was quite large, they were not certain about the size of the synthetic shirt market or about the desire for synthetics at a lower price. To obtain a better feel for the demand for their product, Modern Shirt Company executives interviewed a number of grocery retailers to determine their response to the proposed plan. Much value was attached to their responses, because Tasty Meat Company's market research department had found them extremely reliable in predicting consumer response to various new meat products.

Modern Shirt Company executives were somewhat surprised to find that the majority of small grocery store operators were not interested in the plan. Even when the free display rack was mentioned, little interest was aroused. The operators felt that the turnover would be rather slow, the rack was too large for their store, and their customers would not like to spend $5.00 for a shirt in a grocery store.

As the stores got larger, however, the interest of the retail merchants seemed to increase. Many superette operators showed some interest and almost all supermarket operators were quite enthusiastic, especially in view of the free display rack. Many of the larger operators estimated sales of at least 200 to 300 shirts a year, but some were not nearly so enthusiastic. On the average, the larger superette operators and the supermarket operators felt that they would be able to sell approximately 150 shirts per year at the $5.00 price. Overall, Modern Shirt Company executives were relatively enthusiastic, because they felt that they should be able to obtain the cooperation of about two-thirds of the total of 30,000 supermarket and larger superette operators.

While the executives were interviewing grocery retailers, the economists of the Tasty Meat Company were preparing estimates of demand at various possible prices. The findings resulting from this analysis are shown in Exhibit I. Three-year estimates were prepared, because the Modern Shirt Com-

EXHIBIT I

Demand schedule for Modern Shirt Company shirts

Retail selling price	Quantity demanded per year for next three years
$7.00	1,000,000
6.50	1,500,000
6.00	2,500,000
5.50	2,750,000
5.00	3,000,000
4.50	3,500,000
4.00	5,000,000

pany wished to maintain a stable price policy for at least three years in order to establish buyer confidence.

In view of all the contemplated expenditures and the relatively low price under consideration, the Modern Shirt Company executives felt that they would be more confident about going ahead with the project if additional evidence about consumer preferences and demand for the product confirmed the analysis to date. Accordingly, Tasty Meat Company's market research department undertook the design of a mail questionnaire to be sent to 20,000 persons.

The market researchers knew from experience that the use of more than a few questions reduced response considerably and also that closed end questions were much easier to analyze. Thus, they constructed the questionnaire shown in Exhibit II.

Of the 20,000 questionnaires sent out, 3270 were returned. In order to discover any possible significant difference between those who answered the survey and those who did not, a random sample of 100 consumers who did not reply to the questionnaire were personally interviewed. The findings revealed that, generally, those who did not reply were much less interested in buying white dress shirts than those who did. It was found that only 30 percent of the 100 consumers interviewed answered yes to the question regarding purchase of white dress shirts for regular, or daily, use, as compared to 50 percent in the mail returns. The most probable effect of this finding would be to reduce the mail sample finding by 20 percentage points. The market research analysts, however, felt that there was a 95 percent chance that the reduction would actually be between 18 and 22 percentage points. The answers given to all the other questions by the subsample of 100 respondents were not significantly different from the proportions found in the mailed responses.

Further analysis of the sample via cross-classification methods revealed that 90 percent of those who bought dress shirts for regular use were women and of these about 20 percent were interested in a well-known brand and 80 percent were not. Of the latter group, about 80 percent were interested in buying a miracle fiber dress shirt through grocery stores and supermarkets.

While the market research study was being conducted, Modern Shirt Company's advertising agency pointed out that additional sales could be obtained by investing more in advertising than the $50,000 initially planned. The agency developed four plans that it thought the company ought to consider as means of reaching new consumers not covered by the originally planned promotion.

In evaluating the plans, Modern Shirt Company executives were particularly interested in aggressive, well-directed advertising campaigns. They were interested in the maximum profit per advertising dollar. However, they were also guided by a rule of thumb that had long been accepted by Tasty Meat Company, that total advertising expenditures should never exceed $1\frac{1}{2}$

EXHIBIT II

Survey questions and answers (as percent of response)

1) Do you or does someone in your family buy white dress shirts for regular (daily) use?

Yes	50
No	50

2) Who usually buys white dress shirts in your family?

Man	10
Woman	80
Husband & wife together	10

IF THE PERSON ANSWERING THIS QUESTIONNAIRE IS NOT THE PERSON OR ONE OF THE PERSONS CHECKED IN ANSWER TO QUESTION NUMBER TWO, PLEASE GIVE THIS QUESTIONNAIRE TO THAT PERSON.

3) What influences your choice of white dress shirts most?

Well-known brand	36
Style	5
Material	29
Price	24
None of these	6

4) a. Would you be interested in buying a new miracle fiber dress shirt made available through grocery stores and supermarkets?

Yes	30
No	60
Don't know	10

b. If yes, what is the maximum price you would have paid if you bought such a shirt?

$4.00	7	$6.00	14
4.50	11	6.50	8
5.00	23	7.00	5
5.50	32		

percent of total expected sales. Since the product was new, the company did not feel that it must necessarily be bound by the $1\frac{1}{2}$ percent requirement but, in the absence of any other guide, had accepted it. Modern Shirt Company was desirous of saturating its market to the greatest extent possible with its advertising, while keeping in view the ratio of advertising cost to sales dictated by company policy. With these restrictions in mind, the company executives studied the four proposed advertising media plans submitted by their advertising agency (Exhibit III).

EXHIBIT **III**

Summary of analysis of four media plans

Plan	Effective messages	Cost per 100 effective messages	Total cost
1	33,000,000	$0.55	$181,500
2	10,000,000	0.80	80,000
3	20,000,000	0.60	120,000
4	20,000,000	0.50	100,000

The plans included advertising only in magazines, on radio, and in newspapers—the media thought by the agency to be most effective. The agency's and the company's research suggested that there would be roughly a direct relationship between effective messages and the extra sales to be obtained due to this additional advertising. Every 100 effective messages were expected to increase sales by three shirts at any reasonable price. Effective advertising messages were measured as messages that reached possible consumers. It was assumed that the messages in each of the four submitted plans would have about equal effectiveness.

QUESTIONS

1. Evaluate the marketing research procedure used by the Tasty Meat Company.
2. How much money should Tasty Meat Company be willing to expend on advertising?
3. What price should be charged for the shirt?
4. Should Tasty Meat Company go ahead with its plans to market men's white dress shirts?

VASA CORPORATION

The Vasa Corporation, a diversified manufacturer based in Albany, New York, manufactures process equipment for the chemical, pharmaceutical, dairy, food, brewery, liquor, wine, and soft drink industries, as well as a wide variety of equipment for the softening, demineralizing, filtering, and other conditioning of industrial, municipal, and household water supplies. A world-wide distribution network markets these several products under the direction of several international "area managers" and marketing personnel in each of the company's North American divisions. Manufacturing plants serve these scattered markets from their locations in several U.S. cities and foreign countries.

Vasa Corporation's corporate objectives have been clearly stated by its chairman and president: "The cornerstone of our corporate philosophy is to keep annual per share earnings on a relatively consistent upward path. Our minimum goal is to maintain the 9% compounded growth rate we have experienced over the last five years."[1] A rapidly growing corporation, Vasa has since 1954 acquired, merged, or formed more than ten other companies.

In 1959 Vasa purchased from two inventors the right to develop and market their patented chemical feeding device for fluoridating home water supplies. A simple and inexpensive device for delivering a flow of fluoride solution into the home water supply, this invention subsequently underwent considerable product development until management was satisfied that product "bugs" had been removed and that its safety was assured.

The company felt that they had found in the home fluoridator a product

[1] 1962 Annual Report.

with tremendous potential to enable them to realize their long-standing corporate goal of breaking into the consumer market, whose noncyclical nature would complement their industrial operations. Furthermore, the fluoridator was considered a natural product for leasing, and therefore offered an exciting prospect for future income. It appeared possible to price the lease fee in terms of service provided rather than the manufacturing cost of production. A patented, unique product, the fluoridator had an inexpensive design that would not be subject to obsolescence and had no moving parts to wear out.

Corporate size necessitated entering the consumer market with a limited financial outlay. The limitation represented a major risk of commercialization, since the cost of developing market acceptance (especially for a product concerned with people's health) could be considerable; for example, acquiring professional support, needed to legitimize the product, would take a large expenditure of time and money. Corporate earnings could not be jeopardized; yet the prospect of starving a significant new product was feared.

Other factors affecting the expected success of the fluoridator project were the progress of municipal fluoridation and the growing, widespread use of fluorine pills and drops and fluoridated toothpaste. The latter forms of fluoridation were thought to be vulnerable to strong competitive marketing efforts for the fluoridator, but the first problem could not be dismissed. The success of the fluoridator, then, depended on penetrating those markets in which municipal fluoridation represented no immediately feasible alternative.

During the early planning phase, the major problem confronting the Vasa Corporation was to develop an effective, salable product. Municipal fluoridation had been proven to reduce cavities by two-thirds, while tests had shown that fluoridated toothpaste could achieve a 20 percent reduction. Consultation with dental authorities at a local university indicated that the fluoridator might reduce cavities by one-half. Because research of two or three years duration would be required to prove conclusively the effectiveness of the fluoridator in preventing tooth decay, and because the management of Vasa was anxious to begin commercialization in order to exploit the advantage such an innovation presented, the decision was made to go ahead with market testing.

The original design was used as the basis for a proposal to the United States Public Health Service to design, market, and test a practical home fluoridator. The company was awarded a contract to proceed. Under the sponsorship of the USPHS, market tests were conducted between May 1961 and October 1962, in a suburban-rural area near Pittsburgh, Pennsylvania, where water sources were presumed to come predominantly from private well supplies. Although it was hoped that a dealer could be found to sell the product, Vasa was unable to secure the services of one and was thus forced to market the product itself. The total cost of this test was $142,334

(61.5 percent of which the USPHS had contracted to pay). The original strategy was to conduct the test in Allegheny County, Pennsylvania, and in the state of Virginia in two phases, during each of which 150 units were to be placed at the rate of 50 per month for three months, beginning March 1, 1961. It was suggested by the USPHS that Vasa hold meetings with local county health officers and dental societies in the area. Also considered at this time was the use of women to sell the product door-to-door, but men were used instead. The unsuccessful nature of this test was finally realized after several months of effort to gain a foothold in the area. Only seven units were actually installed, and white deposits were found on five of them, which indicated that the fluoridator had not yet been successfully engineered. Furthermore, the cost of manufacturing the product for this test was $57.78 per unit, compared with the expected cost of $17.70.

In August 1962 it was decided, with USPHS approval, that the test site would be changed to Montgomery County, Maryland (near Washington, D.C.), in October of that year. For this test the company enlisted the services of three part-time and two full-time salesmen to sell the fluoridator door to door. The results of their selling effort are presented in Table 1.

TABLE 1

Fluoridator units sold in Montgomery County, Maryland, November 1962 to May 1963

Total sales by all salesmen	
November 1962	2
December 1962	4
January 1963	11
February 1963	36
March 1963	60
April 1963	61
May 1963	8
Grand total	182

Units sold by full-time salesmen—selected periods

Salesman 1: Date (by)	Salesman 1: Cumulative units sold	Salesman 2: Date (by)	Salesman 2: Cumulative units sold
12/22/62	3	3/21/63	58
1/8/63	4	3/29/63	83
1/19/63	4	4/4/63	91
2/14/63	7	4/12/63	107
2/19/63	21	4/19/63	116
2/25/63	23	4/26/63	124
3/5/63	23	5/3/63	125
4/12/63	33	5/8/63	126

The fluoridator operation was turned over in early 1963 to a newly created corporate division, Water Purification Division, which was formed to administer the fluoridator and water softener operation. By the end of May 1963, 182 units had been placed since November and the test was considered a success. The major reasons for this successful effort were thought to be the high level of health consciousness in the area, the feeling by the professions there that courtesy was apparently owed to the USPHS, the lack of competition in the area from fluoride pills and tablets, and the relative novelty of, and hence lack of objection to, the door-to-door salesman by whom the product was sold. The strategy of putting the available money into salesmen's commissions and local newspaper advertising had now been proven to the management's satisfaction to be feasible, and Vasa felt that it had found a low-cost method for marketing the fluoridator. A call-back survey in Montgomery County conducted between April 27 and May 9, 1964, generally confirmed these beliefs. Of the 182 original customers, the following status was reported:

Wholly satisfied	138
Satisfied, but some complaints	16
Unable to contact	6
Removals, moved or city fluoridation	11
Removals, customer dissatisfaction	10
Removals, deadbeat	1

Encouraged by the test experience of Maryland, the company moved to initiate commercialization as soon as possible. On the basis of the Montgomery County test results, a rough preliminary projection of the national market was made and the number of franchised dealers needed was forecast. Of the 20 million homes with private water supplies, 50 percent had children under 14; it was thought that one-half of this group could be sold. These 5,000,000 units could be placed and serviced by 1600 dealers selling 3000 units each at an estimated profit of $9000 per year; the company's projected profit was estimated at $14,400,000.

Using the experience gained in the Maryland test, Vasa began to plan marketing strategy for full-scale introduction of the home fluoridator. A release for production was expected at the end of April or May with production to be at the rates shown below:

1st month	250 units
next 5 months	500 units/month
next 3 months	750 units/month
next 6 months	1000 units/month
next 6 months	1500 units/month
thereafter	2000 units/month

Cost and profit estimates were calculated under several alternative dealer projections. The final cost estimates prepared prior to commercialization were as follows:

Unit cost	$10.07
Reserve for warranty @ 3%	.30
Reserve for inventory loss @ 1%	.10
Royalty @ 2½% of $40 selling price	1.00
Amortization of tooling ($15,000)	.15
Fill cost	1.34
Total	$12.96

The units would be capitalized on an eight-year life and depreciated on the basis of double-declining balance. Prices for the alternative pricing arrangements of outright sale and lease of the unit to the dealer were determined to be as follows:

Outright sale	$40.00 each, including one fill
Lease	$1.00 per month for three years .35 per month thereafter

Estimates of projected dealer earnings and Vasa's potential profit were next prepared under the assumption that the unit would be rented to the customer for a monthly payment of $3.95 after collecting an installation fee of $15.00. The unit would require servicing two or three times yearly, with the attendant cost of fluoride fills set at $1.00 each to the dealer and $2.00 each to the customer.

Given these pricing and cost assumptions, dealer earnings projections were prepared. Table 2 shows the calculations when 20-unit placements are assumed each month. All categories increase linearly, with the exception of "Rent and utilities" and "Supplies and miscellaneous," which are subject to slight economies of scale.

The immediate marketing problem confronting the company at the conclusion of the Maryland test was the establishment of an effective distribution mechanism. The alternatives considered were (1) to market the fluoridator themselves through only water purification franchised dealers, (2) to utilize a single marketing strategy to sell the fluoridator through water purification dealers and those of a competitive water softener manufacturer, (3) to sell the units to the above competing manufacturer for resale to his dealers, whose independent marketing strategy would directly compete with that of the water purification's dealers, and (4) to sell the rights for marketing the fluoridator outright to the competitor.

The first alternative, to sell through only water purification franchised dealers, was considered to offer the greatest return to the company and would therefore enable the division to establish a strong dealer network that would be useful in marketing their water softening products. This approach would also allow retention of complete control. This direct sales method, however, would be costly and difficult, and would result in lower volume than the other methods of distribution.

Selling through the competitor's more than 1200 franchised dealers in addition to their own would result in greater volume. The cost of dealer recruitment would be diminished, but some control would be lost, for the company would be depending on a competitor for sales coverage. In addition, several practical problems would have to be resolved to initiate such an approach, for example, contract length, pricing, whose name to use, and antitrust implications.

Selling units to the competitor and competing with them directly through franchised dealers offered the advantage of being the simplest way to maximize the dealer network. The risk in this case was that still more control would be lost.

Outright sale of the rights for the unit's marketing would eliminate the risk of commercialization and avoid antitrust difficulties. This approach, however, would undermine Vasa's efforts to build a strong division to strengthen its position in the consumer market and might represent a forfeiture of a product that someday could be very profitable.

The use of a national franchise network of dealers was adopted on a test basis, the results of which would be evaluated at six-month intervals until a decision to drop the product or undertake complete commercialization was made. If management could be satisfied that such an approach would attract dealers whose sales efforts were acceptable and whose service was

TABLE 2

*Franchisee earnings projection**

	Year 1	Year 2	Year 3	Year 4	Year 5	Year 6
Income						
Monthly charges	6,162	17,538	28,914	40,290	51,666	56,880
Installation charges	3,600	3,630	3,705	3,735	3,780	180
	9,762	21,168	32,619	44,025	55,446	57,060
Direct expenses						
Lease costs	1,440	4,320	7,200	10,080	12,960	14,400
Fills	–	–	960	2,400	3,840	5,280
Service; installation	2,400	2,430	2,505	2,535	2,580	120
Sampling	360	1,440	2,520	3,600	4,680	5,400
Maintenance and removals	–	180	360	540	720	960
Selling commission	3,600	3,630	3,705	3,735	3,780	180
Lead and advertising	2,400	2,400	2,400	2,400	2,400	120
Clerical	500	1,000	1,500	2,000	2,500	2,500
Franchisement	150	190	270	330	390	300
Rent and utilities	1,800	1,800	1,800	1,800	1,800	1,800
Supplies and miscellaneous	350	350	350	450	450	450
	13,000	17,740	23,570	29,870	36,100	31,510
Net operating income	(3,238)	3,428	9,049	14,155	19,346	25,550

* Basis: 20 units per month at $3.95 monthly customer payment after installation fee of $15.00. For this purpose, no new units are considered added after the fifth year. Allowance for removals and resells in years 2–6 is included.

of high quality, then this franchise network would become the established distribution system for the marketing of the fluoridator.

Other factors considered in experimenting with a national franchise network were that it would minimize the company's initial outlay for distribution expense and that it could be used with a minimum of promotional support. Management thought that such an approach, furthermore, would eventually produce a valuable, ready-made distribution network for other company products, particularly a home water softener in the developmental stage at that time.

On the other hand, a major problem encountered in initiating such a franchise system was to find aggressive franchisees who would be able to withstand the initial financial burden that limited customer acceptance would impose on them at the outset.

Distribution strategy during this initial phase of commercialization was based on several critical marketing assumptions: (1) That the product was a hard-sell item that could only be successfully distributed by a door-to-door salesman; that is, it would not be bought off a counter or from a catalog; (2) that only a qualified service organization could handle the fluoridator because of problems of installation, water testing, and fill control; (3) that only a "hungry" dealer would promote it successfully; (4) that direct-to-customer selling is effective only when it is single-lined; and (5) that at the outset dealers would be selling a unique proprietary product that would not be subject to price comparisons. The consequence of such a strategy was that a significant volume was required to break even. For Vasa to break even in the third year required the existence of 125 to 150 *successful* dealers. To break even at the start of the third full year of operation, a dealer would have to average 20 units per month.

Shipping was scheduled to begin on a large scale in September 1963 but did not do so until late December, so the product did not hit the market in full force until January and February, a dead buying season. By April 1964, seven months of "full-scale" commercialization had been completed and the results were not encouraging; the Montgomery County experience was not being duplicated and a reevaluation of the entire program was consequently conducted.

Of the 44 original dealers, 19 were doing business at the end of this seven-month period, but only four with consistent activity; 27 had been canceled or were about to be. Significantly, the seven franchisees added later were all active and two were among the top five dealers. Located mainly in the suburban areas of New York City, Boston, and Los Angeles, the dealers were selling one to three units per week at a closing rate of one out of eight to ten presentations (for salesmen to be recruited at 5 percent commission required closing ratios on the order of 1 in 3 or 4). Reasons offered for this unsuccessful selling effort included distrust of a new product, the new concept, and the door-to-door man; the indifferent, often negative, sometimes hostile reaction by the medical and dental professions to a prospective customer's query; the high percentage of families using fluoride pills or tablets; and the intellectual, rather than emotional, appeal of the product that made effective demonstration difficult. The effect of price was also considered to be a possible contributor to the disappointing results.

By the end of April 1964, about 600 units had been placed since the conclusion of the Maryland test (see Table 3). Although 16,500 units were initially budgeted to be placed by December 1964, that projection was lowered to 3800 units, including 3300 shipped on lease. To reach such a sales level required a minimum recruitment of five dealers per month who would progress at average rates of sales of 4, 6, 8, 12, and 20 per month for the first five months and 20 thereafter. Table 4 shows the placement rates during the first six months of operation for the test area and selected successful franchisees. A revised plan of selling to dealers called for the leasing of the units for a straight $1.00 per month with six fills included free.

TABLE 3

Fluoridator sales, May 1963 to May 1964

	Total monthly sales	
Month	Unit sales	Cumulative sales
May 1963–Sept. 1963	54	54
Oct. 1963	60	114
Nov. 1963	37	151
Dec. 1963	30	181
Jan. 1964	106	287
Feb. 1964	93	380
Mar. 1964	104	484
Apr. 1964	100	584

Sales by dealers

Week	Weekly sales	Number of selling dealers	Week	Weekly sales	Number of selling dealers
11/8/63	12	8	2/7/64	24	16
11/15/63	11	8	2/14/64	15	8
11/22/63	7	5	2/21/64	18	8
11/29/63	7	4	2/28/64	36	15
12/6/63	14	9	3/7/64	29	10
12/13/63	10	6	3/14/64	32	10
12/20/63	3	3	3/21/64	19	9
12/27/63	3	2	3/28/64	24	9
1/3/64	9	4	4/4/64	31	12
1/10/64	9	7	4/11/64	22	6
1/17/64	44	8	4/18/64	29	12
1/24/64	13	8	4/25/64	18	9
1/31/64	31	9			

In spite of the foregoing considerations, improvement was still forecast because (1) the presentations were not being flatly rejected, (2) additional promotion (some cooperative) was being planned, (3) the USPHS was scheduled to make an encouraging report in mid-1965, (4) a clinical study to confirm the decay-preventative capability of the fluoridator was being planned, and (5) a pattern of sales radiation was believed to be operative (once a few units have been installed in an area, additional units can be placed with less resistance). Another factor expected to contribute to sales improvement was the program to enlist the professional backing that was being pursued. A professional advertising program, a direct mail campaign, the use of a professional detail man, and the employment of the services of a prominent pediatrician to answer professional queries were the major elements of this effort.

Total investment in the fluoridator at the end of April 1964 was $318,000:

Product development	$ 93,000
Montgomery County	26,000
Allegheny County	14,000
Marketing	185,000

The advertising strategy adopted was to prime a market area to establish an aura of legitimacy for the product and then to greatly reduce the expenditure to cover only expenses of maintenance promotion while the priming campaign was moved to another area. For example, the priming schedule for metropolitan New York called for using the 3 top non–rock-and-roll radio stations, 2 principal dailies, 42 local weeklies, and half-page *Life* and full-page *Reader's Digest* advertisements.

TABLE 4

Fluoridator sales for selected franchises and Montgomery County, Maryland, for first six months of operation of each location

	Month					
Franchise	1 and presales	2	3	4	5	6
Montgomery County, Md.	0	2	4	6	19	60
Dedham, Mass.	8	4	8	12	5	6
Caldwell, N.J.	22	4	2	1	3	4
Paramus, N.J.*	11	2	1	4	5	8
Greenlawn, N.Y.	18	9	17	20	20	35
Hempstead, N.Y.*	0	8	16	—	—	—
Van Nuys, Calif.**	1	10	10	—	—	—

* Division-owned branches.

** Later became a division-owned branch.

Given these introductory problems, the Water Purification Division's outlook was recalculated by marketing management (Table 5).

Vasa's management accepted the risk that the lowered chance of success (judgmentally determined to be 50–50 versus 80–20 at the start of early planning) entailed and decided to incur additional promotional expense of $40,000 per month in an effort to get the product off the ground. At this time a December deadline was set for an exhaustive "go–no-go" analysis and decision. Advertising outlays were increased to an annual rate of $102,000 for the remainder of 1964 (1963 expenditures had been $28,000); in addition, cooperative advertising on a 50–50 basis was budgeted at $6000.

Sales declined following the April reevaluation to only 62 units in May 1964 and 78 in June, bringing the cumulative total placed to 724 by the end

TABLE 5

Water purification division outlook as of April 1964

1. Fluoridator units on sale basis. Franchisees are recruited at rate of 5 per month. Average franchisee sales grow at rate of 4, 8, 12, 16, 20 per month and 20 per month thereafter.

	1964	1965	1966	1967	1968
Unit fluoridator shipments	3,300	17,400	31,800	46,200	60,600
Fluoridator sales ($M)	147	791	1,516	2,332	3,241
Water softener sales	320	630	757	966	1,239
Total sales	467	1,421	2,273	3,298	4,480
Gross margin	205	741	1,227	1,916	2,598
Selling and administrative	460	645	800	960	1,160
Operating net	(255)	96	427	956	1,438
Corporate interest	20	33	40	50	60
Net before taxes	(275)	63	387	906	1,378
Net after taxes	(137)	31	194	453	689
Earnings/share	(.12)	.03	.17	.39	.50

2. Same presumptions as above, but all units on lease basis at $1.00 per month with no fill charge during first three years a franchise operates, starting July 1, 1964.

	1964	1965	1966	1967	1968
Unit fluoridator shipments	3,850	16,500	31,800	46,200	60,600
Fluoridator sales ($M)	58	139	428	916	1,657
Water softener sales	361	630	757	966	1,239
Total sales	419	769	1,185	1,882	2,896
Gross margin	144	377	614	1,093	1,785
Sales administration and depreciation	528	645	800	960	1,160
Operating profit	(384)	(268)	(186)	133	625
Corporate interest	23	33	40	50	60
Net before taxes	(407)	(301)	(226)	83	565
Net after taxes	(204)	(150)	(113)	42	282
Investment tax credit	3	13	26	40	50
Net earnings	(201)	(137)	(87)	82	332
Earnings/share	(.18)	(.12)	(.08)	.07	.29

of June. Conditions worsened still further in July as a result of a crumbling dealer network. By the end of that month, although 23 dealers were carried as active franchisees, only 9 were actually operating and only 2 potential newcomers were on the horizon.

To enlarge the dealer organization, an advertisement was run in *The Wall Street Journal* in July 1964 asking for franchisees outside the northeastern section of the United States. The type of person desired or his location was not specified, and the response was extremely varied (from an evening postal clerk to several unemployed salesmen).

Table 6 shows the sales and profit performance of the Water Purification Division for the months of July, August, September, and November. Furthermore, between April and August, 22 complaints from customers were received, asserting that the product was either flooding or not feeding enough if at all.

In the meantime, Vasa officials decided to enlist the services of an independent marketing consulting firm to evaluate objectively the whole question of the fluoridator's marketing feasibility. Four consulting firms were

TABLE 6

Water purification division sales recaps

	Softener	Fluoridation Sales	Fluoridation Rentals	Totals
Month of July, 1964				
Gross Sales	$20,543	$ 1,058	$ 781	$22,382
Less: Returns & Allow.	584	5,848	–	6,432
Net Sales	19,959	(4,790)	781	15,950
Cost of Sales	13,368	(196)	95	13,266
Gross Profit	$ 6,591	$ (4,594)	$ 686	$ 2,684
Month of August, 1964				
Gross Sales	$18,909	$ 4,446	$(766)	$22,589
Less: Returns & Allow.	350	10,146	–	10,496
Net Sales	18,559	(5,700)	(766)	12,092
Cost of Sales	13,522	992	81	12,611
Gross Profit	$ 5,037	$ (4,708)	$(847)	$ (519)
Month of September, 1964				
Gross Sales	$24,883	$ 9,494	$ 6	$34,383
Less: Returns & Allow.	1,299	4,304	–	5,603
Net Sales	23,584	5,190	6	28,780
Cost of Sales	16,081	298	–	16,379
Gross Profit	$ 7,503	$ 4,892	$ 6	$12,401
Month of November, 1964				
Gross Sales	$18,926	$ 1,351	$ 834	$21,112
Less: Returns & Allow.	285	53	–	338
Net Sales	18,641	1,298	834	20,774
Cost of Sales	7,217	1,028	–	8,244
Gross Profit	$11,424	$ 270	$ 834	$12,530

approached, and one was chosen to conduct a $10,000 analysis, which was to be submitted in August to allow time for consideration before the December reevaluation deadline. The study's objectives were to determine the extent of the market for such a product, to establish a demographic profile of potential users, and to offer advice regarding the kind of marketing strategy that could be employed most effectively and profitably. The key section of the report follows.

Size of the Potential Market for the Vasa Fluoridator

Based upon survey data presented earlier in this report concerning the type of people that would comprise the Vasa Fluoridator market and further modified by taking into account the type of sales deterrents that the product must face, it is possible to compute estimates as to the size of the potential fluoridator market. With this data it is also feasible to discuss and formulate marketing strategy. This section will deal with the size of the market, in terms of number of families, based upon the current marketing strategy of selling through door-to-door salesmen. The estimates presented in this section take into account the following assumptions:

1. That the Vasa Fluoridator will appeal primarily to families with children under ten years of age.
2. That the Vasa Fluoridator will only have appeal in those areas where the community water supply is unfluoridated.
3. That the Vasa Fluoridator will appeal primarily to those families who can control their own water supply and therefore own the one-family dwellings in which they reside.
4. That the Vasa Fluoridator, under the current cost structure, will have its primary appeal among families whose annual income is $10,000 a year or more and considerably less appeal to families who make over $7,000 a year or more.
5. That the Vasa Fluoridator will have little appeal to those families who have unfavorable or apathetic attitudes toward fluoridation.
6. Assuming ideal conditions for a Vasa sale, there will be a certain number of families who will be unwilling to take any kind of action concerning fluoridation for one reason or another.
7. That the current Vasa Fluoridator cannot be expected to appeal to 100 per cent of the families who are willing to administer fluorine to their children. This is based upon the judgment that fluorine pills and drops will continue to be, at least under the current marketing strategy, major competitive factors vying for shares of the total fluoridation market.

Utilizing these assumptions and employing the data presented in the first section, estimates of the potential market for the Vasa Fluoridator are presented below. To facilitate the application of this data to a market-by-market basis if desired, estimates are also presented in percentages of the total number of families.

	Number of Families	Percentage of Total
1. Total number of United States families. Source: Current Population Reports, P-20, United States Census, 1961.	45,435,000	100.0
2. Total number of families with children under 10 years of age. Source: Current Population Reports, P-20, United States Census, 1961.	20,164,000	44.4
3. Total number of these 20,164,000 believed to live in unfluoridated areas. This is computed by multiplying the above figure by 72.9% which is the percentage of United States families without a fluoridated water supply in 1962. (Total 1962 population 189,682,000 minus 51,320,346 receiving fluoridated water in 1962 leaves 138,261,654 without fluoridation. This is 72.9% of 189,682,000.) Source: Task Group 2620 P – Division of Public Health, United States Public Health Service.	14,699,556	32.4
4. Number of these 14,699,556 families who reside in one-family homes that they own, based upon United States Census data (51.4%) and dwelling unit construction data for 1963 (53.2%). Since some renters of single family dwellings might be potential customers, the higher of the two figures is used. (14,699,556 × 53.2%) Sources: United States Census, 1960 and Construction Review estimates based upon authorized building permits issued in 1963.	7,820,163	17.2
5. Number of these 7,820,163 families in higher income groups which might be willing or able to pay for the Vasa Fluoridator. If all families who receive an annual income of $7,000 or more are included, the percentage is 38.6 or 3,018,583. If only families who receive $10,000 annually or more are included, the percentage is 17.7 or 1,381,969. Source: Current Population Reports, P-60, 1962 Bureau of the Census.	3,018,583 to 1,381,969	6.6 to 3.0
6. Number of these 1,381,969–3,018,583 families who have favorable attitudes toward fluoridation. The assumptions are that 70% of $7,000 annual income and over families would be favorable and that 80% of $10,000 annual income and over families would be favorably disposed toward fluoridation. (70% × 3,018,583 equals 2,113,008) (80% × 1,381,969 equals 1,105,575) Source: Judgment based upon survey results.	2,113,008 to 1,105,575	4.7 to 2.4
7. Estimated number of these families who would be willing to do something and take specific action concerning their favorable attitudes about fluoridation. Possibly a third or one half. Range presented is based upon one half of higher figure and one third of lower figure. (2,113,008 × 50% equals 1,056,504) (1,105,575 × 33% equals 368,525) Source: Judgment based upon survey results.	1,056,504 to 368,525	2.3 to 0.8

	Number of Families	Percentage of Total
8. Estimated number of families who might be willing to try the Vasa Fluoridator approach as compared to pills, drops, topical application, or any other method. An optimistic share might be 25% and a conservative share might be as little as 15%. The range presented here is based on 25% of the higher figure and 15% of the lower figure. Source: Judgment based upon survey results and knowledge of other markets and how they divide.	264,126 to 55,279	0.6 to 0.1

The midpoint of the above range probably represents a realistic estimate, since the lower figure is a conservative one and the upper one is an optimistic estimate. The midpoint of this range is 159,702 (0.4% of all families) and represents, in our view, a realistic estimate of the potential market for the Vasa Fluoridator under current pricing practices and utilizing the current marketing strategy.

QUESTIONS

1. Identify each of the major points at which the company was faced with a decision of whether or not to go ahead with plans for marketing the home fluoridator.
2. At each of the points identified in question 1, prepare an analysis utilizing the information available up to that point, including your own past analyses, which would have been helpful to the management in making their decisions.
3. Evaluate the management's understanding of the market target group at each of the points identified in question 1.

BLANKE, INC.

In February 1969 the attention of the officers of Blanke, Inc., of Boston, Massachusetts, was directed to a warehousing problem that was developing in their industry. Blanke, a distributor of office supplies and furniture to business and industry, to nonprofit institutions, and to retailers, found itself operating eight warehouses accumulated through periodic acquisitions. Its largest competitor utilized only one warehouse, and a second, smaller competitor was growing rapidly while operating 20 warehouses. Blanke's management wondered what warehouse configuration would best serve their market.

Company history

Blanke, Inc., was established in 1930 with a single office in Boston. In the following years, Blanke acquired subsidiaries in New York, Buffalo, Washington, Rochester, Roanoke, Atlanta, Detroit, and Columbus. The basis of acquisition of these businesses was an existing market and Blanke management's belief that the territory was a proven source of revenue and profit. No market surveys were undertaken to determine market potential prior to the time of acquisition of each subsidiary. The Roanoke division did not meet expectations and was deleted from the company. Blanke currently defines its operating territory as all of the United States east of the Mississippi River.

Product line

Blanke sells primarily office supplies and furniture. Orders for the 25,000 items of office supplies must be filled promptly in order for the customers to continue their work. The 5000 items of office furniture are not usually required so urgently. In fact, about 10 percent of all furniture items are sold on a special order basis. Blanke does not carry these items in stock but purchases them from the producers as sales are made.

Procurement

Although Blanke has its main office in Boston, each warehouse also has its own buying office. Order points, order quantities, and instructions concerning the purchase of products from other subsidiaries are, however, specified by the main office. Since many products are purchased by several warehouses directly from the manufacturers, there may be a tendency not to take advantage of quantity discounts. Products with a purchase price of $75.00 or more must be cleared with the Boston office before purchase. There is some interwarehouse shipment of products as a means of balancing inventories.

Sales method

Blanke does no manufacturing; rather, it performs the sales and service functions on items purchased from various manufacturers. These items are sold by a group of 48 Blanke salesmen scattered throughout the eastern United States.

Blanke's customers fall into three main categories: business and industry, institutions (mostly educational), and retailers (who resell the products). Customers purchase products from Blanke at prices set by the producer. Blanke cannot cut prices or give quantity discounts; it can, however, give increased service and special consideration to regular customers whom it considers to be important.

Blanke pays freight costs on both the products it buys from manufacturers and those it sells to customers. Truck or parcel post is used for most of Blanke's shipping, since most customers are not distant enough from existing warehouses to warrant faster modes of transportation.

The study

A study was undertaken to help Blanke's officers understand the nature of their problem and to determine how to improve the efficiency of their present distribution system. The ultimate goal of the study was to determine the number of warehouses and their locations such that distribution costs might be minimized and sales and customer satisfaction might be maximized insofar as warehouse locations affected these variables. Primarily because of time limitations, the study concentrated on an analysis of product flow through the system. Clearly, a thorough analysis of the total product flow of 30,000 products was impossible. The solution to this was to study a sample of 150 representative items.

The data

Because items selling for $75.00 or more must be cleared through the Boston office, adequate data were most readily available for such items. Because almost no office supply items fall in this category, the sample of 150 items was restricted to office furniture. The data in Exhibit I show that the

EXHIBIT I

1968 units sales of 150 selected office furniture items

Source (location of manufacturer)	Number of items	Transmitting warehouse							
		Boston	New York	Buffalo	Washington	Rochester	Atlanta	Detroit	Columbus
Allentown	1	6	10	0	3	4	3	9	10
Detroit	5	171	85	48	114	192	52	69	88
Boston	7	213	95	44	60	80	65	177	142
Buffalo	14	39	13	56	12	78	13	27	95
Chicago	45	402	385	156	150	552	180	240	255
Denver	2	0	27	0	3	2	5	15	10
Houston	1	3	8	2	2	4	2	0	10
Milwaukee	1	0	2	2	0	2	0	6	3
New Haven	8	33	53	10	8	86	33	27	35
New York	20	144	180	48	87	200	142	186	83
Rochester	18	447	250	132	105	472	90	336	208
San Diego	1	9	5	8	0	4	5	9	2
Trenton	27	555	462	160	173	534	366	387	285
	150	2022	1575	666	717	2200	956	1515	1226

Boston
Rochester
Buffalo
New Haven
Milwaukee
Detroit
New York
Allentown
Chicago
Trenton
Columbus
Washington
Denver
San Diego
Atlanta
Houston

EXHIBIT II

EXHIBIT III

1968 total dollar sales

Boston	$ 5,103,000
New York	4,567,000
Buffalo	2,042,000
Washington	1,992,000
Rochester	5,508,000
Atlanta	2,993,000
Detroit	4,005,000
Columbus	3,252,000
	$29,462,000

150 items originated in only 13 cities, and that only eight of these cities supplied more than one or two items. Exhibit II is a map identifying those cities that serve as sources and/or present warehouse locations of Blanke. The total number of units in the sample transmitted by each of the eight warehouses is in fairly good agreement with the distribution of total dollar volumes for all products for the same period (Exhibit III).

It took a great deal of time to assemble the data in Exhibits I and III because Blanke at present makes only limited use of electronic data processing equipment. Blanke's management does plan to develop an information system that will provide data about sales, transportation costs, and so on for each of the 30,000 items Blanke sells. However, it will be several years before this information system is established and then at least another year to accumulate the data necessary to conduct a thorough warehouse study. It is the judgment of Blanke's managers that the firm cannot wait several years to explore the warehouse question, particularly in the light of competition. Thus, they would like to undertake an analysis of the warehouse location problem now, even though such a study would have important limitations.

QUESTIONS

In answering these questions, be explicit with regard to assumptions you have made, other sources of information you have utilized, and the characteristics of the models you have employed.

On the basis of information obtained in the sample of 150 items, should Blanke

(a) centralize buying of office furniture?
(b) centralize storage of all office furniture in one or a combination of the existing warehouses?
(c) establish one or more new warehouses to handle all storage of office furniture?

Author Index

Subject Index

A 0
B 1
C 2
D 3
E 4
F 5
G 6
H 7
I 8
J 9